To Deanne & Don,

[signature]

12/6/94

NAPA WINE

NAPA WINE

A History

from Mission Days

to Present

Charles L. Sullivan

ILLUSTRATIONS BY

Earl Thollander

Earl Thollander
Dec 6, '94

.:.

THE WINE APPRECIATION GUILD
SAN FRANCISCO

The Wine Appreciation Guild Ltd.
155 Connecticut Street
San Francisco, California 94107

Library of Congress Cataloging-in-publication Data

Sullivan, Charles Lewis, 1932
Napa wine: a history from mission
days to present. --1st ed, 438pp. 20.4 x 25.5cm
Includes bibliographical references and index.
ISBN 0-932664-70-9
1. Wine and wine making - California

TP557.S78 1994   94-30837
338.7'64122'09794--dc20   CIP

ISBN 0-932664-70-9

The author and publishers will be grateful for any information
which will assist them in keeping further editions up to date. Although
all reasonable care has been taken in the preparation of this book, neither
publishers nor the author can accept any liability for any consequences
arising from the uses thereof, or from the information contained herein.

Editors: Eve Kushner and Sabrina Ferris
Illustrator: Earl Thollander
Copy Photos: Richards Lyon and Paul Mackey
Photo Research: Paul Mackey
Index: Susan De Renee Coerr
Project Chairman: Gordon Williams and John C. Ellis
Historic Photos Courtesy of: Napa Valley Wine Library,
St. Helena Star, Wines and Vines, The Wine Spectator,
Gunther R. Deter, Reginald Oliver, Nina Wemyss and others.

Design by The Digital Table
Ronna Nelson, Lauren Fresk

(A deluxe leather-bound, signed, numbered limited edition is available).

Printed and bound in China

IN MEMORY OF JIM BEARD

ACKNOWLEDGEMENTS

Except for the Inglenook manuscript collection all the important primary sources on which this history rests are easily accessible in public libraries of the San Francisco Bay Area. The most important of these are the Bancroft Library of the University of California (Berkeley), Shields Library of the University of California (Davis), San Francisco Public Library (periodicals and special collections), Napa Public Library (microfilm and special collections), Sonoma County Wine Library (Healdsburg), and San Jose Public Library (California Room). The staffs at these institutions contributed unselfishly to the final product here.

The Napa Valley Wine Library Association is the sponsor of this study and a special thanks is due to several of its members who acted as my editorial advisory board and who afforded me assistance in gaining special access to many important sources from the Library. Chief among these were Gunther and Mary Louise Detert, Stewart and Jeanne Hughes, Richards Lyon, Jack Ellis, and Gordon Williams. They and others in the Association were instrumental in the collection of the graphic materials that enhanced this study. Many Napa wineries are members of the Library Association and made the collection of these materials much easier.

Also essential to my research was the assistance afforded me by Marilee Talley and Bill Brenner of the *St. Helena Star,* who opened the newspaper's historical files to me. My eyes and sanity are better for their help. Also important to my peace of mind was guidance afforded me by my patient mentor, Jefferson Rich Davis, who led me and my historical files into the world of computers.

I am fortunate in having had several specialists in the world of California wine read large portions of this history in draft. My special thanks for their time and suggestions go to Maynard Amerine, Fred Mc Millan, Robert Mondavi, Reginald Oliver, Bernard and Belle Rhodes, Bo Simons, Ruth Teiser, Larry Walker, and Nina Wemyss. This study is far more accurate as the result of their suggestions and corrections. But I did not heed them all. Ultimately the outcome is the result of my own judgment and interpretation. I am not so bold to think that I have avoided errors and I invite readers' suggestions for improvement.

A good portion of the recent history I have written here comes from the materials collected by a tireless group of wine and history lovers whose keen eyes and ready scissors have provided me with a steady flow of periodical and newspaper data for the last twenty years. They are headed in Southern California by Margaret Scott Dealey and in Northern California by my mother, Charlene F. Sullivan. My very special thanks goes to them. And for giving order to this potential jungle of material and for providing the special order a writer needs in his life, I give loving thanks to my wife, Rosslyn Polansky Sullivan.

Charles L. Sullivan
Los Gatos, California
December 2, 1992

Contents

FOREWORD

In Napa Valley we have the soils, climate, the grape varieties and the human resources to make this special place one of the premier wine regions of the world.

Viewed from the perspective of over 7,000 years of wine on earth, our 150 years in Napa Valley is quite short. But the impact on the world of wine has been impressive, and for that reason, among others, a history of Napa Valley should be required reading for vintners and consumers alike.

Charles Sullivan has done a masterful job in pulling this history together. His book depends mostly on local Napa sources, particularly local newspapers going back into the 1850s. The author has read them all, from the earliest days to the present, and this detailed background gives the book great credibility.

Charles draws heavily on personal memories of the leaders of the Napa wine industry, particularly since Repeal. He has used the oral history collections of the University of California's Bancroft Library and local oral histories collected by the Napa Valley Wine Library.

The book is a marvelous resource, telling the story of virtually every Napa vintage from the 1860s to the 1990s. Very special emphasis is placed on the modern wine revolution and Napa's unique contributions since the 1960s, in which we're pleased to have played a part. A series of charts and tables cover 120 years of wine in Napa Valley.

In no place in the Western Hemisphere is historic winery architecture richer than in the Napa Valley. The book ties these relics of the past to the present cultural landscape of the Valley, with its handsome new additions.

Special emphasis has been placed on recent attempts to preserve the unique natural and agricultural environment of the Napa Valley. The author traces these struggles right to the present.

For the first time a wine history book traces in detail and attempts to explain how Napa Valley acquired its unique reputation for fine wine in the 1870s, and how it has retained it ever since. While other regions have also improved enormously, Napa has kept its prominence as America's premier wine region.

The Napa Valley Wine Library Association, with years of accomplishment for all of us, has brought us another great gift. With this book the reader can participate in our marvelous heritage and pride in Napa Valley.

Robert Mondavi

12-6-94

To your health!
Robert Mondavi
Oakville, California

INTRODUCTION

I got to know about the Napa Valley Wine Library when my wife and I took the Association's wine course in the summer of 1968. Jim Beard, one of the Library's founders, was the ever-present spirit of the course, and I was elated to discover a kindred spirit. Besides our mutual passion for wine, we found that we both lamented the practically non-existent state of California wine history, particularly at the local level. We talked then, and later wrote each other, about the means for preserving the historical sources that would eventually act as the basis for the histories that would later be written.

We agreed that, for the moment, the most pressing need was the preservation of the memories of those who could recall the earlier days in the wine industry and out in the wine country. I had already begun searching for the documentary leavings from the past and had learned the truth of Jean-Paul Sartre's observation that "History is made without knowing of its making," at least so far as California wine history was concerned. Little had survived from the past, save newspaper articles, industry periodicals, and government publications. This knowledge strengthened our interest in oral history.

We knew that Ruth Teiser, with her associates, had begun their work gathering recollections from the giants of the California wine industry for the Bancroft Library. Jim and I wanted to gather the memories of people close to the vine and the wine vat, at the local level. I returned to the Santa Clara Valley and collected interviews here and there to underpin my research on winegrowing in that area. Jim's zeal for Napa wine history led eventually to The Wine Library's great four-volume collection of eighty-two interviews, which have acted as a basic primary source for this study.

After he died in 1984 the Wine Library Association determined that a perfect salute to James Beard's contributions to our valley would be a history of Napa wine, from the earliest days to the present. The Association has allowed me to write that history, which is lovingly dedicated to the memory of our tireless, jolly, and sage mentor.

...

Writing the history of Napa wine has required me to use the techniques and discipline of local history. But since writing any kind of history is a process of selection, my original hope to blend the story of the Valley's wine industry with the overall local history of the area has fallen far short of this goal. The size of this study, as originally conceived by the Library Association, was smaller than the end product here. Thus the process of selection has been mostly a question of what must be left out. What I have left out would be a personal embarrassment if there were other histories of Napa that traced the story of the wine industry here from the earliest years to the present. But there are none.

I saw that my primary task was to answer the question all local histories must cope with. That is, "What happened?" This includes a brief story of virtually every vintage from the 1860s to 1993, along with the development, growth and geography of the Napa wine country. All this is tied to the overall story of the development of the California wine industry and the general business conditions of the American economy. But in doing so, and in developing several important historical themes, I have been forced to virtually overlook such matters as labor relations, ethnic and racial relations, and most local color. French historian Leo Loubère once complained that wine histories "rarely give more than passing mention to the human factor." I am sorry to say that this study will not do much to change his mind.

Originally I had hoped to blend the extremely violent nineteenth century history of the Napa Valley to the overall narrative. There were riots, lynchings, and murders in numbers that, for so small a community, might make us wonder at the relative intensity of the violence in contemporary California society. The slaughter from railroad accidents here was almost unbelievable. The racial and ethnic tension, violence, and prejudice make today's Napa Valley seem a mellow melting-pot in comparison.

Even though my focus has been on wine and the men and women who have grown it, produced it, and sold it, I still have had to wield a heavy hand in the process of selection. Many an industry personality and many a winery do not appear in the narrative. And even some aspects of the industry, particularly recent technical developments in the vineyard and cellar, have been touched only lightly because of the adequate coverage available in more general works. Where Napa wine men and women have been on the leading edge of a technical development, I have given the matter a full treatment.

What I have put together does, however, go beyond simply answering "what happened?" My most important theme has been to show the development of the Napa Valley's reputation as the greatest winegrowing area in the Western Hemisphere. This is the history of a perception and its growth since the 1870s has been complex and uneven, but for 120 years clearly manifest. I have taken special pains to show how this perception dimmed and almost died after Prohibition and how it has grown steadily since the 1950s.

I have also focused on the use of Napa land for winegrowing, the relative importance of the wine grape product here, and the recent and so far successful attempts to conserve the Valley's viticultural heritage, in the face of the urban and suburban growth in the San Francisco Bay Area since World War II. In doing so I have used the Santa Clara Valley, the topic of my previous regional wine history, as a contrasting pattern of development. Napa environmentalists have been continually aware of that pattern and have developed a frightening local neologism, "Santaclarafication."

Since much that has passed for California wine history since Repeal has had commercial overtones, often produced to underpin the sales of wineries with historic pasts, many names of Napa wine heroes-past have been lost to the contemporary wine world. We quite rightly remember the names of Charles Krug, Jacob Schram, and the Beringer Brothers. But these Napa wine leaders should stand no taller than George Belden Crane, Henry Pellet, H. W. Crabb, Theodore Bell, and Bismark Bruck. I hope that this study will fill out more properly the pantheon of Napa wine heroes.

Everyone knows that history is supposed to be objective, but anyone who understands historiography must accept the fact that the end product is still a matter of interpretation and judgment. The selection process that underpins this study is by definition a subjective one. I love wine and the world of wine at the local level with a rather uncomplicated passion, which I have tried to keep from intruding onto these pages. But no historian can escape his beliefs, values and tastes to reveal a past, in the German historian Ranke's words, "exactly as it happened. (Wie es eigentlich gewesen ist.)" If my peculiar passion has overstepped the proper bounds of historical good judgment, I take it for granted that my readers will let me know about it.

Charles L. Sullivan
Los Gatos, California
December 22, 1992

LA FRONTERA DEL NORTE

There are large open areas of land quite
proper for the cultivation of the vine.

—FR. JOSÉ ALTIMIRA
(June 29, 1823)

THE HISTORY OF NAPA WINE BEGINS AFTER 1817 WITH THE MOVEMENT OF THE Spanish mission system onto the northern portions of the San Francisco Bay Area. Before this date, for almost half a century, European civilization had been settling the coastal valleys of Alta California. The northern limit of that settlement was a line that one could draw from the Golden Gate across San Francisco Bay to the Carquinez Straits. North of this imaginary line was the *Contra Costa del Norte Este,* the farther coast to the northeast, today the counties of Napa, Sonoma, Solano, and Marin.

In 1769 Franciscan padres had begun settlement of Alta California with their mission at San Diego. By 1777 missions had been established in the Santa Clara Valley and at San Francisco. At the top of the San Francisco Peninsula, facing the yet to be named Golden Gate and the northern frontier, stood a little fortress, or presidio.

The California mission system accomplished its task of converting the natives of the coastal valleys fairly well. Most of these large agricultural establishments were located in spots that guaranteed good harvests. The security of the food supply at the missions was probably the greatest attraction to the neophytes. But one mission did not succeed well in its agricultural endeavors, the Mission San Francisco de Assis. Its crops simply would not ripen properly and its Indian population was unstable. Sickness and low morale complemented the gloomy coastal fogs, which are still a part of San Francisco's modern image.

In 1817, as an experiment, the San Francisco Mission settled a small number of Indians at San Rafael, a few miles north of the Golden Gate. This was the first Spanish settlement on the *Frontera del Norte,* and it was a success, to such an extent that in the following year a permanent *asisténcia,* a sort of branch establishment, was set up at San Rafael. It flourished. The branch mission did everything well that seemed impossible at San Francisco. They raised cattle and sheep, wheat, barley, and beans. And they planted a small orchard and vineyard, the latter from cuttings brought up from Mission San Jose, across the Bay to the southeast. The padres made a little wine here, probably first in 1821.[1]

The Frontera del Norte as drawn in 1889 from a map of the 1820s.

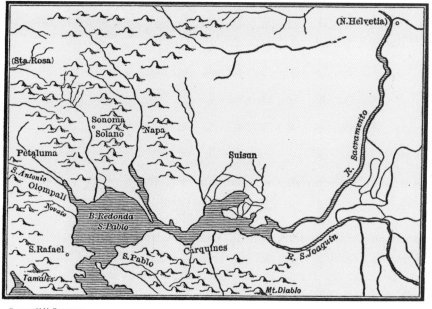

SOURCE: H.H. BANCROFT.

The San Rafael *asisténcia* was not the first European settlement in this part of California. The Russians, in their eastward march of empire, had established a small settlement in 1811 at Fort Ross (Rossiya), about fifty miles north of the Golden Gate on the Sonoma Coast. Later they also settled on Bodega Bay, a few miles to the south. The purpose of these Russian outposts was to raise crops and animals to help supply their Alaskan fur operations and to collect sea otter pelts. Until the 1830s the Russians had no intention of expanding these operations or of threatening the Spanish frontier to the south.

The Russians established ranchos inland where they raised livestock and grew crops. On the Georgy Rancho near Bodega there was a small orchard and a vineyard where vines brought north from Peru in 1817 were planted. They are known to have been bearing in 1823. A historical question arises here as to the first European vines planted in what we today call the North Coast winegrowing region of California. Should the Spanish at San Rafael or the Russians near Fort Ross receive the credit? It is a very close call, but it is likely that both plantations went in during the dormant season of 1817–1818.[2]

The real movement onto the northern frontier took place when a dedicated Franciscan padre dared to defy his religious superiors, who opposed his desire to expand the mission system to the north. His goal was to bring more Indians to the salvation offered by the Church. Father José Altimira had come to the San Francisco mission in 1820 and was numbed by the apathy and lack of progress there. He was born in 1790, a small, tough Catalan, like Father Serra before him. He met Governor Luis Arguello and impressed this official with his ideas and zeal.

In the spring of 1823 they worked out a plan to transfer the San Francisco Mission to the *Contra Costa del Norte Este,* that is, between the Petaluma area and the land east of present day Vallejo, on Suisun Bay. But it is fairly clear from the padre's later writing that he considered the Sonoma Valley the best spot for founding the next Franciscan mission, based on descriptions he had read of this land.

On April 9, 1823 the legislative council in Monterey ordered the transfer of the San Francisco mission to the North Bay and suggested the "Plains of Petaluma" as a likely spot. Arguello then wrote his superiors in Mexico for permission to proceed. Altimira sent a copy of the council's order to his superior, Father José Señan. According to law and tradition, such a transfer could not be made without authorization of Church officials, whatever the determination of the secular governor.

Shooting grizzly bears in old California

SOURCE: HUTCHINGS MAGAZINE.

Altimira and Arguello were now intent on presenting their superiors with a *fait accompli*. In June they organized an expedition whose object was "to examine the land for the establishment of the new Mission San Francisco." On June 25, without authorization from his superiors, Altimira, two of Arguello's officers and nineteen soldiers launched their little expedition from the embarcadero of the San Francisco Presidio and sailed up to San Rafael. The next day they set off on foot across Las Petalumas and on the 27th arrived at "the place called Sonoma." They marveled at the beauty of the situation and the wonderful weather (la bondad de la clima), so much warmer than San Francisco. They were particularly impressed by the abundance and vigor of the wild grapes growing there. Altimira decided that this was "a very proper locality for a mission."

The next day they set off across the rolling hills north of the Bay, today's Carneros region. They probably passed through Brown's Valley and explored the entrance to Napa Valley, much impressed by the herds of deer and antelope they saw there. They thought that this Napa area was a "special place," resembling Sonoma in every way, except that the latter appeared to have a better supply of water. They camped on Napa Creek and in the morning headed off to the east, up Tulocay Creek into Solano County's Green Valley. From there they descended into the Suisun area, shooting every grizzly bear they encountered, ten in one day. "Animals offensive to humans," wrote Altimira. They parleyed with local Indian leaders and decided that the area from here to the east was too far from the Presidio and had no advantages over Sonoma or Napa.

Fort Ross (Rossiya).

From an etching by

an early French visitor.

On the first of July they returned to Napa and rested at their old campsite. Altimira prophetically noted in his diary that there were large areas of land here "quite proper for the cultivation of the vine." In the afternoon they marched back to their camp at Sonoma, taking a more northerly route up Carneros Creek and dropping into the Valley from the northeast. They spent two more days looking over the area, making sure. They tramped up to

Bennett Valley and crossed over the hills into the Petaluma area again. Altimira had made up his mind that Sonoma it would be. It had better wood, stone, and water. The soil was good, and some of it looked perfect for vineyards. (Vemos tierras buenas para plantar Viñas.) The Monterey council had suggested Petaluma, but the padre wanted Sonoma, and that was it.

On July 4, 1823 they raised a huge redwood cross where the site of the mission church would be and Padre Altimira declared this place the "New San Francisco" Mission. On July 6 they were back at the Presidio.[3]

Many historians have argued, with virtually no documentary evidence, that this move to the north was motivated by the "Russian menace" at Fort Ross. It is true that Mexican independence in 1821 seemed to place the unsettled lands north of the Golden Gate in jeopardy, since Russian expansion here would no longer threaten the delicate Russo-Spanish relations of the 1820s. But if such matters ever crossed Altimira or Arguello's minds, there is no such record. Later, in the 1830s, there was something of a threat here from the Russian governor general, who hoped to acquire the mission lands in the North Bay for his company, but he was never supported by the Russian government.

Now Father Altimira had to deal with his own superiors, whom he had bypassed in the matters relating to the new mission. On July 16 he sent a report of his trip to the Father President of the missions, but received no reply. On August 3 he wrote Arguello that there was official opposition to the new mission. He argued that this opposition was mindless since Sonoma "offers more good fortune than any place this side of San Diego."

Apparently with the tacit consent of the governor, the padre put together the first complement for the new mission and set off from San Francisco on August 23. He had twelve soldiers, a two-pound cannon, and a large group of neophyte laborers. To the great California historian H. H. Bancroft the little padre was a man "with a will of his own," animated by a "spirit of independence," that rebelled against the conservative, legalistic attitude of his superiors. To the modern Catholic historian Zephyrin Engelhardt he was a somewhat audacious man of rebellious spirit.[4] Nevertheless, he was certainly a man who accomplished what he set out to do.

The little band arrived at the Sonoma Mission site on August 25 and, without ceremony (that had been taken care of July 4), went to work putting up the first rude buildings. Meanwhile, the president of the missions wrote Altimira that what he was doing was strictly illegal. The padre immediately wrote the governor, fuming over the obstructionist "machinations" of his superiors. He demanded to know whether "these men can overthrow Your Honor's wise provision." Arguello wanted the mission in place and didn't care how the clerics worked it out. So he put together a compromise with the ecclesiastical authorities. Altimira got to keep Sonoma. The San Francisco Mission would retain its function and its independent status, and San Rafael would continue as an *asisténcia* to the older mission. Sonoma would no doubt be setting up its own *asisténcias* in the Petaluma and Napa areas in the years to come. The new mission could not, however, remain "New San Francisco." Accordingly, it was renamed San Francisco Solano, after the Franciscan apostle of the Indies and Peru. This continued to be the official name, although most called it the Sonoma Mission, as will this study.

By the end of 1824 Altimira had a thriving operation, with 623 neophytes having come in for conversion the first year. They raised buildings and brought up cattle from the south. Crops were planted and an orchard and vineyard put in. The latter was propagated from about 3,000 cuttings shipped

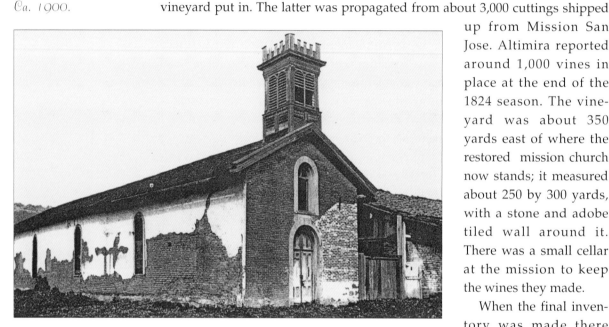

up from Mission San Jose. Altimira reported around 1,000 vines in place at the end of the 1824 season. The vineyard was about 350 yards east of where the restored mission church now stands; it measured about 250 by 300 yards, with a stone and adobe tiled wall around it. There was a small cellar at the mission to keep the wines they made.

When the final inventory was made there in 1836 there were 3,250 vines, but by 1839 the vineyard had fallen into total neglect, a place where cattle and horses were allowed to browse. Still, it served as the mother vineyard for the expansion of viticulture in the Sonoma and Napa Valleys.

MISSION WINES & VINES

At this point it is appropriate to discuss the character of winegrowing in Alta California during these years, since the methods used and the grapes grown at the missions and ranchos were, through the 1850s, those employed by the American winemaking pioneers of the Napa and Sonoma Valleys.

The vine which the padres brought with them from the missions of Baja

Sonoma Mission

before restoration,

Ca. 1900.

California and Mexico is usually referred to today as the Mission variety, although the term Criolla was then often employed. Later, in the 1850s, it was called the "California vine," while others of European origin were termed "foreign." The Mission vine, in fact, is clearly European in origin, a variety of the *Vitis vinifera*. But there is no clearly Old World counterpart today which can be firmly linked to this variety. Since it must have come to the New World in the sixteenth century, whatever the padres brought to Alta California after 1769 had been in the Western Hemisphere for at least two hundred years, plenty of time to have been crossbred accidentally or intentionally with New World vines.[5]

It is difficult today to say just what the Mission vines were that the padres carried to Sonoma and the American pioneers thence to the Napa Valley. None there could have survived the phylloxera pest of the late nineteenth century. The vines of the Mission variety which survive in California today, something over 1,000 acres, are of uniform breed. The plant is vigorous and produces huge crops from large clusters of brownish-red berries. The grapes are good to eat and can be used to make raisins. The wines made from them intended to be red are usually deficient in color and dull to the taste. Dry white wines are equally dull and harsh and tend to oxidize and darken easily. As a base for ordinary sweet wines, Mission grapes have received barely passing marks. But for the traditional California Angelica this variety can be a real success.[6] (This historic beverage will be discussed below.) Mission wines have also been distilled into an acceptable brandy. Such a product, as we shall see, was an important part of early Napa winegrowing.

The historical description of the Mission grape does not give a clear picture. Some writers thought there were at least two different varieties. Those grown in Northern California seemed to have had a more bluish color, which could have resulted from the different climates. And then there was a mysterious white Mission grape which Arpad Haraszthy discussed, but which no one has been able to identify.[7] We do know that there was a white muscat grape grown in some Mission vineyards, but we don't have a clue to its identity.[8]

We do have good descriptions of the mission and rancho wine in these days. Until recently it was thought that the first such wine came from vines that Father Serra brought to San Diego in 1769, and that subsequent mission winegrowing stemmed from this event. This notion has been put to rest by modern scholarship and the use of mission archive manuscripts. The first wine produced in Alta California was probably made in 1782 by Father Pablo Mugártegui, at Mission San Juan Capistrano, from vines brought from the south in 1778.[9] Winegrowing then spread to all the Spanish missions, save one, and became a useful part of mission life. At San Francisco the padres were never able to ripen grapes.[10]

In 1833 Father Narciso Durán of Mission San Jose wrote then Governor José Figueroa, describing the four types of mission wines. There were two types of red for the table, one dry and one sweet, "resembling the juice pressed from blackberries and thus rather unpleasant." There was a dry white wine made from the free run juice of the grape, which picked up a little of the color from the skins. The other white was sweet, made by adding brandy to the partially fermented, or unfermented, grape juice, often called must, and then allowed to age. This is what Californios came to call Angelica, which when aged for several years developed a sweet, nutty flavor that still finds favor among some California wine lovers. The padre added that it was very good with dessert. Well-aged Angelica usually brought praise from early visitors to Alta California, its flavor often likened to that of good Madeira wine. Americans and Europeans were usually rather contemptuous of the Californios' dry wines, which didn't go well with the powerful, spicy California cooking anyway. Sweet wines got much better marks.

A description of the winemaking process employed by the missionaries and rancheros does not communicate the charm implied by Father Durán's discussion of the end product. There are many fairly uniform descriptions from the 1840s and 1850s, the best and most complete by a native Californio who came to Alta California as a youth in 1834. He reported that large-scale winemaking operations employed a sort of platform from which a huge cowhide receptacle was hung. Sewn together hair-down, the hides acted as a sort of large bowl into which the grapes were dumped. Then Indians, well-washed (muy bien bañados) got in and trod the grapes. They wore loincloths and their heads were covered to keep hair from falling into the grapes. Their hands were covered with cotton cloth to wipe away the perspiration and each carried a stick (palo) to keep him from falling into the mess. The juice was gradually drawn off from underneath through an opening and placed in large tubs or tanks, which, when full, were allowed to sit for two or three months while the must fermented. The pulp rode on top of the fermenting mass and was later squeezed in a crude wooden press. This material was distilled into brandy. Little copper stills for making this *aguardiente* could be found throughout the province. Now the red wine was placed in barrels, or jars, or any moderately airtight receptacle handy, to be consumed over the next few months. White wine was made by drawing off a certain amount of the first run juice (el primer caldo de la uva) and placing it in separate containers to ferment.

For smaller operations the crushing was done in cowhides suspended between four large poles or trees. But otherwise the process was about the same. It was when American pioneers in Sonoma and Napa Valleys finally got away from this crude system of production that a real improvement could be tasted in wines produced there.[11]

SECULARIZATION

The years following the establishment of the Sonoma Mission marked a time of chaos in Mexican political affairs, which affected Alta California. The character of the Sonoma community totally changed and the settlement of the Napa Valley began.

Mariano

The anticlerical bias of the Mexican independence movement meant that the mission system in Alta California was doomed. In August 1833 the Mexican government ordered the secularization of the missions. The lands were to be distributed to the Indians and the central mission buildings were to

Guadalupe

Vallejo.

serve as the home for the padres, who would now be the parish priests. On August 9, 1834 Governor José Figueroa ordered the process to begin, and in doing so incited a veritable land rush, particularly along the northern frontier where the Sonoma Mission legally controlled over 700 square miles of land, including the entire Napa Valley. In addition there was much more good land outside the mission domain to be granted for ranchos.

The key person in distributing this land was a young lieutenant in charge of the garrison at the San Francisco Presidio in 1831, Mariano Guadalupe Vallejo. After the 1833 secularization decree, Figueroa ordered Vallejo to set up a new presidio in the Santa Rosa area and to grant land to settlers in order to accelerate the population of the land. Figueroa also ordered Vallejo to take up headquarters at Sonoma to oversee the breaking up of the mission's huge holdings. Sonoma was to become a pueblo and, for the time being, the military headquarters of the northern frontier district. Meanwhile the place filled up with prospective settlers, most of whom had moved from the south in hopes of acquiring some of the newly available land. In the spring of 1834 Vallejo himself was granted the huge Petaluma Rancho, which he was supposed to dole out to settlers, but never did. Nor was there to be a new presidio.

Not all those in the Sonoma area during these months were of Hispanic origin. One such was George Calvert Yount, a native of North Carolina. He was one of the most famous of America's mountain men, those tough individualists who roamed and trapped the western half of the North American continent and began entering Alta California in the 1820s. Yount had arrived here in 1831 and in the same year had passed through Napa Valley. Later he spent some time hunting sea otter in San Francisco Bay and its tributaries. He was attracted by the obviously expanding possibilities on the northern frontier after the 1834 secularization decree and got to know the young commandant of the region at Sonoma. During the building flurry at the new pueblo in 1835, he made himself particularly useful to Vallejo by organizing workers and teaching them the American art of shingle making, something seemingly unknown to the local Californios. The nearby redwood stands proved particularly useful for this task. In 1835 he also went down to San Rafael and was baptized Jorgé Concepción, a step necessary to qualify for land which Colonel, soon to be General, Vallejo would grant him the next year.

In the months after the Sonoma Pueblo was established the region changed from a huge mission domain to an area with large Mexican ranchos and Sonoma as its political and social center. The mission lands were doled out over the next few years to Vallejo's trusted military associates, friends, blood relatives, and in-laws. The legally required transfer of the land to the mission Indians did not take place, except in a few isolated instances. The Mexican government, under the corrupt rule of Antonio de Santa Anna, or his corrupt rivals, had neither the will, the ability, nor the desire to interfere in the marvelous land grab going on all over California.

On March 23, 1836 Vallejo granted Yount the mission's Caymus Rancho, an undeveloped section of the Napa Valley covering 12,000 acres, over eighteen square miles. (Of course, all the Napa Valley was undeveloped and uninhabited by whites.) The grant covered the Valley from just below today's Yountville to about a mile below St. Helena. Yount waited until the spring of 1838 to move onto his land. Meanwhile he continued to make himself useful to Vallejo as an Indian fighter, helping the General wipe out a huge band of horse thieves in the Soscol area south of Napa. The site of this battle was later the home of the Thompson Brothers' famous nursery, which helped supply some early Napa vineyardists with vines.

Before we leave Sonoma to concentrate on affairs in the Napa Valley, we need to take a backward glance at an important viticultural event. In 1836 Mariano Vallejo took over the Sonoma Mission vineyard. He made about 400 cuttings from the untended vines there, which he planted behind the two-story adobe he had recently built on the northeast corner of the Pueblo's plaza.

It was to be his family's new residence. He later expanded the vineyard with cuttings taken from the San Rafael Mission. Since Napa's first vineyards came from Sonoma cuttings and since the mission vineyard there was in disrepair in 1838, it is clear that George Yount's Napa vines, planted in 1838 or 1839, probably came from Vallejo's own plantation and not from the vines of the old mission vineyard enclosure.[12]

NOTES FOR CHAPTER ONE

It is not possible to present documentation for this study in its entirety. Nevertheless, for subjects about which there has been substantial controversy, I have supplied a fairly full set of notes. Citations to contemporaneous materials should be complete enough that a reader can use them to pursue a subject discussed.

ABBREVIATIONS

AESB	Agricultural Experiment Station Bulletin, University of California
Alta	Daily Alta California
AWP	American Wine Press and Mineral Spirit Review
Bancroft	Bancroft Library, University of California, Berkeley
BATF	U. S. Treasury Department, Bureau of Alcohol, Tobacco and Firearms
Bonfort's	Bonfort's Wine and Spirit Circular
Bulletin	San Francisco Bulletin
Chronicle	San Francisco Chronicle
CHSQ	California Historical Society Quarterly
Democrat	Sonoma Democrat
Examiner	San Francisco Examiner
Farmer	California Farmer
NVVA	Napa Valley Vintners Association
NVWL	Napa Valley Wine Library Association.
	History of NapaValley. Four volume oral history.
PWSR	Pacific Wine & Spirit Review (several titles)
Register	Napa Register
Reporter	Napa County Reporter
SBVC	Reports of the Board of State Viticultural Commissioners
Star	St. Helena Star
Transactions	Transactions of the State (California) Agricultural Society
UC	University of California
UCB	University of California, Berkeley
UC Davis	University of California, Davis
USDA	United States Department of Agriculture
VWGJ	Vinifera Wine Growers Journal

1. Hubert Howe Bancroft. History of California (San Francisco 1886-1890): II, 329-331; Jacob N. Bowman. "The Vineyards in Provincial California." Wine Review (May 1943): 10.

2. George Tays. "Mariano Guadalupe Vallejo and Sonoma." CHSQ (September 1937): 232; Bowman (June 1943): 9; Bancroft. II, 637.

3. José Altimira. "Diario de la expedicíon. . . 25 de Junio de 1823." Manuscript in Bancroft; Robert S. Smilie. The Sonoma Mission (Fresno 1975): 6-15.

4. Bancroft. II, 579, 692; Zephyrin Engelhardt. The Missions and Missionaries of California. (San Francisco 1908-1915): III, 178-183.

5. Thomas V. Munson, the noted American vine breeder, believed that the Mission "clearly shows characteristics of the Vitis girdiana." He thought the Mission an accidental cross between this native vine of the American Southwest and some European V. vinifera. See his Foundations of American Grape Culture. (Denison, Texas, 1909): 89.

6. M. A. Amerine and A. J. Winkler. "Composition and Quality of Musts and Wines of California Grapes." Hilgardia, XV:6 (February 1944): 536-537, 557-558; A. N. Kasimatis et al. Wine Grape Varieties in the San Joaquin Valley. *AESB*, AXT-26 (August 1972): 35; Brian McGinty. "Angelica." Vintage (October 1975): 33-37.

7. The story of the Napa Golden Chasselas gives us a hint in this matter. This grape was actually the Spanish Palomino, used in sherry making. Napa wine men knew this but liked the other name and kept it. Probably one way the vine got to Napa was from the Russian vineyard near Fort Ross which contained European vines brought from Peru. Since vinifera vines were brought here as early as 1817, and since John Sutter took cuttings from them in 1841, there may have been several unidentified varieties, white and red, abroad in the province before the American Conquest in 1846.

8. Thomas D. Terry, S. J. "California Grapes and California Missions," in Agriculture in the Development of the Far West (Washington DC 1975): 292-293; Arpad Haraszthy. "Wine Making in California." Overland Monthly (December 1871): 490; Vincent P. Carosso. The California Wine Industry, 1830-1895 (Berkeley 1951): 24; Andrew W. M'Kee. "The Grape and Wine-Culture of California." Report of the Commissioner of Patents, Agriculture, 1858 (Washington DC 1859): 338-339.

9. Edith Buckland Webb. Indian Life at the Old Missions (Los Angeles 1952): 95-96; Roy Brady played the sleuth in putting together Mrs. Webb's data on this matter. See "The Swallow That Came from Capistrano." New West (September 24, 1979): 55-60, and his more detailed essay in the Book of California Wine, 10-15.

10. Herbert B. Leggett. "Early History of Wine Production in California." Master's thesis, UCB (1939): 8-20.

11. Carlos N. Hijar. "Recuerdas sobre California. . . en 1834." Manuscript in Bancroft; Irving McKee. "The First California Wines." Wines & Vines (April 1947): 47-48; Agoston Haraszthy. "Report on Grapes and Wines of California." Transactions, 1858, 312; Edwin Bryant. What I Saw in California. . .1846, 1847 (London 1849): 298.

12. Madie D. Brown. 'The Vineyards of Gen. M. G. Vallejo." CHSQ (September 1957): 241-143; Irving McKee. "Vallejo, Pioneer Sonoma Wine Grower." California - Magazine of the Pacific (September 1948).

PIONEER DAYS

Cultivators of California! Plant your vineyards.
Begin now. No better investment can be made.

— CALIFORNIA FARMER
(January 11, 1855)

AFTER GEORGE YOUNT FIRST TRAVELED THROUGH THE NAPA VALLEY IN 1831, HE recalled that it had been its beauty that impressed him most. It was not distant from whatever European settlements existed in the Bay Area. But it was isolated and completely untouched by the white man. There were perhaps 3,000 natives living in the Valley then and he found most of them friendly. He decided that it was here he would settle down and live out his days.

When he returned in the spring of 1838, he brought some tools, a few animals, a hired hand, and a little Indian girl. He pitched his tent and began building a two-story log cabin/block house, the first in California, for protection from the hostile Indians to the north. He had roamed the West long enough to know that security was not built on hopes or impressions.[1]

During the year he "raised a tolerable supply of vegetables" and built a house and corral. He soon had a hundred head of cattle, the economic mainstay for any ranchero in those days in pastoral California. Later he built a flour and saw mill nearby. He continued to spend much of his time exploring the area and hunting. A large part of that hunting activity consisted of shooting grizzly bears, which might be considered the dominant species in the area before Europeans brought in their high-powered firearms. One day Yount killed eight of the monsters and later noted that seeing fifty or sixty in a day was not uncommon.[2]

Yount was able to deal with the local Indians in much the same way he had seen it done at the missions. He was able to attract a large force of reliable labor with the security of his blockhouse and his muzzle-loader. And there was always a dependable supply of food. He got along very well with most of the Napa Indians, often coming to their assistance when their *rancherías* in the Valley were raided by marauding parties from the Clear Lake area and the Central Valley.[3]

George C. Yount,

Ca. 1855.

As the years went by Yount's agricultural domain grew to a remarkable extent. He had several hundred acres under cultivation in the 1840s, mostly to grain, and there were more than a thousand head of livestock. In later years, more than other grantees in the region, he tended to hold his land together, not selling so much off in pieces as others did.

In 1844 his estate was further expanded when General Vallejo granted him the 4,400-acre Rancho La Jota on top of Howell Mountain, east of today's St. Helena. American settlers had started arriving in Northern California, the first wagon train making it through the Sierra, without their wagons, in 1841. Yount wanted plenty of lumber to meet the coming demand from such settlers and, like John Sutter later in the Sacramento Valley, he went to the nearby hills.

Sometime during these early years, Yount planted a small orchard and vineyard at his adobe residence, near what is today Yount Mill Road, just above the village of Yountville. This vineyard marks the beginning of viticulture in the Napa Valley, but its planting was no special event, since virtually any respectable ranchero in California wanted his own supply of grapes. The cuttings were obtained from Mariano Vallejo, probably from his new vineyard. But it is not certain when they first went into the ground.

This is a matter of some interest for anyone wanting to celebrate the 175th or 200th anniversary of Napa Valley viticulture. J. L. L. Warren, the publisher of *California Farmer* and founder of the California State Agricultural Society, visited Yount several times over the years and reported that the vineyard had been planted in 1839. In 1856 a visiting committee of the Society reported that the vineyard was eighteen years old. This statement was made in 1857, again pointing to an 1839 planting date. This year makes better sense than 1838, since Yount arrived in the spring, normally too late to plant cuttings successfully. A proper inference from these data is that the vineyard was probably planted during the dormant season of 1838–39, with some cuttings very possibly going in before the first of the year. Yount's cuttings were huge, three feet in length and planted two feet deep.[4]

Determining the founding date for Napa's viticulture is nothing compared to the task of dating the first Napa vintage. There simply is no firm date. We can certainly presume that Yount would have squeezed a few grapes from his first harvest, which would have been in 1841 or 1842. He had seen it done at Sonoma, and on a small scale it would have been no difficult task. He almost certainly gave it a try. But it appears unlikely that he was very proud of the result, since visitors who came by over the next few years and then wrote of the fine meals at the rancho never mentioned wine as a part of the Yount board. But he certainly did make wine here in the late forties, at least on a small scale. His little granddaughter watched it being made.

Mary Bucknall lived on the rancho with her grandfather until 1853. Later she recorded the winemaking process as she had seen it in her youth.

> I have a very distinct recollection of seeing the most primitive and earliest methods of winemaking. . . . The grapes were put in rough troughs and the Indians, girt with their loin cloths only. . . trampled out with their bare feet the mass until it was reduced to a pulp. This pulp was then placed in suspended ox-skins. They were hung from four strong stakes sunk in the ground, and when the fermentation process was complete a hole was made in the skin and the wine (so-called) was drawn off.

We shall see that by the early 1850s Yount had become quite serious about making wine and was showing it off at a San Francisco newspaper office.[5]

The natural environment in which George Yount now toiled was as beautiful as it was productive for him and those who later settled there. The Napa Valley is a long and fairly narrow portion of the California Coastal Range system, about thirty-five miles in length from the place where the Napa River empties into its delta to the Calistoga area in the north, where the valley is bluntly pinched off by the surrounding mountains. On the west side the Mayacamas Range rises abruptly from the valley as far south as Napa where it gives way to the rolling hills that serve as the northern margin of the Carneros region. On the east side the Vaca Range extends south all the way to the northern shoreline of the Carquinez Strait. North of the town of Vallejo, this ridge also rises abruptly from the valley floor and becomes quite rugged as one travels north. Northeast of St. Helena it broadens into a plateau-like volcanic hump, Howell Mountain. Several valleys of importance lie on the eastern drainage side of this range: Chiles, Conn, Wooden, Pope, and Foss.

The main valley has a wide variety of soils, with more than forty fairly distinct types. These soils fall into two general groups, upland and lowland. The upland soils stand back from the center of the valley and extend into the narrow foothill belts. On the Mayacamas side good upland soil is also found on Mt. Veeder, Spring Mountain, and Mount Diamond (or Diamond Mountain). Howell Mountain has some excellent soils, as well. These upland soils are generally favored for growing wine grapes. Lowland alluvial soils are deeper and tend more to the center of the valley on each side of the Napa River. But many of these lowland soils also provide very good environments for wine grapes.

A very large portion of the Napa Valley soil derives from volcanic materials, particularly north of Conn Creek. This is also true of the Stag's Leap area on the east side of the valley and on the west side south to Oakville. Pockets of this igneous alluvium can be found here and there even farther south. From the Oak Knoll area south, the Napa Valley soils are simply too complex for a study such as this to discuss in any detail. But over the last 125 years, experiment, particularly in the Carneros region of late, has shown many spots to be favorable to viticulture.

Those whose vineyards today stand on the Bale loam derived from volcanic rhyolite tend to think that their soil has a lot to do with the excellence of their wine grapes. Those whose vineyards stand on other soil types tend to agree with the American (not French) scientific view, which holds that the parent material of soils has not been proven to be a determining factor in the excellence of a wine's flavor.[7]

In the 1850s the pioneers knew that grapes grew well in the Valley. By the

1860s they were fairly sure that some of their wines tasted really good, and that upland grapes seemed to provide better flavored wines. That was about the limit of soil science here at that time.

Climate is a very different matter. The Spanish sailors, who sailed along the California coast for the two hundred years before the padres moved their missions there, knew very well that as they went north the climate became more and more like that of coastal Spain. They were right. The coastal valleys of Alta California have that almost unique Mediterranean climate that brings moderate but usually plentiful rainfall in the winter and spring, and warm, dry summers that ripen crops without the humid conditions associated with east coast climates. Less than one percent of the earth's surface has such a climate, but in Northern California the Napa Valley has it with particularly benign properties. The Valley gets more than its share of rainfall, since it approaches the fairly rainy "marine west coast" designation of northwestern California. When San Jose gets fifteen inches of annual rain at the southern edge of the Bay Area, Napa will normally receive closer to thirty inches. In addition, the Napa Valley benefits from all the warming and ripening effects of a sometimes torrid summer heat. But the cold, upwelling waters along the coast bring a cooling effect in the evenings. And there are also the cooling coastal fogs that penetrate the valleys around the Bay Area. For thirty to fifty days during the summer months, cooling fogs creep into the Napa Valley during the night and sit there in the morning, warding away the heat of the summer until they burn off, usually well before noon. In the Carneros region these fogs are often heralded by cooling late afternoon breezes which moderate the high temperatures experienced earlier in the day.

But in the winter the coldness can be hard. Sometimes the Valley is blanketed by snow. Freezing temperatures are good for the vines when they are dormant. But freezing weather sometimes extends into the spring, as late as May, after the vines have leafed out. Then these delicate vinifera plants can be burned black and their crop cut in half, or less. The average late date of the last spring frost at St. Helena is March 27. The first fall frost averages October 29.

In the fall the local "Cape Verde" climate means that summer temperatures often last into late October. This is important for the eventual maturity of the Valley's grapes. But fall rains can sweep in, particularly from the southwest, and drench the Valley in September and October, an unfortunate situation for the winegrower. Before Prohibition, Napa's Indian summer conditions in the late fall could be a problem for winemakers, since fermentations often "stuck" with October temperatures in the nineties or higher, which can be fairly common.

Since the early days the Napa Valley has afforded its inhabitants a wonderfully moderate climate in which to live and grow grapes. The area stands well removed from the centers of economic and cultural life in the Bay Area. And there are no through routes coursing the Napa Valley. Yet the place is close enough to the heart of Northern California life to serve as a special magnet for those who want the bucolic isolation it affords, but who also want the company of the society that has come to love its wines.

EDWARD BALE — MORE GRAPES

General Vallejo granted portions of lower Napa and the Carneros soon after Yount's grant, but these did not directly affect the settlement of the upper valley. The next grant with significance for this study went to Edward Turner Bale, an English surgeon who landed at Monterey in 1837. He married Vallejo's niece, Maria Soberanes, was naturalized, and received his grant from the General in 1841. The name of the new rancho was Carne Humana (human flesh).[8] This tract was half again as large as Yount's, running north from Rancho Caymus' northern edge to the end of the Napa Valley, well above Calistoga. The Bales did not move onto the land until 1844, and then only after the doctor was almost lynched in Sonoma for attempting to shoot Vallejo's brother in the back. His aim was less than perfect, nicking Salvador on the neck. Vallejo packed Bale off to Napa forthwith.

Edward Bale's

1846 grist mill

as it looked in 1888.

He built an adobe home on what is today Whitehall Lane, south of St. Helena. So far as the Valley's viticultural history is concerned, Bale is more significant for the marriages of his two daughters than for any work he did among the vines. (Carolina will marry Charles Krug and Lolita will marry Louis Bruck. We shall meet these two German families later.) A small vineyard was planted above St. Helena in the early 1850s, but Bale's most important relation to wine was the amount he drank.[9]

Bale and his widow, far more than Yount, were willing to break up and sell portions of this huge domain. That tendency meant that this portion of the upper Valley would develop and move into viticulture sooner than the Rutherford-Oakville-Yountville section. In contrast, several thousand acres of Yount's land remained undivided until the 1870s.

Today, Bale's name is usually linked to the huge gristmill with the distinctive waterwheel he had built in 1846. It has been rebuilt and is one of the Valley's important historical attractions today. The man who did the blacksmith work on the mill was Florentine (Frank) Kellogg, who was paid for his effort with a large piece of land north of St. Helena. He planted vines in 1849 and later made small amounts of wine. His place was purchased in 1871 by William W. Lyman, who built his El Molino (the mill) Winery there.

Others moved into the Napa area in these pre-Gold Rush days and planted Mission vines. David Hudson, John York, and Wells Kilburn on Bale land, and Charles Hopper, who bought land from Yount, are among the best known. In the eastern valley named for him Joseph Chiles also planted a few vines.

Meanwhile California had undergone revolutionary changes. Americans had begun arriving steadily overland after 1841. Then between 1846 and 1848 Alta California became a possession of the United States. In 1848 gold was discovered and the world rushed in. By the 1850s the Indian population of the Napa Valley had almost disappeared, decimated by cholera, smallpox, and the land hunger of the growing American population. By 1860 there were only about 200 Indians left here.

The town of Napa was laid out in 1848 at the ford of the Napa River on the Benicia-Sonoma Road. To this point the river was navigable at high tide. Steamboats connecting the Valley with the rest of the Bay Area were common sights in 1851. By 1852 the place was a little wooden boom town with about three hundred inhabitants. The next year Henry Still bought a piece of Bale land and opened a little store. This would become the nucleus of the future village of St. Helena. Within a couple of years there was a small hotel, a blacksmith, a wainwright, and a little Baptist church.

Napa entered the fifties as a home for livestock. By the end of the decade it was a land of grain. In 1859 Richard Henry Dana wrote that he "never saw so much land under the plough in the same space, except in England. Great fields, level, rich. . . and the distances so great that the men are ploughing by flagstaffs, as a pilot would steer his ship."

But there also was a tendency toward agricultural diversification, as local farmers learned about drought conditions and the business cycle. By the mid-1850s there were about 50,000 grapevines in the Napa Valley; at the end of the decade there were about 200,000. The locals were heeding Warren's call to "Plant your vineyards."[10]

JOSEPH W. OSBORNE & OAK KNOLL FARM

In the Gold Rush years, California attracted a large number of Argonauts from New England, a few of whom had already visited Pacific ports as shipmasters in the old China trade. One such man was J. W. Osborne, who settled in California in 1850 and the next year bought a large tract of land three miles south of Yountville, which he called Oak Knoll. Had he not been murdered by a former employee in 1863, history might well have named him the father of Napa Valley's fine wine industry.

As an active member of the Massachusetts Horticultural Society, Osborne had taken a keen interest in viticulture in the old Bay State, where a profitable hothouse grape culture had developed in the 1820s, growing vinifera varieties under glass for the table. Osborne and Frederick W. Macondray, also a Massachusetts sea captain, brought a large number of these vinifera vines to California in 1852. Osborne planted them in his nursery at Oak Knoll. They included several varieties suitable for winemaking as well as for the table. There were muscat varieties such as the Frontignan and Alexandria. There were also the Catawba, the "Zinfindal," and the Flame Tokay.

By 1854 Osborne had 6,000 vines, half of them foreign. By 1860 his fifty-acre vineyard was the largest in the Napa Valley. In 1856 Oak Knoll was named the best farm in the state by the California Agricultural Society. Year after year Osborne won top awards at various Northern California fairs for his outstanding grapes. He was president of the state Horticultural Society and, with Agoston Haraszthy in 1859, led the way in forming the Sonoma-Napa Horticultural Society. His agricultural library was thought to be the largest in California.

Oak Knoll, the estate of J.W. Osborne. Later the site of the Eshcol Winery.

Osborne was ever the advocate of better wine grapes to replace the almost ubiquitous Mission variety. More than anyone he was responsible for introducing the Zinfandel vine to the Napa and Sonoma Valleys in 1859. But after his death, his 1,800-acre estate lost its experimental character, although grapes were still grown. Later a portion of Oak Knoll became the Eshcol Vineyard, which is the home today of the Trefethen Winery.[11]

Shortly after Osborne acquired Oak Knoll, the Thompson brothers, Simpson and William, took payment for some lumber they had supplied to General Vallejo by taking over 335 acres of land south of Napa on the east side of the Carneros. Soscol Creek gave the area and the Thompson nursery their names. In 1853 they began planting their huge orchards and a vineyard. Grapes were by no means the Thompsons' major concern, but they took a lively interest in them and helped promote the planting of better foreign varieties. Their grape

Thompson Bros. Ranch

collections were usually to be seen at the regional fairs in Northern California in the 1850s, competing successfully with those of Osborne and Macondray. The poorly drained bottom land around Soscol Creek could never have served as a proper home for fine vineyards, but in later years the Soscol hills to the east and southeast did support successful vineyards. Today vineyards are again appearing there, since it is really a sort of eastern extension of the Carneros area.

JOHN M. PATCHETT — NAPA WINE

After having a go in the mines during the Gold Rush this English brewer from Pennsylvania came down to Napa in 1852. He bought a piece of land west of town on which a vineyard had been planted in 1850. He expanded it and by 1856 was making a fairly sizeable amount of wine. The next year, according to historian Irving McKee, Patchett made the first commercial shipment of wine from Napa Valley, about 400 gallons. In 1858 he agreed to have a young German fellow from the Sonoma side bring over a little borrowed cider press and make his wine this year in a fashion more typically European than Californian. Charles King, as Charles Krug was then temporarily styling himself, had done the same on shares the previous year for others in Sonoma. The resulting vintage pleased Patchett enough to build a real stone cellar the next year, the first in the Napa Valley. It was located at First and Monroe Streets in Napa and replaced the little adobe hut he previously used to hold his wine.

Patchett was proud of the white wine that Krug had made for him in 1858 and the following spring he dropped in to see Colonel Warren at the offices of the *California Farmer*. Warren was impressed and thought it tasted like a good German "Hock." (Krug had probably added a little muscat to the otherwise bland Mission.) Patchett then hired the French-Swiss Henry A. Pellet to be his permanent winemaker. Pellet stayed on until 1863. We shall meet him again in St. Helena. By the mid-1860s some considered Patchett's wine, red and white, to be the best in the Valley. Warren also thought his brandy to be superior. Patchett made wine in Napa until 1870 when, at age seventy-three, he sold his business.

The Englishman was not the only one who was thinking about selling Napa wine. George Yount had sent samples of his wine down to San Francisco as early as 1854. The editor of the *Alta California* thought it was probably Vintage 1853, "clear bright red, and bears a good resemblance to the Bordeaux wines, but is better than most of the claret offered in the San Francisco market." The paper went on to say that it would be better if a little older, with "perhaps a little better management."

Yount finally got that better management in 1860 when he took on Charles Krug and his little press to make up his grape crop. Yount had done quite a bit of planting in the mid-1850s, but his wine production through 1855 was only averaging about 200 gallons per year. In 1860 Krug produced 5,000 gallons for him on shares. (In 1859 Krug made wine on the Bale Rancho for Louis Bruck, his future brother-in-law.)

In later years Krug looked back at these three vintages and liked to say that he had produced "the first lot of wine ever made in Napa County." Then he would wink and "correct this statement." At the Bale and Yount ranchos they had given him "a tincup full of 'elegant claret' which was fermented in large cowhides." He owned amusedly that it was a "glorious drink." Actually Richard Henry Dana had thought a little better of Yount's wine when he visited the old pioneer in 1859. The old pioneer gave his visitor a "bottle of wine of his own make." Dana said, "I like it. It has no spirit, but pure juice, pressed by hand." At the 1857 Napa Fair Yount didn't win the first prize for table wine, but his brandy did. The next year he exhibited four bottles of his "Native Wine" at the State Fair.

Before Yount died in 1865, he had become one of the leading wine producers in the Valley. A little village to the south of his place had grown up, called Sebastopol, after the site of the great siege in the Crimean War in 1855. After his death the locals changed its name to Yountville. He was the richest man in Napa County in these years but, in Dana's words, he had "a simple, natural courtesy. . . which is delightful. He is a gentleman roughened by forty years of hardy adventure." In his later years he was annoyed by lawyers and squatters who, he thought, were worse than grizzlies. In all, he was one of the true heroes of the West.[12]

We should take note of two other pioneers of the 1850s. J. J. Sigrist planted his vineyard in 1859 and later built a sizeable cellar west of Napa near Browns Valley Road on the way to Sonoma. By 1860 his forty-five-acre vineyard was exceeded in size only by that of J. W. Osborne. By the end of the decade, Sigrist was making over 50,000 gallons of wine per year. In 1878 he sold his place to George Barth who expanded the operation even further.

The wine pioneer of the Carneros was William H. Winter, who bought 664 acres in 1855 on the Sonoma County line along Carneros and Huichica Creeks. He later expanded his holdings there to over 1,200 acres. Winter was involved in everything from stock raising to olive culture. In the process he planted seventy acres of Mission vines and built a stone winery and distillery. We shall look in here again in the 1880s when the renowned Professor George Husmann comes to Napa.

THE CALIFORNIA WINE INDUSTRY

Nothing in the preceding pages should suggest to the reader that the Napa wine "industry" had any kind of standing yet in the overall picture of the state's industry. At the end of the 1850s, Sonoma had three times as many vines as Napa. Los Angeles had almost ten times as many. In the early 1860s even El Dorado County in the Sierra foothills had twice as many vines as Napa.

Something of an industry had begun in Los Angeles in the 1830s when Bordeaux-born Jean-Louis Vignes became California's first truly professional winegrower. After the American Conquest and the Gold Rush, the new state's appetite for alcoholic beverages of all kinds was astronomical. In 1855 California imported 13,758 barrels and 120,000 cases of still wine (non-sparkling), as well as 18,620 cases of Champagne.[13] Most of this wine came from France. The small steps toward commercial winegrowing discussed earlier were part of a statewide effort by local producers to get a piece of this action.

Since most of the state's vineyards were in Southern California and most of the markets were in the north, the basis for a successful new industry depended on its ability to produce wine in the Los Angeles area and market it in the San Francisco Bay Area. This was first accomplished by Charles Kohler and John Frohling, two young Germans who started their business in 1854. By the end of the decade they had stored over 100,000 gallons of Southern California wine in their San Francisco cellars.[14]

In Northern California the best efforts to take advantage of this market were made in the Santa Clara and the Sonoma Valleys. In the South Bay area the mission and pueblo were the sites of quick development. In the 1850s the well-settled area began attracting many Frenchmen interested in promoting a wine industry. The historic imports of good French vinifera vines by Antoine

Delmas in 1852 and Charles Lefranc in 1857 set the process in motion.[15] In the North Bay we have already seen the glimmerings of commercial winegrowing around the Sonoma pueblo. Then in the 1850s several Americans planted Mission vines. But in 1857 things really started moving. Agoston Haraszthy bought a piece of land here and began pushing for serious commercial winegrowing. General Vallejo hired a Frenchman as his winemaker, Victor Faure. Two Germans, Jacob Gundlach and Emil Dresel, also arrived and imported European vinifera. It was here in Sonoma during these years that the North Bay winegrowing frenzy originated. Ripples from this splash were quickly felt in the neighboring Napa Valley, helped along by the good work of Charles Krug, John Patchett, and J. W. Osborne.

Krug was one of the Germans who came to Sonoma with Haraszthy. He bought a twenty-five-acre piece of land, named it Monte Bello, and planted 6,000 vines. But his experiences in Napa led him to put the place up for sale in September 1860. It is worth noting that in 1860, fifteen of the leading vineyardists in the Sonoma Valley were Germans, an ethnic influence that would soon become clearly visible in the Napa Valley.[16]

In the 1850s Napa was connected to the rest of the Bay Area by steamboats. The Zinfandel went to work in the 1870s.

PASSENGER
AND
FREIGHT LINE
BETWEEN
San Francisco and Napa
STEAMER

ZINFANDEL

H. G. BELL, MASTER,

Will leave Washington st. wharf, San Francisco, every Tuesday, Thursday and Saturday at 5 p. m., touching at all intermediate landings.

RETURNING, leaves Napa Tuesday, Wednesday and Friday, with the tide,

FARE, INCLUDING BERTH, $1.00.

Freight at Lowest Rates.

N. H. WULFF, Agent, Napa, Cal.
Telephone No., Napa, Red 72.
San Francisco, Main 1104

By 1860 the Napa Valley was ready to become winegrowing country. If a person flew over it in a balloon at the beginning of the decade he would have to look closely to find its vineyards. By the end of the decade there were over 2,000 acres of vines.

Napa City was a wooden and brick town now, dusty and boisterous. It had fourteen saloons and six livery stables, three hotels, five churches, sixteen lawyers, and a race track with a "jockey club." The town was now linked to the south by telegraph. It was a little urban center for a leading producer of grain and an outlet for various mining interests to the north. There were even moves to establish resort facilities in the area.

St. Helena was not even a real village yet, with no more than a dozen houses when Krug arrived there in the fall of 1860. By the end of the decade it would be taking on the look of a little American wine town.

To the historian Vincent Carosso, the story of California wine before 1860 was "largely a chronicle of romantic personalities and interesting events." The state wine industry was now to become a significant part of the economy. For the Napa Valley, the decade of the sixties was both a time of romantic personalities and interesting events and a time when winegrowing became a large part of its economy.

Notes for Chapter Two

1. Orange Clark. "George Calvert Yount." 1855 manuscript in the papers of Zoeth Eldredge, Bancroft; Charles L. Camp. George C. Yount and His Chronicles of the West (Denver 1966); C. A. Menefee. Historical and Descriptive Sketch Book of Napa, Sonoma, Lake and Mendocino (Napa City 1878): 125-127.
2. Elizabeth C. Wright. 'Early Upper Napa Valley." Manuscript (1924), Bancroft.
3. There were six villages between today's Calistoga and Soscol. Yount helped keep the peace between them and his blockhouse was the site of many a battle, often a haven for local natives.
4. Farmer, 3/16/1854, 8/10/1860; Transactions, 1856: 10-13; PWSR, 7/6/1892. William Pfeffer, the noted Santa Clara Valley vine breeder, worked on the Yount ranch in 1869, rooting out these old vines for the widow Yount. When he complained of the difficulty such a method of planting caused, she chided him for "speaking in a disrespectful way about Mr. Yount."
5. Mary E. Bucknall. Early Times. Bancroft; Ellen Lamont Wood. George C. Yount (San Francisco 1941): 114; Elizabeth Ann Watson. Sketch of the Life of George C. Yount. Bancroft.
6. There are three "Napas," the city, the valley, and the county. In the early years the little town was always termed "Napa City." This study will refer to it as Napa unless the meaning is not clear.
7. David G. Howell of the U. S. Geological Survey (Menlo Park, CA.) has begun studying the relationship between the volcanic soils of the Napa Valley and wine flavors, particularly of Cabernet Sauvignon. But in his words, he has "barely scratched the surface." He has produced a commercial video on the subject, "Earth Nectar: The Wines of the Napa Valley and the Earth from which They Arise." D. L. Elliot-Fisk and A. C. Noble of UC Davis cast doubt on the relationship between wine flavor and soil-type in a 1991 paper presented at the Miami AAG Symposium on "Viticulture in Geographic Perspective." Proceedings at 45.
8. The Indian ranchería on the Bale grant was variously spelled, usually coming out something like Callajomanas. Bale, according to Erwin Gudde, "with a gruesome sense of humor," twisted the term to the Spanish expression. See his California Place Names (Berkeley 1962): 19, 54.
9. Bale was a hard drinker and had run a saloon in Monterey. His books show he once traded forty sheep for five cases of Madeira wine. In regard to his vineyard, there is a report from one of Professor Bowman's sources that there were vines growing there in 1838. But in 1845 James Clyman stopped at Bale's and noted it "almost destitute of vegitation (sic) no fields garden of any kind of cultivation to be seen. . . ." In Bale's 1849 will there was no vineyard in the large inventory. Bale Family Papers, Bancroft; Charles L. Camp, ed. James Clyman Diaries (San Francisco 1928): 7/16/1845.
10. Appendix to the Journals of the Senate, "Annual Report of the Surveyor General. . . California," Session of 1856: 50. The collection of agricultural statistics in California in the nineteenth century is often laughable. The numbers given in this study are my best guesses, taken from a wide variety of sources.
11. Alta, 9/28/1857, 10/6/1858, 2/12/1860, 10/6/1860; Farmer, 6/22/1854, 8/8/1856, 11/21/1856, 9/18/1857; Transactions, 1858: 241; Ernest Peninou and Sidney Greenleaf. A Directory of California Wine Growers and Wine Makers in 1860 (Berkeley 1967): 34; Irving McKee. "Historic Napa County Winegrowers." California - Magazine of the Pacific (September 1951). For a detailed documentation of the Zinfandel in early California see: Charles L. Sullivan. "A Viticultural Mystery Solved." CHSQ (Summer 1978): 114-129, and "Zinfandel: A True Vinifera." VWGJ (Summer 1982): 71-86; Wines & Vines (February 1977): 17.
12 PWSR, 3/18/1890; Star, 12/27/1878, 12/19/1890; Alta, 2/2/1863; Farmer, 3/18/1859, 8/10/1860; Transactions, 1858: 105.
13. These statistics were compiled by Frederico Biesta in his report to the Sardinian Minister of Foreign Affairs. CHSQ (December 1963): 311-330.
14. Charles Kohler manuscript (5/27/1886), Bancroft.
15. Charles L. Sullivan. Like Modern Edens (Cupertino 1982): 15-31.
16. Alta, 12/6/1859; Farmer, 9/21/1860, 10/10/1860.

BUILDING A WINE INDUSTRY

Krug's wines are pretty good, but rather strong, else I tasted a little too much,
as I found my way to Calistoga, after imbibing a while in his cellar,
only because there is but one road leading up the valley.

—DAILY ALTA CALIFORNIA
March 11, 1866

UNLIKE SOME OTHER PREMIUM WINEGROWING DISTRICTS IN CALIFORNIA, THE Napa Valley is not weighed down with foggy myths about the origins of its wine industry. Napa started late and the two men most responsible for this start lived into the 1890s. They left a good chronicle of those early days when they first heeled in their vines. Both had a strong time sense and an appreciation of the history they made and observed.

Charles Krug was a builder, a soft-spoken, persuasive intellectual with a great will to succeed. He is remembered today in association with the premium winery in St. Helena that bears his name and proudly displays the little cider press that Agoston Haraszthy had loaned him in 1858; Buena Vista presented it to him in 1878 to commemorate his pioneer winemaking efforts in the Napa Valley. He became a leader of the state industry and was one of the several in his community who acted as a conscience for the local industry.

The other man was equally persuasive, an intellectual whose pen was ever at the ready to defend the cause of good wine and sound winegrowing practices. The first to use good foreign vinifera grapes here, he showed that the Upper Napa Valley could make very good wine. He built no huge wine plant that might perpetuate his name. But when Charles Krug looked back to the industry's real beginnings in the 1860s, he recalled that when he first came to settle here, this man took him out to see his new vineyard, "the first planted in Napa County for the purpose of wine making."[1]

George

Belden

Crane

GEORGE BELDEN CRANE

When the *Alta California* complained in 1859 that "the Napa wine exposed to our taste seemed badly made," the correspondent might just as well have said that it seemed to be made from inferior grapes. Mission grapes were the bane of Napa winemakers who used them to produce dry wines. But in 1865 one could now taste wines made from George Belden Crane's foreign vinifera vines, planted in 1861. From then on Napa wine men made a permanent change in their Valley's history. The planting frenzy that began in the early sixties had mostly involved Mission vines. After 1865 varieties such as White Riesling, Sylvaner, Palomino (called "Golden Chasselas" here), Zinfandel, and Black Malvoisie (Cinsaut) were the order of the day.

Crane came to California in 1853 and settled in the San Jose area, where he practiced medicine until 1857. In that year, at age fifty-one, he determined that the upper Napa Valley was just the underdeveloped area he wanted to help develop. He had met

32

NAPA WINE

the Santa Clara Valley wine man, Francis Stock, and became interested in the future of wine in California. He came to the Napa Valley and bought 300 acres of Bale land for about $2,100, just south of St. Helena. In January of 1859 he broke ground, clearing the rough chaparral and planting some Mission vine cuttings on six by seven foot centers. Virtually every cutting in the twelve new acres leafed out that spring, but in the winter of 1859–60 half of them died. He replaced them and got a good take. Next year he got his foreign cuttings from Francis Stock, who had imported the White Riesling and Sylvaner from Germany in 1858.[2]

Crane's first vintage came in 1862. It amounted to 300 gallons from his Mission vines. He then built a small stone cellar and the next year hired as his winemaker Henry A. Pellet, already noted for his work at John Patchett's. In 1864 Pellet made a few gallons from Crane's German grapes, which, the *Alta California* declared, showed how good wine from the St. Helena area could be. In 1865 he had a real vintage and the next year the *Alta* cheered Crane as the leader of this new Napa phenomenon. Even the leading Sonoma newspaper declared that Crane's wines were as good as anything they had made yet on their side of the mountains. Here we see the beginnings of a development that would mature in the 1880s. It was the idea that the upper Napa Valley made the best wines in Northern California, an idea of great importance at a time when it was becoming more and more evident that Northern California would soon take the lead from Southern California in wine production.[3]

Redwood tanks became part of the Napa wine scene in the 1860s.

In 1869 Crane had put in about a hundred acres of vines and by 1874 had boosted his production to 50,000 gallons. By then he was almost seventy years old and was ready to retire from the wine business. Over the next several years, many notable wine men ran his place for him: Albert Schranz, R. W. Lemme, and finally John McPike, his son-in-law. Crane lived until 1898. His articles and letters to the press were constant reminders to his readers that an agricultural community in the Napa Valley might attain most of the elements of high culture aspired to by city folk.

WINE TANKS
IN SHOOKS

The undersigned beg leave to inform the Winegrowers that they are prepared to furnish **REDWOOD TANK MATERIAL** of best quality butt cut, thoroughly seasoned and prepared ready to set up in tanks, at the most reasonable rates. None but the best quality material used. Will also receive orders for tanks complete.

FULDA BROS., 30 to 40 Spear St.,
San Francisco.

FRED S. EWER, Agt.
Office, Steves' Store, St. Helena.

CHARLES KRUG

Charles Krug had the same qualities of intellectual power and integrity as Crane. But where this well-educated young German learned to make wine is not clear. It might have been that living near Agoston Haraszthy in Sonoma for a year was enough. It is unlikely that he learned it at his birthplace near Westphalian Kassel, which is well above the northern limits of German winegrowing.

Krug had a classic German university education at Marburg and was of just an age to be caught up in the political turmoil that swept central Europe in the late 1840s. He had come to the United States in 1847, but returned to Germany in 1848, taking part in the unsuccessful movement for German unification through republican institutions. He typified that remarkable generation of German liberals who came to this country after these events and brought with them education, ideals, and culture, which were of great value to this young republic. Krug was one of the "48ers" and appropriately started out in 1852 as the editor of the *California Staats Zeitung* in San Francisco, a German language newspaper that reflected his liberal views.

In 1854 Krug took up some land near Crystal Springs, south of San Francisco. After eight months of the agrarian life he returned to the city with his neighbor, Agoston Haraszthy. This Hungarian transplant, by way of Wisconsin and San Diego, had acquired a position at the San Francisco Mint from the Pierce Administration in Washington. Krug also worked at the Mint and for a refining company in which Haraszthy had an interest. When Haraszthy was indicted for mishandling the Mint's gold, they headed off to Sonoma.[4]

We have seen Krug's three Napa vintages for others. When he was at the Bale Rancho he met Carolina Bale and on the day after Christmas, 1860, they married. Her dowry was 540 acres of Bale land, north of St. Helena, where the Charles Krug Winery stands today. The next spring Krug began setting out twenty-three acres of Mission vines and built his first "small rude cellar," as he called it. That fall he made his own wine, ironically maintaining his Sonoma connection by using grapes from Knight's Valley. He produced about a hundred gallons.[5]

Like other winemakers Krug expanded his production in the

Charles Krug

late sixties. By 1868, convinced by Crane's success, he was planting foreign varieties. When the expansion years began in the seventies Krug's little winery mushroomed. He built his first large stone cellar in 1872 and the next year had a capacity of 250,000 gallons. By 1876 his production had surpassed this capacity. When he died in 1892 the Krug cellars could hold 800,000 gallons.

At first glance Charles Krug's influence is best seen in light of his early success and the extent of his later great estate. By the late 1870s his name had become synonymous with the great quality successes that were perceived for Napa Valley wine. But the eulogies recited in 1892 did not stress the greatness of his holdings. By then he had gone through receivership, too often ready, it was said, to let his trust and friendship enter into his business arrangements. What the speakers emphasized was his steadying influence on the industry during its times of troubles and during his ten years on the Board of State Viticultural Commissioners, a body that had had more than its share of mercurial egomaniacs.

But more than anything else his friends praised him for his work at home. He organized the Valley's growers and producers and showed the rest of the

Charles Krug Winery

state how to do it. He demonstrated how to take an issue affecting local interests and publicize it through broader agencies. And he showed them how to take state and national issues to the local level, make them understood, and then how to organize a useful reaction. As such, his ten years as president of the St. Helena Winegrowers Association were probably more significant than his tenure on the State Board.

Frederick Beringer delivered Krug's eulogy in German, and was probably well understood by most of those who heard it. Charles A. Wetmore delivered the address at the grave. All there knew they were saying farewell to a very good man. Charles Krug's funeral and procession was the grandest and most somber event in Napa Valley history.

The central American event of the 1860s was the Civil War. Important as it was, it had little effect on everyday life in the Bay Area, or on its perpetual spirit of expansion. There were lots of Southern sympathizers in the North Bay area, particularly around Sonoma, where authorities closed down the local newspaper for its "copperhead" sentiments. On the Napa side the spirit was far more obviously Union, particularly among such wine leaders as Crane, Osborne, and Yount.

The vine planting frenzy which had started in Sonoma continued strong in the Napa Valley even after it had waned some to the west. In 1860 Sam Brannan, the colorful San Francisco capitalist, had headed off to Europe to buy "real" vines for winegrowing. He too was thinking "Napa." Next year, Agoston Haraszthy followed Brannan's lead, leaving for Europe shortly after the first shots were fired at Fort Sumter. Brannan planted his vines on land that he bought around Calistoga. Haraszthy's imports never had much effect on California winegrowing.[6]

J. J. Sigrist was the biggest planter in 1861, but lots of cuttings and vines that went in that year were washed away the next winter when California and the Napa Valley experienced the worst flood in their recorded history. The Valley became a lake, but when the floodwaters subsided in the spring Napa planters were back at work. That they were novices in such matters is evident in their lack of concern for general business conditions, which deteriorated for wine producers in 1862. The real problem was in Southern California where the planting craze of recent years had run amok. Now the newly planted vines were coming into production and there was a glut of California wine. The *Alta* noted that most of the wine being made was poor stuff and wartime inflation had pushed up production costs. The obvious answer was to convert the surplus wine into brandy to fortify sweet wine and to serve as a beverage. But a wartime excise tax on distilled spirits worked against this idea.[7]

As a result, California wine men decided to have a state convention in December 1862. Dr. Crane represented the Napa Valley. For three days in San Francisco they talked about all sorts of vinous matters, but the main concern was the war tax on brandy. Almost as important was their desire to raise the tariff on foreign imported wines, which were pouring into California and were hurting what little East Coast trade the Californians had. They sent off their memorial to Congress on these matters, but relief did not come from that quarter until after the war. While he was in the city Crane got together with Haraszthy and Charles Kohler to see if a better supply of oak staves for barrels could be found on the East Coast.[8]

One of the reasons that Napa grape farmers could continue to expand was their proximity to the fresh grape market in San Francisco. This outlet for their Mission grapes gave them a fairly steady cash flow through the war years. The inflated prices which were hurting Southern California growers raised the price of fresh fruit in Northern California, without pushing up northern costs to the same degree.

Solano County grape men across the hills in Green Valley had similar experiences in these years. In fact, that part of Solano has been historically connected to Napa in their viticultural interests. In 1862 there were about 100,000 vines in Green Valley, most of them tended by German growers headed by Francis Meister, who started his vineyard work there in 1854. In following the history of Napa winegrowing it is important to keep in mind that since early days there has been a connection between the parts of western Solano and Napa, which have similar climates and soil.

Napa's neighbor to the north was Lake County. This rugged region was less physically accessible to Napa than to Solano, but strong connections have existed since early years. In fact, until 1861 there was no Lake County; it was simply the northern portion of Napa County. We have already seen Napa's early relations with Sonoma County to the west. Today the good wine grape growing areas of these counties, plus Mendocino, above Sonoma, comprise the North Coast viticultural district.[9]

Napans learned more about viticulture in the drought years of 1863–64. While the local cattle industry staggered and the wheat crop from over 30,000 acres languished, the established vines survived and produced satisfactory crops. The county fair was held even that year and Charles Krug showed off nine of his new wines.

Next year the planting continued strong. There was good rain and an abundant harvest, really Napa's first sizeable vintage. Perhaps 50,000 gallons were made, and yet a large part of the crop was shipped off fresh to San Francisco on the little steamers that ran between Napa and the city. Some producers made brandy, perhaps a total of 2,000 gallons. But, as we have already seen, people did not look back on Vintage 1865 with great respect, since virtually all the wine was from Mission grapes.

Gradually this situation began changing as everyone marveled at Dr. Crane's success. Patchett tried to sell his wine on the East Coast, but the story this year, and for several years to come, was a bleak one in that market. It was next to impossible to sell there. After a ship ride around the Horn, or on the little railroad across the Isthmus of Panama, between passages through the Tropics, the wine did not arrive in very good shape. Easterners discovered that wines from Northern California could be just as bad as those from Los Angeles.

Most of the things for which Samuel Brannan is famous fit neatly into the narrative history of the Golden State's early years—here with the Mormons by sea, the spark that lighted the Gold Rush frenzy, a leader in the San Francisco vigilante movement. But his remarkable venture in the Napa Valley doesn't often make it into California history books.

Brannan first came to Napa in 1852. He visited the hot springs at the head of the Valley and kept the place in mind for the next four years. Resort hotels had already appeared in the Napa area, at White Sulfur Springs and Soda Springs, when Brannan made his first purchase of up-valley land in 1857. He now intended to build his own resort at the head of the Valley, a place he called Calistoga, implying that it would be California's counterpart to New York's famed spa at Saratoga. He used his huge profits in San Francisco banking to underwrite the venture. By 1860 he had built his Hot Springs Hotel and within two years dozens of little cottages were surrounded by palm trees, exotic shrubbery, and beautiful walking paths. There was even a horse racetrack. Construction of the little town continued for some years.[10]

Meanwhile, the vine planting fever struck the Valley. But Brannan had already been infected. On his 1860 trip to France he had bought 20,000 cuttings and now set them out in his nursery near Calistoga. He bought a huge tract of land here in 1862 from J. S. Berryessa and the vine planting began. The next year he bought another thousand acres of valley and hillside land from Henry Fowler. As the vines developed and approached bearing age, Brannan hit upon brandy production, both from some of his own vines and from the oversupply of Napa Mission grapes. He formed a

Sam Brannan's resort

at Calistoga in the

early 1860s.

partnership with Lewis Keseberg and built a winery/distillery in Calistoga. Meanwhile, he was following any number of other agricultural ventures, even silk culture.

Things got hot for Brannan in 1868. He visited the Valley as Keseberg was getting ready for his first large-scale brandy production. His watch was stolen in Napa. When he got to Calistoga he learned that some property near town over which he was involved in a lawsuit was now occupied by the other litigant. Brannan marched down to the property with some friends and was greeted with a volley of bullets, five of which struck home. He never really recovered fully from these injuries. But the brandy was made, about 20,000 gallons of it, now a profitable deal since the war tax had been sharply lowered. He had it shipped around the Horn to New York, where it got a better reception than most California wine. It was billed "Calistoga Cognac."[11]

In 1870 Brannan's world started coming apart. His wife, Ann Eliza, sued him for divorce and demanded a cash settlement of the California community property. It took Brannan a little time to go under. He added 6,000 gallons of sweet wine and 12,000 of vinegar to his brandy operation. The next year he planted more vines, and even added to his stand of mulberry trees, part of the silk production scheme. But soon the distillery had to close down and in 1875 the foreclosure process began on his Napa properties. The next year the Internal Revenue Service seized the distillery and in 1877 a correspondent of the *San Francisco Post* reported that the place was in a state of decay.[12]

Sam Brannan

Brannan had been able to make his fall 1868 brandy shipments from the Valley by rail, since the Napa Valley Railroad had reached Calistoga in August. He had been one of its founders and his influence on this project was one of the lasting impressions he made on the Napa Valley. By the end of the 1870s, others owned his lands and vineyards. Brannan's great stable was eventually converted into a winery by Ephraim Light and can still be seen at Grant and Stevenson Streets. Brannan himself moved to Southern California after losing his huge estate, living in obscurity until his death in 1889.[13]

The magnetic character of the Napa Valley drew another German in 1861. Jacob Schram had come to America at age fifteen and to California in 1854, twelve years later. When he found his way to Napa, the local vine planting craze was at its height, and Schram joined in. He was born in the well-known Rheinhessen wine district and knew that the best wine often comes from the steepest slopes. He found a likely spot on Mount Diamond in the western hills below Calistoga. He bought virgin land for what he always called "a trifle." His first vines probably went in during the 1863 planting season. There were Missions in his first vineyard, but he had picked up some foreign vines, and as he added to his acreage he expanded his foreign plantings and experimented with as many varieties as he could acquire. He aimed at both red and white wines, but mostly white. It is not known what influence neighbor Crane down the Valley had on Schram, but it is clear that the German was considered something of a local expert on foreign varieties long before they had come to dominate the minds of most Napa vineyardists.

The Schram estate,

from a photo by Frona

Wait in the 1880s.

In 1867 the *Alta* interviewed him and gave a fairly detailed report of his findings, commenting on a large number of varieties, some quite obscure. In the end he gave a strong push for the White Riesling, Burger, and Palomino for whites. And he wisely observed that the new Zinfandel looked like the best grape for clarets. Twenty years later a noted wine writer called Schram "the Nestor of Napa Valley vignerons," a title which he probably deserved for his sage council at this early date.[14]

What made Schram famous in his Valley was not so much his sagacity but his industry and intelligence. Krug ever used him as an example of how a man could make his way in life here through hard work and careful order. Five years after his first vines went in, the local press had singled him out as a poor man who had worked wonders on his mountain. Next year the *Reporter* exclaimed that "the direct want of California just now is more Jacob Schrams."

Perhaps what most interested people was the fact that as he built his little domain, Schram kept up the cash flow by plying his trade as a barber. In 1869 he was still riding over to White Sulfur Springs Hotel on Sundays to shave and crop the visitors there.[15]

It has often been written that Jacob Schram was made famous by Robert Louis Stevenson's visit to Schramsberg in 1880 and memorialized in the Scotsman's *Silverado Squatters* in 1883. A far better explanation would be that Stevenson was taken there by his local friend because of Schram's fame, particularly for the German's excellent white wines. Stevenson tasted them all, red and white, taking special notice of a Schramsberger white, which had "a notable bouquet." How Schram got this effect is worth noting. The wine was made from an ordinary Palomino grape, but the German winemaker liked it "verbessert" with a touch of muscat, which Schram called his "Rhenish Muscateller." He would also mix it into his wine made from the equally ordinary Burger grape. Schram's Rieslings apparently stood on their own legs.[16]

Jacob Schram showed all that hillside vineyards would produce excellent wines in the California environment. He didn't make much wine in these early days, but what he did produce made his name. By the time Stevenson came by, he had already dug tunnels in the mountain to age his wine, a feature of his estate which tended to draw visitors and more attention from the press.

In 1871 he was making 5,000 gallons per year, but by 1882 he was producing 30,000. By then his Schramsberger label was known in many better restaurants and hotels in Northern California. Even Professor Eugene Hilgard, the agricultural wizard at the University of California, owned that he had taken to using Schram's red "Burgundy" at his table. Years before Stevenson had climbed up Mount Diamond, the learned Professor had compared Schram's Rieslings to Franconian Stein wine, "firm, dry and flinty."[17] By 1883

Jacob and Annie Schram

in their later years.

Schram was clearing $10,000 profit per year from his wine operation, a fairly heady sum in those days.

When wine writer Frona Wait praised Schram in 1889, she contended that "His name is a household word among Californians and is known to connoisseurs everywhere." In that same year Schram and his wife began building their beautiful home, which graces the property to this day. It took them three years to finish it.[18] Meanwhile Schramsberger wines were winning awards at almost every imaginable American and international competition. Schram had also taken his son Herman into the business as a full partner. In 1891 Herman joined forces with Charles Bowen to market Schramsberger and other premium California wines. In 1892 the Schrams had 300,000 gallons stored in their tunnels. They also took part in the flush times at the end of the century, planting another thirty acres of vines in Knight's Valley.[19]

SOURCE: LYMAN FAMILY COLLECTION.

After Schram's death in 1905 Herman operated the establishment until Prohibition. Then it passed through several hands, with two false starts at wine production after Repeal. In the 1960s it was restored and is today the home of the internationally famous Schramsberg sparkling wines.

NEWCOMERS

In the 1860s there were a few more newcomers worth noting. Henry A. Pellet was no new hand, having already made wine for Patchett and Crane, when he started his own wine operation near St. Helena in 1866. He called his place Manzanita Vineyard for all the red barked bush he had to clear from his land next door to Dr. Crane's. He made 20,000 gallons his first year from others' grapes and had 15,000 vines in his rocky soil by 1868. Over the years he expanded on his reputation for high quality, although his winery never had a large capacity. Pellet was greatly respected for his technical knowledge and abilities. He was also a successful Valley politician. When he died in 1912 he was the dean of Napa Valley winemakers.[20]

John Lewelling has one of the most famous names among these early Napa wine men, but it is not usually associated with this Valley. He and his brother made their names as Gold Rush nurserymen in California and Oregon. San Lorenzo, in the East Bay south of Oakland, was the site of Lewelling's great agricultural enterprise, but Napa had the climate he loved. He moved there in 1864 and planted the first part of his vineyard. He acquired his winery site on Spring Street in St. Helena in 1876. At first he was far more interested in viticulture than winemaking. He raised the Muscat of Alexandria for raisins in these early years, but was soon hit by the winegrowing bug. In 1878 he was a leading force in the cooperative movement to build a brandy warehouse in town. In 1883 he died, his winery moving through many hands over the years.[21]

Oak Knoll was owned by R. B. Woodward after J. W. Osborne's death in 1863. He kept the wine operation going and hired Joseph Mattos (Matthews) in 1866 as his winemaker. Mattos was from Madeira and knew how to make brandy to fortify sweet wine, which he did at Oak Knoll until 1877. In that year he began building his own stone cellar in Napa City, which he called the Lisbon Winery. He became the Valley's first large-scale sherry producer. However, the credit for Napa's first sherry probably goes to Thomas Pettinelli in 1866.[22]

To the hills on the east side of the Valley, on Soda Springs Road, came Dr. J. H. Wood, probably in 1865. He planted ten acres of vines, all White Riesling. He claimed that the volcanic soils made his "Pearl Hock" particularly invigorating. Dr. Wood's claim sounds suspiciously similar to those of the Hapsburg monarchs explaining why they always drank Tokaj (also from volcanic soils) on their wedding nights. The local press called Wood's wine "Pearl Hawk."[23]

General Erasmus Delano Keyes, the Indian fighter, bought his land next to Crane's property in 1867. He called his estate Edge Hill and began planting vines. The stone winery went up in 1870 and later played an important part in the Valley's wine history. The stone edifice has since been remodeled and serves as the home of Louis P. Martini.[24]

We cannot trace the careers of every new winegrower in the sixties, but one does require special mention. H. W. Crabb came to California in 1853 and settled close to Lewelling near San Lorenzo. There he farmed successfully for twelve years. He followed Lewelling to Napa in 1865 and three years later, at age forty, purchased a 240-acre plot at Oakville. Like Lewelling he was first solely interested in table grapes and raisins, but this soon changed. His Hermosa Vineyard grew slowly, reaching seventy acres in 1873. The year before, he built his first little wooden winery, filling the thick walls with sawdust for insulation. These small beginnings give no indication of the vast stature of Crabb's establishment in the 1880s, which he then called To Kalon, Greek for "most beautiful."

THE VALLEY'S CHANGING FACE

As the 1860s wound down, the size and importance of Napa City became ever more obvious. It was a rough town with plenty of saloons, brothels, and violence. But its schools already had more than 300 children in their classes. One writer said it was just a "little San Francisco," a metaphor not meant to praise. When the railroad worked its way up the Valley everything became more rushed and industrial. And in 1869 all this was linked to the national economy when the transcontinental hookup was made.

There was a real ethnic and racial mixture developing here. Single Chinese workers were everywhere obvious, but there also were several Chinese families living in town now. There was also a small black community with its own church. Virtually every European nationality was represented, but there was a growing Germanic character to the community that could not be doubted, and it continued to grow through the 1870s. The winegrowing success of Krug, Schram, and Sigrist acted as a magnet for others. And Krug was ever ready to hire on a *Landsmann* who needed work. At the end of the decade there were two German brass bands in the Valley. By 1872 the local Germans were able to draw over a thousand countrymen to their picnic at Habermehl Union Gardens. In St. Helena the German population had become so numerous that the high school was able to mount a profitable production of Schiller's *Die Räuber*, quite a feat, since the play is difficult even for Germans to understand.

Besides the railroad, the "Great Earthquake" also hit the Napa Valley in 1868. But the forty-second temblor caused little damage here. The railroad, on the other hand, played an extremely important role in actually changing the demography of the Valley. Soon the pattern of settlement here would be marked by a series of little villages and railroad stops, some of these with wine names like Krug, Zinfandel, Larkmead, and Oak Knoll. Gradually the villages took on their own characteristics and the wines made from the vineyards around them appeared to local folks to have their own special flavors. Today, for some lovers of California wine, it is as important to be able to reel off "Yountville, Oakville, Rutherford, St. Helena, and Calistoga," as it is for Bordeaux aficionados to recite "Margaux, St. Julien, Pauillac, and St. Estephe."

INCREASING PROSPERITY

The vintages after 1865 brought their surprises, rewards, and precepts. The spring of 1866 saw more vineyards planted, with much more emphasis on foreign varieties. May 10 taught Valley growers about late spring frosts. Those off the Valley floor were not so badly burned as those mid-valley. Considering the increased bearing acreage, the crop was short, but the total gallons produced amounted to almost double the production of 1865.

Next spring the planting continued apace, with Zinfandel now the darling. By May the new wood from the spring growth throughout the Valley had already been sold in advance for cuttings for next year's planting. The grape crop was good in 1867, but the late October heat that would not let up taught winery owners about stuck fermentations and the importance of cool cellars.

Planting slowed some when the troublesome '67s proved difficult to sell. By now the Valley had twenty-nine vineyardists with a total of more than ten million vines, with Brannan, Crane, Sigrist, and Krug at the top.[25] The grape harvest in 1868 was very large, but the wine production was a little smaller than the previous year. The reason was brandy. The war tax had been lowered, and it was clear that the brandy still, and the fresh market, were the proper outlets for the Mission grapes. Brannan, William Scheffler at Krug's, and Oak Knoll made most of the Valley's 46,000 gallons of brandy.

Little planting, little rain, and a short crop hurt by mildew characterized 1869. The sulfur bag now became a common sight at most vineyards. The brandy stills kept bubbling and good prices for fresh grapes continued. A local newspaper crowed that "wine will soon be *the* interest of our county." One would certainly think so from the 300,000-gallon vintage of 1870.

Now planting was almost at a standstill, but there were clear signs of some serious stone-cellar building. Outside capital had begun to take a long-term interest in Napa wine. Sigrist was importing large oval oak casks from Germany, and Crane was touting large, shallow redwood fermenters. There was a good deal of groaning at wine and grape prices, since there was a record high state vintage. Profits were down, but there were still profits. Two-thirds of the Valley's wine had been produced by some familiar names: Pellet made 35,000 gallons, Crane 25,000, Krug 22,000, Winter 20,000, and Groezinger 90,000.[26] Who was this Gottlieb Groezinger?

At this point another German enters our stage of vinous history, a leading San Francisco wine merchant and wine producer. In 1869 Groezinger actually made over 100,000 gallons of wine from grapes brought down to the city. Groezinger, perhaps better than anyone else, represents the next important phase in the history of Napa wine.

The post Civil War prosperity of the late sixties had the definite markings of a boom in the California economy. With a soaring population, overwhelmingly male, and industrialization transforming the Bay Area, Northern California had truly become a part of European industrial society, best symbolized by the completion of the transcontinental railroad. Industrialized San Francisco could now produce bottles, barrels, and winemaking equipment. Growing markets on the West Coast, hope for improvement in eastern markets, and the apparent improvement in California wine quality all attracted capitalists to the Napa wine scene.

Groezinger built his huge winery/distillery complex in 1870. An even more complex and attractive tourist center today, it is still visible at Yountville. He also bought 370 acres of land with a few vines on them for $11,000. He started planting in earnest.[27] Soon to follow were capitalists Guiseppe Migliavacca and Peter Van Bever, who built huge wine cellars in the city of Napa. Their production in the years to come would number in the hundreds of thousands of gallons.

Meanwhile, in San Francisco an efficient and powerful group of wine merchants had been developing. They would increasingly have their say in matters concerning the Northern California wine industry. And the Napa producers were keeping pace with developments. Krug's production went from 20,000 to 50,000 gallons between 1869 and 1871. In 1869 Schram put out 18,000 vines. Boom times and industrial expansion were making their marks on the youthful Napa wine industry.

Notes for Chapter Three

1. PWSR, 12/30/1890.

2. Crane got his Mission cuttings in Napa, not San Jose, as is usually reported. For a detailed report of these activities see his letters to J. L. L. Warren (November 1861) in Warren Papers, Bancroft. Also see George B. Crane. A Life History (San Jose 1886): 158.

3. Star, 8/25/1876; Reporter, 1/4/1873; Alta, 3/8/1865, 3/11/1866, 4/18/1867; Democrat, 3/25/1865, 6/10/1865.

4. Krug was never involved in Haraszthy's misadventures at the Mint, and the charges against the Hungarian were eventually dropped. For a detailed analysis of Haraszthy's contributions to California wine see: Charles L. Sullivan. "A Man Named Agoston Haraszthy." Vintage (February through April 1980); cf. Paul Fredericksen. "The Authentic Haraszthy Story." Reprinted by the Wine Institute from the original 1947 series in Wines & Vines. "One More River" is an unpublished Haraszthy biography by Fredericksen (ca. 1961) in my possession.

5. NVWLA III, 5-12. This study of Charles Krug was compiled by Gunther Detert, who was in charge of this project. Also see: Star, 12/27/1878, 11/4/1892; PWSR, 1/26/1891, 7/6/1892.

6. Alta, 8/30/1860; Thomas Pinney. A History of Wine in America (Berkeley 1989): 269-284. Professor Pinney's handling of the Haraszthy legend is a breath of fresh air in a miasma of historical nonsense, which, as he writes, has reached almost mythological status.

7. Alta, 9/25/1862, 11/29/1862; Reporter, 10/18/1862.

8. Peninou and Greenleaf, 57-59; Farmer, 12/19/1862.

9. Carosso, 79-83; Farmer, 12/19/1862.

10. Kay Archuleta. The Brannan Saga (San Jose 1977): 41-54; Paul Bailey. Sam Brannan and the California Mormons (Los Angeles 1959): 217-228; Menefee, 180-191.

11. Bulletin, 7/23/1870; H. H. Bancroft Scrap Books: II, #755; Reporter, 8/15/1868; Alta, 4/18/1868, 1/24/1870; Farmer, 1/26/1871.

12. Alta, 1/20/1871, 1/26/1871, 2/12/1871, 6/5/1875, 9/7/1876, 7/2/1877.

13. Irene Haynes. Ghost Wineries of the Napa Valley (San Francisco 1980): 28-29.

14. Alta, 5/6/1867, 5/13/1867; Frona Eunice Wait. Wines and Vines of California (San Francisco 1889): 131-132.

15. Reporter, 8/15/1868, 10/23/1869.

16. SBVC (1884): 108; Robert Louis Stevenson. Silverado Squatters (London 1901):44-45. James Beard

printed the "Napa Wine" chapter from this work in 1965, with an introduction by M. F. K. Fisher.

17. Maynard A. Amerine. "Hilgard and California Viticulture." Hilgardia (July 1962): 14; Democrat, 12/6/1878.

18. PWSR, 4/20/1892. Writers often incorrectly have Stevenson sampling Schram's wine at this house.

19. PWSR, 9/20/1891, 6/6/1892, 11/20/1893; AWP, 4/1897.

20. Star, 12/27/1878; PWSR, 6/30/1912; Wait, 121-122.

21. NVWLA I: 126-138; Haynes, 6; Star, 12/27/1883.

22. Star, 12/14/1877; Transactions, 1867: 156.

23. Reporter, 10/23/1869; Star, 12/14/1877.

24. Alta, 4/18/1867.

25. Reporter, 8/15/1868.

26. Farmer, 8/3/1871.

27. Alta, 3/29/1867, 11/18/1869, 11/27/1871; Ruth Teiser and Catherine Harroun. Winemaking in California (New York 1983): 93.

THE BUSINESS CYCLE

DURING THE 1870S THE UNITED STATES EXPERIENCED ALMOST FIVE YEARS OF industrial depression, a result of the overexpansion in the years after the Civil War. The bad times were a rude blow to the young California wine industry, but the survivors learned important lessons between 1873 and 1879. Napa producers did not feel the economic distress as severely as those in other districts. Some were even able to expand their operations in the face of generally lower prices for grapes and wine.

For most of the state, planting slowed at the beginning of the new decade, but Napa vineyardists kept right on planting. The spring of 1871 saw more vines go in than any year since 1865. The favorite varieties were Burger, Palomino, and White Riesling.

It was another dry year, but yields held up well until an infestation of quail lowered the expected tonnage. The vintage hit close to a half million gallons and some wines later were praised for their superior quality. For all the planting to better varieties, however, more Mission grapes than better varieties still showed up in the fermenting tanks.[1]

Groezinger's new operation at Yountville again topped the Valley with 80,000 gallons. Pellet was a close second, followed by Krug, Crane, and Sigrist, and a few new names, such as the Swiss T. A. Giauque, who turned out 30,000 gallons at his new cellar south of St. Helena.[2] W. W. Lyman had his first vintage, 12,000 gallons, at his just constructed El Molino Winery near the old Bale Mill. He had bought Frank Kellogg's place and would buy the mill in 1879. Edge Hill also made 12,000 gallons, but it was General Keyes' last vintage, since he sold the place to Richard S. Heath the next year.[3]

There were two newcomers who did not make the published statistics. John A. Pettingill, a dentist, had bought 107 acres near Soda Canyon Road and planted twenty acres of White Riesling. He built a little winery in 1870, which he called White Rock Cellar. He made about 2,000 gallons per year and aged them for four years before selling the wine, mostly to local customers. The second name is John Benson, a San Francisco capitalist, who bought a huge tract of land west of Oakville in the fall of 1871. Soon he had planted more than eighty acres, mostly to hay and grain. Benson was influenced by Lewelling and planted Muscat of Alexandria vines at first. Later, in 1885, he built his turreted Far Niente Winery. The winery's official founding date is 1885, although Benson actually made wine on his ranch in the 1870s.[4]

1872 brought a few more new names of importance into the winegrowing picture. William C. Watson, the Napa banker, founded his beautiful Inglenook and planted fifty acres of Malvoisie. The estate at Rutherford was noted for its artificial ponds, one of which was outfitted like a swimming pool with a diving board. A few years later a certain Finnish sea captain would buy the place and build his world-famous winery there.

Serranus Clinton Hastings, the jurist for whom the law school is named, planted three vineyards in the Oakville-Rutherford area, one next door to Watson. At first he only grew grapes, but in 1884 he put up a winery. He also had important winery and vineyard holdings in Lake County. Further up the road toward St. Helena was the winemaking operation of J. H. McCord, whose Oak Grove Winery was built here in 1880. Before that time he made wine under rather rough circumstances. McCord produced a few oddities in his day, such as a "Sparkling Burger," a blackberry brandy, and a cherry cordial. He shortly acquired a neighbor in Washington P. Weaks, whose Monongo Winery went up in 1876.

On the eastern side of the Valley was the most imposing addition of 1872, Vine Cliff, a great four-story winery up Rector Creek Canyon. The winery and sixty-acre vineyard were financed by businessmen G. S. Burrage and G. W. Tucker, who had started putting out vines here in 1865. The winery, set on the side of the canyon, seemed to a visitor "as though the finger of enchantment had been pointed at the frowning, rocky surface." Within two years both owners died and the winery came under the control of Terrill Grigsby and George Pampel, the latter a Rumanian-born winemaker, who had made wine for others in the Valley. Grigsby would build his huge Occidental Winery in 1878, four miles to the south, in the Stag's Leap area.[5]

1872

A lot of poor wine came out of the Valley in 1872 and the years that followed. People who might have better been in grain and hay made 2,000 gallons here, 5,000 there, much of it in wooden barns without proper equipment or basic winemaking knowledge. How this poorly made stuff kept getting out into the wholesale trade is something of a mystery, but it hurt the Valley's wine image that year and for most of the rest of the decade.

The 1872 season began with moderate planting above Rutherford. There was also a healthy trend toward grafting over some Missions to better varieties. Much of the young planting was destroyed by an ugly April 12–13 frost. The crop was short and there was quite a bit of mildew at harvest. Reds did not color well, even though there were some torrid days during the vintage that caused too many rapid and sometimes stuck fermentations. This was a difficult year, but Napa wines were able to buck all the negative trends in the industry at large. This was a healthy climate in some ways, but it also caused a certain amount of optimism that was really unwarranted. Reality would come down hard in four years.

1873

There was a record state wine crop in 1872, so the planting rage in Napa finally cooled in 1873, except around St. Helena. 1873 also marked the formation of the Napa Valley Wine Company, comprised of several leading producers in the upper Valley. It aimed to market Napa wines directly to the East Coast. Charles Krug, one of the organizers, had now put up a real cellar, raising his capacity to 250,000 gallons. He also imported 5,000 vinifera cuttings from Peru. He decided to keep his original little cellar "to mark the difference between then and now."

The rainy season was rather dry and the spring was again full of frost. It was during this year that Napa vineyardists began to understand the wonderful manner in which the Zinfandel vines set a second crop after a bad frost. The vintage was short, yielding about 20 percent less than 1872. But the quality of the reds was very good. Another precept from nature—a short crop may bring more highly flavored wines.

When Groezinger's big brick complex at Yountville had completed its efforts at the end of the 1872 vintage, Napa Valley had its first individual 100,000-gallon wine product. This German was no newcomer to wine or its manufacture when he purchased the huge Henry Boggs ranch in 1870. Born in Württemberg, he was twenty-four years old when he arrived in New York in 1848. He worked as a waiter at Delmonico's and later as a steward aboard the S. S. Oregon on the Panama run. After arriving in San Francisco he headed for the mines and did well enough to set up a liquor business in the city.

He also began making some wine from country grapes. In fact, he bought some of Agoston Haraszthy's Sonoma grapes in 1858. By the late sixties he was well established, with enough capital to jump into the Napa planting boom. He quickly grafted over the twenty acres of Mission he found on his land to Zinfandel, White Riesling, Malvoisie, and several others. Within a few years there were two hundred acres of vines; by the mid-eighties over five hundred.

The Groezinger Winery.

Today the site of the

Vintage 1870

shopping complex.

Production went as high as 300,000 gallons in the eighties. Groezinger concentrated more than most on foreign markets, selling in London, Mexico, and Central America. Another outlet for his wines was the San Francisco sparkling wine plant of Alois Finke, and after his demise, his widow, the producer of the famous, but never fine, A. Finke's Widow "Champagne." Helping Groezinger keep tabs on his business in these early years was one Claus Schilling, who eventually would control this plant and many other wine and food enterprises as well.

The winery complex was a model of modern efficiency and mechanical wizardry. Everything was up-to-date, hydraulic, and steam-driven. A visit and tour led by superintendent Frederick Schweitzer were de rigueur for touring journalists and travel writers. When the boom of the 1880s started to fade, Groezinger was forced to retire and sold the plant and some of the vineyard to Antone Borel. Groezinger finally died in 1903.

Schilling and his partners later leased the plant and it passed through several hands, finally to the California Wine Association. During Prohibition some grape concentrate was made there and after Repeal several people made wine on the premises. By the 1950s it sat quietly on the highway until the restoration was begun in 1973. Today as Vintage 1870 it greets the eye of almost every visitor to upper Napa Valley. This successful collection of shops and restaurants says much about the recent boom years in the Napa Valley. As one of Napa's great architectural monuments, it also suggests much about the hopes and confidence of those who were leaders in the industrial development of the wine interest here in the 1870s.[6]

1873 – 1877: Depression

When Jay Cook and Company failed in New York on September 18, 1873, a national depression would be set off that would last for five years. The speculative condition of the economy toppled financial institutions and eventually had a deadly effect on the market for California wine. But it took a while for some of the uglier aspects of depression to hit home in the Napa Valley. The ugliest never really touched the lives of people here.

Americans didn't understand macroeconomics in the 1870s. In Napa people's understanding of their plight was seriously flawed, if superficially logical. A look at California exports to the East Coast by rail and sea in the 1870s shows solid growth:

1875	1,030,000 gallons
1877	1,460,000 gallons
1879	2,500,000 gallons

These exports increased at just about the same rate as total statewide wine production. In the same decade the import of competing French wine declined precipitously:

1872	7,100,000 gallons
1875	3,200,000 gallons
1877	2,400,000 gallons

This decline resulted from the phylloxera's devastation of French vineyards

John Thomann

and the lowered demand for foreign wine in the depressed American economy. Neither the growing demand for California wine nor the flagging competition of the French product caused the average ton of Napa grapes or gallon of Napa wine to decline in value. The problem was the overall American economy and the fact that during hard times there is always a great elasticity in the demand for a product like wine.

Napa's leading wine men pinned the problem on the generally low quality of California wine, a result of too many Mission grapes and far too little technical know-how at too many wineries. Men like Krug and Pellet didn't name names, but they focused on the quality of much of their Valley's home product as a major cause for its decline in value. And after the depression years had passed they looked back on those bleak days with somewhat Social-Darwinistic satisfaction. They were not displeased that the conditions had driven out those who had lowered the quality of Napa wine through their ignorance, sloth, or greed. Those who survived, they contended, would be well paid for their toughness and high standards when the good times returned.[7]

1874

The first full year of depression, 1874, was hardly perceived as such in Napa. It was a time of greatly advanced production, with the large plantings of a few years ago coming into production. The wine product was half again as large as the record 1872 vintage. Throughout the harvest it rained so heavily that it was next to impossible to get wagons into the access rows to remove the loaded harvesting boxes from the fields.

Many newcomers had started the year with high hopes. John Thomann, a Swiss-German, had bought four and a half acres of land from Lewelling, south of St. Helena, and started building his winery in the summer. He made 30,000 gallons the first year and was averaging 100,000 in the 1880s. Above St. Helena, near Krug, Jean Laurent from Bordeaux built his first little winery and made 20,000 gallons. He had been in the Valley since 1868 and built a real stone winery on the site in 1877. He averaged about 50,000 gallons in the 1880s. After Prohibition the old building housed one of the Valley's cooperatives.

When Charles Lemme moved onto Spring Mountain, he became the second after Schram to move onto the western hills. He bought and began clearing land in 1874, building a little cellar two years later. Eventually the Lemme winery became part of the Schilling holdings.

A particularly discouraging event, preceding the ugly vintage this year, was the great fire at Charles Krug's place. His new cellar was virtually destroyed and superintendent Jacob Beringer was almost killed fighting the inferno from the blazing roof. They couldn't open the wine storage areas because Krug had the keys and was gone for the day. When the blaze reached the proof spirits, veterans in attendance swore it sounded like an artillery barrage. Krug only had $8,000 insurance on the place. He was able to get started again but the debt hung over him for years.

Guiseppe Migliavacca's construction of a 100,000-gallon winery on Fifth Street advanced Napa's industrial development. He had come from Pavia in 1857 and started his wine and liquor business in Napa in 1866. By the 1880s he was making 200,000 gallons. Based on contemporary accounts, of all such large operations in the area, his product was the best. He retired in 1908 and died in 1911, aged seventy-eight, leaving the business in the hands of two of his ten children.

Wine Cellar and Residence of John Thomann.

CHARLES CARPY AND THE UNCLE SAM WINERY

Northern California's grandest personal wine empire in the 1890s derived from a modest warehouse winery begun in Napa in 1870 when Peter Van Bever sold his fish market and grocery store and started making wine from local grapes. Van Bever and his associates took over a large warehouse in 1872 and made 25,000 gallons. The winery's location in Napa made it possible to purchase both Napa and Solano grapes for processing. When conditions warranted, these wineries also bought from Sonoma and the Sacramento Valley.

The business passed into the hands of Charles T. Anduran in 1881. He had an important and active employee in one Charles Carpy, a native of Bordeaux, who had come to San Francisco as a boy in 1855. He later attended St. Mary's

College and then went to work for Anduran. By 1882 the Uncle Sam Winery at Fourth and Main was making 200,000 gallons; by 1886 it was up to 500,000.

Carpy already had a piece of the business when Anduran died in 1886. He then bought the major portion for $40,000 and formed C. Carpy & Company. His chief brand was La Loma. Carpy's acquisition of the company came at a time when the industry was beginning to feel the effects of overheated expansion. He proved his business genius not only to survive but to prosper in the coming hard times. In 1891 he bought the huge Pacific Winery in San Jose and became Northern California's leading wine entrepreneur. He also bought Napa's Greystone Winery in 1894. When the California Wine Association was formed that year, Carpy, with his country wineries and his San Francisco cellars, became an important member. When good times returned, however, he sold his CWA stock and in 1903 became president of the French-American Bank in San Francisco. He remained a director until his death in 1928 at age seventy-nine. During these years he kept his hand in wine, a sought-after speaker at banquets and a judge at major wine competitions.

Much of Carpy's wine was ordinary cargo stuff, which added little to the

An advertisement for

Charles Carpy's Uncle

Sam Cellars in Napa.

luster of California's high-quality image. But he always maintained a keen interest in quality and was ever ready to buy small lots, at often unheard of prices, from a premium producer. He would keep that wine separate and maintain its special identity. A perfect example of this practice was his purchase of Tiburcio Parrott's famous Cabernet Sauvignon in the 1890s. This wine went into his La Loma brand, which won far more than its share of awards at the great expositions in those years. Today the Carpy name survives in Napa in the person of his grandson, also Charles Carpy, who was instrumental in reviving the Freemark Abbey label in 1967.[8]

1875

The 1875 vintage was similar in size to that of the previous year. Weather conditions were also similar but quality was up. The depression was starting to hurt and the government's tougher attitude toward brandy production made it less likely to find an outlet for an oversupply of grapes. Railroad rates also hurt. It was almost impossible to make good money shipping east by rail. Statistics for these years of increasing eastern shipments show no growth in overland traffic. Krug went east in the spring trying to sell more wine and came home totally discouraged. In his view the situation had nothing to do with the economic depression, but with a glut of poor and mediocre California wine that was a drug on the market.

The tariff also appeared to be a problem but took far more blame for the bad times than it deserved. Import statistics for wine show that foreign competition did not increase in the seventies. Complaints were loud enough that Congress did change tariff regulations in 1875 to the advantage of California producers.

Local wine men were also becoming increasingly aware that cooperation would help solve their problems. At the county level, The Grape Growers Association of Sonoma, Napa and Solano Counties had been meeting sporadically since 1870. Krug and Pellet decided to get serious after the 1875 vintage, calling for the formation of a strictly local organization. The first meeting of the St. Helena Vinicultural Club was held on January 22, 1876. Most of the important locals were there, including a few new men who had recently set up shop in the area. There was John Weinberger, who had just made 50,000 gallons at his place across from Jean Laurent's. Weinberger's stone winery would go up that year. There was also Charles Wheeler, who had planted thirty-seven acres along the highway at Zinfandel Lane. In years to come, his son, John H. Wheeler, would become a powerful leader in the state wine industry. And there was Seneca Ewer, who would also be a formidable industry figure. The chief topic of discussion at this first meeting was eastern markets and their relationship to the high railroad rates.

Napa vineyardists really knew they were in a depression after a meeting of the Vinicultural Club in the spring of 1876. Krug stunned the audience by announcing that he would not buy grapes from independent growers this season. His cellar was still full of unsold wine. He had just come back from another trip to the East Coast where he found that there was some interest in what little really good California wine was available, particularly whites with some age on them. He told a story of visiting an Indianapolis wine dealer who gave him a blind sample of a German style Hock. He couldn't place it, but it was outstanding, he thought. It was Schram's Palomino/Gutedel blend. In Iowa a dealer asked him to identify another good white. It was excellent, but he had never previously tasted it, he thought. In fact, it was one of his own wines with three years on it. But for now Krug had a full cellar. So did Groezinger, who also announced that he would not buy grapes this year.[9]

That summer the Centennial celebration in Philadelphia was dampened by the dreadful economic conditions. Neither the California state government nor the State Vinicultural Society could officially underwrite a wine exhibit. What was done was put together by independent operators for their own benefit. The result was not a happy one. A national writer may have overstated the long term results when he suggested that it took ten years "to remove the bad impression created by that villainous travesty." According to historian Vincent Carroso the wines shown were "coarse, earthy, and full of sediment."[10] These events were a kind of symbolic nadir for California wine men. After the vintage that year things started looking better for them, particularly in the Napa Valley.

After the hot summer of 1876, the grapes came in early. Again, it was a record vintage. Most vineyardists managed to find some kind of home for their grapes, even if prices were rock bottom. The quality of the wines was satisfactory, but the harvest was cut short by October rains. In the midst of it all Groezinger's distillery burned down. But the Valley made over 20,000 gallons of brandy from surplus grapes, much of it by a newcomer who had set up his still at Krug's place earlier in the year.

William Scheffler and his associates bought Edge Hill from R. S. Heath that summer and soon took over the Fulton Winery in St. Helena, after the owner's death.[11] By the end of the decade his wine production had passed 100,000 gallons, but brandy was his chief interest. "Scheffler's Sanitary Brandy" developed a good reputation, until the fiery German went bankrupt in 1887. Scheffler's Swiss winemaker, Eugene Morel, undertook some interesting experiments on the effects of whole berry fermentation, almost a century before this practice became fairly popular in the Napa Valley. After some early successes brought forth wines with remarkable fruitiness, he found that he could not consistently control the biological cleanliness of his fermentations. Eventually there were some rather gruesome results, full of volatile acidity. Other winemakers who followed his much publicized example also found themselves producers of unwanted, high grade vinegar.[12]

Krug didn't have to follow through on his ominous statement. He eventually bought lots of grapes in 1876 and produced over 250,000 gallons. He symbolized the rising mood in the winemaking community at the end of the vintage by hoisting the Stars and Stripes over his newly rebuilt wine cellar after the last load had been crushed. The *Star* was ebullient, reporting that "the crushers of that great establishment have carried through their rapacious maw near two thousand tons of grapes."

Some important new names showed up in this year's production statistics. Franco-Swiss Auguste Jeanmonod made 10,000 gallons at his new place in Oakville. John Benson made 15,000 at his nearby Far Niente. The Fountain Winery on Dowdell Lane had its first crush of 18,000 gallons. It would continue production until 1911. Mrs. Sarah Bourn, whose son would build Greystone Winery in 1889, reported 26,000 gallons at her place west of Crane's winery. And in the Conn Valley the Franco-Swiss Winery of Fred Metzner and Germain Crochet made its first 25,000 gallons, mostly from grapes grown by the twelve growers in that district. Their 60,000-gallon winery went up the next year.

THE BERINGER BROTHERS AND LOS HERMANOS

Over two million Germans came to the United States between 1868 and 1888, more than five times the number of Italians and far more than any other non-English-speaking nationality. There were not many of this huge number who came to the Napa Valley, but those who did had a profound effect on society here in the last quarter of the nineteenth century. The Beringer brothers came to New York from Mainz, where Jacob had worked at winemaking and coopering. Frederick, or Fritz, stayed on the East Coast and developed a malted barley business, while Jacob came to California in 1869, eventually to Napa, where he soon became Charles Krug's foreman. While in New York he had served as foreman at the Truche and Winkenback Cellar.

When Jacob came to work for Krug he saved his money and eyed the partly developed property across the highway, formerly the David Hudson place, which, in 1868, had about 24,000 Mission vines. William Daegener later acquired the land, intending to develop the property himself, but an accident forced a change of plans. In 1875 Jacob and his brother paid $14,500 for the ninety-seven acre ranch.

With Chinese labor Jacob started excavating a winery cellar, finishing it in February 1877. By then these workers had made a good beginning on the spacious limestone ageing tunnels that have become a tourist feature today. That year Jacob made 40,000 gallons in the half-finished winery. By the end of the year the local newspaper declared that it was the best cellar in the Valley, not the biggest, but the best. When they laid the cornerstone Charles Krug dropped a twenty dollar gold piece in the container.

In 1878, with good times in the offing, Beringer expanded his production to 100,000 gallons, added a distillery and further expanded the cellar. Through most of this activity he stayed on at Krug's, but he finally gave up his foreman's job in February 1878. In 1882 Jacob followed Charles Lemme onto Spring Mountain and began planting a vineyard at the thousand-foot level.

Frederick finally came west in 1884 and built his wonderful Rhine House, still an eye-catcher for Valley tourists today. Jacob's friend, Tiburcio Parrott, had also bought land on Spring Mountain and soon built a counterpart to Rhine House in the hills to the west. Parrott's mansion has become famous in recent times as the setting for the Falcon Crest television series. He dubbed the Beringers "Los Hermanos" (the brothers) and suggested the term for their vineyard, a brand name that has stuck to Beringer production through the years.

The Beringer brothers profited from their winemaking skill and business acumen. Frederick had good connections in the east and soon had a string of salesmen there, where they sold most of their wines directly to dealers, bypassing the growing power of the San Francisco merchants. By 1889 the operation had a capacity of 500,000 gallons and produced about 275,000, plus lots of brandy. Andrew Carnegie was known to favor Beringer wines for his table.[13]

The Beringers weathered the hard times of the 1890s and took an active part in replanting the Valley after the phylloxera epidemic. Fritz died in 1901, Jacob in 1915. Unlike most Napa wineries Beringer stayed in family hands through Prohibition, Repeal, World War II, and the beginnings of the second wine boom in the 1960s. In December 1970 the family sold the winery to the Swiss Nestlé Company.

PHYLLOXERA

With the economic slump, not many in Napa took time to notice that reports of a root louse were beginning to cause concern among a few industry leaders. The discovery of the phylloxera was made in Sonoma in 1873, but the bug was certainly in the region in the 1860s.

This nearly microscopic pest is native to the Mississippi Valley and was probably carried to France on cuttings of American vines in the late 1850s. It returned to Northern California in the early 1860s on vines imported from France and probably on imports of eastern North American varieties from the Midwest, particularly the Catawba.

In Europe its spread seemed to outstrip the wind. But in California the bug was slow, "lazy" in the words of some wags. The dry summers appear to have inhibited the development of the winged form, so the bug traveled from place to place on picking boxes, wagon wheels, cuttings, and in the vineyard on plows and boots. The effect was twofold here. Most Californians tended to take a fairly relaxed attitude. But the devastation of the French vineyards was a boon to the California industry, in that French production, and therefore imports to this country, were cut substantially.

One voice that was heard from the moment of the owner's arrival here in 1875 to take his post as Professor of Agriculture at the University of California was that of Eugene W. Hilgard. He first spoke to the State Vinicultural Society in November 1875, outlining the problem in fairly strong words. The infestation he saw reminded him of vines he had handled that were "precisely so circumstanced, thirty years ago, when my father. . . attempted the culture of Rhenish grapes in Southern Illinois."[14]

A few days earlier he had visited Napa looking for evidence of the phylloxera. The bug had already been sighted in Brown's Valley. But most local people didn't want to talk about the problem openly. In bad times like these, knowledge that the pest had struck an area would further depress land values. As the economic horizon cleared, wine men wanted to do nothing to blunt the effects of a strong recovery. In some circles outside Napa Hilgard was attacked as an alarmist.[15]

By the end of the decade a wide variety of cures had been put forward all over the world. This was in part a result of the French government's 1873 offer of 300,000 francs for a solution to the problem. Submerging vineyards in water worked, but was not practical here. Chemical cures, such as carbon bisulfide, offered possibilities, but no long-term solution. Biologically crossing American vines with vinifera vines would transfer some of the resistance of the native vine, but grapes from such vines would make inferior wine.[16] The production of such hybrids has had an important effect on wine production on the East Coast but not in California.

The answer, of course, was to graft vinifera varieties onto resistant native rootstock. The Dresels in Sonoma understood this before the decade ended. In Napa H. W. Crabb contacted a certain Professor George Husmann of Sedalia, Missouri. The next year Husmann sent Crabb several hundred native cuttings, which marked the beginning of experimental work in the Napa Valley. It would be another ten years before the threat was properly appreciated here, and then for many it was too late.[17]

Working with F. W. Morse of the university, in 1880, Hilgard reported on the extent of the phylloxera threat in the Napa Valley. There were several bad spots in the Carneros and in vineyards around Napa. The worst infestation was at the entrance to Brown's Valley, on the road from Sonoma to Napa. There were also spots in Henry Hagen's vineyard northeast of Napa and further up the Valley at Frank Salmina's on the east side. There were a few more spots noted, but Morse concluded that for now the Napa Valley was clean north of Groezinger's property, with one exception. Somehow the pest had gotten into John Weinberger's vineyard north of St. Helena, and it was spreading.[18]

1877

The break in the Napa wine depression seemed to take place in mid-January of 1877, when from out of the blue John Lewelling received an unsolicited order from a Philadelphia dealer for all the wine he could send. There was a fairly healthy burst of planting again. Krug, Weinberger, Crane, and Wheeler were all planting madly by the end of January. By summertime the orders were pouring in from the east and from San Francisco merchants. Between July 1 and August 15 thirty-two cars of wine and brandy rolled out of the little station at St. Helena. The situation was similar up and down the Valley.

That spring Napa really faced up to Jack Frost. Krug had translated a German paper for the Vinicultural Club in February advocating smudging, burning coal tar in small metal pots. Have your cuttings and brush all bundled and ready to burn, spaced evenly through the vineyard, he told them. Watch your thermometer. If it is 35° F by ten o'clock, it is going to freeze. Between April 12 and 23 dense clouds of smoke from the frost-fighting shrouded the Valley. Groezinger was later singled out as the hero of the great battle of the 23rd, personally leading his workers in a successful all-night battle.

The 1877 vintage started early again, in mid-August. It was another record, with very good yields in a year when the state crop was short. About 3,400 acres of bearing vines produced around 1,500,000 gallons. By the first of October the Valley was crawling with eastern buyers, bidding each other up to get remaining lots of the 1876 vintage and trying to secure contracts this year.

The most important new wine operation, Brun & Chaix Winery, was being built along the tracks at Oakville. Dubbed "Nouveau Medoc" by its French owners, it produced only 10,000 gallons in 1877 but was up to 50,000 by 1879. This winery and its additions would be a major force in the Valley until Prohibition.[19]

1877 brought Jacob Schram a couple of new winemaking neighbors on Mount Diamond, Conrad Wegele and Colin McEachran, both making about 5,000 gallons. The latter was immortalized three years later when Robert Louis Stevenson dropped in for a visit. Stevenson was thrilled to be able to exchange a few words in Scots with McEachran and thought he "had the look of a man who succeeds." He did, taking over the operation of the Weinberger Winery after the owner was murdered in 1882.

1878

There was lots of smiling around the Valley at Christmas time. The wines had fermented through without a hitch, most were already sold, and the rain came down in torrents. The spring was almost perfect. Frost was negligible, the berry set was good, and the 1878 vintage was orderly and considered outstanding. The yield was more than four tons per acre, making for a vintage of over 2,000,000 gallons. Again the state crop was short and Napa winegrowers reaped another economic bonus. Napa was also reaping a special image for wine quality. It was the 1878 vintage that really started to give Napa wines a special position in the market, which they have never lost. The clarets, made mostly from Zinfandel, especially turned people's heads. The proof was the prices paid for these wines; it was becoming clear that Napa reds were now commanding top dollar.

Now that prices were on the rise, togetherness came a little more easily. Upper Valley wine men built a cooperative bonded brandy warehouse in St. Helena, finishing it by the end of the year. With other Northern California wine producers they became galvanized by the threat of tariff reciprocity with France. This possibility emerged from the French drive between 1878 and 1879 to promote the so-called Chotteau Treaty. The problems California wine producers faced during the depression and the threat of unlimited, tax-free

Charles Carpy's

San Francisco cellar,

later a part of the

California Wine

Association.

competition from cheap French wines now illustrated to the winegrowing community the importance of working together.

While the 1878 vintage was coming in and the battle over the treaty raged, a series of letters appeared in the *Alta California*. Their author was Charles A. Wetmore, a fiery young newspaperman with a keen interest in California wine. He had been the valedictorian of the first graduating class at the University of California and had left a bright trail wherever he passed thereafter, including being jailed for contempt of Congress in 1875. In 1877 he raised some eyebrows with a letter to the *Washington National Republican*, contending that 90 percent of California's best wines ended up being sold under foreign labels. It wasn't a new complaint, but the medium was unique. He concluded by advising American wine drinkers to buy the best California wines they could find. "Save money and save headache."[20] Next year the State Vinicultural Society sent him to France to represent California at the Paris Exposition. His letters to the *Alta* from July to December were a textbook on wine and its proper production. They became common reading for every serious wine producer in Northern California.

There were some more new names on the local wine scene. On the east side Terrill Grigsby built his Occidental Winery in 1878, with a 275,000-gallon capacity. The structure still looks down on the Silverado Trail on the southern side of the Stag's Leap area. John Stanly (note the spelling) also came in 1878. His Riverdale Farm and La Loma Vineyard in the Carneros district became one of the most important winegrowing operations in the county. And we must add the Valley's second important sherry facility, as John Ramos and Frank Sciaroni began production at the Crane Winery. They later built their own facilities, both still standing in St. Helena.[21]

1879

It was a good thing that prospects were looking up when the 1879 vintage came along. The Valley was flooded in the rainy season, was beset by terrible frosts in the spring, and was treated to ugly weather in May and June, causing poor berry set. None of these conditions produces bad wines; in this case they meant a short crop, down 20 percent from 1878. The end result was a harvest of excellent grapes. Anyone in the business who hadn't noticed Napa in 1878 couldn't miss what happened in 1879. The boom was now on.

By the end of Vintage 1879 everyone was talking boom times. As the demand for land and wine in the Valley escalated, so did prices. Brandy producers were also smiling. The San Francisco *Post* ran a long article on the quality of Northern California wines, happily copied by the *Star*. They deplored the amount of ordinary wine for the eastern trade that went into the cellars of San Francisco merchants and emerged sophisticated and barely drinkable. They marveled at the flavor characteristics of Napa clarets; they definitely lacked that earthiness that seemed so typical of California reds. The whites could be good, as well as some brandies. But those dry reds! The *Star* predicted that there would be 2,000 acres planted in the Valley in the dormant season 1879–1880. Their prediction fell short.[22]

Napa Valley Wineries, circa 1880

The following wine operations were producing, or were about to produce, wine in 1880. The winery is listed by its popular, commercial name or the name of the owners or sometimes both. The letters in parentheses represent the ethnic/national origin of the owner(s). The gallonage approximates the average production in the years to come and is a fair reflection of the winery's relative capacity. Where no gallonage is given, the winery is not yet in production.

ETHNIC/NATIONAL ORIGIN:

(G) - German; that is, the German Empire as of 1871.

(F) - French; that is, the Republic of France.

(Sw) - Swiss; that is, the Swiss Republic, ethnically French, German, or Italian.

(B) - British; that is, English, Irish, Scottish, Welsh, etc.

(P) - Portuguese.

(I) - Ethnic Italian, but not Italian Swiss.

(M) - A combination of ethnic/national ownership.

WINERY	NATIONAL ORIGIN	GALLONAGE
Napa City		
G. Migliavacca	(I)	75,000
Uncle Sam	(F)	250,000
B. Semorile	(F)	20,000
J. Matthews (Mattos)	(P)	10,000
Napa Area and Brown's Valley		
G. Barth (Sigrist)	(G)	60,000
H. Hagen	(G)	35,000
J. Perry	(B)	25,000
Wm. Reed	(B)	8,000
J. Knief	(G)	3,000
S. A. Roney	(B)	3,000
F. Fagler	(M)	7,000
South of Yountville		
Oak Knoll/Eshcol	(B)	20,000

YOUNTVILLE

G. Groezinger	(G)	250,000

CARNEROS

Talcoa	(B)	25,000
J. Stanly (La Loma)	(B)	
G. Groezinger	(G)	250,000

OAKVILLE

H. W. Crabb (To Kalon)	(B)	200,000
Nouveau Médoc Brun & Chaix	(F)	85,000
Far Niente (Benson)	(B)	10,000
De Banne & Bressard	(F)	25,000
A. Jeanmonod	(F)	15,000

MT. VEEDER — NAPA REDWOODS

J. Gartman	(G)	7,000
J. Hein	(G)	9,000

RUTHERFORD

Inglenook (Niebaum)	(Baltic German)	

SILVERADO (EAST SIDE)

Occidental	(M)	60,000
F. Salmina	(Sw)	15,000
J. Pettingill	(B)	5,000
F. Borreo	(I)	4,000
Vine Cliff	(M)	100,000

SOUTH OF ST. HELENA

John Thomann	(Sw)	100,000
T. A. Giauque (Stamer)	(F)	
Sarah Bourn	(B)	15,000
Oak Grove (McCord)	(B)	45,000
Monongo (Weaks)	(B)	10,000
C. R. and J. Wheeler	(B)	

CONN VALLEY

L. Corthay	(Sw)	10,000
Franco-Swiss	(F-Sw)	40,000

SPRING MOUNTAIN

C. Lemme (La Perla)	(G)	15,000

POPE VALLEY

G. Haug	(G)	1,000

MT. DIAMOND

C. McEachran	(B)	3,000
Schramsberg	(G)	30,000
C. Wegele	(M)	8,000

CHILES VALLEY

M. Kaltenbach	(G)	500

Charles Krug	(G)	200,000
Beringer Brothers	(G)	150,000
Edge Hill & Fulton	(G)	125,000
G. B. Crane	(B)	30,000
Fountain Winery	(M)	25,000
J. Laurent	(F)	35,000
W. Leuthold	(G)	10,000
J. Lewelling (Degony)	(M)	45,000
El Molino (Lyman)	(B)	10,000
F. Rosenbaum	(G)	4,000
E. M. York	(B)	20,000
N. Negouy	(Sw)	30,000
J. C. Weinberger	(G)	50,000
O. Schulze	(G)	10,000
F. Sciaroni	(Sw)	
E. Heymann	(G)	20,000
A. Schranz	(G)	
Berretta Bros.	(Sw)	4,000
A. Rossi	(Sw)	10,000
H. A. Pellet	(Sw)	25,000

CALISTOGA

L. Kortum	(G)	30,000
J. H. H. Medeau	(F)	10,000

NOTES FOR CHAPTER FOUR

1. Alta, 1/20/1871, 4/17/1871.

2. Pacific Rural Press, 8/26/1871; Reporter, 12/2/1871.

3. Menefee, 210; Reporter, 1/4/1873; NVWLA I: 141-145.

4. Haynes, 43; NVWLA IV: 44-96. This history of Far Niente insists that Benson did not start making wine until the 1880s. For some of his vintages in the 1870s see: Star, 11/24/1876, 11/30/1877.

5. Haynes, 39; Star, 11/30/1877; Reporter, 1/25/1873.

6. Star, 2/26/1876, 9/1/1877, 9/19/1879; Reporter, 9/28/1883; Bulletin, 9/4/1877; PWSR, 9/5/1891; 11/30/1903; Vintage (April 1974): 49; John Wichels. "Footsteps in the Sands of 1870." Napa Valley Historical Society, 1979; Bancroft Oral History. "Horace O. Lanza." (1971). Ruth Teiser and others have produced an important series of oral histories for Bancroft. See Sources.

7. Farmer, 10/23/1876; Star, 3/4/1876; Reporter, 10/3/1879; Carlo M. Cipollo. "European Connoisseurs and California Wines, 1875-1895," in Agriculture in the Development of the Far West, 299-303.

8. Reporter, 11/2/1872, 4/13/1883, 10/12/1883, 8/27/1886; Star, 12/7/1877; PWSR, 6/6/1892, 6/20/1893; Bonfort's , 5/10/1889; Haynes, 64; Teiser and Harroun, 169-170.

9. Reporter, 1/29/1876; Star, 3/4/1876, 8/5/1876.

10. Edwards Roberts. "California Wine-Making." Harper's Weekly (March 9, 1889): 197-200; Carosso, 98.

11. This winery was built in 1865. For years it was the oldest St. Helena wine cellar, since others of greater age here were actually outside the town limits. The structure finally blew away in a violent

windstorm in 1973. Irene Haynes. "Lost Wineries of the Napa Valley." Wine West (39:3): 14-17.

12. Star, 3/11/1876, 7/2/1876, 12/29/1876, 9/12/1879; Reporter, 12/4/1885. For some excellent descriptions of Edge Hill and other Napa wine operations see: Thomas Hardy. Notes on the Vineyards of America and Europe (Adelaide, Australia 1885). This book is very rare, but the American chapters were reprinted in Wines & Vines (September 1966 to September 1968). Also see: Bonfort's, 10/10/1886. For Morel's experiments see: Charles L. Sullivan. "California 'Carbonic Maceration' in the 1880s." Vintage (October 1981): 50. For an interesting note on Morel's early years in North Carolina see: Pinney, 415.

13. Star, 7/20/1875, 12/22/1876, 3/2/1877, 8/31/1877, 2/6/1878, 1/31/1879, 9/11/1883, 7/12/1905, 10/19/1915; Reporter, 4/21/1882; PWSR, 4/21/1882; Teiser and Harroun, 85.

14. Eugene W. Hilgard. "The Phylloxera or Grapevine Root Louse. . . ." Supplement No. 1 in his "Report to the Board of Regents," (1880), revised and issued as AESB 23 (1876). For a historical discussion of the complicated story of the selection of resistant rootstocks in California see: Charles L. Sullivan. "California's Early Response to the Dreaded Phylloxera Root Louse." VWGJ (Spring 1988): 12-17.

15. Reporter, 10/15/1875; Alta, 9/13/1875.

16. George Ordish. The Great Wine Blight. (New York 1972): 80-92; Star, 11/19/1880; PWSR, 9/14/1883, 1/8/1887.

17. Star, 4/1/1876; Transaction, 1882: 158-166. Husmann has an important paper here on current rootstock work.

18. University of California, College of Agriculture. "Report of the Professor in Charge to the Board of Regents. . . ." (1880). Viticultural Appendix No. 9: 92-108.

19. William Alexander Hewitt , ed. Brun Family, Napa Valley, from 1874. (San Francisco 1989)

20. Alta, 12/20/1877.

21. Haynes, 9, 16.

22. Star, 12/19/1879, 12/26/1879.

THE GREAT WINE BOOM

The wine interest of Napa County
is getting up a little earthquake all by itself.

—ST. HELENA STAR
1880

THE PEOPLE OF THE NAPA VALLEY ENTERED THE DECADE OF THE EIGHTIES FULL of sap, virtually bursting with expansionist energy. By now the Valley had picked up a public image for its beauty and its wines' high quality that it holds to this day. In March an *Alta California* editorial contended that Napa was to most Californians much what the beautiful Valley of Tempe, sacred to Apollo, was to the ancient Greeks. "Nowhere else in California can a traveler go by rail for thirty miles through one unbroken stretch of enchanting landscape." And the weather was next to perfect, evidenced by the State Medical Society's call to establish a hospital for consumptives there. Already there was a state asylum in place and soon to be a veterans' home at Yountville. The mountains were spotted with vacation resorts and health spas. The *Alta* summed it up by claiming that, "Napa is now the leading wine-growing county of California, and . . . St. Helena has become the centre of the most prosperous wine district in the State." And there was even support for this idea from the Sonoma side. In 1883 the *Sonoma Index* concluded that "we are letting Napa Valley get ahead of us. Already her wines are attracting more attention than ours, and the merchants are seeking the wines of Napa at higher prices than they are paying for our wines." We cannot tell whether Napa wines were really so good, but that is certainly what people were thinking.[1]

The planting fever was again concentrated in the St. Helena area during the dormant season of 1879–1880, but there was also heavy activity around Yountville. There is no reliable survey of the acreage planted, but the total was somewhere between 3,000 and 4,000, numbers that rival the massive plantings here in the early 1970s. The demand for cuttings was intense, but for the next season; the wood from this season's canes was long since sold. An important characteristic of all this planting was the emphasis on white varieties, particularly German vines such as White Riesling, Sylvaner, Burger, and something Californians were calling Grey Riesling, not a riesling at all and not German. This emphasis was a reaction to the overall demand for California white wine but does not reflect the growing popularity of Napa Zinfandel claret. In Charles Wetmore's words, it was these whites from German varieties that provided California with its first "victory of quality" in the 1870s.[2] Eastern buyers were most interested in building on that early success. The orders from the east poured in throughout the year. Krug reported cash orders in the spring he could not fill.

The spreading confidence of the local wine men can be seen in the construction of Vintners' Hall in St. Helena, two stories high, with reading and meeting rooms, and a hall upstairs for general meetings and social events. The new State Viticultural Commissioner had called for the formation of local winegrowing associations. The local "Club" conformed to Wetmore's idea of a formal pattern of local organization. The Club now became the Association, which divided the Valley into very loosely defined viticultural districts. The lower Valley and Carneros were lumped into the Napa District. The others carried the names of the central town or village: Yountville, Oakville, St. Helena, and Calistoga. When administrative matters were involved, Oakville and Rutherford were lumped into St. Helena, but the town and village designation became a standard method of reference, along with certain railroad stops, like Larkmead and Oak Knoll. The eastern valleys and Howell Mountain were also administratively combined with St. Helena, but they tended to maintain their separate identities.

Another salutary sign was the growing emphasis on sherry and brandy production as an outlet for the Valley's Mission grapes. The big commercial wineries in Napa, particularly Uncle Sam, also helped to raise quality by giving small producers a place to ship their wines in the spring, before hot weather attacked the wooden barns that far too many used as "cellars." An additional move toward higher quality was the St. Helena winegrowers' decision publicly to condemn the use of sugar during fermentation to raise the alcohol content of wines. Next season they actually signed pledges not to sell grapes to producers who used this process of chaptalization. This issue illustrates a conflict between the German spirit of *Gemeinschaft* (community) and *Gesellschaft* (association or corporation). At one of the Club meetings there was a lusty debate on the issue. William Scheffler of Edge Hill was incensed by the pledge; it was a violation of his freedom as a producer. Krug attacked him roundly, but in a friendly fashion, calling for a broader view and a higher allegiance than narrow self-interest. The primary consideration was the overall needs of the winegrowing community; their reputation depended on the purity of their products. *Gemeinschaft* won out; Scheffler and other opponents signed the pledge.[3]

In 1880 nature counterbalanced the happy spirit in the Valley with a very frosty spring, capped by a remarkable freeze on May 15. The vintage was not as short as feared, with second crop Zinfandel making up a large part of the harvest. But so many second crop grapes in the fermenters made the resulting reds of the vintage rather light. The wineries operating this season numbered forty-nine and the final product was a whopper, close to 3,000,000 gallons. Five wineries accounted for almost half the total: To Kalon, Krug, Edge Hill, Groezinger, and Uncle Sam.

Shortly after the new wine had finished fermenting Professor Hilgard visited Napa Valley to survey the situation and address the local winegrowers. On December 8 at Vintners' Hall he gave an address that came to be called "The Permanent Maintenance of Our Vineyards." In it he offered advice that focused on many of the key issues the Napa wine men would face in the next two decades.

Hearkening to the difficult times of the 1870s he argued that they would return only "by our own grievous

An early Beringer label.

Gutedel was popular for

inexpensive German style

wines in the early days.

fault." To avoid these faults Napa must stress quality instead of quantity. California now must be able to "show its own face in the best of company." That is, California wines must travel under their own labels to compete with the best of the rest of the world. He made it clear that Napa would be a key in presenting this good face. A reputation for fine wine was essential.

Good wines came from better grape varieties, which meant the end of the Mission grape, so far as he was concerned. They must wean themselves from the practice of blending better wines with Missions just to get rid of the latter. Given the right varieties and the proper climate, the key variable to producing good grapes was the soil, a topic on which he was a thorough expert. He advised that they continue to move onto higher ground, to the foothills and upper valleys and pointed to Schramsberg as proof of the advisability. He specifically pointed to Howell Mountain as a good prospect.

He begged them to send soil samples to the university for analysis. And he promised that his laboratory facility in Berkeley would systematically test grapes grown in as many local environments as possible. In other words, the university would provide a practical means for determining which grapes gave what kinds of wine, grown in a wide variety of situations.

He closed with these words. "Now is your golden opportunity; and if you act wisely, energetically and unitedly, you are sure of success."[4]

HOWELL MOUNTAIN

Howell Mt. vineyard

scene from the 1880s

depicted in a French

magazine of that era.

Hilgard had actually received some soil samples from Charles Krug in the summer of 1880. They had been taken from atop Howell Mountain, to the northeast of St.

Helena, a giant volcanic knob that had weathered into a huge plateau looking down on the Napa Valley, out of the reach of most morning fogs. Today we know the predominant soils on the mountain fall basically into four series, mostly stony clay loam well-suited for winegrowing. After he had analyzed them Hilgard gave his approval and advised Krug to go for it.[5]

Much of this highland had been granted to George Yount in 1843 as the Rancho La Jota. The origin of the name is not known. It could derive from the Spanish letter "J" or from the lively dance of Aragon by the same name. There was little economic activity here besides lumbering until the 1870s when Edwin Angwin established his resort. Others found the environment salubrious and built summer places nearby. The Howell Mountain Road cut through the plateau and brought the products of Pope Valley and the upper Chiles Valley down to the larger valley below. But there was little in the way of agriculture on the mountain before Krug began his investigations.

Krug soon started planting and was followed by John Thomann and the Brun & Chaix Winery at Oakville. They were all taking advantage of the good land prices, but there was also the thought of escaping the slow spread of the phylloxera. The Napa Register at the time predicted that "many years will not elapse before Howell Mountain rivals the Napa Valley as a great winegrowing section." Later the *Star* contended that Howell Mountain "would be to California what Medoc is to France."

In 1881 there was something of a land rush. On one day in October over 1300 Howell Mountain acres were sold. A large part of this interest had as much to do with vacation retreats as with grapegrowing. In fact, many Bay Area businessmen combined the two objectives; the local press noted that quite a few took their families up to camp out, while their crews were clearing the land and preparing it for planting. By 1884 much of the prime land on the mountain had been sold off. There were about thirty vineyardists with over 500 acres planted. Krug had put in five experimental acres spaced at a rather untraditional 3.5 x 14 feet. The vines did well and eventually he transferred this practice to his valley planting. The 1884 statistics show that about half the vineyardists had holdings of under ten acres. Brun & Chaix, Krug, and Thomann had the largest plots. Also important were Albert Schranz, William A. Smith, and C. W. Banks; the latter two were Bay Area bankers. Serranus Hastings was also soon to plant vines here, as was W. S. Keyes, the son of the founder of Edge Hill. The name of Captain John Sutter also appears on twenty acres. Later in 1891 his daughter and son-in-law, Caroline and Emil Leuenberger, started a winery on the lower slope of the mountain, reborn Deer Park Winery in the 1930s. In 1906 the Leuenbergers bought the Thomann winery and conferred the Sutter family name on the operation—Sutter Home. (Note that this John Sutter was not the famed pioneer, but a Bay Area businessman and former sea captain.)[6]

In 1884 Brun & Chaix made about 10,000 gallons from their young mountain vines. The result was satisfactory and in two years their 150,000-gallon winery was finished, still visible off White Cottage Road. Next year at the State Viticultural Convention one of their Zinfandels was evaluated. The press noted that the wine excited much interest, while the committee on red wines declared that it "confirmed the expectation" of Howell Mountain supporters. Hilgard was a member of the committee.

The upshot was a *Star* editorial that stated "if any grape-growing region in California deserves to be called a well-defined district it is Howell Mountain." By the end of the 1880s the area had acquired an excellent reputation for its dry red wines. In the 1890s it would develop a world-class reputation for its Cabernets.

THE MOUNTAIN VALLEYS

To the north and east several mountain valleys also developed a small winegrowing interest during these years. Chiles and Pope Valleys were the furthest removed from the main Valley. Conn Valley was more accessible.

The long and narrow Chiles Valley was the base of the Catacula land grant to Joseph B. Chiles in 1844, but he did not settle there until 1854. He planted a few vines and was listed in the 1860 census as having 280 gallons on hand. Before Chiles' death in 1885 a few people had started adding to this small beginning. By 1887 there were about 130 acres, almost half Zinfandel. The only winery here was a tiny affair run by M. Kaltenbach. When George Husmann moved to Chiles Valley things began to pick up. He made 5,000 gallons at Kaltenbach's place in 1885. By 1890 there were about twenty vineyards producing almost five hundred tons of grapes. The next year Francis Sievers built his Lomitas Winery, which dominated the winemaking scene here until Prohibition.

Before the mid-eighties most Chiles Valley grapes went to the Franco-Swiss Winery in Conn Valley. By 1887 this valley had over 650 acres of vines. During the same years about two hundred acres were planted in Pope Valley, although no large winery was built there. Most of the grapes went over to Howell Mountain or down to Lomitas Winery. Gustav Haug did have a little winery here that made about a thousand gallons each year.[7]

MT. VEEDER

To the west of the main valley, on the Mayacamus Range, we have already seen the coming of viticulture on Spring and Diamond Mountains. The move onto Mt. Veeder to the south was less obvious. In many ways this growth was something of a geographical extension of the Brown's Valley beginnings below, pioneered by J. J. Sigrist, whose winery was expanded by George Barth in 1879. Before this date Stalham Wing had planted a vineyard near Dry Creek Road and was making some wine in the 1860s. His place was acquired and expanded by J. A. Bauer in 1884.

The Mt. Veeder area was usually referred to as the "Napa Redwoods" in these early days. It was primarily a resort area, the chief place of comfort run by Herman Hudeman. At one time he owned about 2,500 acres of the mountain as well as a small vineyard and winery, which Robert Jordan later acquired. Nearby, Jordan's good friend Ernest Streich built the Castle Rock Winery. In later years Jordan carried out practical experiments with pure yeast cultures, sulfur dioxide, and cool fermentation equipment in conjunction with Frederic T. Bioletti at the university. Livermore wine man Theodore Gier bought the Jordan property in 1900 and built his winery there three years later. There is much more history here to be told. J. H. Fischer built another winery of historic importance on Mt. Veeder in 1885. It passed through many hands, eventually to become today's Mayacamas Winery. By the 1890s there were about twenty vineyards and six little wineries on the slopes of Mt. Veeder. To most people this was still the "Napa Redwoods" area and had no distinct winegrowing personality in local chronicles. During these pre-Prohibition years the area did not develop a special reputation for first-class wines, a situation that has gradually changed in the period since Repeal.[8]

INGLENOOK

No examination of the growth of the Napa Valley wine industry in the 1880s can go this far without specific reference to Inglenook, the great winery built by Gustav Niebaum. We have already seen that William C. Watson in 1871 founded Inglenook after he bought the mostly undeveloped Koenig farm west of Rutherford. Watson, the banker son-in-law of George C. Yount, developed a pretty estate that acted for a while as a sort of resort-sanitarium. He planted about fifty acres of Malvoisie grapes that he regularly sold to H. W. Crabb.

Niebaum began looking for a winegrowing estate in 1879 and settled on Inglenook, which accounts for the traditional 1879 founding date, although the Captain did not swing the deal until 1880. The

The great Inglenook Winery was completed in 1887. Here Capt. Niebaum is seated in his carriage before the structure. Ca. 1895.

transaction was extremely complicated, the main part of the land passing through several hands before Niebaum finally acquired it. He also purchased adjoining parcels, which gave him an estate of something more than a thousand acres by 1881, extending well up into the hills west of the main house.

Gustav Niebaum was born in 1842 of Swedish–Baltic German lineage in Finland, which was then a semi-independent grand duchy, part of the Russian Empire. He took to the sea and had his first officer's papers at the age of twenty-two. He was in the Russian-Alaskan waters when the United States acquired Alaska in 1867. Thus he was in on the ground floor to make his fortune there, mostly in the fur trade, as one of the founders of the Alaska Commercial Company.

By the end of the seventies Niebaum had amassed a large fortune and decided to develop a landed estate. When he saw the Napa Valley he knew where he wanted it to be. And his interest in wine determined what the main activity on that estate would be. From the beginning he refused to consider his purchase of Inglenook as an investment. It was a diversion, a "hobby," he called it. Actually, it became a very serious avocation. When he died in 1908 he was at the helm of the Alaska Commercial Company, still solidly linked to its offices and his home in San Francisco. That had been his vocation.

Niebaum knew that grape varieties must be selected before the winery went up. He sent right off to a San Jose nursery for a thousand Sauvignon blanc vines. Others of equal quality soon followed. He understood that Watson's Malvoisie would not make a first-rate wine and had these vines grafted over to better varieties. By 1884 the vineyard had been transformed into a model of the best practices employed on Europe's most renowned wine estates. He put in good varieties: Sauvignon blanc, Sémillon, White Riesling, and "White Pinot" for his whites, Cabernet Sauvignon, Malbec, and Pinot noir for his reds. There were also some heavy bearers of good quality: Grenache, Carignane, Mourvèdre, Charbono, Zinfandel, Sauvignon vert, Palomino, and Burger.

The Captain's man-on-the-spot was a longtime acquaintance from the Alaska days, Hamden W. McIntyre, a Vermonter with a background in engineering and, from his New York days, winery operations. Niebaum supplied the philosophy for Inglenook; McIntyre made it work.

Niebaum's first vintage was in 1882, about 80,000 gallons. It was ordinary stuff which he sold off to Lachman & Jacobi, wine merchants in San Francisco. Next year McIntyre began building the first real winery on the property, but not the great edifice that graces the Valley today; that would come later. Until the new vines came to bear, they bought most of the grapes they needed. By 1884 they were making 120,000 gallons.

As the years went by Niebaum's view of the estate evolved. He accumulated information on winegrowing and decided to construct a truly grand winery. McIntyre worked on the basic design and they hired a San Francisco architect to draw up plans. The construction began in 1886 and had progressed enough for the 1887 crush. It was dedicated in 1888, but the hammering and pouring did not end until 1891. By then the wine being made at Inglenook was as stylish as the new building. Niebaum had picked up the French idea of estate bottling and had his best wines put up on the site, ready to ship to the buyer. He had the cork branded and a wire hood placed around the capsule. Bottling at the winery, except for the local trade and home consumption, was unheard of in California. A very few case goods were shipped east from San Francisco merchants, but these wines were blended and bottled in the city.

Niebaum also set about establishing a brand of his own; it had a special label with a complex diamond trademark. Others had tried this idea before, but no one to date had ever put it all together.[9] The success of this Inglenook brand hinged on two essential factors. Niebaum's agents in San Francisco and on the East Coast put together a masterful public relations campaign. They introduced wines at public events and private social affairs. The comments of those noted people who liked them were then well reported to the press. To this was added a parallel campaign that stressed the technical and experimental side of the Inglenook operation.

The second factor, to which Niebaum was zealously devoted, was a methodical effort to make the public image a true reflection of the reality at the estate in Rutherford and in every bottle of Inglenook wine. Niebaum was a martinet in matters concerning cleanliness in the winery. McIntyre seems to have been the perfect man to make this compulsion a day-to-day reality. Niebaum amassed a huge library of the best works on viticulture and winemaking he and his agents could find.[10] He kept his ear to the ground on local vineyard technology and was right in step with Krug's experiments on closer spacing. He also had a keen interest in soils and their various relationships to different grape varieties.

Niebaum made sure that

Gustave Niebaum (on the left) in the offices of his San Francisco distributor.

Inglenook wines were displayed throughout the world during this time of lavish international expositions. His wines, even his brandy, won awards in the nineties in Paris, Melbourne, Atlanta, Berlin, and Bordeaux. His agents and the Inglenook printed ad campaigns made much of these successes. But a San Francisco trade journal was probably correct in stating that "the judgment by swell New Yorkers is worth a dozen medals," referring to one of the dinners that the Alaska Commercial Company mounted on the East Coast to promote Inglenook wines.[11]

Niebaum's great service to the California wine industry was his ability to present a dependable line of wines at the premium end of the price spectrum, and to do it with just the right balance of showmanship to appeal to upscale Eastern customers. There is no doubt that quality was a solid part of that showmanship; when older Inglenook wines were sampled at a dinner of the San Francisco Wine and Food Society in 1939, the secretary of the Society described two pre-1900 reds as frail but "exquisitely perfumed, smooth and delicately rich. . . ."[12]

Niebaum took no public part in all these efforts to boost the image of Inglenook wine as a commercial product. He did grant an interview now and then, but discussed only mundane matters relating to vineyard and winery operations. Never did he publicly attempt to puff Inglenook wines. It is also noteworthy that Inglenook's great surge in popularity came at a time when the California wine industry was experiencing a terrible depression.

The Captain was able to weather the economic storms ripping through the wine industry in the early nineties, but when the situation became a national economic calamity after 1893, he had to cut back. Soon most Inglenook wine was shipped out in bulk, and by 1895 the practice of estate bottling was abandoned. But Inglenook wine was still bottled in glass in San Francisco at the Alfred Greenbaum firm and shipped from the city as case goods.

Production at Inglenook peaked in 1897 at about 80,000 gallons. By 1901 it was down to about 25,000 gallons, primarily as a result of the phylloxera infestation. Niebaum had replanted in the nineties on resistant rootstock, but his vineyard was down to about a hundred acres in 1900. By 1905, however, planting had picked up on the estate, now managed by the B. Arnhold Company of San Francisco. After Niebaum's death in 1908 the winery was closed for two seasons, but started up production again at a level similar to that of the nineties.

Vintage 1881

We left our narrative of Napa vintages with the satisfied growers and producers hearing the words of Professor Hilgard after the 1880 vintage was safely housed. The new year brought an almost unbelievable torrential flood at the end of January. On one day thirteen inches were measured in St. Helena. The bridges at York Creek and Lodi Lane were washed away. The long bridge in Napa was submerged under two feet of water. Schram reported that the road up to his place had disappeared. But this apparent disaster dampened the winter planting frenzy not a jot. By the time the vines were leafing out, more than 4,000 acres had gone in, over a third Zinfandel. In 1881 Napa also helped establish serious viticulture in the Livermore Valley when H. W. Crabb sold 150,000 Zinfandel cuttings to J. F. Black in Pleasanton.[13] Also noteworthy was the formation of the Napa Viticultural Society, an organization which functioned separately from the St. Helena group, but to which most important upper valley growers and producers belonged.

Hot weather and a poor berry set brought the 1881 vintage down to just over 2,000,000 gallons, with a record 70,000 gallons of brandy. Winery owners were concerned about the escalating grape prices. Some, like Beringer, even threatened to use only their own grapes. Prices remained high but stable, as the result of the short crop. There was also more discord over the "glucose problem." W. W. Lyman complained that some producers were not living up to their pledges to keep the sugar sacks away from the fermentation vats.[14]

Toward the end of the vintage a new face was introduced to a growers' meeting. George Husmann, who had visited the Valley that summer, was presented as the new manager of the winery operations on the Simonton estate in the Carneros. His visit to Napa had seduced him from his professorial duties in Missouri.

1882 AND 1883

Planting slowed some in 1882, although the Howell Mountain development moved right along. Beringer Brothers also made a very significant investment in mountain grapes, planting seventy acres on Spring Mountain. There were now about 12,000 acres of vines in Napa County.

Charles Krug on conditions in 1882.

"I need money, more than usually."

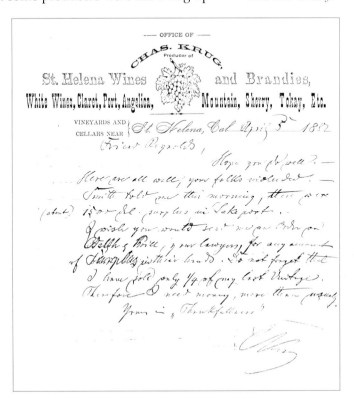

This year the spring frosts were particularly numerous and late, endangering the crop in mid-May. Smudging was general and effective. The summer was quite mild and sugar came up slowly in many varieties; then the rain hit in September. The result was a vintage characterized as low in quality, particularly the Zinfandels. But the Valley's sixty-one wineries generally made money from the 2,600,000 gallons they produced. The brandy stills worked overtime with the low-quality grapes, producing a record 100,000 gallons.

The Napa winegrowers were distracted some by the fact that one of their own was the Republican candidate for governor this year. Morris M. Estee was a noted San Francisco lawyer who bought land on Atlas Peak Road in the eighties and planted vineyards that grew to more than three hundred acres. His campaign managers emphasized his position as a "Napa Valley farmer," but he lost anyway. He did take Napa County, but only by seventy votes. In the coming years his Hedgeside Winery became one of the leading Cabernet producers in the Valley.

Planting was still strong in 1883, but with a marked change in emphasis among the red varieties. Growers were becoming sensitive to the coming prospects of the full Zinfandel crop looming two years down the line. This season the varieties most often mentioned were Carignane, Mourvèdre, and Cabernet Sauvignon. Vineyardists also made good money selling cuttings to growers in other districts.

Windy weather caused poor berry set at bloom time, which, with a bad April 13 frost, held down the yield per acre. But even with a final yield of under two tons per acre, the vintage just about equaled the record production of 1880. Most generally agreed that the state's vintage in 1883 was defective, for a variety of reasons, mostly meteorological. Even though the Napa wines of this vintage were never touted as particularly fine, they impressed reporters and the market with their sound quality in the face of the overall situation. The 35 percent decline in brandy production by Valley distilleries illustrates the local satisfaction in the outcome.

1883 brought the formal incorporation of the Napa Valley Wine Company, with Krug, A. L. Tubbs, Scheffler, Lyman, Estee, and Pellet its major stockholders. It aimed to make it easier to hold wine longer and to sell direct to wholesalers all over the country, bypassing the increasingly powerful San Francisco dealers. To this end the company leased space at Krug's in 1883 and built a large winery in Napa in 1885. E. C. Priber, a German wine dealer from St. Louis, established a link between the company and the east. He visited St. Helena in 1883 and was introduced at a growers' meeting. Priber eventually settled in the Napa Valley and became powerful in the local industry in the nineties.[15]

Even before he visited Napa in 1881, George Husmann had established good connections here with his interest in native rootstock as a means of fighting the phylloxera. During the 1870s he had sold several varieties of such rootstock to H. W. Crabb in Napa and to Julius Dresel in Sonoma. Long before that he had made a name in viticulture. His parents had immigrated to the United States in 1836 when George was nine years old. Like so many Germans they had settled in Missouri, where he planted his first vineyard in 1847. It was located at Hermann, to the west of St. Louis, still a winegrowing area.[16]

After serving as a Union officer in the Civil War, Husmann began his serious investigation of American viticultural possibilities. He published his first work on the subject in 1866.[17] Just before coming to California he published his well-read *American Grape Growing and Wine Making.* After settling in the Napa Valley he issued an enlarged edition with a sizeable section on the California wine scene. There were eleven editions of this work, the final appearing in 1919, seventeen years after his death.

J. W. Simonton had acquired the old Winters ranch in the Carneros in 1879. He aimed at developing a highly diversified agricultural estate, including olive culture, but was concerned by the advance of phylloxera in the area. When he hired Husmann to take over the vineyard and winery management in 1881, the chief task assigned the former professor was to develop a vineyard that would be phylloxera-proof. During the 1881–1882 dormant season Husmann brought in 75,000 native vines, about 50,000 of them from Missouri,

George Husmann

(on the right) in

the Carneros vineyard

of J. W. Simonton.

mostly *V. riparia*. He also bought 25,000 *V. californica* seedlings under the mistaken impression that this local native vine was resistant. Meanwhile Husmann began performing the task for which California winegrowers would owe him a great debt. He became a regular correspondent to many Northern California newspapers, laying out in straightforward, understandable language detailed but practical technical guidelines for winegrowing.

Simonton died suddenly in

1882, throwing the future of the huge agricultural enterprise in doubt. Husmann stayed on and Adolph Flamant, who owned the large ranch to the west, became the executor of the Simonton estate. Flamant was also quite interested in the phylloxera problem and the rootstock solution. During the following year he and Husmann had several serious disagreements, the worst concerning rootstock. Finally, in January 1884, Flamant fired Husmann and there followed a fiery exchange in the local press. Flamant's chief complaint against Husmann was that he refused to pay any attention to the work the French were doing in the field of resistant rootstocks. The former professor's insistence on depending solely on the results of local experience led him in later years to embarrassing pronouncements and a battle with university scientists, which, as we shall see, he lost.[18]

After his sacking, Husmann decided to establish his own wine property, but his limited finances required that he look outside the higher-priced land on the valley floor. He settled on the Chiles Valley and, at the end of the year, bought the Peterson ranch. He first made 5,000 gallons at the little Kaltenbach place in 1885 and proved he could make wine as good as his advice.[19] He began building his own stone winery at his Oak Glen Vineyard in 1889. Today the old place is part of a large Louis Martini vineyard. The winery is gone, but the Martinis were able to save the old engraved keystone.[20]

Husmann continued to fill the newspapers with his practical epistolary advice and acted as an important quality conscience for the entire California wine industry. In such matters he took a very strong stand, along with Professor Hilgard, insisting that making and trying to sell faulty wine was inexcusable, that flawed wine should be recognized as such, and that California's reputation as a wine-producing state depended primarily on the quality and dependability of its best wines. Husmann believed that Napa was one of those blessed places capable of producing such wines, but he was ever ready to promote the good work of other districts making an effort to produce the best they could.[21]

When he died in 1902, he left behind a sound body of practical work and a moral legacy, like Hilgard's, that often made industry leaders bristle. He also left behind his best student from his professorial days at the University of Missouri, his son, George C. Husmann, later a viticultural specialist for the U.S. Department of Agriculture. He was instrumental in overseeing the Department's experimental stations until his retirement in 1932.[22]

PHYLLOXERA VASTATRIX — THE DESTROYER

By the mid-eighties the phylloxera had probably been part of Napa viticulture for at least twenty years, and yet wine production and profits were booming.

But several thoughtful persons had made extrapolations from their observations and understood the danger.[23] Some had begun experimental work in their vineyards by 1881.[24] There were two important questions that needed answering from these experiments. Which resistants should be the choice for Napa's new plantations? And how serious was the problem? That is, what kind of lead time did growers have in unprotected vineyards? Napa growers had no clear answer to either question by the end of the decade.

The danger was clearly manifest in the Carneros, where Simonton, Flamant and Husmann had led the way. A neighbor, John A. Stanly, had acquired his Riverdale Ranch in 1878 and joined his neighbors in planting resistants in 1881.[25]

The upper Valley had not been hit hard yet. Nevertheless, an 1884 examination of the pre-1870 plantings showed that every old vineyard was on the decline, except those just below St. Helena owned by Pellet, Scheffler, and Mrs. Bourn. Krug had previously reported in 1882 that "notwithstanding the presence of phylloxera in many vineyards of my district, the fear of further spread and any serious damage has vanished from our vine growers."[26] Next year the French Agricultural Minister, Henri Grosjean, visited the Valley and remarked that the phylloxera problem didn't appear very serious.[27] Such observations did not move the Valley's vineyardists to face up to the danger. Luckily, California phylloxera spread very slowly.

Less lulling than confusing was the inability of industry leaders and scientific specialists to determine the proper resistant for the various soil situations around the Valley. Most confusing was the almost unbelievable history of the *V. californica* as a resistant stock. Throughout the 1880s industry leaders and scientists touted this native vine as a good source of resistance. Commissioner Wetmore stated in 1884 that "it is surely a resistant vine." Husmann accepted it, as did Flamant and others.[28] Of all people, it was Morris Estee, the politician-winegrower, who publicly challenged the experts and questioned the vine's resistance. But his condemnation fell on deaf ears.[29]

The general acceptance of the *V. californica* can partly be traced to Professor Hilgard's support throughout the 1880s. What seemed to fool the experts was Charles Lefranc's experience in the Santa Clara Valley. In 1857 he had used californica to graft his French imports, not for its resistance but for purposes of propagation. These vines had survived into the 1880s, but only because the phylloxera did not appear in Lefranc's Guadalupe district until the 1890s.[30]

Hilgard went all the way with his error, planting his own vineyard at Mission San Jose with californica grafts. Years later he wrote that "we will have to sell it for its value as bare land, if we can."[31] Why Hilgard persisted in such a belief, even in the face of French scientists' findings to the contrary, is baffling. When Pierre Viala, the French expert, visited the United States in 1887, he found, with Charles Krug as his guide, clear evidence in the Napa Valley that the californica was not resistant. Even before this M. Millardet had rated the vine as totally nonresistant. Such errors tarnished the image of university research in the 1890s in the eyes of many Napa winegrowers, at least on this subject.[32]

By the mid-1890s, when the *V. californica* was finally seen here for what it was, hard times had settled on the Valley's wine men. Charles Krug even stated that the phylloxera had become a friend by holding down production at a time of falling prices. Those who pursued their practical investigations here had come to the conclusion that the best sources of resistant rootstock were *V. riparia*, *V. rupestris*, and the Lenoir *(V. aestivalis/bourquiniana)*. But which and under what conditions were still a matter of conjecture. Also complicating the matter was the fact that California wine men did not understand, and for a while university specialists did not make it clear, that there were a large number of varieties within each species, some useful, others not. This was another lesson they would have to learn from the French, but not until 1897.[33]

1884

The Valley's average winegrower thought little about the phylloxera threat as the 1884 vintage season began. About another thousand acres went in, but many spoke at growers' meetings about planting *really* better varieties. Hilgard and Wetmore both spoke in Napa with this theme predominant in their talks. H. W. Crabb called for more Cabernet Sauvignon and "White Pinot," and less Malvoisie and "Chasselas" (Palomino). He also warned against the misuse of Napa's Zinfandel wines. Good as they could be, he argued, far too many were being used to upgrade poorer quality wines, particularly wine made from second-crop grapes.

Nine new wineries were built in 1884, and many more went into the winemaking business, bringing the total to ninety-seven; there were also 315 vineyardists in the county. Of particular note were the new wineries that Justice Hastings and Christian Adamson put up at Rutherford, and that S. P. Connors built at Larkmead below Calistoga. On Spring Mountain Tiburcio Parrott had bought the Forbes ranch and began planting vines, particularly red Bordeaux varieties, which would produce one of the most famous Napa wines of the 1890s.

The high prices of 1883 had made vineyardists somewhat greedy, for there appeared to be much overcropping this year. Despite June rains there was a large crop set, but the summer was mild and the fall cool, foggy, and stormy. The result was a huge crop with inadequate sugars. Part of it never made it to the fermenters, particularly Zinfandels and Rieslings, which were battered by the fall rains. Many producers sugared their fermenting musts, without a public peep from anyone about "pledges." In a state vintage that was 60 percent greater than the previous year's, this vintage's low-quality deluge broke the market. The record Napa production totaled almost 5,000,000 gallons. Unhappily for local wine prices it was a record that would last only three years. Looking back on the 1884 vintage and its effect on the eastern market for California wines, E. C. Priber stated that it shook "considerably the confidence in our good wines."

H. W. CRABB AND TOKALON

By 1884 Hamilton W. Crabb had the largest winery in the upper Napa Valley, with a capacity of 400,000 gallons. By the end of the decade it could hold double that figure. We have already noted that he arrived here in 1868, apparently keen on producing table grapes. He bought the 240-acre E. L. Sullivan ranch in that year, but by 1872 he had clearly changed the direction of his operation when he built his first little winery at Hermosa Vineyard, as he then called it.[34] In the 1870s his passion for winegrowing and viticultural investigations grew to the point where his vine collection totaled 183 varieties. By the end of the 1880s it approached four hundred; some claimed it to be the largest in the world.[35]

H. W. Crabb

As the years passed, Crabb's reputation for good wine and sound business practices grew. Whenever wines were to be tasted and tested, at industry conventions or international expositions, his were at hand in great number. He was a pioneer in marketing the top varietal wines. Often he blended, but to raise quality, not to mask mediocre wines with a trace of White Riesling or Cabernet Sauvignon. Along with J. H. Drummond of Glen Ellen and John T. Doyle of Cupertino, he promoted the wine varieties from the Rhone region of France and from Northern Italy. One Italian variety, the Refosco, became literally synonymous with his name; many called it "Crabb's Black Burgundy."[36]

By the end of the seventies Crabb had 160 acres in vines, and a winery with a 300,000-gallon capacity. He was, in the *Star*'s words, "a mighty man of vines." But his winery made no pretenses in any area save efficiency and cleanliness. His huge facility was nothing more than a collection of well-insulated one- and two-story frame buildings. The *Star* thought it looked more like a "young town" than a winery. In Crabb's view, if a "good wine needs no bush," a good winery need not look like a fortification or castle.[37]

In 1886 Crabb decided to develop a national brand for his wines. He established agencies in the East, the Midwest, and at New Orleans. From then on he shipped bulk and case goods. The brand name was "To Kalon," a term that was thereafter identified with the winery until it burned down in 1939. To this day the old vineyard is still referred to as To Kalon by some. The Greek term means "most beautiful," but Crabb jokingly told Frona Wait when she visited the place that "I try to make it mean the boss vineyard."[38]

As economic conditions were generally falling apart for the California wine industry between 1889 and 1891, To Kalon's prospects, like those of Inglenook, were improving. Crabb seemed to have a perfect combination of technical know-how, a capital base that enabled him to release his wines with enough age on them, a sound sales force, and a reputation for high quality that held up for years. In 1890 the *Chicago Herald* called him the "Wine King of the Pacific Slope."[39]

Crabb was a quiet, scholarly man, whose only major public vice seems to have been

H. W. Crabb's

To Kalon. "More like

a young town than

a winery."

SOURCE: GUNTHER DETERT.

horse racing. He had a large stable of ponies and a three-quarter-mile track on which to work them. But when the depression of the 1890s lifted, he had it plowed up and planted to vines. He lived to see much of his vineyard land flourishing on riparia rootstock, while large portions of Valley were falling to the phylloxera. When he died in 1899 ownership of the estate passed to the E. W. Churchill family, where it stayed until Martin Stelling purchased it in 1943. Today much of To Kalon is owned by the Robert Mondavi Winery. Since the 1939 fire, virtually nothing remains of the two-acre complex of buildings.

Charles Krug was the Valley celebrity in 1885. First came his sixtieth birthday celebration in March. A huge party of celebrants marched up to the winery, led by the St. Helena Phoenix Band. Fritz Beringer and E. C. Priber made speeches, followed by a great banquet. Krug stood up and announced that there had been a mistake; it was his thirtieth birthday. At the end of the evening the entire company marched over the premises and into the vineyards, led by Krug, arm in arm with J. L. Beringer and G. Bustelli, both former cellar masters.[40]

Then in June came the sickening news that Krug had failed and was in bankruptcy. On July 11 he met with his creditors. His debts came to $236,000, mostly to banks and to Gustav Niebaum. His assets were $181,000. They worked out an arrangement whereby Krug and his family could stay on the property and the winery would continue to function under the guidance of a body of trustees. For several years Krug's wine statistics were recorded under Mrs. Krug's name, since she still held some of her Bale inheritance in her own name.[41]

The huge inventories of wine in the Valley and prospects of another large vintage generated more pessimism. Still, there was some planting and several wineries were built. The most important was the 150,000-gallon structure that Seneca Ewer and J. B. Atkinson built in Rutherford. (The winery would later become the home base for Beaulieu Vineyards.) Hamden McIntyre designed it. He had but two more seasons here before he headed for Tehama County in the Central Valley to supervise the huge winery operation that Leland Stanford was building at Vina.

On Spring Mountain Tiburcio Parrott had begun building his great residence, with rock brought over from Howell Mountain. A. Schröpfer, Parrott's San Francisco architect, had designed the Beringer Rhine House. Today the Parrott estate is the home of Spring Mountain Vineyards. By vintage time there were 102 wineries in Napa Valley ready to make wine.

Drought, frost, and heat held down the 1885 vintage to little more than half the level of the previous year's. But harvest days were torrid, and milk-sour wines from stuck fermentations were a common complaint. Brandy production, understandably, was up 27 percent. But much was made of the many outstanding red wines produced at wineries that followed Hilgard's suggestions regarding cool fermentation techniques. Prices were firm, since state production was down 20 percent from 1884. There was quite a bit of talk about hauling Sacramento Valley grapes by rail to some of the large Napa wineries. The *Reporter* later suggested that now was hardly the time to do anything that might damage Napa Valley's reputation for good wine.[42]

The next season nature was on the Napa winegrowers' side. In 1886, for the first time in five years, rain totals were above normal, and for the first time in almost twice as long there was virtually no planting. More wineries sprang up, the most important being that of Alfred L. Tubbs, north of Calistoga, today's Chateau Montelena. The seeds of another important modern winery had been planted in 1881 when John Tychson bought 159 acres north of St. Helena on Lodi Lane. He and his wife, Josephine, had planted vines and planned a winery, but in 1885 he committed suicide. In 1886 Mrs. Tychson supervised the building of a 25,000-gallon winery. The property eventually came into the hands of Antonio Forni, who built his Lombarda Winery there in 1900. Later this stone structure became the home of Freemark Abbey.[43]

The good 1886 weather continued right into the vintage, which was orderly and long. The final product was just under the 1884 record and the quality of the grapes was excellent. Prices were stable and the concern about possible overproduction was calmed for the moment. Second-crop grapes came in to boost the total, since the good weather lasted into November. Both Krug and Pellet declared this to be the greatest vintage for quality in the Valley's history.[44] Krug himself bought no grapes. He leased part of his cellar to William Bourn, whose name would soon be a major factor in Napa winemaking. The Napa Valley Wine Company moved their winemaking equipment out of the Krug winery to their new facility east of Napa. One can imagine the size of the new operation from the fact that the winery had 250 new 1,000 gallon oak casks.

NAPA WINEGROWING IN 1886

DISTRICT	TONS OF GRAPES	GALLONS OF WINE	ESTIMATED YIELD PER ACRE
Conn Valley	1,390	150,000	2.1
Spring Mountain	400	21,000	1.1
Pope Valley	156	4,000	1.1
Berryessa	150	———	4.5
Chiles Valley	196	6,000	1.5
Howell Mountain	390	40,000	.6
Calistoga	2,600	646,000	1.5
St. Helena	14,387	1,777,000	2.7
Rutherford	4,611	464,000	3.0
Oakville	4,032	800,000	3.7
Yountville	3,960	212,000	2.4
Napa	7,303	348,000	2.2
TOTALS	**39,575**	**4,468,000**	

The drought was back in 1887, with killer frosts in the spring. The desiccating winds in June made for another short crop, under two tons per acre. There was practically no planting, the total county average having leveled off now at about 16,000 acres, a number similar to totals for the early 1970s. Vintage time saw more hot weather and difficult fermentations. Brandy production topped the 1882 record by 50,000 gallons. A large state crop cut down hopes for good prices. People were starting to talk depression.

The only important winery that went up this year was that of Sheriff Henry Harris in Rutherford. Beaulieu's Georges de Latour acquired this property in 1908, shortly after his acquisition of the old Hastings Ranch in Oakville.[45] Another positive move was the Board of State Viticultural Commissioners' establishment of an experiment station at To Kalon. This was the beginning of a long tradition of such facilities at Oakville, later run by the Department of Agriculture and the university.[46]

Prices early in the year had been soft, many producers taking whatever the large Napa wineries or the San Francisco dealers offered them. Some argued that this unwillingness to hold on was breaking the market. When prices dropped even further at vintage time, the willingness to blame merchants was intensified. At the end of the 1887 vintage the *Star* growled that "today many are threatening to dig up their vines rather than suffer the villainous wrong inflicted upon them by the San Francisco wine ring."

The time bomb of previous planting finally exploded on Napa and the rest of the state in 1888 with a vintage here of over 7,000,000 gallons, from a crop that averaged a modest yield of just over three tons per acre. The quality was satisfactory, the whites outshining the reds this year. People continued to argue about the causes of low prices, but steps were being taken to soften the effect. The cooperative brandy operation in the Valley this year boosted production to almost 200,000 gallons. And William B. Bourn led a movement to set up a cooperative wine warehouse. The end result next year would be something very different from the ideas that Bourn and his

Fortune Chevalier's

new winery on

Spring Mt. in 1887.

friends put forth in the spring. Another cooperative effort was started below Calistoga when the Connors/Furniss winery there became the Larkmead Co-op. One of the largest growers selling to the winery was Charles Hitchcock whose daughter, Lillie, was to become something of a San Francisco celebrity in later years, after her marriage to Howard Coit. Her father built her an exotic oriental home out in the vineyard, which she dubbed "Larkmead." It burned down in 1933, but some of its palm trees survived and mark the Three Palms Vineyard today.[47]

Another exotic lady named Lillie came to St. Helena in 1888, the "Jersey Lily," Lillie Langtry. The internationally famed actress had come here to get a California divorce but had to establish residence. She did so by buying a large ranch in Lake County. A huge crowd was on hand at the St. Helena depot on June 1 to observe her well publicized arrival. She and her entourage, which included her current lover, Freddie Gebhard, stayed at the Windsor Hotel and the next day they were off to the ranch by stage. She got her divorce some years later. Up at the ranch some fairly serious winegrowing took place for several years, today the site of the Guenoc Winery.[48]

No number of titillating events such as Mrs. Langtry's visit could hide the grim reality of Napa's economic situation. By now the United States was in the throes of a real agricultural depression. Later, economic historians would characterize the period from 1873 to 1896 as a "long wave" depression, with but eight prosperous years in twenty-four. In agriculture the chief problem was overexpansion of productive capacity in relation to markets. The wine industry had expanded to take advantage of the decline of European imports and to meet the growing demand for wine from the burgeoning Italian and Eastern European immigrant population, who were used to wine as part of their diet. From 1870 to 1890 the rate of immigration from Italy and Eastern Europe had risen by 147 percent.

GREYSTONE

The elasticity of demand for such a commodity as wine is obvious, particularly during an economic depression. For the country as a whole the depression would hit home in 1893. For now the problem in the wine industry was too much wine, but American producers understood little of business cycle theory in these days. For Napa wine men the problem was too much poor wine, and little of it from Napa. They believed sincerely that there was a growing economic conspiracy among San Francisco's chief wine dealers. We have already noted the local grumblings; they grew louder and louder. The *Star* continued to hammer away at the "unholy combination," particularly Lachman & Jacobi, J. Gundlach, and C. Schilling. In January the paper noted that the winemakers' enemies were united in San Francisco; why weren't the winemakers united out in the country?[49] It is true that the merchants' monopolistic actions might have exacerbated the situation, but the problem was overproduction. Arpad Haraszthy had seen it coming eight years earlier when he advised vine planters to take care "lest they overdo a good business." The euphoria of good times had closed the vineyardists' ears to such warnings.[50]

The building of a community distillery near the St. Helena train depot in 1888–89 represents a movement toward more cooperation. Far more important was the project that William Bourn put forward in 1888. At first he envisioned simply a warehouse to make it possible for Napa wine men to empty their cellars without taking up the first offer from wine dealers. By mid-1888 the concept had grown to that of a huge winery that would act as such a storage facility and also make wine for growers. They then could borrow money at the end of the vintage, with the new wine as collateral. By rounding up a large number of investors and gaining bank financing Bourn was able to swing the deal without risking much of his own money.

After making a fortune in mining, William Bourn produced wine for several years in the Napa Valley. His mother had operated a small winery here since the 1870s. He leased the Lewelling Winery in 1885 and later made wine at the Krug facility. The result of Bourn's efforts was to create a corporation ahead of its time, and to build a huge winery. Greystone, just across from the Krug place north of St. Helena, was the largest stone winery in the world, and remains today the architectural centerpiece of the Napa Valley wine industry.[51]

The huge structure started going up in 1888 and was ready to receive wine for storage that year. The finishing touches put the winery on line for the 1889 vintage, with manager Louis Zierngibl making about 350,000 gallons. Bourn let it be known, however, that no Mission or Malvoisie would be allowed in the 2,500,000-gallon facility. He also had a good distillery that converted a large part of the local crop into about 50,000 gallons of brandy.

But you can't beat the business cycle with a large building, and within three years Bourn and his partners, headed by Everett Wise, had given up. In 1892 they leased the place to James Dowdell, who had already established himself in a 100,000-gallon winery south of St. Helena in 1886. Charles Carpy finally bought Greystone in 1894. He made it part of the industry giant, the California Wine Association. In recent years it has been the tourist showplace for the Christian Brothers.[52]

Bad times were pushing Valley wine men to the wall. Scheffler had joined Krug in bankruptcy in 1887. Distillers began cutting corners and were caught by Revenue agents. Krug, Thomann, and Benson at Far Niente were the first to fall. Locals understood their shortcomings to be the result of the Revenue Service's previous winking at brandy shortages, rather than the result of willful wrongdoing.

The *Star* noted that "other distillers who have brandy hidden away are quaking in their boots." The ones who fell later appear to have been far more culpable than those caught in the first wave.

1889

Not all the Napa wine news was bad. Unfortunately the good news did little to raise wine prices. *The New York Tribune* ran an article praising the Napa industry, particularly the efforts of Crabb, Niebaum, and Schram. In addition, several Napa producers had entered their products in the Paris Exposition of 1889 with very positive results for the image of Napa wine. Of the twenty-one medals won by California producers, eleven went to products of Napa vineyards. This pattern continued in the 1890s at other expositions. Producers did take advantage of the advertising potential, but the wine depression had little relationship to the wine drinking public's willingness to buy first-quality Napa wines.[53]

Also appearing in 1889 was Frona Wait's *Wines & Vines of California*, something of a paean to California wine with a special boost for Napa, which she named "the banner wine-making county."[54] On the local scene the *San Francisco Examiner* ran a series of articles on the plight of California wine producers and elicited a wide range of responses from wine men to queries concerning the causes of the price depression. A few had it straight on the relationship of supply to markets, but most settled on scapegoats to explain the situation.[55]

When the vintage started, the Valley's cellars were still full of 1888 wine and morale was very low. The local press and growers themselves had tried to talk up a short crop in July and August, but the upshot was a huge crop of grapes whose quality was about average. When a series of storms struck in early October, about one third of the crop was still on the vine, and most of that stayed there. The rains hit all of California and the resulting shock to the vintage halted the decline in wine prices. As in previous years a few very careful producers made some outstanding wines, which gave 1889 a very good quality image years later, when people were talking about the good old red wines in their cellars.[56]

For the first time there was now serious talk in the Valley about the effects of phylloxera on the size of the final crop. About 25 percent of the vineyards below Yountville were now infected.

Events in 1889 imply that the ax would fall on the Napa wine industry in 1890, but it didn't. Even though several large Valley producers unloaded about half a million gallons to San Francisco dealers in the spring, the result was not a decline in prices, but simply a slowdown in the market. Napa wine and grape prices remained firm throughout the summer. There were even glimmerings of expansion here. Charles Carpy was adding on to his plant in Napa, and the Rennie Brothers, here from Scotland since 1880, built a 90,000- gallon winery near Zinfandel Lane, today the home of the Flora Springs Winery.[57]

Vineyard acreage for Napa County probably peaked this year at a little more than 20,000 acres. There were well over 100 facilities making wine, of which about fifty had stone cellars. In all there were about 600 vineyardists in the county and thirty-five distilleries. These, and virtually all statistics given here for Napa winegrowing in these early days, are my estimates. Statistics for later years are more accurate but are still often educated guesses.[58]

The rainy season was satisfactory in 1889–90, but the spring and summer months through August were very hot, with some July days rising above 110°. Then it became cool and the winegrowers waited and watched as sugars refused to rise. Late September rains, mostly light and misty, also held back maturity and severely damaged the Zinfandel crop. Growers who held on were rewarded by a stretch of Indian summer that went on into November. The resulting red wines were rich and well-colored. Grapes from hill vineyards were declared superb. Carpy, Krug, and Schram expressed themselves in jubilant tones to the press. The long warm spell also brought in a good second crop, pushing up final figures far above predictions. These wine leaders had no long faces now; people here believed in Napa wine. They believed that when they made good wine they could sell it. Plans went forward now for a vintage festival for 1891.

It would have been difficult to perceive any particular fall of an ax in 1891, but at the end of the year conditions had driven Napa Valley wine men to the brink. Throughout the year, reports of California wine shipped east and into foreign markets were encouraging. But prices paid to producers continued to fall. The gloom was heightened by the terrible advance of phylloxera in recent months. At least 3,000 acres expired between Vintages 1890 and 1891.[59]

There were continued signs of consolidation now in an industry fighting to save itself. Charles Carpy added to his wine empire in May when he bought the huge Pacific Wine Company in San Jose. Claus Schilling took over the the faltering Groezinger Winery. But a new winery was being built on Spring Mountain by Fortune Chevalier, a San Francisco liquor dealer who had bought land there in 1884. The winery was to become today's Chateau Chevalier.[60]

The 1891 vintage was an ugly one. Conditions in the spring and summer set a fairly short crop. From July on it was a wild roller coaster ride of soaring temperatures, rain, and scorching September winds. Grapes were low in juice and many fermentations stuck. October rains left about 25 percent of the crop in the vineyards. The distilleries worked overtime. But there was a bright side to part of this situation, since new government regulations made it possible to use fortifying brandy for sweet wines without paying the brandy tax at the time of fortification. A record 275,000 gallons of brandy were made, a good part of which went into the record 130,000 gallons of sweet wine.

The vintage festival in September was a great success, hosted by the local Turnverein. Ducking showers throughout, the merry crowds started out with a concert at the Turner Hall. Herman Schram was one of the vocal soloists. There was a big parade to Edge Hill for a picnic, where about 600 pounds of meat and over 1,000 loaves of bread were served to the hungry folks. Uncounted bottles of wine were consumed. Louis Zierngibl of Greystone was the master of ceremonies and Fritz Beringer the orator. His theme was work hard, organize, and aim for high quality in all you do. Everything was in German. The next day there was a great tour of the Valley, first to Parrott's, then lunch at the brewery west of town, and finally another big dinner, this time at Inglenook.

Then came the rest of the unhappy harvest. At the end the Valley was disheartened by the death of Mrs. Krug. The old pioneer himself did not survive the coming year.

The wine market broke in December when a large Santa Clara Valley producer dumped over a million gallons at a disastrously low price. The day after Christmas the Napa wine men met to consider their plight. By any set of criteria, 1891 was a disaster. The phylloxera was marching up the Valley. Planting was not even discussed. The total yield this year had been low. Prices were rock-bottom. The quality of this year's wines was low.

The first step, they decided, was to reach out to their fellows in the other dry wine districts of Northern California. They must prepare for an all out fight against the San Francisco "wine ring." Krug pushed for deputations to Sonoma and Santa Clara immediately. In his last speech to his Napa friends he cried out, "No agitation. No Victory!"[61]

NOTES FOR CHAPTER FIVE

1. Alta, 3/15/1880.
2. SBVC (1884): 38.
3. Reporter, 7/22/1881, 8/26/1881.
4. There are several sources for this famous address. Krug included it in his December 27, 1880 "Report" in SBVC (1881, 2nd Edition, revised): 75-84.
5. Register, 9/14/1880, 9/29/1880; Wine Spectator, 2/16/1983.
6. Star, 6/3/1884, 10/15/1886; PWSR, 9/14/1888; Reporter, 7/9/1886.

7. SBVC (1887): 44; "The Vineyards in Napa County." in SBVC (1893): 30-31, 42-43; Star, 1/21/1881; 12/11/1885; PWSR, 10/5/1891.

8. T. J. Gregory. History of Solano and Napa Counties (Los Angeles 1912) contains an article by Jordan on his experimental work at 226. Also see: Mt. Veeder, A Concise History of Viticulture and Enology, published by the Hess Collection Winery in 1989; Farmer, 10/4/1864; Reporter, 1/22/1876.

9. Virtually all Inglenook history discussed in this study, and much more, can be found in: Tom Parker and Charles L. Sullivan. Inglenook Vineyards, 100 Years of Fine Winemaking (Rutherford 1979). A good part of this work derives from a manuscript collection unique in nineteenth century California wine history. It includes McIntyre's "Letter Book, 1882-1887," "Cellar Statement, 1889-1898," "Statements of Shipments, 1890-1902," "Pay roll, 1888-1902," "Monthly Ranch Statements, 1893-1908," "Time Book, 1888-1908," and "Cellar Book, 1911-1914."

10. Part of this collection has been recently re-assembled and housed again at Inglenook.

11. PWSR, 7/30/1886, 2/26/1895, 10/8/1895, 3/7/1896.

12. Wines & Vines (May 1939).

13. Livermore Herald, 4/28/1881; Reporter, 4/18/1881.

14. Star, 12/2/1881.

15. Reporter, 8/24/1883; Star, 7/31/1883.

16. For the Hermann, Missouri wine story see: Leon Adams. The Wines of America (New York 1985): 169-171. In 1980 the Treasury Department granted the Augusta area, just to the east, the country's first designation as a viticultural district.

17. For a Husmann bibliography see: James M. Gabler. Wines into Words Baltimore 1985): 135-136.

18. Reporter, 11/3/1882, 10/2/1884, 10/24/1884, 10/31/1889.

19. Star, 1/16/1885, 12/11/1885; PWSR, 3/16/1888, 8/22/1889.

20. Bonfort's 10/10/1889; Haynes, 69.

21. San Jose Herald, 6/20/1885; San Jose Mercury, 8/16/1889; PWSR, 4/24/1885, 6/13/1890, 9/20/1892.

22. AWP (November 1902). For William Laferriere's obituary biography of George Husmann see: PWSR, 11/30/1902. For his son's work see: Wines & Vines (June 1928), (March 1932), (December 1939).

23. For a detailed narrative of the arrival and early spread of the phylloxera in the Napa Valley see: "The Grape Phylloxera in California." USDA Bulletin No. 903 (1921): 7-11.

24. PWSR, 10/9/1885 lists A. L. Tubbs, H. W. Crabb, G. Niebaum, M. Estee, C. Krug, A. Flamant, G. Husmann, G. Schoenewald, and J. A. Stanly.

25. By the end of the century, Stanly's La Loma Winery had developed the best reputation for quality in the Carneros. Over the years he was the most persistent and successful in his use of resistant rootstock there. PWSR, 10/26/1883, 11/6/1885, 3/16/1888; Chronicle, 10/6/1889; "The Vineyards in Napa County." SBVC (1893): 22; Wait, 106.

26. SBVC (1882): 44.

27. Reporter, 1/5/1883.

28. SBVC (1884): 129; Star, 9/1/1883, 10/4/1884.

29. Reporter, 10/5/1883.

30. SBVC (1888): 48; Sullivan, Edens, 85.

31. Amerine, "Hilgard," 4; Bonfort's, 4/25/1889.

32. Viala pulled no punches. "Elle n'aurait donc aucune valeur pour la reconstitution do nos vignobles, malgré sa grande vigeur. . . ." Pierre Viala. Une Mission Viticole en Amerique (Paris 1889): 144-151; Ordish at 212 gives Millardet's numerical rating of resistance, citing Chancrin. Viticole moderne (Paris 1950). Viala's conclusions were transmitted to the SBVC in a document dated 12/27/1887, which was not published until 1890. It is clear to me that the translation, probably by Wetmore, was far less emphatic in its rejection of the V. californica than Viala's original. SBVC (1890): 108.

33. Sullivan. "Phylloxera Root Louse." VWGJ, 13.

34. NVWLA III: 125-136; Star, 10/25/1878.

35. PWSR, 5/4/1891. The Star had earlier asked Crabb for a complete catalogue of his collection, which it printed 10/13/1882. It is one of the most useful documents of its kind in nineteenth century California viticultural history. Sonoma also early praised Crabb's work. Santa Rosa Republican, 5/17/1877.

36. PWSR, 12/24/1886. Refosco and Mondeuse appear to be the same vine. See: Galet, 79. In post-Repeal times the grape was often used in blends of Napa "Burgundy." the most famous of which

was produced at Beaulieu Vineyards. Between 1984 and 1985 the vine disappeared from the official statistics of Napa County, where it had previously been listed as Refosco.

37. Star, 7/25/1879, 8/1/1879, 8/6/1886.

38. Star, 7/8/1889; Wait, 108-109; Guido Rossati. Relazione di un viaggio d'istruzione negli Stati Uniti d'America (Rome 1900): 199.

39. Chicago Herald, 6/29/1890; PWSR, 5/4/1891. For a racy story of Crabb's private life see: Star, 8/2/1889.

40. Star, 3/4/1885.

41. Reporter, 6/23/1885; Star, 7/3/1885, 7/17/1885.

42. PWSR, 9/26/1884; Reporter, 8/27/1886; Star, 8/20/1886.

43. Reporter, 5/27/1887; Star, 8/17/1886.

44. Star, 12/3/1886; PWSR, 12/10/1886.

45. Star, 5/27/1887; PWSR, 9/1908.

46. SBVC (1887): 67.

47. Star, 8/17/1888, 2/15/1907; Wines & Vines (April 1937); Wait, 123; Archuleta, 93-94. Lillie Hitchcock Coit's fascination for members of the city's fire department is memorialized by San Francisco's Coit Tower.

48. Star, 7/22/1887, 1014/1887, 6/1/1888, 6/8/1888; Pierre Sichel. The Jersey Lilly (Englewood Cliffs 1958): 228-247; Suzanne D. Case. Join Me in Paradise (Guenoc Winery 1982); Charles L. Sullivan. "Lillie Langtry," Wine Spectator (July 16, 1982).

49. Star, 3/30/1888, 1/4/1889.

50. Transactions, (1881): 168-175.

51. Star, 4/16/1889, 8/23/1889.

52. Star, 2/23/1888, 4/6/1888, 8/13/1889, 9/23/1892, 6/1/1894; PWSR, 4/13/1888; Teiser and Harroun, 164; Ruth Teiser. "Stone-Age Survivor." Wine Spectator (July 1, 1984).

53. PWSR, 2/17/1889; Star, 8/23/1889. Wine awards went to G. Migliavacca (gold); Mrs. Weinberger, Inglenook, Beringer, and Henry Hagen (silver); Larkmead, Krug, Matthews, Brun & Chaix, and J. Atkinson (bronze). Brandy awards went to Crabb, Hagen, Edge Hill, and Napa Valley Wine Co. The United States received a total of twenty-eight medals for wine. The number won by other countries is revealing: e.g. Switzerland (21), Australia (36), Portugal (289), France (950). Reports of the United States Commissioners to the Universal Exposition at Paris (Washington DC 1891): IV, 726-732.

54. The book was re-published in 1973 under the auspices of the Napa Valley Wine Library Association. For a caustic review of the book see: Bonfort's, 12/10/1889. This national publication accused Wait of "untruthful abuse" of European wine. "It is these ridiculous, exaggerated statements that make California contemptible in the eyes of the world and render it almost impossible for true friends to gain for her wines the recognition their merits deserve." However exaggerated, the book is a useful journalistic examination of California winemakers in the 1880s.

55. Examiner, 7/23/1889, and in many more issues for the next five months.

56. PWSR, 7/8/1889, 8/22/1889; SBVC (1892): 55-59; Reporter, 12/6/1889; Star, 11/15/1889. The local press tended to predict the Napa vintage at least a million gallons below actual production.

57. Star, 8/15/1890; Haynes, 57.

58. SBVC (1890): 48-50; cf. SBVC (1891-1892): 55-59.

59. PWSR, 2/14/1891, 7/8/1891; Bonfort's, 12/10/1891.

60. Lindy Lindquist. "A Castle on a Hill." Vintage (August 1975): 35.

61. Star, 1/1/1892.

THE DISMAL DECADE
DESTRUCTION AND RESUSCITATION

*Our Vineyards are melting away
as the mist before the morning sun.*

—E. C. PRIBER
1892

IF ONE WERE TO VIEW THE NAPA VALLEY, ITS VINEYARDS, AND ITS WINERIES, AS the second half of the 1890s got under way, it would have been difficult to predict anything but a grim future for this once-great land of vines. Such a prediction for the West Side of the Santa Clara Valley should have been equally grim, and fairly accurate. That once-great sea of vines never recovered. Profitable agriculture did survive there, but the vineyards were scattered here and there among the prunes and apricots.

Napa seemed to hang by a thread. Prunes, pears, and walnuts were now planted in large number. But in the wake of the greatest national economic collapse in history, climaxed by a bloody financial war within the wine industry itself, and in the face of a seemingly unconquerable pest, the Napa Valley's wine industry came back by the early years of the new century and was flourishing.

1892

The 1892 season was another unhappy one for most. As the vineyards died, few gave thought to replanting. Growers generally understood that the experts couldn't agree on which resistant stocks would work, so why go to the expense? The morale of local vineyardists can be gauged by their reaction this year to the terrible frosts that blackened the Valley in April. The ubiquitous dark clouds of smudge smoke did not appear. Why spend money to save grapes whose prices would hardly pay for their harvest?

And yet the image of Napa wine was steadily on the rise, at least the best Napa wine. Prices for "Medoc" blends, basically Cabernet Sauvignon and Malbec, were surging. Producers of established brands, such as Beringer, Crabb, Schram, and Niebaum, were having no trouble selling their dry table wines in the east. And those who had developed a reputation for quality but sold to dealers could also expect good prices. Such a one was Tiburcio Parrott, whose Cabernet Sauvignon was the basis for Charles Carpy's La Loma brand Medoc.

In March Andrew Carnegie gave the Valley a boost when he toured here in his private railroad car. It was the perfect time to visit. Everything was bright green, with the fruit trees in flower. The large party went off to visit Parrott's place, guided by Morris Estee. The *Star* reported that Carnegie was "wild with enthusiasm over the beautiful view of the valley." Later Carnegie told a San Francisco reporter that Napa surpassed in beauty anything he had seen in California. Next they went off to Beringer's for a tour of the tunnels and a wine tasting. The steel baron

Schram and Carpy.

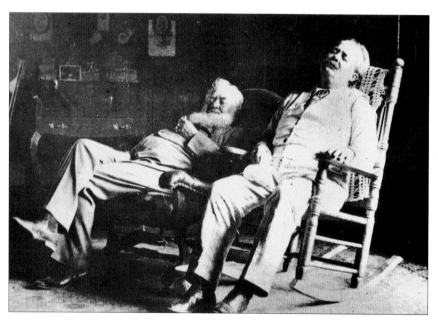

thought the 1888 Beringer Riesling one of the best wines he'd ever tasted and followed through with a large order next month. Then they were off to Krug's place where the old pioneer shared a glass with his fellow immigrant.[1]

Visiting the Napa Valley and its wineries became a must for tourist groups to Northern California. In the 1890s it grew into a tradition that lasted until World War I and began again in the 1950s. It didn't always go smoothly. In June a group of 600 newspaper editors was scheduled to see the sights, but their hosts in Solano County didn't get them back to the train on time, not even close. Eventually the locomotive pulled out of Vacaville leaving seventy of them behind. They could stop for only thirty minutes in St. Helena, and the trip to Parrott's place, which had been tricked out for a fancy luncheon, was canceled.[2]

The 1892 vintage was quite short, down 38 percent from 1891. With prices still down and large inventories remaining in most wineries, many Napa vineyardists simply could not make the interest payments on their bank loans. It was clear to those hurt worst, independent growers, and small, narrowly financed producers, that the end was near. And the phylloxera continued its advance up the valley.

SELECTED NAPA WINERIES CIRCA 1891

The following Napa Valley wineries were in operation in the early 1890s. This is far from a complete list of the approximately 140 winemaking operations functioning then. Given the turbulent times, a complete list would be next to impossible to construct. There were rapid changes in ownership, numerous bankruptcies, and many wineries that suddenly decided simply to become grape producers.

I have chosen the wineries on this list for their historical significance and often because there are physical remains today. See Irene Haynes' *Ghost Wineries of the Napa Valley* for maps and photographs. Wineries marked (r) either have such remains or have been physically revived in some manner. Those marked (*) still operate or have been revived as wineries. When a modern successor operates under a different name, the new name is given in the second column. Gallonage indicates a typical vintage for these years and is a fair indication of relative capacity.

LOCATION/1891 WINERY	CURRENT WINERY	ANNUAL GALLONAGE
CARNEROS		
J. Stanly		50,000
E. Bressard		30,000
P. Priet /Debret (r)		20,000

NAPA CITY

G. Migliavacca		250,000
J. Matthews (*)		50,000
Uncle Sam/C.Carpy (r)		300,000
Napa Valley Wine Co.		300,000
J. Baxter		20,000

NAPA AREA/BROWN'S VALLEY/MT. VEEDER

H. Hagen		40,000
A. Carbone		15,000
F. Fischer	Mayacamus	10,000
J. Knief		10,000
E. Streich (r)		4,000
R. Jordan	Hess	4,000
J. Hein		10,000
M. Pond		8,000

SOUTH OF YOUNTVILLE

Eshcol	Trefethen	100,000

SILVERADO (EAST SIDE)

Hedgeside	Quail Ridge	100,000
Bay View/Borreo (r)		20,000
J. Vopt		20,000
White Rock/Pettingill (r)		5,000
Occidental (r)		45,000
F. Salmina		8,000
L. Banchero (r)		15,000

YOUNTVILLE

Groezinger/Schilling (r)		100,000
J. Frye		30,000
M. Meyers		25,000
E. Bressard		30,000
T. Fawver		40,000

OAKVILLE

To Kalon	Robert Mondavi	250,000
Brun & Chaix		100,000
Far Niente (*)		35,000
A. Jeanmonod		20,000
J. Davis		40,000

RUTHERFORD

Inglenook (*)		65,000
Ewer & Atkinson (BV)		100,000
C. Adamson (r)		100,000
H. Harris (r)		90,000
C. La Rue		50,000
C. Beerstecher		30,000

CONN VALLEY

Franco-Swiss (r)		100,000
Corthay		20,000
Mountain Cove (r)		10,000
E. Hall		20,000

CHILES VALLEY

Lomitas/Sievers		20,000
Oak Glen/Husmann		20,000

SOUTH OF ST. HELENA

J. Thomann	Sutter Home	100,000
Stamer Bros.		30,000
Oak Grove/McCord		40,000
Rennie Bros.	Flora Spgs.	50,000
Monongo/Weaks		25,000
J. Wheeler (r)		150,000
T. Amesbury(r)		30,000
H. Helms (r)		20,000
C. Brockhoff (r)		20,000
Olive Hill/ H. Lange		20,000

ST. HELENA

Charles Krug (*)		100,000
Edge Hill	L. Martini	75,000
Mrs. J. C.Weinberger (r)		25,000
B. Ehlers	Ehlers Lane	20,000
Beringer Bros. (*)		200,000
Greystone		350,000
W. Castner (r)		15,000
J. Dowdell (r)		100,000
Mrs. J. Laurent	Markham	40,000
A. Rossi		25,000
G. Schoenewald	Spottswoode	20,000
F. Sciaroni (r)		30,000
Mrs. J. Tychson	Freemark Abbey	10,000
E. Zange (r)		25,000
G. B. Crane		25,000
H. A. Pellet		30,000
G. Fountain (r)		20,000
J. McPike		50,000
W. Lyman	El Molino	10,000
E. York (r)		35,000
T. Ink		50,000
F. Kraft (r)	Spottswoode	20,000
D. Cole (r)		10,000

SPRING MOUNTAIN

R. Lemme/ La Perla (r)		20,000

Miravalle/T. Parrott	Spring Mountain	15,000
M. Hueschler		5,000
P. Bieber		5,000
P. Conradi	Keenan	20,000
F. Chevalier	Ch. Chevalier	25,000
MT. DIAMOND		
Schramsberg (*)		40,000
L. Zierngibl		15,000
R. Schmidt	Sterling	15,000
A. McEachran	Schramsberg	10,000
HOWELL MOUNTAIN		
Brun & Chaix	Ch. Woltner	75,000
Liparita/W. S. Keyes (*)		5,000
Spring Hill/ G. Mee		15,000
W. Geiselmann/Hastings		20,000
O. Norman		7,000
R. Chabot	Forman	10,000
POPE VALLEY		
G. Haug		10,000
CALISTOGA		
J. Grimm	Storybook	60,000
V. Courtois		50,000
Larkmead	Rombauer	150,000
Kortum & Fulscher		60,000
G. Lange		20,000
E. Light (r)		25,000
A. Tubbs	Ch. Montelena	45,000
C. Pickett		10,000

SELLING NAPA WINE

Save for the dilemma of quality, the most serious problem facing Napa winegrowers in the nineteenth century was marketing. A hundred years later Napa producers would likely place marketing right at the top.

The two problems were closely intertwined in these early years, since the satisfactory delivery of wine to the consumer, whatever the package, was ever tied to the fragile chemical nature of the product. The marketing pattern developed in the 1860s, whereby Southern California wine was brought to the cool cellars of the San Francisco dealers, was changed little by the shift of the industry's productive center to Northern California in the 1870s. Typically, Napa wines were sold to San Francisco merchants, who blended them to suit their local and eastern customers' tastes. They then shipped them out in bulk. Except for the California market, which was always sizeable, these barrels and casks were shipped by sea to New York and New Orleans. After California was linked to the east by rail in 1869, a growing percentage of this bulk traffic went through in large casks aboard unrefrigerated box cars. By the 1890s about 60 percent of the state's wine exports went by rail, a figure that grew to 70 percent by the end of the decade. Of the total wine exported in the 1890s, only about one tenth of one percent, or about 40,000–50,000 cases, went out bottled.

The bulk wine thus shipped was usually sold to local bottlers after it reached its eastern destination, but a fairly large percentage of this wine was bottled by the San Francisco merchants themselves, many of whom maintained sizeable receiving and bottling facilities in several large cities east of the Rockies. These merchants were thus able to establish their own brands and reputations, with virtually no recognition of the source of such wines, or the grapes that produced them. As Napa's reputation grew, however, it became more and more common for dealers to incorporate a mention of the Napa origins onto some of their labels.

Napa itself was directly represented by San Francisco dealers rooted in the Valley's past. The most important were Charles Carpy and the Napa Valley Wine Company in the 1880s, and later Claus Schilling. In 1894 all three became part of the industry's "wine trust," the California Wine Association.

From the beginning Napa winegrowers saw the potential economic benefit of bypassing the dealers and selling directly to customers outside California. Thus, several producers in the 1870s hired eastern jobbers and salesmen and even set up eastern depots as sales outlets, none of which proved particularly successful. The main problem they faced was the generally poor quality and poor reputation of California wine in the east. Pioneers in these attempts such as Krug and Pellet did benefit from these early connections when times improved after 1878. Having German contacts in St. Louis opened the Midwest to Krug and became an important aspect of his business in the eighties. Crabb had the same advantage in Chicago.

A particularly hurtful situation developed in the east in the 1870s, partly due to California's poor reputation for quality. Eastern merchants who found good California wine also found they could sell it far more easily under a foreign label. This deception helped sell good California wine, but it did nothing for the Golden State's sorry wine reputation. It was a long, uphill task to convince easterners, who were willing to pay a premium price, that the California label could be trusted. By the 1890s what California wine men called the "eastern prejudice" had been broken. We have seen how several good Napa Valley brands were well received during the depression years after 1893. Cargo wine of poor quality continued to appear under foreign labels until the passage of the Federal Food and Drugs Act of 1906.[3]

Selling California wine overseas was a very important part of the wine industry's public relations image, particularly during the heyday of the Viticultural Commission in the eighties. Some Napa producers occasionally made important sales. Both Groezinger and Carpy were able to open the London market on occasion. In 1894 Carpy actually made a single sale of 256 barrels to a London customer.[4] In 1895 Schram began selling wine to the North German Steamship Line. But in the nineties about 85 percent of the California wine leaving the state by ship ended up in East Coast markets.

The overseas shipments were well scattered. Most of them went to Pacific basin ports, half to Mexico and Central America. Hawaii often took more than Mexico. Ten to 15 percent went to Japan and China. Tahiti took 5 to 10 percent. By the turn of the century foreign business had grown by about a third since the eighties, most of that growth measured in shipments to Great Britain and Germany.

Here are some fairly typical examples of such foreign shipments. On December 2, 1892 the coastal steamer *Newbern* headed for Baja California and points south with 4989 gallons of California wine a small part of her cargo. These were shipments from ten different Northern California dealers. One of these was Charles Carpy, who sent 842 gallons to customers in various ports, packaged in fifty-three kegs, thirteen octaves, thirty cases, and a barrel. On December 18, 1897 the *S. S. City of Peking* left for the Far East with 2131 gallons shipped by eight dealers. Aboard were eight barrels of Beringer wine to be dropped off in Yokohama and forty-one cases from the Napa and Sonoma Wine Company, destined for Shanghai and Hong Kong. But far more typical was the *S. S. Louisiana* posted for New York in 1892 with 2537 barrels from seven San Francisco dealers.

Selling Napa wines in hotels and restaurants was difficult anywhere in the United States, including Napa itself. The problem was that Americans were not wine drinkers, and the people who ran these establishments usually sold wine with little interest or conviction. At the typical hotel there was a red and a white, which were bottled on the spot from barrels purchased from a local dealer. At your dishonest "swell establishments", Napa wine might be available, but it probably came to the table in a bottle labeled "Chateau Latour" or such. Invariably it would appear at the table already open, having just been drawn from a ready cask in the "cellar." This practice accounts for today's seemingly pointless tradition of drawing the cork at the table and presenting it to the customer. At high-class, honest eating places that is just what the waiter did; in those days it was really the customer's only "guarantee" of authenticity.

Outrageous prices were another part of the restaurant swindle. Wine that the owner probably bought for less than fifty cents per gallon would often sell for as much as a dollar per bottle, a markup not unheard of today. Charles Wetmore called such businesses "the worst enemies of California wines." At Napa's Palace Hotel he asked for a California Zinfandel and was told they had none. Eventually he had to settle for a "spurious imitation of Chateau Margaux." "When I go to Napa I always growl; the idea of being forced to pay the price of a dinner for five cents worth of wine. . . ."[5]

But in some large cities there were high-class establishments that eventually took up the cause of good California wine and made places on their wine lists for some brands. San Francisco was no better than many big cities in these matters, but the Palace Hotel was an exception. Here manager C. H. Livingston had a small but representative choice of California wines that included a Cabernet and Sauterne from Hedgeside, and Schramsberg's Riesling. And there were Zinfandels, listed as such, from Inglenook and the Napa Valley Wine Company. At a dollar a bottle Mr. Estee's Hedgeside Cabernet cost the same as a shipper's "St. Julien-Médoc."

R. L. Stevenson and Hawaiian King Kalakaua in 1889. Stevenson had Napa wine shipped to the Pacific Islands after he left the valley.

Where the manager was a real wine connoisseur, the result could be even better for California wine. The head man at the Hotel Del Monte at Monterey in the eighties was George Schoenewald. His wine list included a wide range of California wines, again with Hedgeside and Schramsberg in the forefront. In a few years Schoenewald would be a noted Napa Valley winegrower.

Few wineries, in relation to the total number of California wine producers, were able to market their own brands. Still, more local wine traveled under the Napa label than on the product of any other California wine district, at least until Sonoma's Italian Swiss Colony practically took over the brand name business in the late 1890s. The same was true of the case goods business, where a fairly high percentage of the bottled wine shipped out of state came from Napa Valley.

An overwhelming number of California producers, however, and most of those from the Napa Valley, had no choice but to sell their wines to the dealers. We have already seen the growing antagonism against the San Francisco merchants, even in the best of times. As the wine depression grew in the nineties, and as retail wine prices held firm, declining prices to producers became an obsessive concern for Napa Valley wine men. Most were certain that a conspiracy was afoot. This spirit was loose all over the land, as farm prices generally declined while retail prices remained stable. It was the time of the Populist revolt, which saw Midwestern wheat farmers and Southern cotton growers band together to attack a perceived conspiracy of American capitalists who were, they believed, bent on squeezing "all that traffic would bear." Agricultural producers saw themselves "under the lion's paw."

There was little interest in the Populist campaign in California or the Napa Valley, but the discontented were well-represented out west. A striking parallel between the California wine situation and the Midwest was the growing belief here that an apparent omnipotent power in the form of international bankers was calling the economic shots throughout the Western world. In the Midwest the image of the "international Jewish banker" became a common whipping boy of Populist orators. Among California's country wine producers this theme was taken up in a sort of growling resentment toward the San Francisco dealers, many of whom were Jewish.[6] The ill will burst into a fury of ethnic name calling at the Viticultural Convention in May 1892, as charges flew back and forth between leading merchants and the wine men from the country districts.[7]

1893

Almost half the vineyards in the Napa Valley had some evidence of phylloxera infestation at the outset of the 1893 season. There were about 2,000 acres on resistant rootstock. But more than 10,000 acres were dying. Winegrowers who had a strong capital position—Niebaum, Crabb, and Beringer the most obvious—put out new vines, but most were neither planting nor replanting.

There were two big stories this year. The most dramatic was the Columbian Exposition in Chicago to celebrate 400 years of European civilization in the New World. The other story should have turned the heads of many wine men, but didn't.

For a country on the gold standard to have its gold reserves drop 20 percent below what most businessman considered an absolute minimum, should have been cause for concern. On May 5, as insiders sensed the situation, the prices on American stock markets declined sharply. The crash took place on June 27, ushering in, but not causing, to be sure, until then the greatest industrial depression in American history. Credit would now be tight, prices would decline, immigration would plummet. In fact, reverse immigration took place for a period of time. Thousands of Italians and eastern Europeans returned to their homelands in the face of rising unemployment here. All this would hit the California wine industry at a time when conditions were bad in the first place. The ill effects of wine and grape oversupply would now be exacerbated by a general condition of industrial overexpansion and financial contraction. It is not clear that Napa wine men realized anything special was happening until a few weeks before the vintage.

Most people had their eyes on the great spectacle taking place on the shores of Lake Michigan. Many Napa folks actually made the trip. The display of Napa wines was in the charge of Louis Zierngibl, who had been given a fairly generous $1,000 to spend. After a year's preparation the state industry had put

Country wine making

in Napa was not all

romance in the 1890s.

together a large display. The overall effect seems to have been highly beneficial to California's image as a wine land, particularly so far as future sales on the East Coast were concerned. The wine competition was important, and, of course, California wines won a treasure trove of medals. Far more important was the individual evaluation of California wines by Charles Furley Oldham, a noted English connoisseur and London wine merchant. His observations will be discussed in the next chapter.

California wineries won seventy-seven awards, twenty-two of which went to Napa producers. Sonoma was next with eleven. Commissioner Wetmore was not impressed by these awards, which he considered "too numerous to be considered prizes of distinction." Carpy led the way with four Napa awards, followed by Beringer and Crabb with three each. Ewer & Atkinson, Zierngibl, and the Napa Valley Wine Company had two apiece. One each went to Schram, Estee, Brun & Chaix, Migliavacca, Otto Norman (Howell Mountain), and Tiburcio Parrott, the latter two for their delicious Cabernets.[8]

The 1893 vintage started with a good crop on still healthy vines, but late September rains hurt the Zinfandel and Riesling. The wine grape deal this season was dramatized by all kinds of special situations resulting from the sudden disappearance of credit usually available to producers. Now the Valley was aware of the Panic of 1893. Lots of wine was made on credit to the grower's account, since it was next to impossible for wineries to get the normal cash advances from local banks. In other words, growers now had to wait for their money until producers were able to sell the wine, a situation not unheard of in recent years.

Another characteristic of the 1893 vintage was the serious labor oversupply resulting from the hard times in Bay Area cities. Workers, mostly white, began flocking to St. Helena in late August. Then contract Chinese labor began arriving by train in early September. The anti-Chinese spirit in the Valley among the working classes was rekindled. The town marshal had his hands full with numerous outbreaks of violence against the Chinese contract labor.

The end result was a good vintage on the vines that were still healthy, about one-third higher than in 1892. Prices were flat and low. The backlog from previous vintages had become a drug on the market, even for sound Napa wines. Many Valley growers and winery owners were starting to calculate the difference between returns on an acre of wine grapes and on an acre of prunes. The numbers for prunes were looking better and better at the end of 1893.

THE CALIFORNIA WINE ASSOCIATION

Morale among Napa winegrowers could hardly have been lower than in the first half of 1894. A price war in the industry was developing as San Francisco dealers competed by dumping their surpluses in the New Orleans and New York markets, further depressing prices. As summer advanced, the country was hit by a national railroad strike, which clogged what commerce there was. The blockade hit home when the Napa national guard unit was called up and hustled off to San Francisco to help maintain order.

The rainy season was quite dry this season and May frosts further cut a crop that would come from at least 2,000 fewer acres, as the phylloxera kept up its northern march. Napa came close to losing Jacob Schram in June when he was almost killed driving home from Parrott's place. His sixty-eighth birthday party had to be called off. Later in the year Parrott himself died, at the height of his great successes in Cabernet quality.

A hot August got the vintage started early and the grapes came in fast, although the quality of the crop had been hurt by growers' overcropping when they did their pruning. But with all the over-cropping the yield was the lowest since 1881, barely more than 2,000,000 gallons. Prices were still low, but the seemingly endless skid was halted by a generally short dry wine crop throughout Northern California.

Before the vintage the long-expected move by the San Francisco dealers to consolidate their marketing operations took place with the formation of the

"The Wine Press"

was created for the San

Francisco Midwinter

Fair in 1894.

California Wine Association (CWA), what its enemies in the wine country would come to call the "wine trust". For good or ill it would dominate the California wine industry until 1920.

On August 10 the CWA's papers of incorporation were signed, combining the forces of seven powerful wine houses. Consolidation was becoming the watchword for American industry. The CWA was the brainchild of Percy Morgan, whose accounting firm had been handling the books for S. Lachman & Company, one of the founding firms. Morgan had convinced the dealers that consolidation was the only logical way to avoid the bloodthirsty price-cutting that was destroying profits at all levels of the industry.

At first this action did not meet with open hostility from the producers in the

countryside. In fact, two of the firms involved were Charles Carpy & Co. and the Napa Valley Wine Company, headed by E. C. Priber and Alfred Tubbs. The spirit of consolidation was surely in the air. Producers themselves decided to form their own combination, incorporated two months later as the California Winemakers Corporation (CWC). Its Napa leaders were John Wheeler and Seneca Ewer. Actually, the main source of energy in forming this entity came from the Sonoma side, particularly from the Italian Swiss Colony at Asti.[9] For a while the CWA and CWC made a go at working together to stabilize the chaotic conditions in the industry. But so far as most Napa producers were concerned, the CWA's main purpose was to crush the winegrowers.

This year, 1894, was also a time for a pair of new names on the Napa wine scene. One was Theodore Bell, elected as a Democrat to the office of District Attorney for a thoroughly Republican county. We shall come to know Bell more intimately over the next quarter century, not so much as the son of a St. Helena winegrowing family, but as the great advocate of Napa and California wine in the face of Prohibition. The other was Felix Salmina, who bought the Larkmead Winery this year. He would act as one of Napa's important transitional personalities between the pre-Prohibition days and Repeal.[10]

1895

Except for the fact that more Napa Valley vine land was dying, 1895 was a better year than the last. Wine prices were actually firm and a bit higher. But south of Oakville the only signs of viticulture on anything but resistant rootstock were dead stumps. Spring planting was mostly to prune trees.

The vintage started in mid-September after a day of rain. Foggy weather persisted for a while and then it heated up, so that the short red wine crop produced a vintage that gave this year a fine reputation a decade later, particularly for wines in the "Medoc" style. But it was clear, from the talk in the Valley and from the increase in local press coverage of the "green and dried" fruit market (e.g. pears and prunes) that a large part of the winegrowing community thought Napa's vintage days would soon be over.

A historic casualty of 1895 was the Board of State Viticultural Commissioners. It is difficult to assess the total effect of the Napa Valley's role in the commission's demise, but it certainly attracted a lot of attention. As early as 1893 the St. Helena growers had called for the abolition of the state agency. Their logic was clear; Wetmore and his cohorts had consistently belittled the local concerns about overplanting. The commission had been able to do almost nothing to effect a decision on what resistant rootstock to plant. Napa wine men were simply asking, what good has this commission done?

The rest of the state's wine industry howled when the St. Helena resolution was presented to the State Legislature. The leading industry journal called for the transfer of the California home for the feeble minded from Glen Ellen to St. Helena. Arpad Haraszthy termed the resolution an "outrage." Crabb owned that St. Helena folk were often "a bit cranky." But the move was in line with a growing discontent among those who disliked the commission's demeaning attacks on Professor Hilgard and the university. Many had come to see the commission as a tool of the San Francisco dealers. Soon the influential Rural Californian joined the movement. The State Legislature sentenced the commission to death on March 27, 1895 and ordered it to hand over its effects to the university. Hilgard, to the satisfaction of many upper Napa Valley wine men, was now in charge of all state-sponsored viticultural research.[11]

1896

The 1896 season appeared cursed from the outset. In April a black frost fried the Valley's vineyards. One journal called the frost "the most killing visitation in the history of the viticultural industry in California." Really, it was nowhere nearly so devastating as the 1880 chill. But it did help cut the vintage to just over a million gallons, the smallest Napa vintage since 1876. Phylloxera contributed as much to the short tonnage as the frost. More chilling conditions during flowering caused a poor berry set, and a searing August finished off the meteorological disaster. To top it off, when the fermentations had finished, most people didn't think the wines were very good. But prices for what there was were up. In addition, the Napa Valley, along with businessmen in the rest of the country, breathed a sigh of relief when William McKinley easily defeated William Jennings Bryan in the presidential race, putting an end to what American capitalists thought was a disastrous call for an overexpanded money supply. There would be no free coinage of silver. The German element in Napa usually leaned toward the Democratic ticket, but not this time. A huge McKinley parade in San Francisco had a good representation from the wine industry. Inglenook had a grand float, and the Napa German community had one with a banner proclaiming, "Der Teufel hole schlechten Wein und schlechtes Geld." (The devil take bad wine and cheap money.)[12]

At the end of the vintage and after the election results were in, the wine people in the Napa Valley who had survived this ugly decade clearly looked toward survival and recovery. Part of the new confidence came from the fact that better times were happily coinciding with what appeared to be a solution to the phylloxera/resistant rootstock dilemma. In November Professor Arthur Hayne of the university spoke at the Napa Farmers' Institute. He declared that the answer lay in employing a particular variety of a certain species of native American vine.

Little had been done to clear up the confusion concerning resistant rootstock, at least not in this country. But between 1895 and 1897 the tension over the situation increased, particularly in Napa. The cause for this anxiety was the growing hope that good times lay ahead, and that with the good times would come an increased stimulus for planting and replanting. But in 1895 no one could answer the question that stood like a brick wall in the face of those who optimistically considered replanting—on what?

The answer was eventually supplied by a combined effort of a university scientist and a group of Napa vineyardists. The *St. Helena Star* lit the fire in 1895 when the editor called for Northern California wine men and the scientific community to get together and answer the question once and for all. He asked for all those experienced with resistants to write the newspaper, which would act as a forum to help resolve the question.[13] For the next three months the paper was full of correspondence and a very useful movement toward resolution was under way.

In December of 1895 Professor Arthur Hayne sent in his recommendations. His thesis was that French scientists had been attacking the problem systematically for years. Their findings clearly showed that there was a wide range of resistance within the native species, particularly those of the *V. riparia* and *V. rupestris*. He called on Californians to understand this situation and to work with the specific varieties that the French had found most useful. He argued that it was foolish to send off to Missouri or Nebraska to buy something called "riparia" without knowing which variety of riparia one would receive. It was as if a person wanted to make claret and sent off to the nursery for cuttings of *V. vinifera*. A week later George Husmann roundly attacked Hayne's approach. He felt as if he personally were being attacked for the riparia he had sent Crabb and Dresel almost twenty years earlier. Husmann argued that the practical experience in the local vineyard is where they should turn for their answers. The old professor now set out on a three-year letter-writing campaign, denigrating Hayne's ideas and rejecting the French approach.[14]

Phylloxera vastatrix (J. E. Planchon). – Female specimens and their eggs. a and a, antennae; b and b, horns or suckers; c, egg plainly visible in the body of the insect; d, the egg; f, winged form of the insect. All greatly magnified.

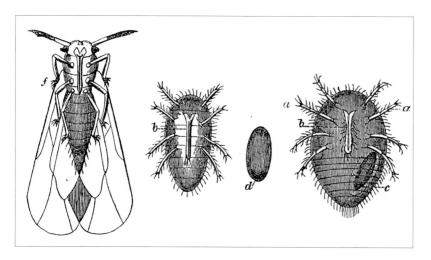

Hayne sailed for France in 1896 to observe the French experiments and published his findings the next year.[15] He came home convinced that the rupestris variety, named the St. George (du Lot) by the French, was the best all round resistant for California vineyards. It suckered less than others, it was an erect grower, and, above all, it was a variety that would grow well in a large number of soils and climates. He also liked several riparia varieties, particularly the Gloire de Montpellier.

This point of view had drifted into Napa before Hayne's findings were published. Crabb was already aware of the several varieties within the rupestris species, having learned of them from the Texas vine breeder, Thomas V. Munson, a friend of French expert Pierre Viala.[16] C. L. LaRue, the Yountville grower, had made the acquaintance of a South African vineyardist named Herzog in 1893 and through their correspondence had been apprised of the characteristics of several riparia and rupestris varieties. John Stanly had also been experimenting and had acquired samples of several varieties and hybrids, such as the AxR-1, from France.[17] Even before Hayne had returned from France, a letter from Rutherford grower, A. H. Frazier, gave Napa readers the resistance ratings that Viala had published earlier in France. Throughout these epistolary exchanges, George Husmann kept up his attack on the French experimental work in general and on Arthur Hayne specifically.[18]

Hayne carried his message directly into the North Coast wine country by talking to growers in Santa Rosa and Napa. He pulled no punches in advocating the St. George. Meanwhile, the first sizeable commercial importation of St. George vines was made by George Schoenewald. He was now a St. Helena vineyardist; his Esmeralda Winery was on Hudson Street, later the Montebello Winery after Repeal. Within a short time, more importations were made by the Beringers and Bismark Bruck, Krug's nephew, now managing the old Krug Winery for the owners.

Bruck became the most audible advocate of the St. George over the next two years as he and Schoenewald reaped the profits from their large French importations.[19] George Husmann kept up the

Eugene W. Hilgard,

Professor of Agriculture

at the University

of California.

attack, but on a visit to Paul Masson's Santa Cruz Mountain estate he observed the Frenchman's success with the St. George. Then he examined the Beringers' St. George grafts, finally writing that the brothers had gained "the greatest success from cuttings I have ever seen." He even praised Hayne's close ally, George Schoenewald. But he kept up the attack on the Berkeley professor as an "incompetent." With the Spanish-American War on now, Hayne had joined up. Husmann hoped in print that the young professor would "make a better soldier than viticulturalist." It was a sorry and rather cranky close to Husmann's useful career, which finally ended with his death in 1902.[20]

By the turn of the century, the Napa Valley was the scene of a spirited replanting, virtually all of it on the St. George, now declared the savior of the California wine industry. During the 1900–1901 planting season over 600,000 vinifera vines, grafted on rooted St. George cuttings (benchgrafts) were sold in the St. Helena area alone. Over half of them were from Bismark Bruck's nursery at the Krug winery. He made large sales to Brun & Chaix, To Kalon, and Georges de Latour, among others. Schoenewald and the Beringers were also important suppliers. The pattern was the same all over Northern California's dry wine districts. By 1903 Paul Masson in the South Bay and Georges de Latour, both with solid connections in France, led in the sale of the St. George.[21] In this year Masson alone imported two tons of benchgrafts. As the years went by the St. George would prove to be something less than the universal rootstock California vineyardists hoped for.[22] For now, however, if one can envision a humble native vine as a knight in shining armor, the Rupestris St. George was it.

Angelica was a popular

wine in the 1890s.

1897

Even though prices remained low for grapes and wine, the buoyant attitude in much of the upper Napa Valley could be seen in the planting season of 1897. Almost a thousand acres went in, over 80 percent on resistant stock. This year planting was general. The *Star* listed fifty-nine different growers taking part. Most of the 150 acres planted on own-root vines were in the Calistoga area, where the full force of the phylloxera had not yet fully been felt.

The big news of the year was the outbreak of the long expected "Wine War" between the San Francisco dealers (CWA) and the CWC (producers). Napa wine men tended to hold no grudges against CWA Napa leaders Carpy and Schilling, reserving their ire for Lachman & Jacobi. The war was triggered by the high inventories of California wine at the beginning of the 1897 vintage. The situation moved the CWA into a "no buy" position with the CWC. This pushed the producers into a dumping competition with the stronger and better organized CWA. Napa's Crabb and LaRue worked as part of a peace committee within the CWC, but CWA president Percy Morgan would have none of it. He promised that "there will be no compromise." In April Charles Carpy had had enough and sold off his CWA holdings, taking off for an extended European vacation. He was too closely tied to Napa Valley folks to take an active part in the coming bloodletting. The situation was complicated by Brun & Chaix and John Wheeler, who apparently bought up cheap Central Valley wines and dumped them in the New Orleans market, while maintaining their leadership positions in the CWC.[23]

Vintage time at Far Niente Winery. Wagons with boxes of grapes wait their turn to unload onto the conveyor.

In Napa the vintage was up almost 50 percent from the miserable 1896 showing. Yields were fairly good, considering the fact that probably half as many acres were producing as in 1893. Some vineyards now bearing on resistants had wonderfully high yields. At Eshcol there were so many more grapes than predicted that they ran out of cooperage. But some of the extra tons came from the blatant overcropping of vines around Calistoga. The quality was mixed and sugar sacks were in evidence at some wineries. The large state vintage and the continued high inventories further depressed wine prices. But there was, nevertheless, a spirit of revival in the air.[24]

St. Helena went right ahead with its lively wine festival. Over two thousand showed up to celebrate and heard a local clergyman recite:

We thank Thee for the vineyard, where
Clustering grapes hang on the vine;
Let joyous chords swell the air.
All hail the vintner and his wine.

It was a grand barbecue, with Bismark Bruck in charge of beans and potatoes. Before the feed Cogswell College beat the St. Helena football team 4–0, but the victors had used two ringers from the university. One would hardly have thought that prices for grapes and wines were still low and that there was a cutthroat price war raging in the industry.

THREE DECADES OF NAPA WINE — 1880-1910

The following chart indicates the ups and downs of Napa Valley winegrowing during three turbulent decades. Note that "mixed" years for quality always indicate generally poor or mediocre quality, but good wines from a few careful producers.

DATE	NEW PLANTING	QUALITY	PRODUCTION	PRICES
1880	High	Medium	High	High
1881	High	High	Low	High
1882	High	Low	Medium	Medium
1883	High	Medium	Medium	High
1884	Medium	Low	High	Medium
1885	Medium	Mixed	Low	Medium
1886	Low	High	High	Medium
1887	Medium	Medium	Low	Low
1888	Low	Medium	Low	Low
1889	Medium	Mixed	Medium	Medium
1890	Low	High	Medium	Medium
1891	Low	Low	Low	Low
1892	Low	Medium	Low	Medium
1893	Medium	Medium	Medium	Low[A]
1894	Low	Medium	Low	Low
1895	Low	High	Low	Medium
1896	Medium	Medium	Low	Medium
1897	High	Mixed	Medium	Mixed
1898	Medium	Medium	Low	Medium[B]
1899	Medium	High	Medium	High
1900	High	High	Medium	High
1901	High	High	Medium	High

1902	High	Medium	High	High
1903	High	High	Medium	Medium
1904	High	Low	Medium	Medium
1905	High	Mixed	Medium	High
1906	High	Medium	High	High[C]
1907	High	High	High	High[A]
1908	High	High	Low	Low
1909	Low	High	Medium	Medium
1910	Low	High	Medium	High

A=Financial panic, B= Spanish-American War, C=Great Earthquake

1898-1900

The next year, 1898, was one of distractions for the Napa folk. The rainy season was almost totally dry, producing a drought like nothing since the 1860s. The Wine War lingered and gathered fewer and fewer interested parties in Napa. By the end of the year good times seemed sure and the CWC retired, leaving the field in the hands of the CWA, now a full-fledged monopoly, which would ride herd over the industry for the next twenty years.[25]

On the plus side the university established a two-acre experiment station on the Krug estate. This station was the result of the cooperation between winery manager Bismark Bruck and Professor Hayne, who had resisted efforts to establish the operation in Sonoma County. Of particular importance would be the practical instruction afforded vineyard workers in grafting techniques.

The greatest distraction of 1898 was America's "Splendid Little War" with Spain, which was over almost as soon as it started. It brought a surge of patriotism to the Valley in April, when Congress declared war. The red grapes, what few there were, had hardly colored in August when the fighting ended.

Planting in 1898 was down some from the previous year. And the scorching spring and summer killed off many of the young vines planted. There could have been no more than 5,000 acres still bearing in the Valley, with a crop of little more than a ton per acre. The vintage came in at less than 1,000,000 gallons. The berries seemed to be all skin and seed, with little juice. Some Napa wineries were able to buy Sonoma grapes. Surprisingly, the wines, even the hardy clarets, were thin. The short crop did boost prices, and the huge state inventory, certainly not huge in Napa, was cut substantially at the end of the season by growing demand.

Along with the rising prices and increased demand came the end of the Wine War. The CWC was beaten in the marketplace and was humbled in court when its case against CWA went against them. Ultimately the CWC was forced to pay the Association $130,000 for breach of contract. Most Napa wine men accepted the result, after the populist idealism of the corporation's leaders had collapsed in favor of personal self-interest. The biggest loss in the Napa Valley was John Wheeler's personal reputation. Many people, including those on the court, thought that he had attempted to profit personally from his position in the CWC.[26] At the end of the year the CWA bought out the CWC's remaining inventory.

Almost everyone in the Valley was now concentrating on recovery. Morale was definitely on the rise. There was lots of planting, and the demand for St. George rootstock far exceeded supply. The 1899 vintage was short, as the drought continued into the spring. But for the first time in years there was active competition for Napa Valley grapes, with buyers in the field well before the first picking box was filled. Several Valley wineries again bought Sonoma grapes, particularly the large operations in Napa City. Migliavacca's production was up more than 50 percent from 1898.[27]

The state vintage was short, but this year's short Napa vintage was outstanding in quality. The reds had great color and plenty of alcohol, the Cabernets were later remembered for their lasting quality. Unfortunately much of this excellent red wine was used to "stretch" lesser reds from other districts.

With national recovery a well-established fact and the demand for wine on the rise, the drive to replant the Valley was about to take off, facilitated by the understanding that the rootstock mystery had been solved. There was plenty of financial credit now available and the wings of the CWA were there to protect its allies, so long as flush times continued. In Napa the tendency was to get into the nest.

The nineteenth century ended with what some then and later called the vintage of the century. By now, well over half the 4700 acres of vines in the Valley were newly planted and nonbearing. Thus, 1900's million-gallon crop was viewed almost as a miracle. This total would have been disastrous six years earlier.

There was enough rain, for a change, and no more frost than usual. After June the weather was almost perfect. The final result was excellent grapes and outstanding wines. They were rich and powerful, particularly the clarets. Again, the CWA used much of the vintage to raise the quality of the average bottle of red wine, since the general quality of the state vintage was rather lackluster. What wasn't used in this way, mostly the product of independent producers, brought a wonderful reputation to the Napa red wine of 1900.

The lavish attention paid to the redevelopment of the upper Napa Valley vineyards after 1898 is an important clue to the quality of Napa wine, so far as investors were concerned. Before the end of the depression in 1897 the picture here was similar to that of the West Side of the Santa Clara Valley, where there was some interest in replanting on resistant stock, but much greater interest in alternative fruit and nut crops. In the South Bay the prune was the fruit of the future.

In Napa the prune was also important in the replanting, along with some pears and walnuts. Below Yountville the pattern was quite similar to that in the Santa Clara Valley. Some lands in the south valley did go back to grapes, but the overall pattern was that of a well-mixed agricultural landscape. It was a picture of intensive orchard and vineyard culture, mixed with large stretches of fodder crops and grazing land. In the Carneros area, except for those very few vineyards early reestablished on resistant stock, the viticultural landscape gradually disappeared, not to return until the 1960s and 1970s.

But the process of change did not transform the upper Napa Valley, as it did the West Side of the Santa Clara Valley between Los Gatos and Mountain View. Within five years the land north of Yountville was again a sea of grape vines. Clearly, the demand for Napa wines and the higher prices paid for them, particularly for the reds, account for the vigorous replanting of this part of the Valley. It was not a spirit of romance that resuscitated these blighted acres, but a view of future profits based on previous experience.

Notes for Chapter Six

1. Star, 3/11/1892, 3/18/1892; PWSR, 4/5/1892.
2. Star, 5/27/1892.
3. James Harvey Young. Pure Food. (Princeton 1989): 104, 141.
4. PWSR, 11/20/1894; Star, 6/7/1895.
5. SBVC (1881): 69; PWSR, 11/21/1884, 6/18/1886, 11/8/1889; Charles L. Sullivan. "Wine Sting in California - One Century Ago." Wine Spectator (August 1, 1982).
6. Star, 7/22/1892; PWSR, 5/20/1892; San Jose Mercury, 9/11/1892; Democrat, 3/21/1891.
7. SBVC (1891-1892): 135-138.
8. Final Report of the California World's Fair Commission (Sacramento 1894): 76-77, 120-121; Rossati, 149; Carosso, 162-164.
9. PWSR, 8/6/1894, 9/6/1894, 11/20/1894. Teiser and Harroun give a particularly lively portrayal of these events and the subsequent "Wine War" at 155-160. Also see: Pinney, 355-363. For Napa's role in the CWC see: Star, 9/14/1894, 11/30/1894; PWSR, 11/6/1894.
10. NVWLA III: 99-105.
11. Star, 2/10/1893; PWSR, 2/20/1893; Rural Californian (November 1894): 393; (April 1895): 196; AWP (April 1895):5. Commissioner Wetmore threw a big party for legislators in Sacramento on February 28, serving up a chilled barrel of Cresta Blanca Sauterne. PWSR, 3/7/1895 called the attack on the Commission a scheme manufactured by "University politicians, headed by Professor Hilgard, whose opinions on matters viticultural no one respects. . . ." This journal calmed down some after the matter was settled. See: 3/21/1895. Carosso gives a good story of the commission's demise at 141-144.
12. Star, 11/13/1896; PWSR, 11/9/1896.
13. Star, 9/27/1895.
14. Star, 12/20/1895.
15. Arthur P. Hayne. "Resistant Vines." University of California College of Agriculture, appendix to Viticultural Report, 1896. (Sacramento 1897): 15-16.
16. PWSR, 10/8/1896.
17. Star, 11/29/1895. In the 1960s this AxR-1 superseded the St. George as the darling of California vineyardists. In the 1980s UC Davis changed course again, rejecting the far less resistant AxR-1.
18. Star, 1/3/1896, 1/17/1896, 1/24/1896.
19. Register, 1/28/1898; Star, 2/25/1898.
20. Pacific Tree and Vine, 4/31/1898; Register, 8/12/1898; PWSR, 12/31/1899; "Official Report of

the Twenty-Fourth State Fruit-Growers Convention. . . ." in Transactions, 1899 (1900): 104-111; "Seventh Annual Report of the State Board of Horticulture. . . 1899-1900." (Sacramento 1901: 172-181, and also found in the same Transactions.

21. Star, 2/1/1901, 1/10/1902, 4/25/1902; San Jose Mercury, 12/9/1902, 2/21/1903; AWP (March 1903). An interesting sidelight to this story is the number of persons who later claimed to have been saviors of the industry for introducing the St. George. Most such stories were simply family stories told years later. An amusing tale named Georges de Latour as such a savior, citing his imports of benchgrafts as the introduction of the rootstock, years after Schoenewald's and Bruck's work, and Hayne's recommendation. See: Wines & Vines (September 1975): 42.

22. F. T. Bioletti et al. "Phylloxera Resistant Stocks." UC College of Agriculture, AESB 331 (1921): 83-85, 130; Lloyd A. Lider. "Phylloxera Resistant Rootstocks for the Coastal Valleys of California." Hilgardia (February 1958).

23. PWSR, 2/22/1897, 4/23/1897, 8/14/1897.

24. Register, 11/5/1897; Star, 12/3/1897.

25. Star, 12/16/1898; PWSR, 10/31/1898, 11/30/1898, 11/30/1899; AWP, 10/1898; Teiser and Harroun, 157-159.

26. PWSR, 10/31/1898.

27. Register, 10/27/1899; Star, 9/22/1899.

NAPA WINES & VINES
IMAGE, QUALITY, AND TECHNOLOGY

The generic term "California wine" is a very elastic and much abused term.
Of course California does produce a quantity of bad wine. But this state also
produces considerable quantities of very good wine.

—CHARLES M. LOESER
(1893)

T HE IMPORTANT STEPS TAKEN TO RAISE CALIFORNIA WINE QUALITY BEFORE 1870
did not come from Napa. The Sonoma and Santa Clara Valleys had the
lion's share of the technical improvements in the cellar, for the
upgrading of viticultural practices, and for the importation of the best French
and German vines. We have seen the sound beginnings of the Napa Valley's
pioneers in the sixties, but J. W. Osborne's death in 1863 robbed the Valley of a
crusading spirit similar to that of Sonoma's Agoston Haraszthy. Krug,
Schram, and Pellet were solid, steady men, but crusaders they were not.
Crane's foreign varieties made an important impression, but at the end of the

decade most Napa wine was still coming from almost 2,000 acres of Mission vines. The brandy still remained one of the local winemaker's best servants. Although the Zinfandel was catching on, Napa wine men still had an unclear focus on the usefulness of the varieties available to them, with the exception of the better German varieties.

Vineyard acreage grew from about 2,000 to about 3,500 acres in the seventies, with yields of two to three tons per acre when conditions were satisfactory. Production grew from around 300,000 to well over 1,500,000 gallons.

The seventies saw Napa wine attain an image of superior quality that persists to this day. This study, of course, aims to trace this early climb and to account for the persistence of this perception among wine lovers today.

A common complaint about early well-made California table wines had been a certain earthiness, even in the whites. But in the early seventies we begin to hear that Napa wines lacked that earthy character. The *Alta California* early commented on this special quality and the *San Francisco Post* later looked back to this factor as the basis for Napa wines' increased popularity in these years. *The Post* thought it Napa's "chief claim to fame." During the seventies the Napa and Sonoma white wines made from good German varieties, and often blended with the heavy bearing and fairly neutral Palomino, turned the heads of some eastern dealers and made a dent in the so-called "prejudice" against California wine. Jacob Schram's efforts on his hillside acres were most often cited as critical in helping to create a positive perception of Napa white wines.[1]

In the seventies, Napa reds were also perceived as light and lacking earthy heaviness, particularly reds made from Zinfandel in a light claret style. Arpad Haraszthy, with roots in Sonoma, early contended that the Napa Valley was "claret country."[2] Unfortunately a large percentage of red wine acreage there was also planted to the Malvoisie (Cinsaut), a heavy-bearing variety best suited for blending in very warm climates. But in Napa it was too often used to blend with Zinfandel, not because of its usefulness but because it was here and something had to be done with it. In his first state report (1880), Commissioner Charles Wetmore lamented this tendency and called on Napa wine men to plant real Bordeaux varieties, such as Cabernet Sauvignon and Malbec. In fact, Napa Valley red wine production in the seventies was rather chaotic, with Zinfandel the only really successful vine planted in any number. There weren't enough real Bordeaux varieties to produce a barrel of wine.[3]

The lamentable position of California red wines in relation to the perceived quality of the state's whites was a topic of special concern in the 1874 report of R. S. Carey, President of the State Agricultural Society.[4] So far as Napa was concerned, getting the Missions out of the fermenting vats had to be a primary goal. Charles Krug was still hammering away on this point as late as 1876. Eventually, using Missions to produce brandy and sherry did much to correct this situation. By 1878 the *Star* could claim that less than 10 percent of the table wine produced in the St. Helena area was "infected" by the juice of the Mission grape.[5]

In 1876, Napa producers started seeing a real interest among eastern dealers in their white wines of Germanic pedigree.[6] Zinfandel was soon to follow, in terms of public perception. Looking back on these years from the 1890s, Charles Wetmore contended that this perception shifted the state's quality leadership in red table wine production from Sonoma to Napa, particularly after 1879. By the early eighties local wine men felt secure in thinking that the real prosperity of the Napa wine industry came from these light red wines.[7]

But it would be a mistake to infer from these later perceptions that Napa producers were clearly on the path to superior red wine production. When the St. Helena Vinicultural Club held a tasting of recent vintages in 1882, the whites were well received, particularly those made to be "Hocks" or "Rhine" wines. The reds were another matter. A wine from "Upright Burgundy" was declared the best claret. A red from Swiss grapes by H. A. Pellet was "splendid." A Carneros Mission was applauded. Krug's "Black Cluster" variety was "excellent." A rich and tannic *V. californica* was praised, while a Pinot noir and a Mourvèdre were found defective. Just about the only red wine well-rated that makes any kind of sense today was a Carneros Zinfandel. (Even that one calls for a bit of head-scratching.) A few weeks later Krug announced his new plantings for red wine on Howell Mountain. They would include Trousseau, Pinot noir, Chauché noir, Charbono, and something called Troubadour. Napa's later reputation as the claret capital of the North Coast was still in the process of evolution.[8]

THE EIGHTIES

The eighties were a decade of technical revolution in the best Napa Valley wine cellars. The influence of the new State Viticultural Commission was everywhere apparent, as Charles Wetmore and his regional commissioners pushed basic ideas

Zinfandel was one of the few bottled Napa varietals before the 1930s. Label Ca. 1895.

that would eliminate seriously flawed wine from the California product. But the thrust of the commission's work did little to make that product competitive with the best wines of Europe. What gradually turned things around in Napa was the influence of Hilgard's work at the university and the individual efforts of numerous Napa Valley producers. This ideological dichotomy, as we have seen, would eventually place Napa producers in the vanguard of those who brought down the commission. From this situation it should not be inferred, however, that the university staff showed any special preference toward the Napa wine men. In fact, if Hilgard leaned in any particular geographical direction, he probably thought that the Mission San Jose/Warm Springs wine district in Alameda County's East Bay had the greatest potential for producing world-class table wines.

As has always been the case in the world of wine, much of the very best produced in a region stays close to home. And much of that which was really good and did leave California had to travel under a foreign label. Henri Grosjean, the French Agricultural Minister, made this point when he visited the Valley in 1883. He had never met California wine he thought much good under a California label. But what he tasted in Napa turned him around. Napa wines were "very good." To a local newspaper he said, "I have completely changed my mind since my arrival here in regard to your wines. . . ."[9] During the next four years eastern dealers became more willing to sell Napa wines, particularly the German-style whites, under their own colors. But the foreign label situation was only improving and had not been totally corrected, as Jacob Schram discovered on his trip east in 1887.[10]

Many Napa Valley producers carefully followed and copied Hilgard's work on proper fermentation techniques in the 1880s. Philosophically the vocal Napa leaders stood with him on the general question of quality. Hilgard was strictly opposed to what he called "the good old style" of California wine, which he thought should be "definitely consigned to the rubbish pile." By this he meant reds picked at very high sugar with deficient acid, fermented in huge containers at uncontrolled temperatures. He also meant whites picked at similar levels, often fermented partially on their skins and exposed to the open air until their aldehyde levels reminded him of poor sherry. He rejected the idea that California could develop a positive wine reputation if 95 percent of the state's production was cheap cargo wine, however sound.[11]

These were not words that industry leaders in San Francisco wanted to hear coming from the university. Arpad Haraszthy thought that the discovery of California's Lafites and Chambertins had to be left "to chance or future generations. For now we must content ourselves in securing abundant yields of really good table wines with satisfactory moneyed returns."[12]

Hilgard's response to the *San Francisco Examiner*'s query on the causes of the current wine depression made Wetmore and Haraszthy see red, and they never let up on the Professor after that. Hilgard put the blame squarely on the "poor quality of the larger part of the wines made in California." This simplistic generalization makes little sense when viewed in light of the previous high prices paid for the same quality of wines from California in the early eighties. Quality didn't suddenly plummet. But Napa wine men, now more insistent on quality than ever before, were attuned to such arguments. Napa's support of Hilgard helped focus critical attention around the state on the Napa Valley as a source of high premium wines.[13]

The vines planted in Napa between 1879 and 1882 more than tripled the Valley's vineyard acreage and raised the potential quality of Napa wine, since, as mixed as they were, save for Zinfandel, they were generally classic European varieties that produced first-rank wines, such as White Riesling, or good quality wines, such as Grenache or Mourvèdre. When these vines came into production in the mid-eighties and producers made their grapes into wine using Hilgard's approach to logical sugar levels and fermentation temperatures, the result was the beginning of what some have called the "Golden Age" of Napa Valley wines. These were the wines to which Wetmore would look back when he attempted to identify the moment when Napa wines finally surpassed those of Sonoma in quality. These were the wines that moved Frona Wait in 1889 to name Napa "The Banner Wine-Making County," which had come to "lead the State in table wines."[14]

The State Viticultural Convention at San Francisco in 1888 firmly established Napa's popular and industry-wide reputation for high-quality table wines, an image that has lasted more than 100 years. A wide range of California wines had been evaluated at other conventions, but never before had the conditions for the evaluation been so carefully handled or the panels so thoughtfully organized. At first the state board had asked the San Francisco Wine Dealers' Association to provide an evaluation committee, but they refused.[15] The board had also planned to have county screening committees for the first round of evaluations, but this idea was dropped and all entries were accepted into the finals. There was much emphasis on the fact that this year the judges would not know whose wine they were evaluating, which was not the case in previous years.[16] In the process most Sonoma producers decided to boycott the proceedings, a fact noted by the press but never publicly explained.[17]

The table wine panels included an array of unquestionable talent and expert zeal. In fact, their makeup appears a bit severe for an industry-dominated event. The red wine committee included Napa's H. A. Pellet, a no-

nonsense expert on fermentation practices and an outspoken critic of incompetent winemakers and their wine.[18] A. G. Chauché was a native of Graves and a future star of Livermore Valley claret production. There was J. B. J. Portal, the Cupertino Burgundy specialist, and J. A. Stewart, the hard-nosed Santa Cruz critic of poor California reds. The white wine group was headed by Professor Husmann and Frederico Pohndorff, a noted European wine merchant. There was also E. C. Priber, a German with a long history as a wine dealer in St. Louis, and Julius Paul Smith, the mercurial owner of Livermore's famed Olivina Vineyard.

Forty-eight California producers exhibited their table wine, seventeen from Alameda County and fourteen from Napa. There were three awards possible for wines in each classification, although some classes did not receive first awards, mostly whites. When the dust had cleared, in categories recognizable today, Napa had received twenty-five awards for its reds and nineteen for its whites. Alameda won twenty-two for reds and six for whites. Sonoma totaled eight awards. Those going to other counties were few indeed. Napa received a total of twenty-one first awards; Alameda, fourteen.

The red wine committee was particularly impressed by the Bordeaux-style reds, headed by the Cabernets. Top marks were split about evenly between the Livermore Valley, Mission San Jose, and Napa. The top Napa "Medocs" came from John Stanly's Carneros winery, Morris Estee's Hedgeside, J. H. Goodman's Eshcol, Charles Krug, and the Napa Valley Wine Company. C. C. McIver's Linda Vista at Mission San Jose received top marks for its other than Cabernet Sauvignon "Medocs," that is, Malbec, Merlot, Verdot, and Cabernet franc. Napa had the top Cabernet Sauvignons.

The committee also made special comment on the good ageing potential of the better Zinfandels. The best Napa Zins came from Ewer & Atkinson, To Kalon, Courtois & Co. (Larkmead), and John Stanly. Burgundies, which might be made from almost anything, did not get raves from the committee, but Napa did receive most of the awards. In other categories that make sense today, Napa took first awards for Carignane, Grenache, and Syrah. First awards went to Livermore for Mourvèdre and Mondeuse and to Mission San Jose for Charbono.

In the white wine competition Napa did even better, although the judges were not as impressed by this general category. Older whites tended to be in poor shape, but the 1887s showed the effects of better fermentation techniques and had not succumbed yet to poor cellar practices. At least half the whites exhibited from earlier years "proved clearly neglect on the part of cellarmen . . . . California wine men have learned pretty well how to make wine, but most of them have yet to learn a great deal about how to handle and keep wine."

That more than two-thirds of the first-place awards went to Napa wineries indicates that there had been some learning going on during the decade.

The Sauterne category pleased the judges most. The wines were praised "most emphatically." First awards went to Eshcol and To Kalon. Most of the awards for German-style wines went to top Napa producers, but the committee was put off by the many different varieties subsumed in the "Riesling" category. R. M. Wheeler, Husmann, To Kalon, the Napa Valley Wine Company, and Ewer & Atkinson won first awards here.[19]

The convention was front-page copy and the San Francisco press covered the outcome of the evaluations well, although the German Kaiser's death on the second day was a major distraction. *The Examiner* treated the whole thing as if the entries were race horses at a county fair.[20] When the prizes were announced W. R. Hearst's popular journal headlined "Zinfandel and Bordeaux Varieties the Favorites." Later his *Examiner* claimed that Napa clarets and Burgundies "take the lead and they certainly have no equal in the State." This was quite an admission from a man whose father just a month earlier had bought a large wine estate between Glen Ellen and Sonoma. But Hearst did add that there would be exceptions "in the best wines of Sonoma and one or two other choice sections."[21] The *Post* headed its report, "Alameda and Napa—The Banner Wine Counties of the State," and then charted the awards, showing the two had won 81 percent of the 126 citations.[22]

To imply that the outcome of these tastings set the California wine world afire would be a gross exaggeration. But Napa's image for premium table wine production was firmly established and has held steady to the present. We shall see that image was further enhanced in years to come, even as the local industry reeled from the effects of depression and phylloxera.

THE PRICE PICTURE

Another way to measure the public's opinion of an area's wine is by examining the price paid to wholesalers. It is impossible to track bulk sales, since no suitable records survive these years. But the prices paid wholesale for case lots in glass are available.

In 1889 Rieslings from the St. Helena district brought top dollar in Northern California. But those from the rest of the Valley averaged slightly lower than those from Sonoma. Sauternes from St. Helena, Santa Rosa, San Jose, and Livermore brought the best prices in this category. Prices paid for St. Helena Zinfandel were tops, about 25 percent higher than for Sonoma Zins. Oakville Zinfandel, which really meant To Kalon, was close behind. The prices paid for Zinfandel from other parts of Napa did not vary significantly from those paid for the same wine from other coastal valleys. Top dollar for

Burgundies went to St. Helena, Santa Rosa, and San Jose.[23] As yet there was no traceable market for what was coming to be called "Medoc-style" wines, usually Cabernet Sauvignon and blends with other red Bordeaux varieties. This situation would change in the next decade.

From these prices we can see that, for certain categories, particularly Rieslings and Zinfandel clarets, the St. Helena district led the way in perceived quality. But for other categories no Napa preeminence is evident. Table wines from the St. Helena district were the most valuable in the state. In future years the extent to which Napa wines were generally perceived in the same light as those from this mid-Valley district would be a measure of the growth of the Napa Valley reputation.

WINES FROM THESE GRAPES

Red Wine

Miravalle. Spring

Mt. Vineyards today

the site of Falcon Crest

television series.

By the 1880s Napa wines were almost always produced as varietals but were rarely marketed as such. By now the sometime method of fermenting different grape varieties together had been abandoned. After fermentation and preliminary cellar treatment, the wines were usually sold to dealers in San Francisco or Napa City. They blended these wines for their market and sold them under traditional generic terms such as Burgundy, Claret, and Riesling. Some were sold as varietals, but rarely. A few that reached the public under "varietal" labels were Johannisberg Riesling, Zinfandel, and Cabernet. By the

1890s it was common to market some varietals under more prestigious generic terms, such as "Medoc" for Cabernet Sauvignon or "Chambertin" for Pinot noir. Of course, there was no legal check on the veracity of these labels. We have seen that several Napa Valley producers developed their own brands and bypassed the dealers. Nevertheless this general nomenclature was still generally adhered to.

Claret* (See Appendix I)

In the earliest years of the California wine industry, the producer and dealer profited from successful price competition with foreign imports. These wines, mostly from France, flooded the state from the 1850s until the early 1880s.[24] To compete with these imports wine men here and on the East Coast found it necessary to employ the regional and generic terms under which these foreign wines were sold. Cheap reds from France, sometimes from Bordeaux but more often from warmer southern districts of that country, were the most popular table wines in the San Francisco Bay Area market. They sold as "claret." In the early years Napa producers attempted to compete with these imports with "red" wine made from Mission grapes. They sometimes remedied weak color by chemical adulteration. These early Napa reds were not an important element in the wine trade here. Eventually the solution to the problem of trying to make red table wine from Mission grapes appeared in the form of the mysterious European vinifera, the Zinfandel. It came to Northern California from Massachusetts where it had been grown in hot houses as a table grape. Captain F. W. Macondray brought it to the Bay Area in 1852. It was introduced to the Napa Valley by his New England friend, Oak Knoll's J. W. Osborne.[25] Much of the Napa planting in the sixties was to Zinfandel, but almost as much Malvoisie was set in. The unhappy Napa practice of blending the two endured until the eighties.

When the planting boom began in the late 1870s, Zinfandel was by far the most popular red grape, particularly around St. Helena. Over the years Napa Zinfandel, particularly that grown above

Tiburcio Parrott. The master of Miravalle on Spring Mt. He produced California's most expensive Cabernet Sauvignon in the 1890s.

the rich mid-valley soils, became the backbone of Napa claret. Zinfandels from Spring Mountain and Howell Mountain also had fine reputations.

Early in the eighties several Napa winegrowers began taking Wetmore's advice and planted red wine varieties from France's Bordeaux region, the home of what Englishmen had come to call "claret." Such vines had first been brought to Northern California in the 1850s by Santa Clara Valley Frenchmen, Antoine Delmas and Charles Lefranc. The latter made the first commercially successful California "Medoc" in the sixties, which he called "Cabernet-Malbeck."

It appears that Glen Ellen's J. H. Drummond planted the first plot of useful Bordeaux vines in the North Coast in 1878. He was soon followed by Napa's H. W. Crabb. By 1885 virtually every major producer here who was interested in fine claret had a stand of Cabernet Sauvignon. Many also grew blending varieties such as Merlot, Malbec, Verdot, and Cabernet franc. At first, Crabb favored Malbec to soften the sturdy Cabernet Sauvignon but later turned to Cabernet franc. Niebaum planted his Cabernet Sauvignon in 1886 and first used Merlot and Verdot for blending. Cellar records indicate that he later favored Malbec. For a while there was talk of using the Tannat as a Cabernet blender, as practiced in Madiran, southeast of Bordeaux. Even though Hilgard recommended it as a "sturdy keeper," this variety never caught on and is still virtually unknown in California today. In 1885 Hilgard, Drummond, and Pohndorff issued a favorable report on the progress of wine from Cabernet blends, but noted that there was "still a long way to go." Over the years producers experimented with such varieties as Carignane, Mourvèdre, Grenache, Refosco, Beclan, Aramon, Mondeuse, Charbono, and even Pinot noir to soften the powerful Cabernet.[26]

Meanwhile, blending Zinfandel and Cabernet Sauvignon became another sometime approach in Napa claret production. In fact, some producers liked to start a Zinfandel fermentation on Cabernet pomace, which usually meant early picking a batch of underripe Cabernet. Another important aspect of claret production was the discovery that Zinfandel, with a few years of bottle age, began taking on some of the characteristics of aged red Bordeaux.

Later George Husmann summed up what a good Zinfandel might be when grown above the valley floor: "With all its faults we love it still. . . a good Zinfandel claret from locations best adapted to it, carefully made, is good enough for anyone."[27]

The Red Burgundy Style*

Napa Valley red Burgundy was whatever the producer wanted it to be; it could be made from practically anything. If claret was to be light, Burgundy should be bigger, and a bit richer and fruitier, with deeper color. Most of what was called red Burgundy in California in these years had to have been a severe disappointment to anyone familiar with the authentic French product. But this is not to say there wasn't good wine produced in Napa under the Burgundy rubric. Hilgard found some of it very good. But no one was able to make wine from any of the Pinot noir clones available that consistently resembled its French counterpart. In his first report in 1881 Commissioner Wetmore contended that what passed for Burgundy in California then was really any heavy claret. Three years later he was even more doubtful. "The term Burgundy. . . is probably now purely conventional and has lost among our people its original meaning." He thought that California could never produce a real Burgundy in the French style.[28]

Most Napa producers didn't care one way or another. They sold their wines to dealers who then made their Burgundy blends. But those here who established their own brands did their own blending. Some apparently did a good job. Very few tried any of the Pinot noir clones because of the almost universally low opinion of their productivity. Actually, the most success came from varieties we associate with southern France today, particularly the Rhône and Provence.

Wetmore early suggested the Mourvèdre for Burgundies, and it did become fairly common in Napa vineyards under its Spanish name, Mataro. The Grenache also had advocates, particularly for its ability to give a little more fruitiness to heavier colored varieties. Carignane was also planted here and there for the same reason, especially around St. Helena. It is quite natural that such varieties should have caught on in the upper Napa Valley where heat summations today are similar to those of the Rhône region of France.

Cooler-climate French Jura varieties like the Trousseau and Plousard were tried and generally rejected. The Chauché noir was a variety that seemed to have possibilities, but was often confused with other vines. Scheffler had it at Edge Hill in 1882 and blended it with the Pinot Meunier. The locals were genuinely astonished at how close it came to an authentic Burgundy. But he was never able to duplicate this success. Crabb had several Pinot noir clones in his nursery collection but was never able to do anything with them on a commercial scale. Hilgard took some of their grapes in 1884 and made a small batch at the university, which turned out very well, but nothing ever came of it. Actually, Hilgard was never able to recommend any particular Pinot noir clone he tested in the eighties.[29]

Two vines that did catch on in these years were the Refosco and the Duriff. Crabb had very good success with the former, so good that the vine and its product were often called "Crabb's Black Burgundy." The Refosco is the same as the Mondeuse, grown in France's Savoie. Later statistics for the Valley often listed them separately.

The rise of the Duriff as the basic blending grape in Napa red Burgundy is not easily explained. Today that variety is usually referred to as the Petite Sirah in California. This name brings to mind the Syrah grape of France, a shy bearer noted for producing the great red Rhônes of Hermitage and the Côte Rotie. J. H. Drummond imported this true Syrah to Sonoma in 1878. Crabb and Krug picked it up and by the mid-eighties were making praiseworthy wines from that variety. During these early years this Syrah was often referred to as the Petite Syrah, with several different spellings. The wines produced by Crabb, Krug, Drummond, and Mission San Jose's Charles McIver received plaudits, but the low yield doomed it for typical growers. Crabb blended it with Refosco to produce what he labeled "Hermitage."[30]

McIver imported the Duriff in 1884 and began calling it Petite Sirah. Crabb was concerned that the grape should be incorrectly identified, but he certainly liked its wine, particularly for its coloring qualities and for its heavy yield. By the 1890s the Duriff had caught on with several more producers in Napa, particularly Inglenook. Then, when the great replanting of the Valley took place around the turn of the century, the Duriff, now generally dubbed Petite Sirah, was one of the most popular Burgundy blenders. Meanwhile, virtually all the original plantings of the true Syrah had been destroyed by the phylloxera and were not reintroduced to commercial California vineyards until the 1970s.[31]

Napa's best success in producing "Burgundy" came from the use of grapes normally associated with the French wine country south of Burgundy. Crabb, like Drummond, even raised a few Marsanne and Roussanne whites to blend with his Syrah. Many of these blends were very popular, particularly when the Duriff was involved. But they all had to play second fiddle to the delicious Napa Zinfandels and the Cabernet blends.

White Wine

We would have discussed white wines before red if early reputation were the primary criterion. Even though the fame of Napa clarets eventually surpassed that of Napa white wines, the Valley's Rieslings and sauternes continued to gain full marks right up to Prohibition. We have seen already that the climb to eastern acceptance after the troubled seventies came on the basis of the apparently excellent German- style wines.

Searching for the Rhine and Mosel*

It was certainly understandable that the ideal of good German-style white wine should have been utmost in the minds of many of the founding fathers in Napa, as well as Sonoma. There were so many Germans and so many who, in the words of the thoroughly Francophile Charles Wetmore, "adhered more closely and persistently to their enterprises" than most other national groups.

Emil Dresel's 1859 importation of White Riesling, Sylvaner, and Traminer vines to his Sonoma Rhinefarm from his family's holdings at Geisenheim acted as the basis for the early propagation and spread of German varieties in the North Coast. Later, in 1861, Agoston Haraszthy brought in all manner of German vines, including a spiced (gewürzt) Traminer. But it does not appear that these vines made it into commercial vineyards other than Buena Vista.[32]

In the Napa Valley the Germanic ideal was firmly fixed by the 1870s. But no matter how good the wines produced were, they rarely attained this ideal. The problem was the climate of the upper Napa Valley, where most of the area's best wines were produced. It simply was too warm. Wetmore early noted that good Riesling was only going to come from vineyards where "over-maturity is difficult to obtain." Hilgard put it this way at the 1886 Viticultural Convention: "When a Riesling must be rushed through a four or five days' fermentation, under the influence of a hot September in the Napa Valley, it is no wonder that its relationship to the produce of Johannisberg is scarcely suspected."

On the cooler Sonoma side Dresel and Gundlach were able to approach the ideal more closely. Jacob Schram on his cool hillside, with his cool, hand-hewn cellars, appears to have been the only early Napa producer who consistently came so close. His was the only Riesling served, in fact the only Napa white wine served, at the 1891 dinner for President Harrison at the Palace Hotel in San Francisco.[33]

But many of Schram's fellows in Napa knew well how to make good wine. Their table wines from German grapes won consistent praise from critics who understood that they were as far from their European counterparts in flavor as Napa Burgundies were from their French counterparts.

Napa Rhenish-style wines fell into three basic categories. There were ordinary blends, sometimes lightly flavored with White Riesling, but mostly from the productive Burger, Gutedel, and Palomino. Other wines used in such blends included Folle blanche, Grey Riesling, and Green Hungarian. Such wines were usually labeled "Hock" after the British tradition. Riesling blends, labeled "Riesling," and often considered quite good, were usually combinations of White Riesling and Franken Riesling (Sylvaner). It was considered improper by most Napa producers to include the bland Grey Riesling in such blends, since it was known to be no Riesling at all. At the time it was thought to be the French Chauché gris, but is probably the Trousseau gris. As in the case of clarets, premium producers needed some term to indicate that their wine was made from the classic varieties that connoisseurs associated with the best European tradition. Thus wine made entirely, or mostly, from the White Riesling of the Rhine and Mosel, came to be labeled Johannisberg Riesling. After Prohibition this tradition gained the backing of law, but in the early days only the producer's good name could act as a guarantee.

Occasionally Traminer (or Red Traminer) traveled as a varietal. After his 1884 importation of the spicy or Gewürztraminer vine, Charles Krug was best known for the production of this highly flavored varietal. Sonoma producers, however, tended to receive the top marks for their wines from this variety right up to Prohibition.[34]

White Burgundy*

On the subject of white wines best grown in cooler regions, some comment should be made concerning Napa attempts to produce "White Burgundy." Most often the generic term "Chablis" was applied to such wines. But their distance in character from their French counterpart is a unifying thread that ties together the few evaluations available from neutral critics. These wines might be made from anything, but most producers seem to have aimed at some tartness, definite dryness, and some vinous flavor.

So far as Burgundian varieties are concerned it appears that few Napa growers knew about them or grew them. Wetmore mentioned in his 1884 report that the "Chardenai" should be tried. It previously had appeared in Crabb's nursery list as "White Pineau–Chaudenay." Later he listed it in vine cuttings for sale as "Pineau Charennay." Inglenook also had something they called "White Pinot" growing in 1889. There was no discussion of Pinot blanc in Napa before the turn of the century, although there was such a vine at Italian Swiss Colony and in Paul Masson's Saratoga vineyard. There is a good chance that Tiburcio Parrott made his "Montrachet" from Chardonnay, but we hear little of it except that he showed it at the Columbian Exposition in 1893 and that it was in bad condition when Charles Oldham tasted it.[35]

Sauterne*

If a region has a climate that encourages the production of red table wine in the style of Bordeaux, it follows that dry white wine styled to Bordeaux's white wines might also be successful. Such was certainly true of wines in the Graves style produced in the Napa Valley before Prohibition. But "sauterne" was the generic term that caught on and stuck until the 1960s when varietal designations took over.

The white wine district of Sauternes was well known to European wine lovers by the eighteenth century, but it was not until the early decades of the

1800s that its name became synonymous with the luscious sweet wines that are its hallmark today.[36] For our wine history it is important that Californians thought the best white wine from Bordeaux came from Sauternes in the 1860s, for this term, without the final "s," became a standard generic expression on bottles of certain California white wine. This wine could be dry or sweet (often termed Haut Sauterne) and had the characteristics of what in the nineteenth century was entering this country as white Bordeaux wine. There were no real attempts actually to copy true Sauternes before Repeal, since the necessary action of the "noble rot," or botrytis cinerea, was not understood here.

The introduction of the Sauternes varieties, Sauvignon blanc and Sémillon, to Livermore in the 1880s is an oft-told story.[37] Their introduction to the North Coast is not so clear. Haraszthy imported them in 1861, but they never seem to have left Buena Vista. Lefranc at New Almaden had white Bordeaux varieties in the 1870s, which Wetmore discussed, but he only mentions the Sauvignon vert (Sauvignonasse), a heavy bearer whose wines often have a slight muscat flavor but lack the range of flavors associated with white Bordeaux wines.

J. B. J. Portal imported the Sauvignon blanc to the Santa Clara Valley in the

Taking in the grapes,

Ca. 1910. The large

shoulder clusters suggest

these are Zinfandel.

1870s. Within a decade H. W. Crabb and J. H. Drummond had both the Sauvignon blanc and the Sémillon, but we do not know where they got their vines.[38] Crabb pioneered good sauterne in the Napa Valley with these varieties. At first he stretched them with Palomino or Colombard, but settled finally on Sauvignon vert as the best base wine.[39] This became the pattern for other local producers, who began receiving good marks in the late eighties (e.g. Inglenook, Eshcol, and Larkmead). At the 1888 Viticultural Convention the white wine committee singled out Northern California sauterne as a wine that "could be shown with pride. . . anywhere in the wine-drinking world." This solid reputation continued and grew in the nineties.

In The Vineyard

Until a detailed history of the early California wine industry is published it seems highly unlikely that a definitive technical history of vineyard and cellar will ever be compiled. Certainly this study can do no more than suggest certain practices and their modification, with particular emphasis on practices aimed at improving wine quality. Most practical innovations in nineteenth century viticulture aimed to protect the crop rather than raise grape quality. But we shall see that some Napa pioneers were willing to spend some time and treasure in pursuit of quality.

Vineyard location was one of the first considerations that led to better wine grapes in the Napa Valley. The move to the higher slopes on both sides of the Valley, as early as the 1860s, powerfully established the concept of upland viticulture in the mind of the Napa wine community. Jacob Schram's success above Ritchie Creek and the later triumphs of Howell Mountain wines were ever cited to support such location of vineyards.

In the early years planting new vineyards was something of a hit-and-miss affair. Setting out new vines as cuttings brought the greatest

The Napa Valley Wine Co. became part of the CWA in 1894. This brochure (Ca. 1900) emphasizes the valley more than the company's wines.

SOURCE: REGINALD OLIVER.

NAPA WINE

number of misses. Easier in the short run, such a practice was often cruelly rewarded by a frigid spring. By the 1870s most growers were more likely to root cuttings in a protected nursery and position them in the vineyard the following year. When resistant vineyards were planted in the 1890s the question of whether to graft the vinifera buds onto rootstock in the field was rarely considered. Today such field budding is common and economical. But a hundred years ago benchgrafting and then planting the grafted vines was the accepted procedure.

The spacing of vines was mostly an individual matter in the early years, one distance naturally controlled by the width of the horse-drawn vineyard equipment. About twelve feet seems to have been the most common width. We can see some early attempts to emulate closer European planting practices as early as 1860 when J. J. Sigrist chose an eight-by-six-foot pattern for his new plantings near Napa City. Charles Krug later set in about the same number of vines per acre on his original Howell Mountain plantation by using a three-and-a-half-by-fourteen pattern. He later employed this approach in the Valley to accommodate a two-horse team. Gustave Niebaum apparently was more interested in raising grape quality when he began his experiments on close spacing in the 1880s, particularly with Cabernet Sauvignon. Nevertheless, when replanting began in earnest in the late nineties the common plan was a six-by-twelve-foot setting.[40]

Napa's grape vines were usually trained fairly low and head-pruned into the classic "goblet" shape still visible in the Valley in the 1970s. They were usually supported by redwood stakes in the early years. Exotic training systems developed in Europe in the nineteenth century (e.g. Chaintre and Guyot) were introduced to California but never caught on in Napa. But the gradual discovery that some varieties set better crops when the vines were cane pruned led many producers to set up single and double wire trellises where appropriate. George Belden Crane had his White Riesling on wires in the early 1870s. By the eighties Sauvignon blanc, Sauvignon vert, Refosco, Cabernet Sauvignon, and Duriff were commonly set on wires.[41]

More than any other cultural practice, proper pruning was the key to grape quality in the nineteenth century. The crop level of a vine is partially determined by the number of buds left when last year's growth is cut back during the dormant season. Greed, a previous short crop, extremely high prices, or the idea that the vineyard might be on its last legs due to phylloxera often led vineyardists to leave too many buds. Such a practice hurt the flavor intensity of the grapes. But it also often led to crops that could not reach proper maturity when fall weather turned ugly. Time and again in the eighties and nineties the local press reported horror stories of unharvested grapes hanging in the rain at less than 18° Brix. But stories appeared almost as often about those who were able to bring in the same variety at proper sugar levels because they had not overcropped their vines. In this matter the leadership of Crabb, Krug, Crane, Pellet, and Groezinger applied an essential moral lever to their neighbors in favor of a community approach to the quality of their Valley's wines.

Pruning technique also could affect vine protection. Save for phylloxera, which had no cure, spring frost was the chief threat to a prosperous vintage. In the 1870s it was discovered that partial pruning to canes when spurs were eventually desired caused vines to leaf out first at the canes' extremes. When a mid-April freeze hit a vineyard, the further portions of the cane, which were unwanted anyway, would be the first to have leafed, and could now be cut back to the desired length of the spur. This approach was particularly successful with Zinfandel, which tends to throw a good second crop of berries.

But the great defense against frost was the smudge pot. In the late 1860s and early 1870s piles of brush piled up in the vineyard often served as fuel for fires that helped circulate the air on those frigid nights after the passage of a cold front, when clear skies brought convectional cooling that laid pockets of freezing air all over the Valley floor. In the seventies the smudge pot, fueled with petroleum oil, became the central tool in the protection system. The trick was to get the system operating before Jack Frost could raise havoc. Several in the Valley put together warning systems that set bells ringing when the mercury dropped too low. The frosts between 1870 and 1900 were so common and so severe as to suggest that the spring weather we experience today in Napa is a faint fellow to that of bygone years.

Growers used other techniques to beat the cold. John Stanly planted lines of eucalyptus in the Carneros. The Beringers tried to protect their grapes by staking their vines high. Springtime in the Napa Valley was always an exciting period, when care and tenacity could save a ton or more of grapes per acre.

The vintage is at its height. Here the wagons wait their turn at the crusher.

One could tell when this resolute spirit was abroad from the dense and dark clouds of smoke that often hovered over the valley to meet the rising sun.[42]

Another threat to grape quality was mildew. Napa vineyardists learned to deal with this threat by applying elemental sulfur in the vineyard. This practice was well-established by the sixties, having been introduced by Santa Clara Valley's Antoine Delmas.[43]

Vineyard culture did not go much beyond the practices discussed here. Weeds had to be kept down, sometimes by plow and harrow, as often by hand and hoe. Careful growers might thin a crop that appeared too large, but most let nature take its course. In the early days some irrigated, but there was usually enough rain in the Napa Valley for established vines. Krug, Thomann, and others brought water down by sluice from the western foothills when they needed it. By the late 1880s it was understood that part of the Napa mystique for wine quality lay in the fact that the Valley's vines were usually dry-farmed.

The harvest atmosphere was always enlivened when there was stormy weather on the horizon. Before the 1890s most grape-picking was done by contract Chinese labor. The availability of pickers could always apply additional tension in these fall weeks. Picking itself was done into specially built boxes, holding forty to fifty pounds, which the picker carried from vine to vine. Filled boxes were loaded onto wagons, which stood in the access lanes found in all sizeable vineyards. Selective picking was rare, but some premium producers such as Parrott and Schram gave pickers special instructions for certain varieties. Typically, first-crop bunches were harvested in the first pass through the vineyards of highly particular wine men. Except for the Zinfandel, however, most varieties were harvested in one pass.[44]

In the Cellar

Historical generalizations about Napa cellar practices are far more tenuous than those for viticulture. There were huge industrial operations, tiny backyard affairs, and everything in between. It would be a mistake to concentrate solely on large producers, since some of Napa's best wines came from relatively small operations. Thus, we must base the following examination of the nineteenth-century Napa winery on principles rather than details.

Seemingly every critic of California wines before the 1880s hit upon their earthiness, heaviness, harshness, their heavy alcohol content, and their low acidity. We have already seen that Napa's early fame stemmed from the perception that its wines lacked those ubiquitous earthy flavors. A good part of the California problem lay in the tendency to harvest grapes too late, when sugars were high and acids low. This tendency came partly from a

European tradition in which cool fall weather led producers to let their grapes hang as long as possible. In the 1870s the Northern California press thoroughly discussed this problem. Before the eighties most Napa producers had found a solution.

The lack of technical literature appropriate for the Northern California climate, with its drawn out, warm autumn weather, added to Napa's winemaking problems. The coming of Hilgard in 1875 and the state board in 1880 provided an institutional base for the spread of useful winemaking information. Publications by the university and the board provided a continual flow of information specifically useful to Napa wine men. The board's promotion of local organization did nothing much for Napa, which already was well organized viticulturally. But the board's promotion of state conventions and the publication of their proceedings was a definite boon. Another plus was the 1883 publication of Emmett Rixford's *The Wine Press and the Cellar*, a practical guide for the California winemaker that brought together Old World knowledge and the California environment.

Potential winemakers also needed someone with a knowledge of industrial design and winemaking technology to draw up winery plans. Such a man was Hamden W. McIntyre, who came to Inglenook with Gustave Niebaum. He laid out the Seneca Ewer Winery (Beaulieu), Inglenook, Far Niente, Greystone, and Eshcol (Trefethen). All these fine edifices continue to decorate the Valley's landscape today. They were gravity-flow operations, laid out on such logical principles of production management that they served as models for wineries built here later and in other sections of the state.[46]

Gravity-flow wineries worked best when their two or more stories were cut into the hillside so that grapes could be delivered easily to the top floor, where crushing and fermenting usually took place. From there the wine flowed on to lower floors for finishing and ageing. Being nestled into the earth also aided in maintaining moderate winery temperatures.

Typical large cellar.

Redwood storage and

blending tanks with new

oak barrels. Ca. 1010.

High fermentation temperatures led to inferior wines, due to the destruction of fruit flavors and to the tendency of hot fermentations to "stick," leaving milk-sour wines fit only for the distillery, if that. Hilgard set out early to help dry wine producers understand this problem, and a large number of the most influential Napa producers supported his sentiments.

Greystone has just been finished. The workers now build the visitors' archway. 1890.

The whole question of correct fermentation techniques became the most important topic discussed by Northern California dry wine producers in the 1880s. In these years the solutions developed by such as H. A. Pellet and H. W. Crabb called for smaller, less full, fermentation tanks, so that a protective layer of carbon dioxide could help protect the must from acetification. Handling the fermentation "cap" of pomace on red wines was another problem, since it too was a potential promoter of unwanted wine vinegar. Some placed a false cover on their tanks to hold the cap under the must level, out of the dangerous oxygen and away from the fruit flies. Others advocated punching down or stirring the cap several times per day. Hilgard warned against leaving wines too long on the pomace. He even supported pasteurization of California wine, so poorly had so many held up in their shipment east. Napa never went for this idea.

White wines presented additional problems. Here the question of oxygen contact went far beyond simply avoiding vinegar production. It was rare to find California dry or semi-dry whites in the nineteenth century that were not highly oxidized, thus lacking the freshness associated with the best of their European counterparts. Since the use of pure yeast strains was rare before 1900, most wine-makers thought that long contact with the skins was necessary to complete the wine's fermentation. Such practices did little to promote delicacy in White Riesling. And how to retain a small amount of residual sugar and still produce a stable white wine that could be bottled a year after fermentation was never worked out here in this century in any satisfactory fashion.[47]

Temperature control continued to be a lively subject on into the twentieth century. University scientists worked on the problem and developed many practical solutions. By the end of the 1890s Professor Hayne announced the development of a simple transfer machine that helped hold down fermentation temperatures. Napa's J. H. Wheeler and James Rennie assisted him in his experiments.[48]

By the late 1870s the crushing and stemming operations at the major wineries had taken on an appearance that would easily be recognized today. Steam-driven crusher-stemmers had become the order of the day. Thomas Hardy noted that all wineries he visited in 1884 had such machinery, mostly built at the Heald Foundry in Vallejo.

Cooperage was a matter that became fairly settled even before the 1870s with the discovery of redwood as a fairly good, neutral construction material for larger storage tanks. But American oak supplied staves for smaller "packages," as they were called. This material was brought in from the Midwest and later from Canada, to be assembled into barrels here. California oak was too tight-grained ever to be considered seriously. Oak was used for its construction characteristics, not for the flavors imparted by storage in new containers, as is popular today. Oak barrels and puncheons of all sizes were highly prized as long-lived, neutral, and dependable.[49]

The chemistry of cellar activities was very primitive compared to today. Sugar was measured in the must with a hydrometer, but few even had the basic equipment to titrate for acid levels. Fermentations proceeded through the activity of wild yeasts. Not until the turn of the century did the introduction of pure yeast strains become common.

The wild yeasts were then subdued with sulfur dioxide. The most common chemical corrections in California wine musts came from adding sugar to raise the final alcohol content in deficient vintages, or adding water to cut overalcoholic wines made from overripe grapes. As we have seen, such practices in Napa after 1881 became matters of public outrage, usually.

At many wineries by the 1890s it had become common to clear or "fine" better wines. Gelatin and isinglass were preferred agents in clearing white wines, while egg whites were the overwhelming fining agent of choice for reds. On some estates the quantity used was so great that consuming the supply of egg yolks was a large part of local housewifery. The result was gobs of mayonnaise, custards, plentiful French toast, and an oversupply of material to paint Christmas cookies.

Basic to all proper cellar operations was cleanliness. Hilgard's vivid descriptions of the stench that he found at some wineries prompted the tidy German and Swiss wine men of Napa to keep an ever-watchful eye on such matters, as much to ward off the telling glances of their neighbors as the telltale swarms of the ever-present fruit flies. Men like Niebaum, Estee, Crabb, and Carpy developed reputations as absolute martinets in matters of cleanliness. Visitors like Frona Wait and Thomas Hardy vouched for a sound tradition of such cleanliness in most large Napa wineries by the mid-1880s.

NOTES FOR CHAPTER SEVEN

1. Alta, 6/3/1872; Star, 12/19/1879 cites and comments on the Post's views.

2. Reporter, 12/23/1871.

3. SBVC (1881): 65.

4. Transactions (1874): 7.

5. Star, 3/4/1876, 12/27/1878.

6. Reporter, 9/2/1876; Star, 1/29/1876.

7. PWSR, 2/7/1896; Star, 12/19/1879, 2/21/1884; SBVC (1884): 38.

8. Reporter, 3/17/1882; Star, 5/5/1882.

9. Reporter, 1/5/1883.

10. Reporter, 4/22/1887.

11. San Jose Herald, 2/15/1887; Report of Experiments on Methods of Fermentation. . .1886-87. AESB, 1889:4; Bulletin No. 75. (November 1887): Bulletin No. 77. (December 1887). Hilgard was still hammering away on this matter fifteen years later. See: Official Report of the 26th Fruit Growers' Convention. . . California. December 3-6, 1901. (Sacramento 1902): 62-70.

12. SBVC (1887): 38.

13. Examiner, 8/8/1889; Teiser and Harroun, 106-108; Amerine, "Hilgard," 12-16; PWSR, 6/5/1885; 3/4/1887, 1/8/1889, 8/22/1889, 2/8/1890, 3/31/1892, 1/6/1893; San Jose Times, 6/26/1887.

14. Wait, 98, 103; A recent article has attempted to downgrade the wines of the late 1880s and 1890s by concentrating on the complaints aimed at the typical wines of the period and all but overlooking the burgeoning praise for the top 10-20% of the coastal valley wine on which this historical reputation is soundly based. See: Bob Thompson. "The Golden Age: California Wine, 1880-1900." The Journal of Gastronomy (Autumn 1988): 65-75. cf. Carlo M. Cipolla. "European Connoisseurs and California Wines, 1875-1895," in Agriculture in the Development of the Far West. (Washington DC 1975): 294-310.

15. Chronicle, 3/6/1888.

16. Alta, 3/6/1888, 3/14/1888.

17. Historically the absence of such as Dresel and Drummond did nothing to diminish the impact of Napa's success. Only Kate Warfield made a sizeable and successful entry from Sonoma. Except for Isaac De Turk the other Sonoma entrants were minor figures in the picture of Sonoma's premium table wine production.
San Francisco Post, 3/15/1888.

18. At the 1889 Convention, when the battle between the state board and Hilgard's supporters became fully public, one of the professor's allies stated that one could count the really outstanding winemakers in Napa on one hand, and Pellet was the thumb. Examiner, 8/16/1889.

19. Report of the 6th Annual State Viticultural Convention. (Sacramento 1888): 173-177; Reporter, 3/16/1888; Star, 3/1/6/1888; PWSR, 3/16/1888.

20. Examiner, 3/9/1888.

21. Examiner, 3/14/1888, 8/13/1889.

22. San Francisco Post, 3/15/1888. Also see: Bulletin, 3/16/1888; Alta, 3/14/1888; San Francisco Call, 3/14/1888. The Chronicle had the most complete coverage of the proceedings, with material not actually published in the official report.

23. PWSR, 4/26/1889.

24. There is no reliable source for California wine import statistics. From time to time the Alta published useful summaries; PWSR often supplied good numbers. For the nation as a whole good data are available in: U. S. Treasury Department, Bureau of Statistics. Commerce of the United States with European Countries from 1790 to 1890. (Washington DC 1893).

25. In the 1880s a lively debate developed over the first introduction of Zinfandel to California. Arpad Haraszthy erroneously attributed it to his father, Agoston. But contemporary witnesses made hash of this claim. The best explanation came from William Boggs in the Star (6/8/1885). He had been a neighbor of the elder Haraszthy and knew the story well. Arpad's high position in the industry helped set his false claim in historical cement, only recently broken up. Also see: Bulletin 5/1/1885; Sullivan, "Zinfandel." VWGJ (Summer 1982): 78-79; Pinney, 280-282. Professor Pinney's view of the Haraszthy/Zinfandel legend is succinct. "It is not true." Napa's H. W. Crabb even classified Zinfandel in his huge nursery collection as an "Eastern Variety." See Star, 10/13/1882 for his catalogue.

26. Star, 10/13/1882; Reporter, 5/18/1883; PWSR, 11/7/1884, 3/27/1885, 4/9/1886; Bonfort's, 4/10/1889; Wait, 117-118; E. W. Hilgard. Report of the Viticultural Work during the Seasons 1887-1889. (Sacramento 1892): 32-48; San Jose Herald, 6/13/1885; Charles L. Sullivan. "Claret/Cabernet Sauvignon-The Ideal of Red Bordeaux," in Generic/Varietal Investigations. Wine West (January 1985): 4-7

27. George Husmann. American Grape Growing and Wine Making (New York 1902): 201-202.

28. Charles L. Sullivan. "California's Generic Tables Wines: Their Rise and Decline." American Wine Society Journal (Summer 1981): 34-37; SBVC (1881): 66; SBVC (1884): 121-122.

29. Star, 10/13/1882; Reporter, 5/18/1883; PWSR, 3/27/1885; SBVC (1884): 123; Hilgard. Report... 1887-1889, 91.

30. PWSR, 4/4/1884, 3/13/1885, 3/27/1885, 3/16/1888, 8/22/1889.

31. For Krug on the situation see PWSR, 4/20/1892, and Crabb PWSR, 1/8/1897. The Duriff, or Durif, had been selected as a seedling of the French Peloursin (Gros Beclan) in 1880. See Galet at 68 and 82. For a historical discussion of this confused story see: (Charles L. Sullivan) "Petite Sirah." Connoisseur's Guide to California Wine (5:1): 2-3. Also see: Wines & Vines (November 1983): 116; Practical Winery (September 1984); Wine Spectator, 5/16/1979, 6/1/1979, 6/16/1979. W. H. Wolfe and H. P. Olmo suggested the similarity of identity between Duriff and Petite Sirah in a paper presented to the American Society of Enologists on June 23, 1977 and published in the American Journal of Enology and Viticulture (27:2): 68-73. Nevertheless, recent research employing DNA "fingerprinting" by UC Davis Professor Carole Meredith and John Bowers suggests that this identity is not as sure as previously supposed. They still have more work to do on these varieties before they can reach any firm conclusions in this matter. Carole P. Meredith to author, 7/7/1992.

32. SBVC (1881): 65; (1884): 105, 117, 144; Reporter, 7/4/1884; PWSR, 1/1908; Charles L. Sullivan. "The Germanic Ideal," in Generic/Varietal Investigations, Wines of the Americas (formerly Wine West) (November 1985): 4-7.

33. The other table wines came from the Livermore and Santa Clara Valleys. Bonfort's, 5/25/1891.

34. Bonfort's, 5/25/1884; PWSR, 3/16/1888. It is probably a coincidence that after World War II Traminers under the Charles Krug label, produced by the Mondavi family, dominated the California State Fair competition in this category for many years.

35. Edmund Penning-Rowsell. The Wines of Bordeaux (London 1985): 394-395. There is a controversy as to when Sauternes producers began making these sweet wines with grapes withered by the action of botrytis cinerea. A former owner of Château d'Yquem thought it began in the 1860s, but Cyrus Redding describes the process in detail thirty years earlier in A History and Description of Modern Wines (London 1836): 156-157.

37. Wines & Vines (October 1935) has Louis Mel's first-hand account.

38. SBVC (1881): 65; (1884): 140; San Jose Times, 10/30/1881; Star, 10/13/1882.

39. Reporter, 5/18/1883; PWSR, 3/27/1885.

40. Farmer, 8/10/1860; SBVC (1888): 45-46; Star, 7/3/1884, 4/9/1886, 9/14/1888; Husmann, 194.

41. SBVC (1884) Appendix I; Reporter, 12/23/1871, 7/29/1886; Star, 6/30/1884, 8/17/1886; Husmann, 215.

42. Star, 2/16/1877, 7/27/1879, 10/7/1881, 4/29/1892; Reporter, 4/19/1873; Alta, 4/12/1875; PWSR, 4/20/1892; Husmann, 224.

43. Farmer, 11/9/1860; Alta, 8/22/1860.

44. Thomas Hardy gives excellent descriptions of workaday vineyard operations in the Napa Valley in the 1880s. See above, Chapter 4, Note 12.

45. Alta, 6/3/1872.

46. PWSR, 5/8/1885, 3/26/1886; SBVC (1889): 83-89; Wines & Vines (May 1978): 58.

47. PWSR, 5/18/1885, 3/26/1886, 5/27/1885, 10/9/1888, 6/7/1889, 8/22/1889, 1/26/1891; Hilgard, Methods of Fermentation, 3-42; Amerine, "Hilgard," 15; Husmann, 242-243.
48. AESB, Bulletin 117 (July 1897); AWP 7/1909; Mt. Veeder, 7-9.
49. Democrat, 8/10/1872; Alta, 8/9/1875; Reporter, 3/20/1872, 7/20/1872, 8/3/1872, 6/19/1885, 6/22/1888;Star, 6/22/1888, 3/1/1889, 12/19/1890.

INNOCENT YEARS

*There are not as many fine wine grapes, nor as much choice wine
in the state now as there was twenty-five years ago.*

—CHARLES A. WETMORE
1911

CHARLES WETMORE'S OBSERVATION ON THE STATE OF CALIFORNIA WINE BEFORE
World War I looks back to the idealistic and experimental days of the
1880s with a pioneer nostalgia that has a ring of truth. Great wines
seem to derive from a mixture of technical skill and idealistic fervor. What
appears to have declined in the years of the new century was the fervor.
Technical developments already under way in the 1890s meant that the
average bottle of Napa wine was probably more chemically sound than in the
eighties. And the replanting of the Valley meant that a far more orderly
selection of tried and true grape varieties would be available. The end of the

Wine War certainly meant that a far more orderly pattern of capital organization would control the destiny of the Napa wine industry than in previous years. Wine producers and vineyardists would make far more money here for the next two decades than they had made in the previous two. It was a good time for American agriculture in general, years to which New Deal economists would later look back to establish price parity for the depression years of the thirties. But no historian can tell for sure whether the best Cabernets of 1910 from the CWA or Inglenook were better or worse than those of Morris Estee or Tiburcio Parrott in the nineties.

TOURING THE VALLEY — 1905

Before we examine the transformation of the Valley in the new century, it would be worthwhile to make an imaginary up-valley trip for a swift overview of some of the important activities and personalities, particularly those that would later make an imprint on Napa Valley wine history.

Below Napa in the Carneros the early advance of phylloxera has converted most of the older vineyards to other, more extensive agricultural activities, particularly dairying. The notable exception is Judge John Stanly's La Loma. Stanly died in 1899, but the family has hired H. A. Pellet to run the winery. Its reputation for good clarets has not sagged, with Inglenook and Gundlach-Bundschu having a lock on their production. The Stanly vineyards will still amount to about three hundred acres during Prohibition. The old winery burned down in 1936.[4]

In Napa itself Migliavacca and the two CWA plants give winemaking in town a distinctly industrial look. All three produce small lots of prizewinning wines, but most of their production is fairly ordinary stuff, a good part of it

California Wine

Association after the

1906 Earthquake.

made from Sacramento Valley grapes. In certain years there are also large shipments of Sonoma grapes to these urban winery complexes.

A very small part of the land between Napa and Yountville is planted to grapes. But at Oak Knoll the Eshcol Winery and its two hundred acres of vines stand out from the surrounding prune orchards. Napa bankers James and George Goodman acquired the property in 1882, once part of the huge J. W. Osborne estate. They built the large wooden winery on the property in 1886. Now, at the turn of the century, Eshcol is run by James C. Fawver, who continues the Goodman tradition for good wine until Prohibition. Today this great wooden rarity is the Trefethen Winery.[5]

The Redwood district to the west of Napa, on the slopes of Mt. Veeder, produces more income from its resort industry than from winemaking. The tiny Streich and Fischer Wineries still operate, but large-scale production is soon to begin in the redwoods with the arrival of Theodore Gier, a German-born Oakland liquor dealer with extensive wine holdings in the Livermore Valley.

On the eastern slopes and up in the numerous valleys, wine production is declining steadily as winery operators find it to their economic advantage simply to sell their grapes in the greater valley. The phylloxera is gradually making its way into Conn, Foss, Chiles, and Wooden Valleys, production is declining, and the urge to replant is mostly lacking. One exception is Anton Nichelini, who built his little winery above Chiles Valley in 1890. Today, it is a rare mountain survivor of these early years, still run by the Nichelini family.

The decline is also apparent on the lower slopes closer to today's Silverado Trail. In fact, dairy cattle become more common than grapes as the years move toward Prohibition. An anomaly is the Stag's Leap Winery, which Horace Chase built east of the trail and south of the Yountville Crossroad in 1893. Later, the manor house will become famous as a resort. The winery today is a handsome ruin; the manor house is a private residence.

Back across the road to Yountville we find the huge brick wine and brandy plant G. Groezinger built just west of the little hamlet, today's "Vintage 1870" complex. In 1889 Groezinger sold a large portion of his interest to Antoine Borel. Subsequent bankruptcy sent the plant through several hands, eventually to those of C. Schilling.[6]

Heading north past the Veterans' Home we can perceive the effects now of the concentrated vineyard replanting taking place. As we approach Oakville the widespread winery buildings of To Kalon come into view. Founder H. W. Crabb died in 1899, the estate passing into the hands of the E. S. Churchill family, where it remained until 1943. In the years before Prohibition, under managers Hans Hansen and Lafayette Stice, To Kalon maintained its reputation. In 1904 it was dubbed "the largest resistant vineyard in

California." But another side of its operations can be seen in a 1906 industry ad that boasted "heavy wines for blending a specialty." The winery survived Prohibition but burned in 1939. Today the To Kalon vineyards, owned by Robert Mondavi and others, produce grapes that have developed a solid modern reputation.[7]

Nearby stands the Nouveau Medoc Winery of Brun & Chaix, which has just passed into the hands of the CWA after the 1902 death of Jean Chaix. This modest 100,000-gallon plant will have its capacity raised in the next few years to more than 400,000, the CWA's workhorse in this part of the Napa Valley, operating as the French-American Wine Company.

As we head up the highway toward Rutherford, we can see Inglenook standing out among the little wineries around that tiny village. Since the turn of the century Captain Niebaum has cut back production, using only his estate grapes, but demand and prestige are still high. The old seaman now spends almost all his time and energy conducting the affairs of the Alaska Commercial Company and is rarely seen in the Valley. He has lost much of the early zeal for his Napa "hobby" and leaves the business in the capable hands of Benjamin Arnhold. When Niebaum dies in 1908, winemaking here ceases for two years. After 1911 the old energy and high quality return.

Just to the east another important wine operation has just started up, actually a cream of tartar works, run by a certain Georges de Latour. The history of his famed Beaulieu Vineyard (BV) must have its own place later in this chapter. Frederick Ewer's Valley View Winery, across the way, will become the main BV plant in 1923.

The village of

Rutherford, Ca 1904.

Today the center of

a newly approved

viticultural district.

North of Rutherford, winegrowing becomes absolutely dominant and new planting is everywhere obvious as we approach St. Helena. At Zinfandel Lane we pass the Wheeler Winery, now run by John H. Wheeler after the death of his brother Rollo in 1889. John was an early leader in the Viticultural Commission and took an active and controversial role in the Wine War. To the left is the Thomann Winery, whose founder died on a trip to his native Switzerland in 1900. Four years later the Thomann family sold the operation to the Leuenberger family who have run a winery on the lower slopes of Howell Mountain since 1891. They name the Thomann place Sutter Home, capitalizing on Caroline Leuenberger's maiden name. Her brother, Albert Sutter, takes charge of the winemaking operations in 1906 and will begin bottling Sutter Home wines at the winery the next year.[8]

The Conradi family girls (Spring Mountain) share wine coolers with the Beringer girls. Ca 1910.

Just up the road on the right, on today's Dowdell Lane, we see the (1875) Fountain Winery, which will operate until 1911. Across the street is the spot where the important Bornhorst & Ebeling Winery will be built in 1909. Both structures still stand, as does James Dowdell's winery (1886) just up the street. The owner, who once ran Greystone in the nineties, died in 1902. In fact, the grim reaper had a field day with the second wave of Napa wine pioneers in a ten-month period when Dowdell, Frederick Beringer, George Husmann, Jean Chaix, and Frank Sciaroni all died.[9]

Our selective tour of the Valley can give no justice to the large number of wineries still operating in the St. Helena area, although the number has come down quite a bit since the nineties. Greystone, now operated in grand fashion by the CWA, is the dominant production center in the upper Valley. Across the way, the Charles Krug Winery is now controlled by the Moffitt family, important in paper manufacturing. The man who has brought the old winery back to health is Bismark Bruck, Louis Bruck's son and Krug's nephew, and now Napa's representative in the state assembly. He will run the place until his death in 1926. Bruck is making good money selling grafted St. George rootstock, in addition to his winemaking operations. Nearby the Beringer Winery sustains its high quality and remains a very important independent producer.[10] On up the road at Lodi Lane, Antonio Forni has just finished the first phase of his hand-hewn stone Lombarda Winery. He acquired the Tychson property in 1895 and will finish building his 300,000-gallon facility in 1906, reborn after Prohibition as Freemark Abbey.[11]

Winegrowing in the mountains east and west of St. Helena is on the decline. On Spring Mountain some vineyards are dying from phylloxera and are not replanted. Toward the summit, above Mill Creek, a hiker in 1993 can walk through what appears to be first-growth forest, suddenly to find ancient grape stakes in line among the huge conifers and madrones, old but not so fragile reminders of early viticulture here.

The Lemme and McPike vineyards have come under the control of San Francisco's C. Schilling & Co. and were incorporated in 1903 as the Spring Mountain Vineyard Company. The winery to be built here will be known as La Perla, handling the product of about 320 acres of Schilling vineyards. Today these viticultural jewels are renowned as the York Creek Vineyard of Fritz Maytag and the La Perla Vineyard of Jerome C. Draper. Nearby we can see the winery of Peter Conradi, who began growing grapes on Spring Mountain in 1891. Once a simple wooden affair, the winery was replaced by a fine stone structure in 1904, which survives today as the Robert Keenan Winery. Further down the mountain the Chevalier family has sold off the winery's cooperage and sells their grapes to others.[12]

East of the Valley on Howell Mountain winegrowing is still important, although on the decline. Certainly the results of the 1900 Paris Exposition should augur a long and wonderful history. The CWA now runs the Brun & Chaix plant, but the chief names on the mountain now are individuals, W. S. Keyes and Frederick Hess, both with wineries on the old La Jota Rancho. Keyes is the son of Edge Hill's E. S. Keyes. His Liparita Winery is now producing Napa's most-sought Cabernet Sauvignon, following his gold medal at Paris. Hess, the Swiss-German publisher of the *San Francisco Demokrat*, built his pretty stone winery in 1898, just up from Keyes' place on Las Posadas Road. Both structures survive today, the Hess Winery operating again as the La Jota Vineyard Company since 1982.[13]

By now the area north of St. Helena around Larkmead Lane has developed something of a winegrowing character of its own. The Valley is much warmer here and the soils are quite different from those to the south. Larkmead has its own stop on the trolley line and the old Larkmead Winery has had new owners since 1895 when John Battista and Felix Salmina, his nephew, bought the place from Mrs. A. C. Furniss. In 1905 these Italian-Swiss natives replace the 1884 cellar with a modern stone structure, which survives today as the home of Hanns Kornell's sparkling wines. The Salmina family will remain a powerful factor in the Valley's wine community until well after Repeal.

Lifting one's eyes to the hills west of this point in the Valley, one might see Schramsberg, were it not so well-hidden by the trees and rugged landscape. Here the old pioneer Jacob Schram lives on, with son Herman running his business and winery and marketing Schram's still much-loved wines with San Francisco entrepreneur Charles Bowen. The old man dies in 1905 and at Prohibition wine production will cease, the estate going through several hands before its modern resuscitation in 1965.

Further north, around Calistoga, the winegrowing situation is complicated and somewhat confused. Here the deadliest blows from the phylloxera have come late. The planting boom here has had far too many of the local growers replanting on unprotected vinifera stock, a shortsighted policy that will have its obvious, ugly results in the next decade. Meanwhile, old and new names have come to dominate the wine production picture here. The Tubbs family continues to own Chateau Montelena after the death of founder Alfred Tubbs in 1896. Now the wine is marketed through CWA and, after empty cellars during Prohibition, will be reborn in 1934 under grandson Chapin Tubbs.

To the west of town, at Kortum Canyon, is the winery of Louis Kortum (1875), a leading independent in the area.[14] The dominant operation is that of Ephraim Light in Calistoga. In 1903 his Mt. Helena Winery at Grant and Stevenson Streets became part of the CWA and the home for a large percentage of local production until Prohibition. After Repeal this old structure, said to descend from Sam Brannan's stables, will become the first home of the Napa Valley Cooperative Winery.[15] Northwest of town, Grimm's Vineyard and Wine Vaults stand against and into the hill where Jacob Grimm's Chinese laborers began carving three ageing cellars in 1888.

Felix Salmina's Larkmead Winery between St. Helena and Calistoga, more recently the home of Hanns Kornell sparkling wines.

This 140,000-gallon facility is another important independent producer and in 1976 is reborn as the Storybook Mountain Winery.

This impressionistic tour of the Valley implies that important changes are in the making. For the wine industry the powerful concentration of the CWA has brought peace and apparent prosperity to Napa's winegrowers. The number who are willing to suffer the trouble of independent production is declining yearly as more and more are attracted to the stability afforded by the wine trust's benevolent power. Some of the CWA wineries keep their labels and their names and give the appearance of competition to the outside world. In all, between 1902 and 1911, the CWA wineries of the Napa Valley crushed an average of about 7,000 tons per year, producing more than a million gallons of wine at a time when the Valley's average production was less than two million gallons.[16]

Another transformation is taking place in the use of Valley land. By 1913 Napa will be California's number four county in prune production. When Prohibition arrives there will be more acres in prunes than in grapes. In these years, the visitor to the area below Yountville must look closely for the grapevines to comprehend why Napa Valley has such a reputation for viticulture. And in the mountains east and west of the Valley, as the phylloxera spreads, rarely, if ever, is an important vineyard replanted to grapes.

The people of the Valley are also changing. No longer is the pronounced German character of the population so apparent. By 1900 less than one third of St. Helena High School's graduating seniors had German last names. But the German element and the sense of Teutonic ethnicity is still strong. At Frederick Beringer's 1901 funeral the services were in English and German. In 1910 the census will show that the German foreign-born who own farms in the Napa Valley outnumber any other ethnic or national group, except the native-born. Before this date when an Italian name was attached to a winery operation, the person was most probably Italian-Swiss. By 1910 an Italian name meant a person was most likely from Italy itself, the number two homeland of Napa County's foreign-born farmers.[17]

These innocent years in the Napa Valley are seeing another change taking place in its people. The area was known for its resort possibilities since the 1860s, and this aspect of life here has picked up considerably since the turn of the century. The Napa region has also become more and more a place that the wealthy seek for their summer and weekend homes, or for retirement. It was the beauty of the place that had so dazzled Andrew Carnegie, and in these years that beauty acts as a powerful magnet. Many winegrowing estates, such as the Parrott and Chevalier places on Spring Mountain, are sold as their owners die or move closer to San Francisco. On Howell Mountain the Angwin resort has been converted to a religious college and community.

Part of the attraction for affluent new residents is that Napa is now nowhere nearly so isolated as it was a few years ago. The new century brought trolley cars up from Vallejo and a swarm of automobiles that is nearly driving many oldtimers to distraction. Telephones are now everywhere and electricity is available in all but the most humble or isolated situations. But there is little evidence that Napa's wine industry has anything to do with these developments. As we shall see, many of these gentile newcomers consider wine little more than booze, which much of middle-class America increasingly perceives as a serious social problem.

1901 — 1902

We left our narrative at the end of the 1900 vintage, a time of rising prices, outstanding quality, and buoyant spirits. The *Star* crowed about the coming "era of good feelings." Credit became available again to the wine men, who could now pay the growers in spot cash. In general, the demand for California wine on the East Coast was surging, shipments in 1900 up 76 percent from the 1895 level. The demand for Napa wine shipped as case goods had also surged, a clear sign of the growing respectability of the Napa label in the east.[1]

Planting in 1901 was still at a frenzied pace, just about every vine now going in as benchgrafts to St. George rootstock. But lots of new prune and walnut planting added to the Valley's growing total fruit and nut acreage. Three horrible days of spring frost, one as late as May 18, hit the grape crop. Prices had risen again and the vintage was orderly. A very large percentage of grapes crushed in Napa were not grown here, coming by rail from the Sacramento Valley. Half of the 3,000-ton Greystone crush arrived from the Folsom/Natoma area. This pattern continued for several years, until the new Napa vineyards being planted and replanted had come to bear.[2]

The vintage was bracketed by two sensational fires. One in August virtually destroyed the town of Calistoga and later another in St. Helena burned down the local Chinatown. By now Chinese performed a very small percentage of the vineyard work in the Napa Valley. But the Japanese presence here in these years was beginning to provoke the same kind of ugly racism that had raised its head in the eighties against the Chinese.[3]

The good prices and generally buoyant business conditions brought an explosion of new planting to Napa during the 1901–02 dormant season. Over 1,500 acres went in, while statewide planting amounted to more than 10,000 acres. The growing conditions were ideal from spring to vintage. Grape and wine prices soared. The yield here on the 3,500 bearing acres was almost 3.5 tons per acre. The local wine product was about 1,700,000 gallons. Late

October rains wiped out the second crop of Zinfandel and dampened the euphoria somewhat—but not much.

Many smiled and cheered when it was learned a few days later that Theodore Bell had been elected to Congress. He was a local Democrat from a winegrowing family in a Republican Valley in a general Republican landslide. Congressman Bell's first contribution at the next session was to offer a national pure wine bill with rigid restrictions against sugared and pomace wines. Bell, Bismark Bruck, and several other Napa wine men had written the bill in St. Helena shortly after the 1902 vintage. It had little chance of success, as progressive as it was in this progressive age of reform. But New York and Ohio congressmen were not likely to let such a bill out of committee. Sugar wine was a way of life for American wine producers outside of California. Bell went on to run as his party's candidate for governor in 1906 and 1910. We shall meet him again in the Prohibition fight.

GEORGES DE LATOUR AND BEAULIEU VINEYARD

In December of 1902 a newcomer to the Valley advertised that he had St. George rootstock for sale. Georges de Latour had been here since 1900 and his jump into the rootstock market was typical of his keen understanding of the economics of the wine industry, from an entrepreneur's point of view. In 1883 he had come to this country from near Périgord at the age of twenty-nine. Trained in chemistry in France, he settled in San Jose in 1890 after a stint working for a mining concern in the Sierra foothills. His San Jose operation was a "cream of tartar" business in which he collected the potassium tartrate crystals from wine casks and processed them for later production as a component of baking powder. He also ran a distillery in the South Bay town.

Georges de Latour

and family in 1912.

De Latour got to know John Wheeler in these early years. This Napa wine man was also engaged in a cream of tartar operation related to his work at an East Bay chemical company. De Latour did business there, met one of the secretaries, Fernande Romer, and married her in 1898. The de Latours then packed up and headed for Healdsburg in Sonoma County, where Georges set up another cream of tartar operation. During these years the Frenchman made good money, pretty much having a lock on scraping wine casks in that area. He kept up his contacts with Wheeler and when the business upswing was in full flower he characteristically made another move. This one put him in position to become the baron of Napa Valley premium winegrowing thirty years later.[18]

He started rather simply in 1900, selling the Healdsburg business and buying a four-acre plot of land in Rutherford from Charles P. Thompson, where he foresaw the site for another tartar works. The agent who swung the deal was also the publisher of the *St. Helena Star*, a friend of Wheeler's. From then on the local sheet was full of the story of de Latour's rise.

The newcomer also saw the potential profits from selling St. George rootstock and set about establishing solid contacts in France to acquire benchgrafted vines. Within three years he was the leading factor in their sale here. So profitable was this side of his business that oldtimers, looking back, recalled that he had had a hand in the introduction of the St. George in Napa, which, of course, was not the case.[19]

De Latour swung right into the Napa tartar business and built a small distillery on the property as well. He also began brokering bulk wine produced in the Valley. He even set up a fruit-drying operation and kept a hand in the East Bay as a part owner of Berkeley's Golden West Distillery.[20]

The 1902 vintage and its marvelous wine and grape prices convinced de Latour to get into the production side of the wine business. He had his chance after the planting season in 1903 when the rest of the Thompson ranch became available. He bought the 128 acres and sent off to France for grafted vines that went into the ground the next planting season. A glance at the list of vines de Latour imported that year clearly indicates that the wine bug that bit him was not of the high premium species. Aramon, Alicante Bouschet, Carignane, Grand noir, and Grenache led the reds. He aimed considerably higher with his whites, which included Sauvignon blanc, Sémillon, Ugni blanc, and Sylvaner. Next year he incorporated his business as Beaulieu Vineyard.[21] In 1904 he rented the Thomann cellar to make up his wine. In 1906 he converted his tartar works into a full-fledged winery, and leased the old Henry Harris Winery in Rutherford, built by the former sheriff in 1887. De Latour also gained control of the surrounding 146 acres. The Thompson place became BV Vineyard #1; the Harris ranch was to be called BV Vineyard #2. In 1910 when he bought BV #2 outright he had 250 acres in vines.

Georges de Latour had all the ordinary grapes he needed before he acquired the Harris place. That a change in his thinking had taken place is indicated by the twenty acres of Cabernet Sauvignon and fifteen acres of Pinot noir he planted there in 1907.[22]

Part of de Latour's dynamic approach to business affairs created lots of friction, as we can see from the heat that often resulted. In 1904 he was arrested for embezzlement on charges that were later dropped. The next year Felix Salmina sued him for performance on a grape contract. He won that one but later lost one and had to pay up. In San Jose he had been cited in a suit for what today would be called environmental pollution. But he came out of these conflicts with a good reputation. He always paid up in the end and tried to maintain good relations with those whom he scraped a bit.[23]

The growing interest in California sparkling wines gave de Latour another bright idea. Several Northern California establishments were making money producing carbonated wines by what was then called the "soda pop" method. He learned of a good machine for the job in France and bought one in 1908. The next year he was producing sparkling Moselle, Sauterne, and Burgundy. This lasted several seasons, although in 1911 the Department of Agriculture began pressuring producers of such "carbonated" wines to stop putting the term "sparkling" on the label.

BV added to its Pinot noir planting in 1909 by putting in 10,000 more vines under the supervision of Joseph Ponti, who was to run the vineyards from 1907 to 1950. There were also huge additions of cooperage at the Harris place. By 1913 the capacity there had been expanded to over 300,000 gallons. By 1914 the winery's capacity hit half a million and de Latour had set up a depot in New York for BV wines. The year before, he took another step toward higher quality by hiring the later famed A. J. Perelli-Minetti as his winemaker.

Meanwhile de Latour had picked up another scent in the economic winds. Between 1905 and 1907 California sweet wine production soared by more than 40 percent. In 1906 a new Federal Sweet Wine Law eased the taxes on fortifying brandy. As a result the master of BV decided to take a large plunge into the production of dessert wines. Part of his eventual success came from BV's ability to take over a large portion of the wine business of the San Francisco Archdiocese. De Latour built a new distillery in 1908 and began planting sweet wine grapes, particularly muscats. In 1915 de Latour ran an ad in an industry journal boosting his sparkling wines and declaring his "altar" wines a specialty. This sweet wine business would carry BV through Prohibition in good fashion. But after Repeal the product of the better varieties on the old Harris ranch would bring Beaulieu national acclaim for its dry wines.[24]

In a time when individualism and entrepreneurial idiosyncrasy were fading into a sort of industrial homogeneity, a new German came to Napa at the turn of the century who seemed to hearken back to earlier years. We know little of Theodore Gier before the 1880s, except that he was born in Germany and opened a small wine and liquor business in Oakland in 1883. He made enough money to join the swelling crowd planting vineyards in the Livermore Valley in the early nineties. In 1900 he bought the old Hudeman place on Mt. Veeder from Rudolph Jordan. "Lotus Farm" became the site of a large vineyard and the first really important wine operation on Mt. Veeder. The big winery was finished for the 1903 vintage. Soon Gier's "Sequoia Vintages" became an important part of the Napa wine scene. Gier's game plan was to maintain his Livermore operation for "sauterne" production and to use the Mt. Veeder estate for Rieslings and clarets. His solid capital position, his sound business sense, his understanding of the beverage industry, and the generally profitable character of premium winegrowing in these years paid off to a degree he probably never imagined.[25]

The Napa operation was so profitable that Gier was soon operating on the Valley floor, first making wine in St. Helena at the old McPike place, then renting the Sutter Home facility, and eventually taking over the Edge Hill property. He finally acquired the Bergfeld Winery just south of St. Helena as a permanent plant in the area. (Today this is the site of the Napa Valley Cooperative Winery.) By 1909 he controlled about 1,000 acres of grapes in Livermore and Napa, with almost 500,000 gallons of winery capacity. The Alameda County wine was produced under his "Pride of Livermore" label. His Napa clarets and Rieslings appeared under the Sequoia and Giersburger labels. They won their share of medals in the years before Prohibition and were a very important part of the independent wine production for the Napa industry. When the country went dry in 1920 Gier had already disposed of his valley holdings, but he held on to the Mt. Veeder property, selling it in 1930, the year before he died.

Other than good wine and the development of a historic wine property, Gier brought an element of style to Napa that helped maintain something of an air of the good old days, a reminder of the image of Napa's Teutonic "Gemütlichkeit." His Mt. Veeder estate was ever the site of excursions by his business associates, his lodge fellows, his political chums, and by tourists to the Bay Area from all over. He used the place much as Andrea Sbarboro used the Italian Swiss Colony at Asti, to promote both his psychic well-being and the image of his wines. Each year after the vintage he brought up the Oakland Turnverein singing society to the Valley for a serenading tour that moved from one trolley stop to another, with trips up to a winery at each stop to sing a carol and cadge drinks.

Gier was flamboyant. He loved a bright uniform and a martial air. He was proud of his shooting ability and somehow got himself appointed a Lt. Colonel on the Governor's militia staff. When World War I came he almost landed in jail for singing "Hoch der Kaiser" with a group of German cronies at a Livermore winery. He later claimed they were singing "Les Marseilles." During Prohibition he was arrested and served time for breaking the dry laws. We would remember him if he made only good wine. We should also remember him as a colorful, somewhat outrageous character, whose solid winegrowing sense created what was to become the Christian Brothers' Mt. La Salle estate and is today the site of the Hess Collection Winery.[26]

1903 — 1905

The next three vintages (1903–1905) saw Napa vineyards grow to over 7,000 acres, with fairly good crops and wines of satisfactory quality. Prices and quality fluctuated around the state, but the steady hand of the CWA maintained a somewhat heady prosperity for Napa's wine men. As the planting binge throughout California continued, voices arose reminding all of the overplanting of the 1880s. The San Francisco *Chronicle* took up the subject as early as January 1902. But it was generally understood that really good wine was in demand and moved easily in the market, whatever was happening throughout the state's industry.

Napa certainly continued to maintain its historic image as the home of really good wine. Each year seemed to underline the perception. In 1903 statewide prices softened after two consecutive large dry wine vintages. Napa made almost two million gallons, but in the spring of 1904 demand for local wine was intense. In the fall of 1904 a September combination of searing heat and heavy rain conspired to produce thin, poorly-colored reds here. But they sold at good prices. The quality of California wines in 1905 was rather ordinary, partly due to widespread overcropping. But a sizeable percentage of Napa's vineyardists apparently resisted the temptation. The result was a red wine vintage here that became famous in years to come. The press was full of the story—a short, mediocre state vintage, but Napa's reds are marvelous. Actually, the better wines all over the northern coastal valleys were excellent, but Napa again got more than its fair share of the publicity. At the end of the vintage a top story told of independent producers in a no-holds-barred fight with CWA to acquire Napa's few yet uncommitted reds. The *Star* insisted editorially that the Napa industry's motto must continue to be "Quality not Quantity."

Another feather in the Valley's viticultural cap was the 1903 establishment of a USDA experimental station at To Kalon, in Oakville. It would concentrate on resistant rootstock, under the general supervision of George C. Husmann, the professor's learned son. Although stationed in Washington D.C., Husmann was ever a Napa fan and a regular visitor. On his visit here in 1906 he applauded the wonderful quality of local table wines and declared that Napa was fast becoming "one of the most famous grape growing valleys in the world."[27]

But change seemed more obvious than continuity during these years in Napa. By 1906 it looked as if the Valley were being overrun by automobiles, the new plaything of the rich and near-rich. One could buy a 7-1/2 horsepower Oldsmobile in Napa for $500. Wine men bought their share of the new machines. John Wheeler was the first, with a lively little Rambler. Georges de Latour, of course, purchased a more conspicuous seven-passenger Locomobile. But many of those clogging the roads were folks from other areas out for a drive. Bloody accidents were soon a regular topic in the local press. Things got so bad in 1905 that the County Board of Supervisors banned all automotive traffic from roads above the valley floor between 6 A.M. and 9 P.M..

EARTHQUAKE

The planting season in 1906 was as frantic as in the previous years of the century. About 10,000 Napa acres were now planted to wine grapes, just about equal to the mid-nineties figure after the phylloxera had started its work. Independent capital contributed to this growth, particularly at BV, Larkmead, and Lombarda. One searches in vain for some dramatic foreshadowing of the great temblor that so thoroughly shook Northern California that its wine industry was changed forever.

When the earth heaved before sunup on April 18, oldtimers recalled the "Great Quake" of 1868. That earthquake had toppled chimneys and elicited panic, but the 1906 quake was bigger, causing extensive damage. When the dust cleared, however, Napa folk

Almost every chimney in St. Helena fell during the 1906 earthquake. Here is the result at the Beringer Rhine House.

could smile at their good fortune. In modern days the Rodgers Creek fault west of the Mayacamas Range and the little Carneros fault have not displayed any real vitality. And until one of them does, it appears that Napa must content itself with the role of onlooker when seismic cataclysms tear up parts of the rest of Northern California.

Many Napa Valley wineries were damaged. The front wall of the Lisbon Winery in Napa came down; the Migliavacca plant was badly battered. Up the Valley, Oakville's French-American plant (Brun & Chaix) suffered the greatest financial loss when several large tanks burst, spilling out about 100,000 gallons. The Beringers had the most severe winery damage and the roof of their historic Rhine House was smashed by a falling chimney. (The *Star* guessed that about 80 percent of the chimneys went down in the St. Helena area.) John Wheeler's place was hard-hit, as was Frederick Ewer's Valley View Winery in Rutherford (BV today).

The CWA's Winehaven plant in 1908. Still in use today as a U.S. Navy supply depot.

The most serious losses to Napa people resulted from damage to their property outside the Valley. Claus Schilling, Benjamin Arnhold (Inglenook's agency), Theodore Gier, and the Napa & Sonoma Wine Company all had their storage facilities wiped out in San Francisco. In fact, all but three of the important cellars in the city were destroyed, the most important survivor being the Italian Swiss Colony warehouse at Greenwich and Battery, which still stands. The industry's biggest loser was the CWA, which lost 5,000,000

gallons in its San Francisco cellars alone. Charles Carpy, W. S. Keyes, and Frederick Hess also suffered terrible financial losses. Hess lost his newspaper and printing establishment.

Some new arrangements were quickly put together. Schilling leased the almost unused Groezinger plant at Yountville. San Francisco wine mogul Amandus Repsold quickly acquired Napa's Lisbon Winery (Matthews). But the great arrangement was the CWA's decision to build a giant, multi-million-gallon wine processing plant in the East Bay at Point Molate, near Richmond.

The basic idea had been in the works for some time, but it took the quake's destruction and the collected capital from insurance claims to get the wheels rolling. Tied to the almost isolated cellars in the city at the tip of the San Francisco Peninsula, the state's wine industry had not been rationally connected to the logistic reality of California wine production. The great San Francisco merchant establishment had grown up like Topsy and could now start over. The ideal situation would be a large plant that could process grapes from the Central Valley, would be close to the premium dry wine districts, and would have direct sea access to the ports of the world, backed up to the transcontinental railroad at Richmond with its connection to the East Coast. The Point Molate spot was perfect; they would call it Winehaven.[28]

The $3,000,000 complex was erected on the double and dedicated September 2, 1907, just in time for the vintage. It had a capacity of 10,000,000 gallons, 20,000,000 by 1915. Meanwhile CWA's Napa facility at Greystone would act as the great collection point for the trust's dry wines. The huge winery also began acting as a bottling facility. But as the years passed, the Winehaven plant more and more acted as the first home for much of the Napa grape crop.

In the days following the quake, life in the Valley went on much as before, except that the quake and fire had made thousands homeless. Like most Bay Area communities Napa pitched in to help care for these refugees.

The earthquake changed the balance of supply and demand for California wine. More than 15,000,000 California-produced gallons had been lost, causing a serious wine shortage. Prices jumped up immediately and buyers thronged to the Valley before spring had passed, searching for uncommitted lots of unharvested grapes.

There was plenty of spring rain to water the more than 2,000 acres of new vines. The vintage started early, as Central Valley grapes poured into Napa during the first week in September. Lots of Napa grapes also went into the crusher early, but not because of high sugars. Prices had risen to a point where producers were taking in underripe grapes and dumping bags of cane sugar into the fermenting tanks. They were taking no chances that a fall storm might undermine the coming bonanza. By the end of the vintage Schilling and the CWA were requiring independent producers to certify the purity of their wines. Another problem was the shortage of pickers due to the inordinate demand for workers in San Francisco, where the rebuilding process had begun in earnest. Napa pickers, many of them school children, were making up to $3.00 a day at the height of the harvest. In all, Napa grapes produced over 2,000,000 gallons in 1906; the Valley entered the Christmas season in flush times. Andrew Carnegie added to the feeling of well-being with a $7,500 Christmas gift to St. Helena for a new library.

1907 — 1914

On January 1, 1907 the new Federal Food law went into effect. CWA President Percy Morgan proclaimed that "nothing in the way of legislation could have more greatly benefited the California wine industry." Napa vintners, early led by Theodore Bell, had supported it all the way. But Napa would gain little from a stringent regulation of the pomace wine. The law did not outlaw the sugaring of wine, but California law did. Actually, the kind of concocted "wine" deemed illegal was not a competitor for Napa wines.

We can learn much about the direction of Napa Valley's wine industry by looking closely at the situation here in 1907. As in previous years there were huge importations of Central Valley grapes, mostly from Yolo County in the Sacramento Valley. The vintage of Napa-grown wine came in at almost 4,000,000 gallons, the highest since 1891 and for the next ten years. But this total was now the product of forty wineries. In 1891 there had been about 140 wineries. Thus, the average Napa producer made almost 100,000 gallons in 1907, whereas the average had been only about 30,000 in 1891. True, the CWA's huge plants were now dominant. Their Brun & Chaix plant made over 400,000 gallons this year. But Salmina's brand new Larkmead Winery had a 500,000-gallon capacity, and BV, another independent, was growing every year. Meanwhile the Chevalier Winery on Spring Mountain closed its doors in 1907 and began selling its grapes to Greystone.

The 1907 vintage was much praised for its quality. Just about everyone called it "the best since. . ." his or her favorite year. It certainly was the best vintage of the decade, particularly for clarets. According to Theodore Gier, it also was special since it came almost solely from vines planted since 1897. Many of these vines were now old enough to produce superior wine grapes.

Things started to get back to normal in 1908. The post-quake euphoria came down some, as did the prices for grapes and wine. There was more talk of the threat of overplanting, as winery inventories started to creep up. Nevertheless, planting in the Valley was as hot as ever. It is actually difficult to tell just how many acres of grapevines were standing at the end of the dormant season. A good guess is about 15,000 acres.

Gustave Niebaum died just before the vintage began. Sonoma's Andrea Sbarboro addressed the Napa grapegrowers a few days later and saluted the old sea captain. He went on to say that "Napa was the first county in California to bring to the attention of the world the fact that as good wines could be produced in California as in any country on earth."[29]

The technology revolutionizing Napa's highways and rails entered the vineyards in 1907 when John Wheeler had the Holt Manufacturing Company build the Valley's first "gasoline traction engine" in Stockton. The first self-propelled steam tractor had been patented in 1901 and by 1907 several inventors around the country had brought out a gas model. Wheeler's was a twelve-ton monster, but its noisy engine was the voice of the future in Napa Valley's vineyards.[30]

The swarms of autos and the coming of the trolley to Napa brought the first active movement among Napa wine men to promote tourism at the wineries. Bismark Bruck and Theodore Gier took the most interest in the new movement. The *Register* copied an article by Bruck circulated in the eastern press encouraging tourists to "visit the wineries." A banquet celebrating the extension of the electric train service had Gier toasting the new era of wine and tourism and predicting that it would revolutionize the Valley. Of course, it did, but not in these early years. For now it was a matter of insuring that whoever was in charge at the plant greeted visitors warmly, showed them around, and offered a glass of wine. Tasting rooms and tour guides were a long way off.[31]

The 1908 vintage was thirty percent less than the previous bumper crop. It had been a dry year and the grapes were short on juice, but the quality of the Napa product was excellent. Again, the reds were remarkable, with concentrated flavors and good ageing potential. The *Star* used one of the President's favorite terms to describe the dry wine situation—"bully." Actually, there was quite a bit of grumbling when it became clear to growers that a crop of less than two tons per acre with lower prices meant a substantial reduction in income. Rising inventories and more acreage coming into production were dark clouds on the horizon. Horatio Stoll of Italian Swiss Colony warned all concerned to be prepared for 7,000 new California acres of winegrapes coming into production next year.

Napa did its share in holding down production in 1909. January saw twenty-seven inches of rainfall, turning the Valley into a lake and virtually killing off the planting season. Then a mild spring coaxed luxuriant growth that was battered on May 15 by a deadly black frost. Vines from Larkmead to

Calistoga were burned to the stump. A hot summer and some September storms added to growers' anxiety. Yields were low, but the vintage was orderly and the quality was high. The state harvest, as Stoll predicted, was up sharply and prices sagged. As more Napa vineyards came to bearing, the need for grapes from outside sources diminished. This year the CWA facility at Napa, the old Carpy plant, made 650,000 gallons, Greystone made 400,000, and the old Brun & Chaix plant made 300,000. The Valley's thirty-nine wineries totaled about 3,000,000 gallons.

A big story for Napa wine in 1909 came from Howell Mountain when Edwin Angwin sold his 1,700-acre estate to the teetotaling Seventh Day Adventist Church. He had settled here in 1874 and established a popular tourist facility that became the hub of the mountain's development. People such as Ambrose Bierce had passed their time among Angwin's pines and at his great swimming pool. The *Star* offered that this was the biggest real estate deal in Napa County history. The sale was settled in August and a month later doors were opened to the students at the church's new Pacific College, later Pacific Union College. The phylloxera also arrived on the mountain and the difficulties of transporting grapes and wine to the Valley had grown with the years. W. S. Keyes' death in 1907 had been a blow to the winegrowing community here, as well. Much of Rancho La Jota was now owned by E. C. Aiken, editor of *Sunset* magazine, but no winegrower. Fred Hess and others continued to produce some Howell Mountain wine, but the great days of the district were over—for now.

Wine for rail shipment is pumped from the tank on the truck into large wooden tanks inside the railroad car. Ca. 1912.

All the new acres coming into production in California and Napa in 1910 should have clobbered prices, but the European vintage was a disaster. André Simon recalled that there was "practically no good wine." He thought it was "one of the worst vintages."[32] As a result Eastern demand for California goods held firm. The Napa crop was short, as usual, but the quality was deemed excellent. John Wheeler thought it the best in his memory. Gier said that it was the best since 1886. The vines planted since 1900 had come to maturity. Certainly the focus on wine grape varieties was far more orderly than before the phylloxera had sorted things out. In 1910 less than a dozen varieties made up more than 90 percent of the Valley's red wine production; in 1890 more than a score would have gone into the same percentage.

The Napa vineyard stabilized between 1910 and 1911 at about 16,000 acres. From this point to 1920 there was a gradual decline in acreage, due to concern over Prohibition and the attraction to other fruit and nut crops. Something more than 5,000 acres of wine grapes would disappear from the Napa Valley in the next decade, but gradually, as the result of many additional agro-economic factors.

We have already discussed the revolution in Valley life occasioned by the automobile, trolley, telephone, and other things electric. But there was no demographic revolution in the Valley. The county's population had begun the century at about 16,000 and by 1910 was up to not much more than 19,000. Over half the population lived in Napa (7,000) and St. Helena (3,500).

The county was in step with the political wisdom of this progressive age. Women's suffrage, the initiative, referendum and recall all went on the books and Napa supported them all. In 1912 St. Helena got a new high school and paved its main street. Many of the Valley wine cellars now had electricity.

The 1911 vintage year was short again in Napa, with a total yield of little more than a ton per acre. A cool summer and low sugars hurt quality but not prices. The use of cultured yeasts and sulfur dioxide in fermentations had now become common throughout the state and was a boon to wine quality. The CWA signed up Napa growers for long-term grape contracts, sometimes for five years, which enhanced the growers' economic sense of well-being. In an era of general price stability in agriculture, such contracts helped increase the number of locally-owned automobiles on Valley roads.

Another sign of the times was the growth of Napa wine sales in glass instead of bulk. Between 1905 and 1910 this aspect of the local trade grew by sixty percent. But wine wasn't Napa's only prosperous industry. The value of Napa's prune crop was slightly higher than that of wine grapes. Actually, money earned from production of butter, cheese, and poultry products amounted to more here than for either fruit product. And if one wanted to spend some of these agricultural dollars in San Francisco, a person could catch the 6:24 morning trolley out of St. Helena and be in the city by 9 AM, by way of the Vallejo ferry.

Theodore Gier expanded his holdings on the Valley floor in 1911 when he purchased the Bergfeld Winery. Inglenook was now back on line, its cellar operating again with lots of new planting, particularly to Petite Sirah, the current darling for blending quality "Burgundy" here. Expansion continued to be the order of the day at BV, although de Latour's personal bad luck seemed never-ending. His home burned down in 1910 and next year he was almost killed by a runaway. But he was soon on the rails for the East Coast pushing Beaulieu's wine sales in glass.

The 1912 vintage was another ugly one in Napa Valley. The dry spring had cut the crop. Then the weather had been just bad enough in late May to ruin the berry set. The resulting short crop was forced in early by September rains that hurt the quality of the Zinfandel wines. The final count again showed little more than a ton per bearing acre and barely 2,000,000 gallons of mediocre wine.

The September deluge just missed the St. Helena Vintage Festival, called off last year for want of interest, but pushed heartily in 1912 by the local winegrowing community. It lasted four days with parades, concerts, exhibits, and banquets, presided over by Queen Inez Forni. The award for the best exhibit went to the Krug Winery, which displayed the old press that Charles Krug had first used in 1858. It was a lively and happy celebration of a really ill-fated event—Vintage 1912.

After the grapes were in, the *Star* broached a very serious matter. The short crop again had seen local wineries purchase lots of Central Valley grapes. The turmoil now stemmed from the fact that a good part of this wine was leaving the Valley as "Napa wine." The newspaper called for the creation of a "winemakers' Roll of Honor," and encouraged local producers to sign a pledge of honesty in the matter. Virtually every major producer did sign up, including the CWA, but the pledge did not cover grapes from Yolo County, where several Napa producers had vineyards. The thing that was making people mad were the grapes from the San Joaquin Valley. Yolo grapes in Napa wine were almost as traditional as the *Star*.[33]

The Napa viticultural magic worked again in 1913. In the face of generally poor quality and a short state vintage, the local product was up 25 percent, still rather short, but widely acclaimed for its quality. There had been almost no rainy season and the spring frosts were bad, but harvest conditions were perfect and everyone except those with long-term CWA contracts was smiling; prices for the 1913 grapes jumped up about 25 percent above contract level. This year Vintage Queen Montana Bohler was able to reign over a much happier and prosperous throng.

No sooner had the festival concluded than the worst forest fire in Napa history whipped through the eastern hills. Centered in Chiles Valley, the blaze destroyed homes and structures all over the area, taking two lives and severely roasting several mountain vineyards. If the fire's heat didn't capture a person's attention at vintage time, he couldn't miss the torrid smell of corruption coming from St. Helena the same week as the fire. A Napa sheriff's detective was arrested at Madame Selowsky's notorious Pope Street Stone Bridge Saloon, a local brothel, for accepting a bribe from the lovely proprietress. She had tipped off the St. Helena police, who obviously were no strangers at her establishment.[34]

The 1914 vintage year began with the heaviest storms the Valley had experienced since 1877. On the first day of the year the Valley was under water. Barrels floated out the doors at Larkmead to be recovered days later a half mile away. On the last day of 1913 seven inches of rain fell on Napa.

There were the usual spring frosts, coupled with a cool summer that seemed to bode no good for the coming vintage. But the eyes of Americans everywhere were riveted now on events in Europe. The assassination in June of an Austrian archduke by a Serbian youth at some place called Sarajevo had thrust European civilization into one of the greatest military conflicts in its history. For now Americans looked on with detached interest to the dramatic events that culminated on the French River Marne in early September. But this war, which was to last four more years, would have a terrific impact on Napa's wine industry. But Napa wine men did view the situation with unconcealed anticipation. "Profits will naturally be greater. . . . California stands to benefit greatly," said Theodore Gier, who well understood that Rhine wine on the tables of New York consumers would be scarce indeed for some time.

The Wilson Administration's September war tax laid twelve cents duty on each gallon of American wine, but the gloom lifted very soon as the demand for California wine leapt up dramatically. When the war broke out Cresta Blanca's Clarence Wetmore was in London and reported that Britain would soon be lapping up California Rieslings. After the Germans captured Rheims on September 3, California sparkling and carbonated wine producers began taking a special interest in the effects of the conflict.[35]

A very warm September saved the quality of the Napa Vintage 1914, which amounted to about 3,500,000 gallons. Very good prices prevailed, although quality was nothing better than ordinary.

THE INNOCENT FAIR

The idea was to add another international exposition to the growing list and to have the opening of the Panama Canal act as the unifying theme for the occasion. The San Francisco supporters began organizing in 1909 and put together a very powerful campaign against New Orleans, the most powerful contender. On January 31, 1911 Congress gave the nod to

California and work toward the 1915 Panama-Pacific International Exposition (PPIE) began in earnest.

Everyone in Northern California knew full well that part of the purpose behind the effort was to show the world that the city on the Golden Gate, and Northern California in general, had risen from the devastating effects of the 1906 Earthquake and Fire. Another theme that would become important was the hope for universal peace, since the 1915 fair took place but six months after the "guns of August" had ushered in the gigantic armed conflict which kept many nations of the world from participating in the event.

The final result was surely a statement of the hopes and beliefs of the American people, still largely agrarian but fully thrust into the later stages of the industrial revolution. It was a marvelous fair with virtually every aspect of early twentieth-century life exposed in an atmosphere of wondrous splendor and beauty. In columnist Herb Caen's words, it was "the most ambitious project of its kind to be carried off in style" by a city San Francisco's size. For the California wine industry it was certainly a symbolic statement of where it had been and what it had become.[36]

The wine judges at the Panama-Pacific International Exposition in 1915. Second from the right is Charles Carpy.

An exhibit association for the California wine industry was formed in July 1912 with Gier, de Latour, Salmina, and W. W. Lyman representing the Napa Valley. Horatio Stoll, the renowned industry publicist who later founded *Wines & Vines*, traveled all over the state putting together a series of movies depicting life among the vines and in the cellars of California's winegrowers. These acted as an attractive centerpiece for the California viticultural and wine exhibit.

Over 100,000 people watched the bucolic scenes carefully edited by Stoll to represent wine and viticulture in their purist state of innocence. They particularly admired the extended scenes from last year's St. Helena Festival. As we shall see, the specter of prohibition was now hovering over the state's industry and everything California's wine men did at the fair aimed to represent

California wine as the product of happy, solid farmers and dedicated entrepreneurs, whose tidy wineries placed a sound beverage on the table of ordinary Americans. There was virtually no emphasis on the growing industrial character of wine production in California, and none on grape brandy and fortified ports and sherries regularly sold in most of the country's saloons.[37]

July 14 was Bastille Day, and at the PPIE it was also Wine Day. An international jury was installed to evaluate the hundreds of California wines on exhibit. They handed out awards by the bushel. There were twenty-one "Grand Prizes" and forty-eight "Medals of Honor." Then came 167 gold medals, the third-highest award.

Napa producers reaped their share of the medals, but it is somewhat difficult to determine which wines were actually made from Napa grapes, since the growing industrial character of Napa wine now tended to wash away precise origin. What counted was the brand name, particularly wine made by the CWA. One can identify their Greystone Hock, which won a grand prize, but who knows how many Napa grapes went into the blend? One could not even be sure that it was made at Greystone.

Other Napa Grand Prizes went to Inglenook for its sherry and to Krug for its Sauvignon vert. Larkmead captured three Medals of Honor, Brun & Chaix and Inglenook one each. In the gold medal category Inglenook, now operated by the Arnhold Company, went wild with twenty awards. Beringer and Larkmead received three each.

What is remarkable about the contestants and the award winners at the PPIE from Napa, and from other Northern California dry wine districts, is the paucity of entries from such dedicated enthusiasts who submitted wines in great number twenty-two years earlier in the wine competition at Chicago's Columbian Exposition. Gone were the names of such proud individuals as Morris Estee, Seneca Ewer, Charles Carpy, H. W. Crabb, Louis Zierngibl, Otto Norman, Tiburcio Parrot, W. S. Keyes, and Jacob Schram. Many family-controlled survivors, such as Beringer and Larkmead, were now large-scale producers. De Latour did not enter the competition.

The Napa pioneers and most of the second wave were now gone. The last leaf had fallen with the death of H. A. Pellet in 1912. There was now little left to suggest the individual enthusiasm which had marked the Valley's wine scene in the eighties and nineties. The days when the members of the St. Helena Vinicultural Club met at Vintners' Hall to sample one another's wares were gone. Now when Napa producers and growers came together it was most likely an industry-sponsored event pitted against the threat of prohibition.

One might wonder why another wave of enthusiasts had not settled in the Valley. The answer comes from an examination of the dominant spirit of the times. This was the Progressive Era, when large numbers of Americans were persuaded to look at the evils of society and to correct them, most often through government action.

In the fifteen years prior to the PPIE, Americans had come to be especially conscious of the evils of drink, particularly the evils of the saloon and its effects on the American family. The California wine industry had done next to nothing during the formative years of this movement to disassociate its image from that of the saloon. Now it was too late. Few Americans drank wine and all alcoholic beverages were associated in the popular mind with the evils of drink. It was no longer an attractive thing to establish, or even to own, a wine estate. People with such money to invest had become sensitive to the stigma attached to any kind of participation in the liquor trade. Napa's wonderful wine estates were changing hands, but more often than not, the new owners were primarily interested in the beauty of the land and could not care less about growing wine grapes. And they did not need a degree in economics to see that prunes paid more per acre than grapes. The 30 percent decline in the acreage of Napa wine grapes between 1914 and 1920 reflects these changes.[38]

Historians often picture the almost euphoric and certainly prosperous years from 1898 to 1915 as an age of innocence, one which ended suddenly with the realities of the Great War. The scenes in Horatio Stoll's movies certainly created portions of that image. But these scenes would soon become a truly nostalgic image of the Napa Valley and its wine industry's past. Napa would face up to the war much like any rural American community. But this war would also bring the reality of national prohibition, an institution that would destroy all but the most slender threads of continuity in the history of Napa wine.

NOTES FOR CHAPTER EIGHT

1. Star, 1//5/1900, 2/1/1901, 3/15/1901; Register, 2/23/1900.
2. PWSR, 9/30/1901; Register, 10/11/1901.
3. Register, 8/9/1901, 1/31/1902, 3/28/1902. This paper was among the first to announce that the "Japs Must Go!"
4. Star, 9/7/1900; PWSR, 1/31/1905. Recently the Carneros Quality Alliance put together a good in-house history of the district.
5. Peninou and Greenleaf, 34-35. Eshcol was a brook where Moses' followers are said to have cut a cluster of grapes so large it was born "between two upon a staff." Numbers. 13:17-24.
6. John Wickels. "Footsteps in the Sands of Vintage 1870." Napa Historical Society, 1979.
7. Transactions, 1904; PWSR, 3/31/1903, 12/31/1905; Star, 10/19/1906, 6/2/1939; Register, 3/7/1902; Wines & Vines (August 1943).
8. Star, 7/6/1906, 3/15/1907.
9. NVWLA I: 79-90; Haynes, 11-12.
10. Lorin Sorensen. Beringer (St. Helena 1989): 70-72.

11. NVWLA II: 79-90; Star, 6/22/1903, 4/8/1904, 9/20/1907.

12. NVWLA I: 123; II, 283-296; Star, 5/31/1903, 4/8/1904, 9/20/1907.

13. Star, 2/1/1901, 2/15/1901; Haynes, 49-52. The visitor was greeted at Hess's Pine Crest by a sign on a large pine tree. "I reign over fields and hills/ While Frederick Hess foots all the bills." The Brun & Chaix Winery on White Cottage Road has come back to life as the Woltner Estate Winery. Liparita was back in production in 1989.

14. Vintage (July 1974): 44-49; (August 1974): 46-51 is a good historical series on this winery.

15. NVWLA I: 53-102. This oral history by John Ghisolpho has excellent detail on Calistoga from 1900 to the 1930s.

16. Register, 10/21/1912.

17. Star, 6/8/1900, 7/19/1901; Theodore Saloutos. "The Immigrant in Pacific Coast Agriculture, 1880-1940," in Agriculture in the Development of the Far West, 185; Charles L. Sullivan. "California Wine Has German Roots." Wine Spectator (June 16, 1983).

18. Star, 12/5/1902, 4/16/1912; San Jose Mercury, 4/3/1899; PWSR, 12/20/1893, 6/9/1894, 9/23/1895; San Francisco News, 10/16/1939.

19. See Chapter 4, Note 21.

20. PWSR, 12/31/1900, 1/31/1901; Star, 1/10/1902; AWP 9/1902.

21. PWSR, 9/30/1904; Star, 9/21/1906.

22. Register, 9/22/1906; Star 4/29/1910.

23. PWSR, 12/31/1905; AWP, 6/1904; San Francisco Call, 5/12/1897.

24. AWP, 6/1906, 2/1908, 1/1912, 5/31/1914; PWSR, 1/31/1915; Star, 9/18/1908, 11/25/1910, 4/24/1914.

25. Register, 2/6/1903; PWSR, 6//30/1903, 4/30/1905, 3/31/1907, 2/29/1912; AWP, 7/1903; Livermore Herald, 8/17/1901, 11/17/1903.

26. Star, 11/8/1912; PWSR, 6/20/1914; San Jose Mercury, 5/23/1922; AWP, 8/1913; Livermore Herald, 9/13/1918, 1/9/1931; Wines & Vines (November 1932); Teiser and Harroun, 186.

27. Star, 4/23/1903, 1/19/1906. Husmann had nine California stations under his supervision. The others were at Sonoma, Geyserville, Lodi, Cucamonga, Mountain View, Livermore, Concord, and Fresno. PWSR, 3/31/1904. A good picture of his work can be seen in USDA Bulletin 209 (August 6, 1915) and in the Star, 8/10/1906. He retired to Napa in 1932 and died there in 1939.

28. PWSR, 6/1907; Star, 12/26/1906, 1/11/1907, 12/20/1907. This great complex still stands, now a naval storage facility with few hints at its former function. Charles L. Sullivan. "Winehaven." California Winelands (August 1985); Chronicle, 12/26/1971.

29. Star, 8/14/1908.

30. USDA Yearbook, 1960, 24-25; Star, 5/15/1908.

31. Register, 4/1/1907; Star, 1/17/1908. Numerous articles aimed at California's new tourists encouraged winery visits. See: Outing (February 1906); Overland Monthly (September 1908); Sunset (February 1910).

32. André Simon. Wine and Spirits (London 1919): 272, and Vintagewise (London 1945): 91.

33. Star, 11/15/1912.

34. Star, 9/26/1913, 3/8/1990.

35. PWSR, 8/31/1914, 9/31/1914; Star, 9/15/1914.

36. Ben Macomber. The Jewel City (San Francisco 1915): 12-14; Frank Morton Todd. The Story of the Exposition (New York 1921): IV, 302, 366-367; Chronicle, 5/20/1990.

37. PWSR, 7/1912, 8/1912, 10/31/1913, 6/30/1915.

38. Napa's official county exhibit at the PPIE emphasized its stone bridges, with virtually no mention of Napa wine. Official Guide, PPIE (1915): 111.

DRY YEARS

The land used in producing grapes should be allowed to relapse into wilderness …
Pension the men engaged in the wine industry …

—C. A. WHITNEY
1913

THE SEEMINGLY CHANCE CONVERGENCE OF THREE HISTORICAL FACTORS
brought national prohibition to the United States in 1920. A long and
not particularly successful temperance/prohibition crusade was at
work at the turn of the century when the Progressive movement took off,
attempting to deal with the nation's problems through corrective public
policy. Then, when interest in prohibition seemed to be waning, America
entered a war that challenged every citizen to sacrifice for a common cause.
Out of the tangle of ardent patriotism, mixed purposes, and cunning deceit
came an amendment to the Constitution and a federal enforcement law that

gave the country an almost bone-dry public policy. Prohibition was imposed on California and the nation by a well-organized league of zealots who took advantage of the historical moment.

California never succumbed to the lures of the prohibitionists. Offered this policy in election after election, starting in 1914, the Golden State's voters turned down every prohibition proposition on the statewide ballot, even rejecting a state enforcement act in 1920 meant to support the national Volstead Act. When the dust cleared in January 1920, the American people had been saddled with laws that they were willing to try, in a sense of public sacrifice and in hopes of solving a very serious social problem.

THE ATTACK ON SALOONS

Prohibition made little headway in California before 1900. The right of communities to ban liquor, their so-called "local option," was introduced in 1873, but was later thrown out by the courts. Still, restrictions on the sale of liquor were generally accepted as legitimate public policy here. Napa folks understood and accepted this principle in the dry zone set up around the State Asylum there in 1874.

In California the national Prohibition Party, formed in 1869, and the Women's Christian Temperance Union (WCTU) never had a strong following. But in 1893 the founding of the Anti-Saloon League (ASL) in Ohio brought a strong national dry leader into the field. It was one of the most effective national pressure groups in American history. Its first California chapter was formed in 1898.[1]

The ASL's most fertile field here between 1900 and 1920 was in Southern California. There the population explosion since the 1880s had peopled a region that, by 1910, was overwhelmingly white, Protestant, and predominantly Midwest in origin. In contrast, Northern California had been a cosmopolitan demographic mix since the 1850s. In 1910, 68 percent of San Francisco's population was foreign-born and the Bay Area was predominantly Roman Catholic. The new immigration that had flooded the American shores since 1880 had originated mostly in southern and eastern Europe. By far most of these who made it to California settled in the north. In 1910 about 30 percent of Napa County was foreign-born, half of these from Germany and Italy in almost perfect numerical balance. But if one includes the sons and daughters of the foreign-born in the calculus, most Napans were not more than one generation from their Old World origins.

The ASL attack in California was aimed at the saloon and the roadhouse, which most Americans, even most Northern Californians, resented. They had good reason for their concern. Between 1870 and 1915 the U. S. per capita consumption of alcohol had risen almost 50 percent, and most of this rise came in the category of distilled spirits.[2]

After 1900 the country united in attacking political corruption, economic monopoly, and moral disintegration. It was logical that one of the targets of some Progressive leaders would have been the saloon and liquor trade. Progressive muckraker journalists ripped at the corrupt influence of the liquor industry. After 1902 state after state east of the Mississippi passed laws outlawing the saloon. By 1919 every western state allowing women to vote, except California, had accomplished this goal. The Progressive attack aimed at the corrupting plutocracy of the distillers and brewers, who controlled over 70 percent of the nation's saloons before 1917. But this attack remained quite narrow at first. Senator Morris Sheppard, the author of the Eighteenth Amendment, declared, "I am fighting the liquor trade. I am not in any sense aiming to prevent the personal use of alcoholic beverages."[3]

THE CALIFORNIA DRY CAMPAIGN

In California the Progressives tended to be dry in the south and wet in the north. Certain technicalities in California law made it possible after 1902 for counties and unincorporated areas to eliminate saloons and, by 1907, large areas of Southern California had done so. The next year the ASL began an all-out campaign to give California a real local option law.

The California wine industry's response to the dry movement's gains was to form the California Grape Protective Association (CGPA), led by Andrea Sbarboro of the Italian Swiss Colony. His goal was to separate the wine industry from the brewers and distillers in the public mind and to promote wine as a wholesome temperance drink. But for now most wine industry leaders were not listening and formed a common cause with the liquor interests in opposing local option.[4] In August of 1908 Napa's CGPA chapter was formed, led by W. W. Lyman, John Wheeler, Jacob Beringer, and Felix Salmina.

In 1910 the Progressives captured control of the California Republican Party and nominated Hiram Johnson for governor, a supporter of local option but a mild opponent of prohibition. His democratic opponent was Napa's Theodore Bell, whose attitude toward prohibition needs no discussion here. Johnson won and in the historic 1911 legislature one of the many reform bills passed was a measure that became the Wylie Local Option Law. In 1912 this statute brought the dry crusade into almost every local election campaign in the state. Also on the books now were women's suffrage, initiative and referendum, all supported by Napa voters. Women's votes strengthened the dry forces; initiative and referendum would bring to California ballots a continuous flood of prohibition propositions until 1924.

The first local option elections under the new law took place in April 1912. Sbarboro and Horatio Stoll covered the state carrying the CGPA message. The results were a mixed bag. Most communities voted wet but there were also many in the dry column, particularly from the Central Valley and Southern California. What startled many wine men were the votes of some communities where the wine industry was of great importance. In Northern California, Los Gatos and Mountain View, both important wine towns, voted dry. In Southern California some local option elections meant that several wineries could produce wine but make no retail sales in their area.

The real test for the North Coast wine region came in the fall elections. Napa County dry petitions placed the retail sale of alcoholic beverages on the ballot in three rural districts. At a time when public opinion polls were not even in their infancy, the outcome of almost any election was in doubt until the votes were counted. St. Helena actually had an ASL chapter that asked voters, "Are not your homes, your boys, your girls and your community of more value than the few gallons of your wine used in the resorts affected by the votes in your district?" In the southern part of the county the battle was heated. Here it was understood that the question was not whether a few swell spas for the rich would lose their liquor licenses, but whether the sordid roadhouses below Napa around Soscol and on the Sonoma Highway would be shut down. Large anti-dry meetings were held here, addressed by Stoll and Gier. The local press was full of correspondence on both sides, the dry forces attacking the wine men as defenders of roadhouses and saloons.

The end result was a not particularly over-whelming wet vote of 58 percent in Napa County. Only 1,777 people actually voted; a switch of 150 votes would have placed most of rural Napa County in the dry column. It is clear that even in the wine country many were impressed by the evils of the saloon and were willing to get rid of them. In Sonoma they did just that, at least in the countryside. But the Sonoma ordinance was strictly an anti-saloon proposition and was not meant to touch the wine industry there. When the voting was over Napa remained the only county in the Northern California

Theodore Bell.

Gun toting Napa

district attorney and

wine industry leader

in the fight against

prohibition.

wine country in which every local option measure had been defeated. By the end of the year California had twenty-two dry towns and seventy-eight dry supervisorial districts.[5]

In 1913 the CGPA was able to get a new Viticultural Commission through the Legislature, proving for the moment, at least, that ASL opposition was not the kiss of death—yet. Not a Napa man was appointed to the new board, which is not surprising, since Napa wine men had been instrumental in destroying the old board in 1893. In the public discussion of the matter the state WCTU called for the destruction of the California wine industry, "which is responsible for so much that is inimical to the highest welfare of our people." Really what these women were complaining about were the millions of gallons of fortified wines and beverage brandy sold in the country's saloons, which the wine industry was always able to overlook when attacked as part of America's liquor problem. It didn't take California's wine men long to get the gist of the ASL program.[6] Their motto said it all. "California Dry in 1914—The Nation Dry in 1916." In February the CGPA was reorganized with lots more fighting money. Napa's Bismark Bruck was elected vice president. It was decided that he would run for the State Assembly, so that wine men would have one of their own on the floor of the legislature. Theodore Bell hit the lecture circuit, taking part in a series of heated public debates with dry leaders. CGPA began publishing a monthly bulletin, "The California Grape Grower," written by Horatio Stoll. This mimeo sheet was the forerunner of his *Wines & Vines*, which began formal publication in 1919 as the *California Grape Grower*.

The big fight in 1914 concerned the statewide prohibition initiative that went on the November ballot. It was soundly defeated, with almost 60 percent of California's voters saying NO to "California Dry." In Napa the wet vote was 5,328–2,040, in St. Helena 551–93. Some thought that the wet victory came primarily as a result of the high repute of the wine industry and the effectiveness of the CGPA campaign. Bismark Bruck was easily elected to the Assembly and Theodore Bell became the full time legal council of the CGPA. For him the election had been too close. He was now determined to "take the drunkenness out of drink." He was convinced that the California wine industry had to take a strong hand in trying to reform the liquor industry. If this meant that the saloon had to go, so be it. Otherwise the wine industry would be overwhelmed by the same wave that would destroy beer and spirits. But wine industry leaders in the CGPA refused to back his position.[7]

The dry campaign began to intensify after the ASL was able to get two state propositions on the 1916 ballot. One was bone-dry and the other aimed only at the saloon. Theodore Bell saw the handwriting on the wall and again asked the wine industry to disassociate itself from the liquor trade and the saloon in the coming fight. At first the CGPA leaders seemed willing to go along, but in the end were cowed by the economic pressure placed on them by the liquor interests, which controlled a large part of the distribution network for California wine in the east.

Meanwhile the ASL decided to oppose any attempt by the wine industry to take part in the reform, limitation, or elimination of the saloon in California. The league's president made their purpose clear: "We naturally prefer to fight saloons unsupported by the wine men, and then turn around afterwards and finish off the wine men." Bismark Bruck's bill for saloon reform never came to a vote in the legislature, opposed by the liquor interests and the drys.

The CGPA put together an enormously effective campaign against the two 1916 dry ballot propositions. Stoll and his crew produced four one-reel movies which concentrated on the wholesome life of California's small vineyardists. These were distributed free to movie houses. Prizes were awarded to schoolchildren for the best essays on the importance of saving California's vineyards. Along country roads, throughout the state, a billboard would announce the coming demise of the vineyard surrounding the sign. The CGPA stress on this contented and bucolic aspect of winegrowing infuriated the drys, but they could do nothing about it. The CGPA campaign worked. Both propositions went down to defeat, but it was closer than in 1914. Now it appeared that 45 percent of California's voters were willing to sacrifice the state's wine industry, if doing so would destroy the saloon. In Napa the bone-dry initiative lost 5,261–1,985. The anti-saloon measure was a little closer, 4,922–2,329.

In November 1916, Woodrow Wilson was returned to the White House for a second term, but ASL leaders were most concerned with the Congressional races. The election upped the number of dry legislators to a point that seemed to promise enough dry votes to pass a prohibition amendment to the Constitution. In California the ASL turned to the national campaign. Their president conceded that "We are much more ready for national prohibition than state prohibition in California." In other words, so far as the ASL was concerned, Californians were going to get prohibition whether they wanted it or not.[8]

Finally California wine men got the picture. They now rushed to separate themselves from the image of the saloon and liquor trade. When the CGPA met in San Francisco after the holidays, Bruck, Salmina, and Ewer joined other directors in declaring: "This Association is not wedded to the American saloon." So belated a decision for divorce was doomed to failure. Bruck again introduced his saloon reform bill, which passed the Assembly but failed in the Senate. Meanwhile, John Wheeler didn't need anyone to tell him what a smart Napa vineyardist should be doing that dormant season. He was ripping out vines and planting prune trees. Over 100,000 prune trees were planted in the

Valley this season. The number would skyrocket in the next two years, as more than 2,000 acres of Napa vines were uprooted.

The drive toward national prohibition was accelerated when President Wilson called Congress into special session to ask for war against Germany. He got it on April 6, 1917. The fact of war now called for greater efficiency and sacrifice from everyone. Foodstuffs could not be wasted on booze. Our "boys" had to be protected from the evils of drink when they were away from home. Women and girls had to be protected from the evil bred by booze while the "boys" were away. By the end of the summer Congress forbade the use of foodstuffs to produce beverage spirits. For the moment wine and beer were exempted.

In California in the fall the big political question was the Rominger Bill, a proposal that would outlaw the saloon and spirits, but would keep table wine legal. Much of the wine industry, including the CGPA, supported it. But radical drys saw this as a trick to save the wine industry from the ax. Moderate drys were for it. The bill passed the Senate, but failed in the Assembly by three votes. Now the CGPA decided to place the bill on the ballot in 1918, but Napa wine men balked. The fact that the ASL was supporting the measure was enough to convince Bismark Bruck that this was the first step on the road to statewide prohibition. Except for Napa, the entire California wine industry got on the Rominger bandwagon next year. Napa's wine men continued to oppose these attempts to change the industry's image at this late date. Napa's Frank Busse argued that this proposition "deliberately proposes to protect the rich man's table and to send the poor man to the bootlegger." Cranky as ever, Napa wine men would have none of it and in August voted to quit the CGPA.[9] The Napa leaders' opposition appears to have been ideologically based, really quite idealistic. It certainly did not derive from self-interest. Bismark Bruck's opposition was typical of Napa's independent producers. In June 1918 they canceled the upcoming vintage festival.[10]

In fact, all this sound and

While the fight over prohibition raged, the St. Helena Vintage Festival continued.

fury in California meant almost nothing. The Sheppard prohibition amendment had just sailed through the Senate 65–20. It set forth an almost bone-dry national policy that would outlaw everything about beverage alcohol except legal possession by private individuals for home consumption.

Behind the overwhelming support in Congress was a fear of appearing anything but totally patriotic. A jingoistic anti-German campaign fueled the anti-liquor fires. The drys simply needed to read off the names of the German owners of the great breweries. In Northern California this frenzy was whipped up by such as Stanford's President David Starr Jordan who accused German brewers of having "rendered thousands of our men inefficient and thus crippling the Republic in its war on Prussian militarism." From Britain the words of Prime Minister David Lloyd George were happily spread by the ASL: "Drink is doing us more damage in the war than all the German submarines put together." It would take a Congressman with a very secure seat to stand against the amendment. In December the House voted 282–128 to submit it to the states for ratification. Five of California's nine representatives voted NO.[11]

1914 — 1918

We left our narrative of Napa vintages in 1914 and the good times in the following summer at the great exposition in San Francisco. Life went on much as before in the wine country, whatever the threat from dry forces. The Great War in Europe was always on people's minds as it gradually settled into a gigantic stalemate. In the 1914 wine grape season the number of freight cars loaded with lugs of California grapes and headed for eastern markets and home winemakers rose significantly. To date this trickle had not been noticed much by industry leaders, except in Lodi and Fresno, where most shipments originated. The first refrigerated car in this trade had headed for Chicago from Lodi in 1910. By 1915 the number would reach 750 cars. We shall see more of this trade later.[12]

1915 brought a sudden crash in the state industry that depressed grape and wine prices to levels of the nineties. The downturn was the result of high inventories and overall decline in demand. Actual U.S. wine consumption in 1915 was about 40 percent below the 1910 level. It would rise again during the war, but not to previous levels. The CWA at Greystone honored its contracts but wouldn't buy an additional grape. Much of the white wine crop was not even picked. The general gloom this fall was increased by the death of Jacob Beringer in October. Frederick, the other Beringer brother, had died in 1901.

The Napa vintage in 1916 was a short one. A May 7–8 killer frost destroyed many young vineyards. It was the worst freeze since 1887. Prices rose to more than double the unpleasantly low 1915 levels and the grapes were almost all in when the October rains hit. The resulting wines were of excellent quality with attractive flavor concentration.

Meanwhile the demand for California wine soared and prices went through the ceiling. The war had virtually cut off wine imports from Europe. About 3,000,000 gallons per month were shipped out of the state during the last half of 1917. Napa wineries were virtually empty when the new vintage got under way. Every Napa grape had been sold before one was harvested this year. Weather conditions were good and the tonnage was double the 1916 crop. It was common knowledge that the Valley's winegrowers, to a man and woman, were able to pay off their mortgages this year. Also noteworthy were the 4,000 carloads of California wine grapes shipped east this season, a trade in which Napa was not yet a participant.

In the first months of 1918 all eyes were focused on events in Europe. American troops were pouring into France by the hundreds of thousands. But people still had to tend to business. Vineyards in Napa continued to disappear, 110,000 new prune trees taking their place this season. John Wheeler replaced thirty more acres of grapes, this time with currants. The CWA had given up and was liquidating its huge assets as quickly as possible. Their president stated glumly that "further pursuit of business with a future so uncertain is unwise."

THE EIGHTEENTH AMENDMENT

The course of the war knocked almost everything else off the front page of newspapers in 1918. But the back pages told how dry forces in Congress pushed for full statutory wartime prohibition, to include beer and wine. They finally put it through Congress on November 21, making production of all alcoholic beverages illegal on July 1, 1919. Many wondered at the logic of this measure, since the Armistice had been signed ten days before Congress passed the bill. Dry forces argued that the war was still a technical reality until a peace treaty was signed. A compliant Congress had bought this idea. Logic had nothing to do with the matter.

State after state ratified the prohibition amendment. The South and Midwest led in the first wave. In California the dry movement worked overtime on the question. ASL spokesman Franklin Hichborn called on his fellow California drys to go over the top, "take the last trench."

In California the vote on the state prohibition propositions took place four days before the Armistice. At this moment the country was being swept by the worst epidemic of influenza in its history. In Napa the weekly list of sick and dead was appalling. The statewide voter turnout was 35 percent smaller than in the previous off-year election. Both the bone-dry and the anti-saloon measures were defeated.

When the 1918 Napa vintage began in September there was a lot of talk here about the prospects for shipping grapes east—next year. For now it was all pure profit.

Grape quality was ordinary, with a cool fall full of rainstorms. Pickers, mostly in masks to guard against influenza, made wonderful money, working long hours to get the grapes in early. Low sugar was no problem for grapegrowers with these kinds of prices. Throughout the Valley there was a great Armistice celebration after the harvest. But in Rutherford, at the end of the vintage, most of the commercial area of the town burned down.

For all the good times the future looked ominous. Theodore Bell advised Napa growers to prune, cultivate, and hope. He was sure that something would be done to get around the wartime prohibition rule. Meanwhile, the national prohibition amendment still had only fourteen of the necessary thirty-six states on line.

But on January 2, 1919 Michigan ratified. Then between January 7 and 9 five more states came over. In California the Senate ratified on January 10 with a 25–14 vote. The Assembly put it over three days later, 48–28. It took three-fourths of the states' approval to get national prohibition, but in individual states a simple majority was sufficient. In historian J. S. Blocker's words, "skillful use of prohibitionist minorities created legislative majorities."[13]

Then came the deluge. Between the 13th and 17th nineteen states ratified the Eighteenth Amendment, and it became law, to go into effect January 16, 1920. To this day no historian has put together the story of how this five-day burst of dry energy was harnessed.

Napa wine men didn't know what to do. The overwhelming rush of dry victories had come in a period of but nine days. No neutral observers had predicted this result. The *Star* lamented that "the beautiful vineyards that have been the pride of the state are doomed." On February 28 a huge group of growers and producers met at the Liberty Theater in St. Helena. Theodore Bell spoke to the crowd but could offer little but illusory hope. For now the big question was the 1919 vintage; what would happen to the grapes after the July wartime prohibition law went into effect?

CWA tested the waters on July 11 by making a huge shipment of Greystone wine under a bill of lading marked "sacramental and medicinal." No one complained. Meanwhile local eyes were really starting to focus on the eastern wine grape market. A representative of an eastern shipping firm arrived in the Valley in mid-July offering top dollar for red wine grapes. Suddenly there was a huge demand for wooden shook to make lug boxes for shipping.

The crop was in great shape, the largest of the century. Frank Cairns and F. J. Merriam, both local men, led the field here in lining up and organizing grape shipments. Cairns had 200,000 lug boxes ready to go when the Napa grapes started coming in. Their first carload left the Valley on September 12. Within a few days buyers from all over the Bay Area were arriving in the Valley with trucks to haul grapes to Oakland and San Francisco for on-the-spot sale.[14]

People wondered whether the government was actually going to allow home winemakers to produce wine. And what about wineries that did not have special licenses for sacramental wine production? On August 22 Theodore Bell called the office of the *Star* to say that winemakers should go ahead and make wine. The IRS was apparently holding fire, not knowing the proper course themselves and far more concerned with controlling the flow of hard stuff.

Gradually the wineries started making wine. On September 12 the CWA began accepting grapes from regular suppliers. Then Larkmead and Lombarda started crushing. To Kalon began making "non-beverage wine" on September 26. By the first week of October buyers from the Bay Area were literally cruising the Napa Valley looking for any lots of grapes not yet sold. On October 3 Bell telegraphed the *Star* to spread the word that home winemaking would be allowed and that the IRS was staying out of the whole wine scene now, so long as the tax revenue laws were obeyed.

When it was all over at the end of October, Napa winegrowers took a deep breath and surveyed the vintage. Lots of wine had been made. It would work its way into various commercial channels, getting around the prohibition rule, but it all had to be done before January 16. Several, like Louis Kortum and Bismark Bruck, made grape juice to be sold as such. John Wheeler had built a copper vacuum evaporator and condenser to produce grape syrup. If the buyer added four parts water and some yeast, a certain chemical reaction would probably take place. There was lots of talk about alternative uses for wine grapes, but for now the obvious use was eastern rail shipment. This season no less than 9,300 carloads of fresh California wine grapes headed for Chicago, New York, Boston, Newark, and other eastern cities with large ethnic populations that were not about to give up their table wine. And for Napa the San Francisco market also looked very good.

THE FRESH GRAPE DEAL

The newly amended Constitution now outlawed the production, sale, and transportation of intoxicating alcoholic beverages. But Congress had to decide what "intoxicating" meant. In fact, Congress had to put together a comprehensive policy to make the Eighteenth Amendment work. The National Prohibition Act, introduced the previous November by Congressman Andrew J. Volstead, was actually written by Wayne Wheeler, the national director of the ASL. Congress could have allowed light wine and beer, but

Wheeler drew the line at 1/2 percent alcohol, thus destroying, as he had promised, the American wine industry. But sacramental and medicinal wines were to be legal.

The way Wheeler wrote the Volstead Act it was bone-dry, but Congress altered it in two ways. First, persons who owned alcoholic beverages before January 16, 1920 could use them in their homes. Also, heads of households were permitted to make cider and fruit juices in their homes. They could not be intoxicating, but they were not strictly held to the 1/2 percent rule. Congress decided that it had to be proved in court that a beverage in question was in fact intoxicating. Thus the salvation of the California wine grape industry.

On January 17, 1920 the *Star* mourned the dawn. "A new order is upon us, for prohibition is here. It came to us while we were sleeping last night and was a reality when we awoke this morning." For Napa and St. Helena residents, whatever their feelings about this new order, most were happy to see the demise of the most obviously outrageous manifestations of the liquor trade in their towns. For the time being the whorehouses and their attendant open bars had to go underground. At first things stayed fairly dry in the Valley, except that wine was everywhere. It was all right as long as they didn't try to sell it. Only occasionally in the first dry years did IRS or Prohibition agents make arrests for illegal wine sales.

Most up-valley Napa vineyardists were busily making money in the first dry years. From 1920 to 1925 wine grape prices in the Napa Valley never fell as low as the boom level of 1918. While America suffered a general agricultural depression from 1921 through the 1930s, Napa vineyardists did not feel the hurt until after 1925. The "fresh grape deal," as it was called, took almost everyone by surprise in 1919, but no one failed to understand the nature of the bonanza.

There seems to have been something almost magical about the home winemaking craze that hit many cities in the twenties. Economic logic seemed to demand that grapes be converted into some easily shipped form, such as a grape concentrate, then be packaged and sent east for sale. Such production was a modest part of the California grape industry in the twenties, but it never gained any kind of enthusiastic following. Most people wanted to see the grapes themselves. There was some kind

Carloads of grapes

were shipped to

Eastern cities for

home wine makers.

Chicago market, 1930.

Source: Wines & Vines.

of aesthetic to the whole operation that never seemed to make very good sense from an economic point of view. But at the bottom line it made perfect sense.

One thing that people at both ends of the deal learned early was that all grapes did not ship the same. Thin-skinned varieties had to be sold in California or not at all. Another quickly learned fact was that white grapes, except for the Muscat of Alexandria, didn't sell. An overwhelming majority of these home winemakers wanted to make a heavily colored, dry red table wine. By 1920 the thick-skinned hybrid Alicante Bouschet was the darling of the eastern trade. Its opaque product resulted from the fact that its free-run juice was dark purple. It was a rare *teinturier,* or dyer, grape. The criteria for keeping a vine in your vineyard now were: thick skin, heavy color, and heavy yield. Other varieties approached the Alicante in these characteristics. Zinfandel qualified for yield and flavor. So did Carignane and Mourvèdre (Mataro). Petite Sirah (Duriff) made it, particularly for color. If one were really interested in flavor, all these latter varieties beat the coarse Alicante. The Muscat was sold in great volume, used mainly to blend with the Alicante to get a little more flavor and to soften the red grape's astringent tannin. By the end of Prohibition the Alicante and Muscat were each making up about 30 percent of California's eastern shipments, Zinfandel about 20 percent, Carignane about 12 percent, and everything else about 8 percent. For Napa the percentages at the end of the planting frenzy in 1926 were: Alicante 40 percent, Petite Sirah 30 percent, Zinfandel 16 percent, Carignane 13 percent, and all others less than 1 percent.

This list obviously mentions practically none of the varieties associated today with the highest quality table wine. One of the negative outcomes of Prohibition in California was the virtual disappearance of almost all first-rate wine grape vines, either ripped up or grafted to shipper varieties. Such grafting was particularly common in Napa. But in parts of Sonoma, Napa, and

A box end from Zinfandel grapes. Cesare Mondavi began shipping grapes east to home wine makers many years before sons Robert and Peter took over the operations of the Charles Krug Winery.

the Livermore Valleys this process was not complete. The San Francisco and Oakland markets were close at hand and here the Alicante was not so popular. In San Francisco the Zinfandel and Carignane were the champions of flavor, and Petite Sirah was desired for color. The Alicante had little following here. Among San Francisco's North Beach connoisseurs it was considered little more than a junk grape.

The Bay Area market used an average of well over 2,000 carloads of Northern California wine grapes each season during Prohibition. This accounts in part for the fact that some prime vineyards in Napa were not completely converted to shipper varieties. There was always a small market for Cabernet Sauvignon among buyers who flocked to the box cars along Drumm Street and along the Embarcadero tracks. You could even sell a little White Riesling or Sémillon, but not much.[15]

In 1920 there was no hesitation in Napa concerning the proper viticultural strategy. There were no more pull-ups. In fact, almost a thousand new acres were planted. For once John Wheeler had been wrong. In June the IRS made the legality of home winemaking unmistakably clear. Every head of a household could make two hundred gallons of fruit juice a year. If the juice fermented the government would have to go into the home and seize it, and then had to prove to a local jury that the fermented juice was "in fact" intoxicating. This was simply not going to happen. Again the Valley was full of grape buyers before the vines had leafed. Merriam and Cairns continued to lead the organization of the market here. Growing conditions in 1920 were favorable and the vineyardists overcropped their vines mercilessly when they did their pruning. The crop was the largest in the Napa Valley since 1891, secured from far fewer acres. Prices were more than double the 1919 level. Many a Napa vineyardist wondered if perhaps Prohibition was such a bad thing after all. Grapes were so valuable that Sheriff Harris was kept hopping, following up on complaints of picked lugs being stolen as they sat in the vineyard.

Napa voters were given a chance to show whether they were willing to change this bonanza for what then appeared to be a possible return to legal light wine. In 1920 the Wright Enforcement Act was placed on the November ballot, sometimes nicknamed the "little Volstead Act." At the time many voters thought that a NO vote might be a sort of first step in the de facto legalization of light wine in commercial channels. The drys were out in force, denouncing opposition to the proposition as a sort of treason against the Constitution. But again the people of California defeated prohibition enforcement, this time by a wider margin than in 1918. Napa said NO 3913–1981. Sonoma was a bit closer, 6564–3534. As it turned out the result did nothing to make light wine legal here.

Planting all over the state continued at a frenzied pace in 1921. In Napa about 700 more acres of Alicante and Petite Bouschet were put in. The crop amounted to less than half the 1920 yield due to terrible spring frosts. Prices remained high, but never in the twenties did they again rise to the heights of 1920.

A Grape Growers Exchange opened in San Francisco to help organize the market during the shipping season. Only about one in five Napa growers took part. This year about 450 freight cars of Napa grapes headed east and about 150 went to the Bay Area market. Just about 10 percent of the local crop was crushed for grape juice, concentrate, and non-beverage wines. Times were so good that the St. Helena Vintage Festival was held again. Governor W. D. Stephens, a dry man through and through, dropped by to crown the queen.

Planting continued apace all over the state in 1922. There was another big crop and prices remained good, but down from last year. Part of the decline came after about a quarter of the crop was caught in fall rains that made swamps of vineyards. Much of the Napa Zinfandel had to be sold for giveaway prices. Just before the vintage the Valley was stunned by the news of Theodore Bell's death in an automobile accident. For Northern California wine men, particularly those of Napa, Theodore Bell was a hero. He had been a no-nonsense law and order district attorney who packed a six-shooter on occasion. He had once actually gunned down a pair of stage coach hijackers. But it was as the legal voice of California wine that he was most admired. He was a political man with the moxie to stand up personally to such as William

Batista Scansi in his newly-planted Petite Sirah vineyard in 1922: site of present day Shafer Vineyards Winery in the Stags Leap District of the Napa Valley.

Jennings Bryan of his own Democratic Party and denounce the Great Commoner as the paid spokesman of those who would deprive Bell's father of the livelihood of his St. Helena vineyard. He was afforded a hero's funeral on September 9 at the Native Sons pavilion in St. Helena.

After the vintage and more than a thousand freight cars laden with Napa Valley grapes had

headed out, the voters were again asked to approve a statewide prohibition enforcement act. This time it finally passed by just over 2 percent. Los Angeles County alone carried the state for the drys. Napa and the wine country of Northern California, except Santa Clara, again voted against enforcement.

The pace of planting finally slowed some in 1923. Since the Napa name rarely accompanied grapes sold outside California, Napa vineyardists were affected like everyone else by the overall condition of the market. Vineyardists at the beginning of the decade had vastly overplanted, especially in the Central Valley. They had been excited by high grape prices, particularly because they stood in stark contrast to the general level of agricultural prices, which began declining in 1920. Thus, many vines came to bear in 1923 and this overplanting eventually brought prices down. 1923 prices held surprisingly firm, but again rain disrupted the market, this time by a five-day downpour in late September. Still, 1,392 cars left the Napa Valley, a little more than 6 percent of the state's total.

In 1923 the county sheriff started hitting the country roadhouses that were popping up. St. Helena and Napa began sprouting soft drink parlors, and several of these started offering something stronger than root beer. Some wineries did get into trouble. Gier was the champion. Perhaps runner-up status should be awarded to Chiles Valley vintner Anton Nichelini, who was hit several times. No one really made much of such matters. Napa folks who were willing to stomach Prohibition had not done so to keep such as Nichelini from making a living. Most thought if you paid your fine, everything was square.[16]

BEAULIEU VINEYARD AND PROHIBITION

We last discussed Georges de Latour during the war years. Like Paul Masson, his countryman in Santa Clara, he found it hard to conceive of a land willingly destroying its commercial wine industry. But like Masson he was able to make more than the best of the situation. De Latour had already made money producing good dessert wine, much of it for the altar trade. With Prohibition he was able to expand this business and increase profits. In 1921 he enlarged his bottling plant and built a swimming pool at his Beaulieu estate. In 1923 he was able to buy 110 more acres of vineyard land from the nearby St. Joseph Agricultural School, which would become BV Vineyard #3.

More important, he determined to consolidate and modernize his winemaking operations. Fred Ewer was now in his sixties and was willing to sell de Latour his big winery in Rutherford, built by his father, Seneca Ewer, in 1885. De Latour transformed the four acres on the east side of the highway into a modern plant, whose outlines can still be seen in the BV operation today. By the end of Prohibition the master of BV would have a million-gallon winery ready to step smartly into the tumultuous California wine world of the 1930s.

De Latour took wide aim in his production goals in the twenties. He produced lots of inexpensive muscatel, bringing up carloads of muscats from the Central Valley.

But he also made an elegant Muscat de Frontignan, which, after Repeal, helped promote a picture of fine diversity in BV products. He did not rip up all the Cabernet he had planted years before. Some of these grapes he sold in the local market, others went into a dry red table wine that winemaker Ponti incorporated into BV's altar wine product line. De Latour also made highly successful dry and sweet white wines in the Bordeaux style. He had some Sémillon and Sauvignon blanc vines, but he could sell more wines from these varieties if he could acquire more grapes. So he struck up a deal to acquire wine from these varieties from the Wente family's famed vineyards in Livermore, whose vines descended directly from cuttings made at Chateau d'Yquem in Sauternes. But in 1926 they ran into IRS resistance to transferring the wine from the Wente plant to BV. So the two families worked out an arrangement whereby Wente Winery became Beaulieu Bonded Winery 898.

When Repeal came, BV was ready to enter the premium sweet and dry wine market with a plant capacity, source of grapes, and an experienced staff unmatched by any other California winery. In Ernest Wente's words, "They were *the* label. They were in the driver's seat when Repeal came."[17]

And what of all the other great Napa wineries? Which ones approached BV's achievements in the dry years? Simply put—there were none.

The large industrial wine operations in Napa closed down during Prohibition. Carneros had long since given up serious winegrowing, except at the old Stanly Ranch. Eshcol made wine for two years, but closed down in 1922 and became another grape ranch. To Kalon followed the same pattern. Inglenook had always been a highly diversified agricultural operation. Now the grape side of production declined in favor of prunes. The great winery closed down in 1919. Mrs. Niebaum lived on in San Francisco but rarely visited the old estate.

The Brun & Chaix plant at Oakville declined in wooden dilapidation until de Latour bought the land in 1925. On the east side of the Valley viticulture almost disappeared during the dry years. There was a vineyard here and there, but dairies and prunes were far more common. Stag's Leap Manor continued as a popular resort. The vineyards in the area did develop something of a reputation for their Petite Sirah grapes, greatly loved by local home winemakers who knew their sources.

Theodore Gier continued to make headlines from his brushes with Prohibition agents. His vineyards still produced grapes, many grafted to Alicantes. In 1930 he sold his Mt. Veeder estate to the Christian Brothers order in Martinez. Gier's old Bergfeld place south of St. Helena became a vinegar plant run by Charles Forni during Prohibition.

John Wheeler ended commercial winemaking in the twenties, but had enough vines among his prunes and pears to retain a voice in Napa viticulture until his death in 1939, fifty-two years after he had taken over Charles Wetmore's position as head of the State Viticultural Commission. His home on Zinfandel Lane was the site of many a reunion of his old friends in the wine industry and his classmates from Berkeley. Wheeler, who could play a solid piano, was stone deaf in his later years, but it was always part of the festivities that he should bang out the old Cal fight songs as his fellow Bears sang along to strains of "Hail Blue and Gold" and "We Are Sons of California."

Operations at the Krug estate became quiet in 1926 with the death of Bismark Bruck. He started managing the place in 1894, and leased it from the Moffitt family in 1918. Many years would pass before another important wine operation would plant its roots here. Across the way all was quiet at CWA's Greystone Winery, purchased by the Bisceglia family in 1925.

On Spring Mountain viticulture at La Perla gradually declined, although the estate continued to supply grapes to the successors of the Schilling operation for years. Here, and across on Howell Mountain, the lack of a specific market for hillside-grown wines meant a further decline in mountain vineyards, with rarely a vine replanted.

Besides de Latour, the Beringer family probably had the greatest winegrowing continuity on an older estate in the twenties. Their grapes were part of Napa's eastern shipments every year. But they did not graft over all their better vines. They made wine and sold it under bond to others, particularly to Beaulieu. Thus they kept a fairly high level of quality in parts of their vineyard plantation, particularly with some good white varieties. At Repeal Beringer was one of the few wineries with good white grapes.

At Larkmead Felix Salmina had one of the most prosperous operations in the Valley. His Zinfandel and Petite Sirah grapes were always in demand among Northern California home winemakers. Salmina's grapes had a reputation similar to those from Italian Swiss Colony among local cognoscenti.

Farther north, near Calistoga, Chateau Montelena became Tubbs Ranch, until its wine operations were temporarily resuscitated after Repeal. Calistoga itself continued to reacquire the character of a tourist spa that it had originally developed sixty years earlier. Here W. F. Bornhorst and William Ebeling ran the old Light Winery for a while; it reopened in 1933 under Charles Forni and Adam Bianchi.

VINTAGES 1923-1929

It would be fifty-two years until the Napa Valley had a drier "rainy" season than 1923–24. There was still more planting, with Prohibition acreage now peaking at a little more than 12,000 acres. The crop was short, prices were firm, and the first grapes were shipped on August 29. One thousand five hundred and forty cars left the Valley in 1924, with Petite Sirah now the grape in most demand here. A good part of this crop was trucked out to Bay Area cities.

After the vintage, for the first time in twelve years, Napa voters could go to the polls without seeing another prohibition proposition on their ballots. The drys in California seemed content for the moment, since the new Wright Enforcement Act had received voter approval in 1922. Still, ASL voices could still be heard attacking the fresh grape deal, which one dry leader called part of an international conspiracy to thwart Prohibition.[18]

In 1925 the previous years' huge plantings caused a shocking decline in the prices of fresh grapes headed east. September rains almost ruined the Zinfandel crop, and when grapes started arriving in poor condition on the East Coast, the box cars full of unsold and rapidly decaying fruit literally lined the tracks for miles. Napa growers were not hit hard. Much of their Zin crop sold in

Anton Nichelini in his Chiles Valley vineyard in 1923. The Napa sheriff visited the winery often during the dry years.

SOURCE: GREG BOEGER.

DRY YEARS   199

the Bay Area at a good price. But this would be the last boom year for Napa vineyardists in the twenties. The season ended when Prohibition agents forced Theodore Gier to dump 20,000 gallons of illegal wine.

The total acreage of California grapes in 1926 was not again attained until the boom years of the 1970s. In February Napa growers met to discuss the coming collapse from oversupply and were reminded of the situation throughout the spring as the usual buyers failed to make their annual appearance. At the state level the California Vineyardists' Association (CVA) was formed to head off the disaster by bringing order to the annual snarl of freight cars heading east with their perishable loads. But each year overproduction continued to drag down the entire industry. When the economic crash hit in 1929, the CVA's task became hopeless.[19]

The 1926 crop was a good one, although Zinfandels in Napa were short. Quality was outstanding but prices were down 30 percent from 1925. A record 1,641 cars left the Valley. After the vintage California voters were again treated to an attempt to revoke the Wright Act. It was close. Fully 48 percent of California's voters were willing to call an end to California enforcement of dry laws. Every Bay Area county except Santa Clara voted wet. Napa was as wet as ever (61.3 percent).

There was hardly a vine planted in 1927 in Napa or any other place in the state. According to an industry analysis, this wine grape depression was now "more acute than in any other farm industry in this State." The credit position of the average grapegrower in California was flat against the wall. Most of the state's vineyards were mortgaged far beyond their real worth in terms of 1927–28 prices. But such was not yet the case in Napa. Here things were difficult, but it was far worse in the Central Valley.[20]

The 1927 crop level was about the same in Napa as in the three previous years. This season far more emphasis was given to the local market. The trick, particularly so far as the San Francisco market was concerned, was to make sure that buyers knew the grapes in the freight cars came from Napa. (This was also the case for Sonoma grapes.) By now it was next to impossible to sell a lug of Alicantes in San Francisco. Close to 4,000 tons of Napa grapes sold in this market, about 20 percent of total production.

In 1928 Napa prune crop was worth more than twice as much as wine grapes and had an acreage about equal to that of grapes, just over 10,000 acres. There were also 2,600 acres of nonbearing pear trees in the Valley, another sign of the direction of agricultural winds. The CVA came in for a lot of criticism for its handling of grape shipments this year. The California crop was huge; the Napa crop was the highest since 1923. Weather at vintage time was terrible. The condition of the grapes leaving the state only exacerbated the oversupply. Napa vineyardists received an average price more than 40 percent lower than in 1927. A wholesale lug of standard Zinfandel brought $2.00 in the New York City yards in 1922; this year you were lucky to get a dollar. Oldtimers in Napa were beginning to retell horror stories from the 1890s.

HOOVER'S LOAN AND FRUIT INDUSTRIES

At the end of the vintage Herbert Hoover was elected president. He was also a Central Valley vineyardist, a Californian, and a man deeply sympathetic to the problems of the American farmer. Napa had supported him solidly over Democrat Al Smith, who had called for repeal of the Eighteenth Amendment. Following his inauguration Hoover supported the passage of a farm relief act which was supposed to help the farmer by supporting farm prices. The approach is often referred to as a "trickle down" policy, with loans going to corporate farm organizations, which were supposed to stabilize prices. To get a piece of the action, the Grape Products Division of CVA reorganized itself and formed a giant marketing corporation dubbed Fruit Industries (FI). Mainly, this was an attempt to save the embattled grape farmers in the Central Valley. No CVA/FI officers were from the Napa Valley, but many Napa growers became authorized agents for the organization. Wheeler, Gier, Cairns, Forni, and Tubbs made the agency list. Two others from the Central Valley, but later associated with Napa, were Louis M. Martini of Kingsburg and Cesare Mondavi of Lodi.[21]

The 1929 vintage was taking place when the stock market crashed in October, but that event had no noticeable effect on the fresh grape deal. In fact, Napa vineyardists did better than in 1928. Prices were steady, if low, the crop was good, the vintage orderly. Actually, this was the last satisfactory Napa grape crop in terms of tonnage for the next five years.

Napa grapegrowers didn't have much to do with FI, and in 1929 most were glad they hadn't. In order to insure that dry forces in Congress would not set up a fuss over the multi-million-dollar government loan to FI, the CVA leadership came out squarely for maintaining Prohibition. FI intended to produce a grape concentrate for home winemakers labeled Vine-Glo, which was supposed to help soak up the oversupply of California grapes. CVA President Donald Conn infuriated Napa growers by contending that there was nothing in the offing to suggest that the American people would reject Prohibition. He called for "legal and proper enforcement of the law." To Napa wine grape men this sounded more like the harangue of an ASL orator than the voice of the chief executive of the organization supposedly dedicated to the best interests of California grapegrowers.[22]

By 1928 the image of Prohibition as an institution set in historical concrete was undergoing a national metamorphosis. Now the opposition to Prohibition did not come strictly from those who would benefit financially from its demise. Many businessmen who had hoped that closing saloons would stimulate worker productivity were now concerned by the spirit of lawlessness that was becoming acceptable in many parts of the nation. It almost seemed that the moral fiber of society was being eaten away. The saloon, as it had been before 1920, was dead. Thus, for many voters Prohibition had served its purpose.

National public opinion polls now clearly indicated that a majority of the American people wanted a redefinition of the term "intoxicating beverage." This meant that people were now willing to accept light wines and beer as legal under the Eighteenth Amendment. There is much evidence to suggest that most had been willing to accept this definition from the beginning if the death of the saloon had been guaranteed. In California this spirit had always been dominant, at least north of Bakersfield. There was also a growing interest in outright repeal. This would mean overturning an amendment to the Constitution, a feat never before accomplished. For now the Eighteenth Amendment was simply being nullified in many parts of the United States. But for most middle-class Americans in the 1920s such an approach was not acceptable.[23]

The evils of Prohibition were brought home to Napa folk in the early months of the Great Depression. First a Prohibition officer was shot dead in Yountville. Several months later three oldtimers from the Yountville Veterans Home died from drinking liquor poisoned with denatured alcohol. On the national scene the American Bar Association called for Repeal in 1930 based on a

Products of the

California wine

industry during

prohibition.

Concentrates,

jelly, and medicinal

wines head the list.

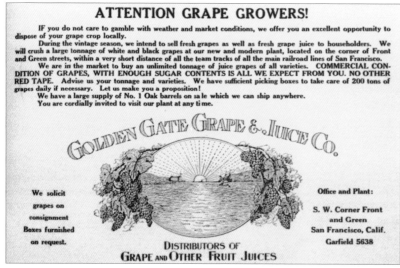

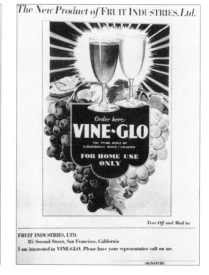

vote of 13,799–6,340. The *Literary Digest's* national poll found that only 30.5 percent of the Americans interviewed now supported Prohibition. More than 40 percent wanted outright repeal. Nullification of the Eighteenth Amendment was an accepted fact in San Francisco and many other Bay Area communities. By mid-year local federal officials admitted that prohibition enforcement

was now aimed only at large-scale producers and distributors of distilled spirits. The president of the CVA did not exactly have his ear to the ground.[24]

Sutter Home Winery

in 1930. Note the

sign and the word

"winery" covered.

SOURCE: SUTTER HOME.

VINTAGES 1930 — 1933 AND THE DEPRESSION

The loan to FI could not stave off the evil results of the national depression. A glut of grapes was now offered to a population with rapidly sinking consumer buying power. It was a population, whatever its ethnic background, that did not place winegrapes above the basic essentials of life. Grape prices hit such depths in 1930 that support dollars did virtually nothing to help any but raisin producers. The Federal Grape Control Board set up to oversee the program ceased operations at the end of the disastrous season. At the end of the 1930 harvest the average price paid Napa growers was only about one third what it had been five years earlier. Again, more and more Napa grapes left the Valley by truck for local markets. To make matters worse, the crop was the shortest since 1921. This year the value of the Napa grape crop was less than one third of the value of the local prune crop.[25]

The next year saw some changes on the Napa wine scene. The Christian Brothers transported the wine cooperage from their old Martinez establishment to the new facility, now termed Mont La Salle, the former Gier Winery on Mt. Veeder. Next year their training school for novitiates was dedicated. Greystone, owned by the Bisceglia family since 1925, was sold again, this time to a Chicago-based firm, but nothing of substance happened at the great winery.

The 1931 vintage was another disaster. Near-drought conditions, followed by a torrid summer, gave a crop of little more than a ton per acre.

Prices in the east dropped another 25 percent from their 1930 low. This year more than half the Napa crop was sold locally, but more than the usual amount of wine was produced at BV, Beringer, Larkmead, and a few others. The whole country was talking about low farm prices and their cause and the talk always came back to Prohibition as a major reason. Thousands of tons of grain would suddenly be in demand if beer and whisky were again legal products. Next year was an election year and the Hoover Administration was in trouble on the farm, and everywhere else, for that matter. The spirit of repeal was in the air, and no place more obviously than the Napa Valley, where, in anticipation of the event, the large wineries had been stepping up production.

In April 1932 Chapin Tubbs chaired a vociferous anti-prohibition growers' meeting in Rutherford. The next month House Speaker John Nance Garner took the Democratic presidential primary in California, but Napa was solidly for Franklin Roosevelt.

The 1932 vintage was the all-time price catastrophe for Napa Valley. Most of the grapes that went to market were sold for no more than ten dollars per ton. Over 2,000 tons were not harvested. But even more grapes were crushed for wine than in 1931. About 40,000 gallons were made at the old Brun & Chaix plant by a newcomer from the Central Valley, Louis M. Martini. He was considering buying an old established winery, but finally decided to build a new one. He had come to Napa with the idea of making premium dry table wine. The Beringers also got very serious about winemaking this year, hiring a young Santa Clara winemaker, Fred Abruzzini, to take charge of their plant. Salmina and de Latour also started refurbishing their facilities.[26]

At the national convention the Democrats nominated Franklin Roosevelt for president and in their platform demanded outright repeal. Hoover and the Republicans equivocated. The Democrats would offer America four Rs to help end the depression— Relief, Recovery, Reform—and Repeal. Roosevelt carried almost every precinct in Napa County. California voters were again given a shot at the state's "little Volstead Act" and this time wiped it off the books. Napa and the rest of Northern California were happy to stay solidly in the wet column.

The people of the Napa Valley now joined the rest of a desperate nation in suffering through the winter of 1932–33 as the Great Depression bottomed out, the national economy in apparent ruin. When March came, a new wet Congress and the President took charge, bent on "putting people to work." Napa winegrowers looked hopefully into the new year and were correct in thinking that things surely could not get much worse.

1. For a good bibliography of American prohibition see: Norman H. Clark. Deliver Us from Evil (New York 1976): 227-235. Joseph P. Kett. "Temperance and Intemperance as Historical Problems," Journal of American History (March 1981): 878-885 is the best discussion of recent prohibition historiography.

2. Clark Warburton. The Economic Results of Prohibition (New York 1932): 23-72; W. J. Rorabaugh. The Alcoholic Republic (New York 1979): 232-233. High as this figure was in 1915, that for 1830 was 177% higher. In 1990 it was about what it was in 1915.

3. Clark, 95; James H. Timberlake. Prohibition and the Progressive Movement (Cambridge, Mass. 1966): 156-157.

4. Sbarboro published several pamphlets on this theme, e.g. Wine as a Remedy for the Evil of Intemperance (1906); The Fight for True Temperance (1908); Temperance vs. Prohibition (1909).

5. Register, 10/26/1912, 10/27/1912, 11/4/1912, 11/6/1912; Star, 10/25/1912, 11/8/1912.

6. SBVC. Report for the Years 1913-1916 (Sacramento 1917); PWSR, 1/31/1912, 8/131/1913, 11/30/1913.

7. Gilman Ostrander. The Prohibition Movement in California (Berkeley 1957): 135-138; Arno Dosch. "California Next?" Sunset (March 1916): 22-24; Star, 11/6/1914, 11/20/1914; PWSR, 11/30/1914.

8. New York Times, 3/27-4/4/1926; Ostrander, 134; Peter Odegard. Pressure Politics (New York 1928).

9. Star, 3/2/1917, 8/17/1917, 8/31/1917.

10. NVWLA II: 233; Star, 2/22/1918, 4/19/1918, 6/7/1918; Chronicle, 3/5/1918; PWSR, 3/30/1918.

11. Clark, 124-125; Odegard, 70.

12. San Jose Mercury, 9/25/1910; PWSR, 1/31/1915.

13. Jack S. Blocker. American Temperance Movements (Boston 1989): 106-119.

14. Star, 2/28/1919, 7/1/1919, 8/22/1918, 8/29/1919, 9/12/1919, 9/26/1919, 10/3/1919, 12/19/1919; Chronicle, 10/11/1919, 10/16/1919.

15. A. J. Winkler. "Viticultural Research at the University of California, Davis, 1921-1971." Bancroft Oral History, 1973: 3-10; California Department of Agriculture. Black Juice Grape Varieties in California (Sacramento 1929); R. L. Nourgaret. The California Grape Industry - 1919. California Department of Agriculture Report No. 1 (Sacramento 1920); L. D. Mallory et al. "Factors Affecting Annual Prices of California Fresh Grapes." Hilgardia 6:4 (September 1931): 101-129; S. W. Shear. "Economic Status of the Grape Industry." CAES Bulletin 429 (June 1927); Chronicle, 10/11/1919; John R. Meers. "The California Wine and Grape Industry and Prohibition." CHSQ (March 1967): 28-29; NVWLA I: 116, 240-246; II,:64, 92, 288; IV: 152, 331-336; Teiser and Harroun, 182.

16. Star, 7/2/1920, 12/29/1922, 1/19/1923, 6/22/1923, 8/17/1923, 4/11/1924, 9/18/1925; Wine Country (February 1982): 11.

17. NVWLA II: 33; Star, 9/17/1926; Ernest A. Wente. "Winemaking in the Livermore Valley." Bancroft Oral History, 1971: 21-23, 65-66; André Tchelistcheff. "Grapes Wine, and Ecology." Bancroft Oral History, 1983: 38-41.

18. San Jose Mercury, 7/21/1924.

19. Teiser and Harroun, 181; Star, 2/26/1926, 6/26/1926.

20. Jessie Schilling Blout. "A Brief Economic History of California wine-Growing." Wine Institute mimeo, ca. 1945.

21. Wines & Vines (July 1929); Blout, 10; San Jose Mercury, 7/14/1929.

22. Leon Adams. "Revitalizing the California Wine Industry." Bancroft Oral History, 1974: 15-23, 28-30; Wines & Vines (September 1, 1929).

23. David E. Kyvig. Repealing National Prohibition (Chicago 1979).

24. Star, 2/14/1930, 2/27/1931; New York Times, 7/31/1930; Kyvig, 117; For a remarkable picture of the collapse of Prohibition enforcement in the Bay Area see: R. A. Kelley. Liberty's Last Stand (San Francisco 1932).

25. Star, 6/6/1930, 9/19/1930, 1/16/1931; Blout, 10-11.

26. Louis M. and Louis P. Martini. "Wine Making in the Napa Valley." Bancroft Oral History, 1973: 30; Sorensen, 106-107.

DIFFICULT BUT HOPEFUL YEARS

Northern California, which produced the best dry wines of the West Coast before Prohibition, cannot produce wine of comparable quality now and will not be able to for some years.

—FRANK SCHOONMAKER

1934

PROHIBITION WAS DOOMED IN 1933, BUT IT WOULD TAKE MANY MONTHS FOR THE Twenty-first Amendment to work its way through the states. Nevertheless, Congress could change the definition of "intoxicating beverage" without amending the Constitution, and this it did on April 7. To California wine men the result was something of a joke, since the new law allowed beer and wine to be produced with a limit of 3.2 percent alcohol. But several California wineries eventually did produce some of this 3.2 wine, usually sweet and slightly carbonated, a sort of wine cooler/Cold Duck concoction. Nobody in Napa took it seriously, although Beringer did sell a few thousand gallons of wine to the Rainier Brewery in Seattle to use in manufacturing the beverage.[1]

The actual repeal process went faster than most had suspected. Californians voted wet by a four to one margin in the June advisory. In St. Helena the vote was 557–54. The same sympathy swept the rest of the nation. On December 5 Utah became the magical thirty-sixth state to ratify. The word was quickly flashed to the country and at 2:31 P.M. the great siren on the San Francisco Ferry Building cheerfully announced the end of the "great experiment."

The next day the *Chronicle* had a huge wine section with a long article on Beaulieu and another on the new Louis Martini Winery. There were photos of Beringer and the Charles Krug estate. There were articles on other districts and ads from wineries around the state. But Napa got the best press, by far.

NAPA AT REPEAL

What was the Napa Valley at this moment in history? The population had not changed much in the dry years. About 23,000 lived in the Valley in 1933, up only 2,000 since World War I. The foreign-born now made up 18.5 percent, down from the century high of 27 percent in 1910. Just over half of these came from Germany and Italy, again in almost equal numbers. But a very obvious ethnic fact of life could now be seen in land ownership. At Repeal, immigrants from Italy and their children were as obvious in the Napa Valley as Germans had been in the 1880s.[2]

Viticulture was still important but was now a far less significant factor in Napa agriculture. Fruit and nut culture accounted for almost half the county's farm income in the thirties, but rarely did grape income make up as much as 30 percent of the total for this category. Eggs and dairy products were both more valuable than grapes in these years. It would not be until 1944 that wine grapes were again a more valuable crop than prunes.[3]

The decline of viticulture had done nothing to damage the image of the Napa Valley and its uplands as a modern Eden, beautiful, restful, and but a few hours from the cultural amenities of cosmopolitan San Francisco. People often linked the gentrification of the area that had started in a small way in the late nineteenth century with the good life associated with wine culture. Between 1900 and 1930, newcomers had not necessarily perceived this connection. Napa County real estate interests put out several well-illustrated pamphlets promoting the area to affluent settlers between 1900 and 1915, as did Sunset magazine's Homeseekers' Bureau, often with virtually no reference to grapes or wine production.[4] Between 1919 and 1933 lovely estates increasingly tended to come into the hands of families with no interest in growing grapes. We shall see that, with few exceptions, the people who would revive the Napa wine industry in the 1930s were not the retired capitalists or moneyed dilettantes so obvious here between 1880 and 1900.

Prohibition most obviously affected the Valley's vineyards and wineries. But these ills could be corrected. The awful physical condition of the vineyards resulted from the collapse of the fresh grape deal, not directly from Prohibition. The ordinary shipper varieties now common on the Valley floor could be grafted over or rooted out, if the demand reappeared for wine as good as had been made here through 1917. Napa really was in relatively good shape in terms of standard red varieties such as Zinfandel, Petite Sirah, and Carignane. Perhaps there was too much Alicante Bouschet and Grand noir, but certainly not as much as in other districts. Some small stands of Cabernet Sauvignon survived here and there. But high-quality white grapes were almost nonexistent. The dilapidated condition of the Valley's wineries actually proved a far more serious problem than the condition of the vineyards. In Professor Harold Winkler's words, "we were about at the same point in 1934 as they were in 1880."

Another great problem facing Napa winegrowers was national in scope; tastes had changed. The great bulk of America's regular table wine drinkers had taken to drinking homemade and bootleg wine, too young, too coarse, and almost devoid of flavor beyond the most rude vinosity. An immigrant generation that had at least known an occasional bottle of fine wine had learned to live without it. During the years of the Great Depression they would continue to do so. From 1932 to 1937 the number of freight cars headed east full of California grapes for home winemakers averaged more than 10,000 per year.

In addition, drinkers of commercial wine had developed a sweet tooth, due in part to the meteoric rise in popularity of bottled soda pop in the twenties. By 1935 the California wine industry had become overwhelmingly a sweet wine industry. Napa producers would have to adjust to this new situation.

Americans' general eating habits had also changed. The twenties saw the final triumph of canned and packaged foods. This was also the era of the self-service cafeteria, the luncheonette, and food service at the soda fountain. Middle-class American women were spending far less time in the kitchen, which symbolically had grown smaller. The radio and movies gave women things to do other than spending the day over a hot stove. And far more women worked outside the home. These changes were not directly related to Prohibition, but were all part of the heritage of the twenties with which the reborn California wine industry had to cope.

And what of that important element of middle- and upper-class urban America that had started to develop a taste for continental, particularly

French, cuisine between 1890 and 1915? Fine wine had been an absolutely integral part of this increment in taste, including a small but important part of California wine production. Napa wine had had more than its share of this market and Prohibition all but killed it. Wine writer Julian Street declared in 1931 that "the art of noble dining. . . was assassinated under legal process on January 16, 1920."[5] According to Historian Harvey Levenstein, "Here and there, notably in San Francisco and New Orleans, islands of Francophilia survived in the dining rooms and restaurants of the older upper class, but for the most part those who hied to the French tradition in the rest of the country felt adrift in the rising tide of culinary Babbitry."[6]

Was it, then, any great tragedy that there were so few fine wine grapes growing in the Napa Valley in 1933? What if 20 percent of Napa's vineyards had been planted to Cabernet Sauvignon? Where would these 4,000 tons of grapes have gone in the 1930s? Easy enough. When a grower brought a small load of Cabernet Sauvignon to Louis Stralla at the Krug Winery in these years, he got his $15 per ton and the grapes went into the tank with the Alicantes and Zinfandels.[7]

The great hurt dealt the Napa Valley by Prohibition was a blow to American tastes. Paul Verdier, of San Francisco's City of Paris department store, said it in 1933: "The people of America must be re-educated to an appreciation of fine wines."[8] When the demand developed, the fine vineyards would be planted. Before the siren on the San Francisco Ferry Building blew on December 5, 1933, a youthful but important American interest in fine food and premium wine had all but vanished from the land.

PREPARING FOR THE 1933 VINTAGE

The Napa Valley wine industry faced two difficult tasks as it braced for the 1933 vintage and those of ensuing years. First, the product of the Valley's 11,500 acres of vineyards had to be converted into drinkable table wine, perhaps some sweet wine too. Whatever vines were in their vineyards, Napa growers were not going to rip them up in the depth of the Depression. For now and for years to come these shipper varieties would be the basis of the Napa crop. There were a few acres of top varieties and some producers and growers were willing to accept the lower yields from such vines. These men wanted to regain a piece of the tiny premium wine market that had somehow survived in America. The recovery of that market was the second great task facing the handful of Napa wine men willing to take such risks. It was going to be a difficult decade, a "roller coaster ride" in the words of wine historian Ruth Teiser. In 1933 "the California wine industry limped out of the chaos of Prohibition into the Depression-ridden chaos of the 1930s."[9]

Not a freight car of grapes left the Valley during the 1933 harvest. In fact, thousands of tons were brought in from Solano County and the Central Valley. Prohibition was still a fact, but everyone knew that California wine would be for sale across the nation in 1934. The crop was very short and grape prices shot up to more than double those of the previous two years. The glow would not last. Napa wine grape prices did not exceed the 1933 level again until the middle of World War II. Most of the grapes were made up into rough table wine, which would shortly leave the Valley by tank car, headed for bottlers east of the Rockies. The search for white grapes was frantic and next to hopeless. The few to be found went for almost double the price of red varieties. When the vintage was over Napa wineries had made about 5,000,000 gallons of wine. There were about sixty Napa wineries in the field this year, mostly small operations whose owners hopefully leaped at the opportunity of Repeal. Many had no real experience at commercial wine production, had too little capital, and would soon leave the production arena when the hard realities of wine economics came down on them. Some historic operations deserve our attention. Equally important are a few of the newcomers who would survive and eventually prosper.

Winegrowing in the Carneros stayed alive on the old Stanly ranch, where wine was made for three seasons until the winery burned down in 1936. Nearby John Garetto began building his small winery that would be in operation for the 1935 vintage. North of Napa James Fawver reopened the old Eshcol Winery and made 160,000 gallons this year. The rebirth was short-lived, but Fawver's grapes later became an important part of Beringer's production. The Churchill family still owned To Kalon, which went back into production this year. It continued to produce bulk wine until the winery burned down in 1939. The Covick family now owned the old Brun & Chaix plant where Louis M. Martini had made wine last year. Next door the Bartolucci family had begun building a large winery, which went into production in 1934.

At Beaulieu Georges de Latour had been increasing production since 1930, anticipating Repeal. He had an inventory of about a million gallons and made another

The first ad for the new Martini Winery. 1934.

200,000 gallons this year from his own grapes and from muscats he imported from the Central Valley.[10] Across the way the good news was that Mrs. Niebaum had decided to reopen Inglenook Winery, placing the operation in the hands of Carl Bundschu, a man with deep roots in the North Coast wine industry. Inglenook made about 100,000 gallons this season.[11] South of St. Helena Louis M. Martini rushed to place his new winery in operation for the 1933 vintage. The million-gallon facility was ready to go when the grapes began arriving. It held almost a half million gallons at the end of the crush.[12]

St. Helena itself was bustling with activity, as more than a dozen wineries opened for operation. The expansion of the John Riorda winery by the owner and Charles Forni marked an important development. They called it Sunnyhill Winery, but changed it to Sunny St. Helena Winery. Later in the decade the Cesare Mondavi family would also become involved in the operation.[13]

In the hills east and west of the Valley there was little winemaking activity. Most of the old vineyards were gone and few of the old cellars were reopened. Probably the best surviving vineyards were on Spring Mountain, where the old McPike and Lemme properties were located. Here there were still about two hundred acres of vines. The most important upland wine events took place on Mt. Veeder, now that the Christian Brothers had acquired the Gier Winery and vineyards. At the moment, however, the Brothers were more intent on the operation of the new Novitiate there, which had been dedicated the year before.[14]

There was a bit more winery activity on the east side. On the lower slopes of Howell Mountain John Ballentine made wine at his Deer Park Winery, the original Sutter Home operation. Nearby, Peter Stark was making wine at the old Rossini Winery, which would become Lee Stewart's Souverain in the forties. The Nichelini Winery continued producing above Chiles Valley, as did the Sam Haus Winery in the Pope Valley. Back on Spring Mountain the Conradi family opened their old cellar for a short time.[15]

On the north side of St. Helena the activity was furious. C. W. Connor and Walter Martini leased the Forni/Lombarda Winery. The giant and almost empty Greystone was now back in the hands of the Bisceglia family after the winery's eastern buyers had gone bankrupt. Next season the great stone winery would be back in production under the supervision of Lawrence Abruzzini. His brother, Fred, was now in charge of the Beringer cellars and had raised the historic winery's capacity to almost half a million gallons. With the best distillery in the Valley, the Beringer Brothers Winery was one of the few in the North Coast able to convert early to the sweet wine demand that had taken over the industry. By 1936 Beringer was able to market more than half of its production as fortified dessert wine.[16]

Across the way the long silent Charles Krug Winery was brought back to life by a man who saw the economic potential in the Napa Valley vineyards with their shipper varieties. Louis Stralla had made money during Prohibition operating a gambling ship outside the three mile limits in Southern California. In July 1933 he came to Napa, looked around, and went down to San Francisco to talk to J. K. Moffitt, the owner of the Krug estate. He talked the paper magnate into letting him lease the place for eight seasons, even though Stralla, in his own words, was "a total pilgrim in the wine business." He went down to BV and talked to J. J. Ponti, who steered him to a retired winemaker, Rufus J. Buttimer, who had previously run the Ewer and Atkinson cellar and was now in his seventies. In Stralla's words, "Ponti used to drag hoses for old man Buttimer." The two of them hired a work crew and got the Krug plant into condition to make up 400,000 gallons of wine in 1933, most of it what Stralla termed "heavy Paisano red." He sold it by the tank car to eastern bottlers and made plenty of money. But not enough to buy the old winery when the lease ran out in 1940 and Moffitt wanted to sell the place. Instead Stralla bought the Covick (Brun & Chaix) Winery in Oakville and continued his bulk operations there until 1945. Louis Stralla mastered the first great task of the Valley wine industry as well as any other in Napa after Repeal. But he had almost nothing to do with the second task. "I wasn't in the wine business from the standpoint of romance. . . .The only interest I had in fine Cabernet was to drink it."[17]

Salmina entry carries array of children and vintages.

To the north the Salmina brothers at Larkmead, Felix and Elmer, were also ready to go, with some of the best standard red wine grapes in the Valley, and some Cabernet to boot. They made 200,000 gallons in 1933, mostly for the bulk trade, but with an eye on reviving the Larkmead premium label. Farther north, at Calistoga, John Ghisolfo, a hotel owner with an interest in wine, opened the Calistoga Wine Company and made almost 100,00 gallons. Libero Pocai was one of the small producers here, and one of the few such who survived these first Repeal years. Even the old Jacob

Wine Float In Calistoga Parade

SOURCE: ST. HELENA STAR.

Grimm Winery went into production for the moment, as did the Tubbs Winery (Chateau Montelena), but this revival also did not last.[18]

After the 1933 vintage Carl Bundschu had a huge open house at Inglenook to celebrate Repeal and the return of commercial winemaking to the Napa Valley. On hand was St. Helena's A. N. Bell, who had attended the dedication of the great old winery in 1888.

1934 — 1936

A lot of wine was shipped out of the Napa Valley by tank car in the early months of 1934. Beaulieu and Stralla both totaled over 50,000 gallons. Most of it was red and dry, some brand new, some from 1932 and 1931. A portion was quite old, dating back well into Prohibition, often blended into the new wine to give it a touch of age. Quite a bit of it wasn't very good. There was a real quality problem statewide, one which tarred Napa with the same brush of disgust that generally blackened the reputation of California dry wine for the next four years. Much of the old wine from the twenties should have been consigned to the distillery.

The price of and the demand for California dry table wine was battered for some time by the volatile stuff dumped on the market this year. Lots of it was poorly made by inexperienced greenhorns. When industry leaders viewed the wreckage at mid-year, it was too late. E. A. Rossi of Italian Swiss Colony growled that a large part of the California dry wine placed in the New York and New Orleans markets was "not only inferior in quality, but in reality is not wine at all." Industry leader E. M. Sheehan felt that the terrible slump in prices had at least one good side to it. It was a "weeding out process" that would drive off the incompetents, the ignoramuses, and the fly-by-nights. All this hurt Napa producers. They were crushed by the general situation, whether they had contributed to it or not. One thing that did operate in Napa's favor was the strong California market for good bulk dry wines. About half of the state's production stayed right here. The big problem was one of national reputation.[19]

Some quick help came from UC Berkeley in the form of Professor W. V. Cruess's short course in basic fermentation principles. The Christian Brothers sent their new young winemaker, Brother John (Stanley Hoffman), to

Napa supported

FDR in 1932.

But this 1936

cartoon in the

St. Helena Star

indicates a

change of mind.

WE WERE JUST GETTING ESTABLISHED IN NATIONAL MARKETS WHEN ALONG COMES MR. ROOSEVELT AND OPENS OUR DOORS TO FRENCH, SPANISH, ITALIAN AND OTHER WINES. WE ARE CERTAINLY ANTI-ROOSEVELT

take advantage of the opportunity. At the industry level leaders began working to establish a statewide trade organization to protect the interests of California wine. A general conference was held in June 1934 at the Del Monte Hotel near Monterey under the auspices of the State Chamber of Commerce. Napa was represented by Charles Beringer, Carl Bundschu, Louis M. Martini, and John Daniel, Jr., Gustave Niebaum's grandnephew, who would take over the Inglenook operation in 1939. Later in the year the industry's Wine Institute was formally established, with Bundschu and de Latour Napa's leading representatives in the formative talks.[20]

The federal government was also involved in the wine industry's woes. Under the National Industrial Recovery Act the New Deal hoped to establish codes of fair play in all industries. And as an agricultural product wine grapes were involved in the development of the Agricultural Adjustment Act. Under Secretary of Agriculture Rexford Tugwell visited the wine country in July 1934, stopping at Beringer and Beaulieu and addressing a meeting of growers in Calistoga. But the Roosevelt Administration was most interested in the situation in the Central Valley, where a huge surplus of raisin and table grapes was hammering grape prices. So long as the market failed to discriminate between the cargo wine of the Central Valley from that produced in the coastal wine districts, the latter would suffer from the problems of the former.[21] In the long run most of the work done on these federal programs by California wine men went for naught after the courts declared major portions of the NRA and AAA unconstitutional.

Independent Napa Valley vineyardists could clearly see the ugly problem facing them in the current market. Wineries could not buy their grapes in 1934 if inventories were locked up by an almost dead dry wine market. The answer was a cooperative movement. Agricultural co-ops had some very favorable tax advantages under federal law. And co-ops gave growers a home for their grapes in times when high winery inventories could leave them out in the cold. Between 1934 and 1936 the spirit swept the state, as fifteen grower co-ops were formed, with a productive capacity of 42,000,000 gallons.

Napa County Agricultural Advisor Herman Baade called organizational meetings during the summer, and on August 6, 1934 the formal papers organizing a cooperative winery were signed. Charles Forni would manage the operation in Calistoga at the old Ephraim Light Winery. About seventeen growers signed up originally, but the number grew to 142 in 1937 as co-op prices everywhere in the state tended to better those for grapes on the open market. Next year Forni put his old vinegar plant into operation as a second facility, the old Bergfeld/Gier winery below St. Helena. Through the thirties the Napa Co-op was able to crush and market about 40 percent of the Napa

Frank Schoonmaker

in 1934. He campaigned

for varietal labeling of

California wines.

Valley grape crop. By the mid-forties the organization was returning an average of more than $1,000,000 per year to its members. Thus, Napa wine men accomplished the first task—producing and selling the product of the shipper grapes that Prohibition left behind.[22]

For all the troubles Napa wine men were having, case goods sales from a few wineries were doing very well in the first year after Repeal. This can be seen partly in the wines that California hotels served in these months. Beaulieu and Beringer were in most top San Francisco places, but outside of San Francisco BV ruled the roost, from the De Anza Hotel in San Jose to the El Cortez in San Diego. A somewhat better sign that Napa wineries were ready to move bottled goods onto the market was the rather informal wine competition held at the State Fair in 1934. Beaulieu, Beringer, Lombarda, Inglenook, Larkmead, and the Christian Brothers (Mont La Salle) had entries.

The 1934 vintage itself was of good quality, but prices collapsed from 1933's euphoric heights. About 3,000 tons were shipped out of the Valley fresh for Bay Area home winemakers. In the long run the most important aspect of this vintage was the great pair of Cabernet Sauvignons produced at Beaulieu and Inglenook. "Great wines," recalled Professor Maynard Amerine a half century later.[23]

The state of the Napa wine industry in 1935 and for the next four years was much like that of the country at large. Times were tough, there was lots of hope and plenty of hard work. Prices remained poor throughout these years but demand did grow. For Napa the two great problems were not yet solved, but the Co-op and bulk producers like Louis Stralla kept local growers afloat. And the seeds of the Valley's premium wine revival were beginning to germinate.

The most serious concern, directly related to low prices, was the low demand for dry table wine. Sonoma's Robert Rossi estimated that at least 23,000,000 gallons of homemade wine were produced in the United States in 1934. Napa growers and producers met several times during the year to discuss the problem. In 1936 they launched a campaign to get the slogan, "Serve Famous Napa Valley Dry Wines," printed on the business stationery of every company in the county. The fledgling Wine Institute was also concerned. Co-founder Leon Adams came to the Valley several times in 1935 promoting membership and listening to growers' concerns. By the end of the year most of Napa's major producers had joined up. The most notable exception was Louis M. Martini who held out until 1941, because of a personal dislike for one of the Bank of America people involved.[24]

The hopeful spirit in the Valley in 1935 manifested itself in the the St. Helena Vintage Festival. Newsreel cameras took in the event and recorded the spirited wine-oriented competition between the wineries, including Roy Raymond's triumph in the barrel-rolling contest. But the vintage was not so happy; it was short and the Central Valley grapes imported by some wineries rankled many local growers. The situation promoted more signups at the Co-op. Grape quality was mediocre, primarily because of overcropping, but some 1935 Cabernets were remembered for their excellence and staying qualities.

At the State Fair the few Napa producers who entered won the county sweepstakes for wine production; Alameda was second, as had been the case in the 1880s. Prizes for Cabernet went to Lombarda and Inglenook, to BV for Chablis, and to Beringer for Riesling. Beaulieu won an award for its sparkling wines. It was a good showing, since now only eight Napa wineries were marketing their wines in glass. (Sonoma had five, Santa Clara seven.)

There were more hints here and there of the growing interest in California premium table wines. In July the San Francisco Wine and Food Society featured 1926 Napa Valley clarets under the Beaulieu and Inglenook labels. Earlier, Carl Bundschu had announced the introduction of Inglenook "Cabinet" wines, special bottlings "for the connoisseur." By mid-year the Southern Pacific was serving BV wines in its dining cars. Another hopeful, but somewhat negative voice, was raised in favor of California premium wine by Frank Schoonmaker, whose Complete Wine Book ripped the quality of 90 percent of California's wines, but he argued for replanting to better grape varieties in coastal counties like Napa and Sonoma. He also insisted that labels on such wines should specify the district in which they were grown and the predominant grape variety used in their production. In other

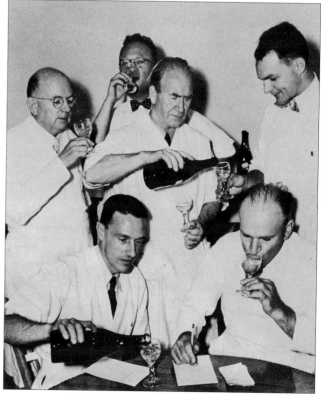

Experts who served on both the 1937 and 1938 Wine Jury, California State Fair.

TOP ROW (LEFT TO RIGHT): LOUIS S. WETMORE, M. A. JOSLYN, W. V. CRUESS, M. A. AMERINE. SEATED (LEFT TO RIGHT): GEORGE L. MARSH, A. J. WINKLER.

SOURCE: GUNTHER DETERT.

words, he was calling for varietal labeling and appellations of origin. The goal was to gain the confidence of the country's knowledgeable wine drinkers and to give California's really good wines a dependable and understandable label. Most of the wine industry scoffed at such an idealistic goal, but several Napa producers took Schoonmaker's words very seriously.[25]

1936 marked the beginning of a turnaround in national dry wine consumption. Californians consumed 3.36 gallons per person, a figure fairly close to the state's average in the early 1970s. The Bank of America concluded that dry table wine was on the rise. And in Napa there was an obvious surge in demand for dry wines in bulk and by the case. In September the Co-op made a 150,000-gallon shipment east at what was called a very good price. Louis Martini also sensed the turnaround, as evidenced by his 1936 purchase of the Mt. Pisgah Vineyard, planted by Samuel Goldstein in the late 1880s. This 580-acre plot on the Sonoma side of the Mayacamus Range had 350 acres of vines, mostly Zinfandel, but with valuable white acreage in Sémillon, Sylvaner, and Folle Blanche. The Martini family called the place

Bertha Beringer

"launches" a cable car to

inaugurate "wine week"

in San Francisco.

Monte Rosso, still an important part of their operation.[26]

The 1936 Napa vintage was short and uneventful. Prices were up a little and the Co-op, operating now at two plants, simply hummed, handling about 175 tons per day. Members received about four dollars per ton more than the Valley average this year. More than a quarter of the total Valley crop went to sweet wine production now that the Co-op had a large still in place.

At Beaulieu there was a new face this season, that of Leon Bonnet, a good wine chemist, formerly of UC Berkeley's Agricultural Department. De Latour wanted a more focused effort on the winery's Cabernet Sauvignon this year; Bonnet was the man to start the process. André Tchelistcheff finished it when the wine was released in 1940 as BV's first Private Reserve Cabernet Sauvignon.[27]

At the State Fair this year the judging was more systematic and carefully ordered than in the previous years since Repeal. All wines were tasted blind by a distinguished panel. Again Napa won more than its share of medals for dry table wines. Over half the golds and silvers in these categories went to Beaulieu, Beringer, Larkmead, Mont La Salle, Inglenook, and Lombarda.

THE CHRISTIAN BROTHERS ON MOUNT VEEDER

In 1937 a certain Alfred Fromm came to California to look at the state's wine industry. A native German from a Franconian wine family, he was now a partner in the importing firm of Picker-Linz, later known as Fromm and Sichel. This firm could see the war clouds forming in Europe and felt they should find a source of good California wine. Fromm visited several California wineries and was particularly attracted by what the Christian Brothers were doing on Mt. Veeder. They had acquired some good wine when they bought the Gier Winery and now under winemaker Brother John were making good wines themselves. The Mont La Salle product was mostly altar wine, sweet and dry, but the label had acquired a certain retail following, having won several State Fair awards.

Fromm's offer to enter a marketing agreement at this time seemed a godsend to the Brothers' local order, which, in 1936, was on the verge of bankruptcy. They were unable even to meet the interest payments on the bonds sold to bring the Novitiate to Napa. Fromm, for his part, was overjoyed to acquire such a source of good wine with such a marvelous potential. He felt that Americans knew little or nothing about wine and would gain "a certain sense of confidence" from a label with an ecclesiastical relationship. From now on the wines from Mont La Salle would bear the Christian Brothers label, making that connection clear to the consumer.[28]

This relationship between the Brothers and Picker-Linz was not always a smooth one. Advertising could be a problem, particularly after the La Salle Institute became involved with brandy production in 1940. At one point an official of the Institute complained that the agency was "selling not only our wines and brandy, but the good name of the Brothers and the good name of the Catholic Church in America." But the relationship was a benefit to both parties. The Brothers' historian later concluded that they "decided quite deliberately to exercise tight control over (the winery operation) in order to insure the quality of the product and to protect the good name of the Christian Brothers congregation." There was always a certain amount of tension among Institute officials on how large the winery operation should become. They always felt they must keep in mind that the work of the Brothers, since the order's founding in 1680, had been to educate youth, particularly the underprivileged. It was to this purpose that the order's profits were directed, and still are, even though the winery and distilling business were sold off to Heublein in 1989.[29]

IMPORTANT NEWCOMERS

Nineteen thirty-seven also brought Cesare Mondavi and John Riorda's incorporation of the Sunny St. Helena Winery. Mondavi had been shipping grapes from the Lodi area since 1923 but was interested in the future of table wine in California. They expanded the winery's capacity to about 500,000 gallons and were shortly a major factor in the Valley's bulk wine trade.

Cesare's son Robert Mondavi became active in the new operation. Sunny St. Helena would serve as a kind of apprenticeship for him before his father acquired the Charles Krug Winery in 1943. The current product was ordinary bulk wine, shipped to bottlers in tank cars. In addition to dragging hoses Robert Mondavi did the basic laboratory work and enjoyed comparing his wines with those of the "Big Four," Beaulieu, Inglenook, Beringer, and Larkmead. He was enticed by the style of these historic producers. Later he remarked, "I bowed my head as I went by Beaulieu and Inglenook." But he was convinced that the Mondavis could produce wines in the same league with the Big Four.[30]

Robert Mondavi

played rugby at

Stanford University

in the 1930s.

Shipments of California table wine leaped up in 1937 to more than double the 1936 level. For the first time since Repeal there was something of a sense of economic well-being in the Napa Valley. The consumption of California sweet wine was soaring as well, but Napa wineries only produced about 150,000 gallons of sweet wine in 1937. They also made close to 5,500,000 gallons of dry wine, of which about 1,000,000 were white. Another million was made from grapes coming from outside the Valley. The upswing in demand brought new calls from Georges de Latour and Herman Baade for Napa growers to plant more first-class varieties. But few of the Valley's 811 independent growers were willing to take the chance.

But there was clear evidence that Napa's reputation for preeminence in table wine production was returning. This year at the State Fair Professor Winkler headed a solid crew of UC professors who handed out forty-two of the eighty-three possible table wine awards to Napa producers. Even the Co-op won a medal for its Sauterne. Alameda County was second with sixteen awards.[31]

There was a flurry of planting during the 1938 dormant season, about 500 acres, primarily by established wineries. Most of the new vines were good standard varieties, Petite Sirah and Zinfandel, with a few Cabernet Sauvignon. White Riesling and Sylvaner were the favored whites. To a great extent this planting resulted from the encouragement that Farm Advisor Baade and visiting UC professors gave these winegrowers. The two professors most commonly seen in the Valley during the 1930s were Amerine and Winkler, who were finding out what varieties were planted where and collecting grape samples at harvest time for experiments at the UC Davis campus. They also talked to and advised everyone who would spare them a few minutes. Their message was clear—plant better varieties in places where they are suited. They stressed better winemaking practices as well. Amerine later commented on the primitive facilities that passed for fermentation rooms at wineries as prestigious as Beaulieu and Inglenook. The thrust of the UC winemaking advice aimed at cleanliness and avoiding the seemingly ubiquitous volatile acidity that had plagued the California wine image since Repeal. They pushed for cooler fermentations, the careful use of sulfur dioxide, and the control of secondary fermentations (malolactic). They promoted the use of pure yeast strains and advised against the old-fashioned habit of targeting overripe grapes at the expense of good acid levels. They also warned against the iron and brass fittings they saw in many Napa wineries. Eliminating these would cut down on the bottle haze that so often turned off potential customers.

The university had many allies in Napa. At Beaulieu J. J. Ponti and later André Tchelistcheff were always willing to help, although it took a while before de Latour got used to seeing the academics "snooping about." John Daniel, Jr. of Inglenook, the Salmina brothers, Louis M. Martini, and Brothers John (general manager) and Timothy (plant superintendent) at Christian Brothers all were later remembered for their contributions to the university efforts here. Wine industry technical and trade journals were full of articles by numerous Davis scholars, generally aimed at practical methods of increasing wine quality.[32]

ANDRE TCHELISTCHEFF AT BEAULIEU

In 1937 Georges de Latour signed a contract with the firm of Park and Tilford to act as the marketing agent for an expanded case goods operation on the East Coast. In the first years after Repeal, BV's image for its case good wines had been solid, though most BV wine was still shipped out in barrels, often through trade channels established during Prohibition for the sale of sacramental wine. It was then bottled in New York and other cities east of the Rockies.

The contract with Park and Tilford would concentrate on wines labeled

Chablis (Ugni blanc and Sémillon, more in the style of Grâves than Chablis), Riesling, Moselle (Sylvaner), Burgundy (Mondeuse, Gamay, and Cabernet Sauvignon), and Cabernet Sauvignon. There would be numerous sweet wines as well. The first shipments were a disaster. A large portion of these wines were returned with high levels of volatile acidity and various microbiological problems. De Latour was fit to be tied.

At the same time Leon Bonnet had become seriously ill and had retired. Beaulieu did have a solid, old-fashioned "practical winemaker" in J. J. Ponti, but he was not up to the laboratory tasks necessary to produce case goods for cross-country shipment. De Latour needed a first-rate wine chemist to set things straight. Thus, in 1938 he and his son-in-law, Henry Galçerand (Marquis de Pins), headed for France to find one.

They went to the viticultural-enology station of the Institute of National Agronomy, just outside Paris, and consulted Professor Marsais, the successor to the world-famous viticulturalist Pierre Viala. Marsais suggested a thirty-six-year-old Russian with a wide background in agricultural research and a solid academic and practical preparation for wine cellar and vineyard. He was just the "research man" that de Latour was looking for. An interview led to a job offer, which led to a confused series of events that got the Russian scientist his American visa. But de Latour had to pull every string within reach to bring it off. He got Leon Adams at the Wine Institute to contact UC people to support André Tchelistcheff's entry as an enologist. It didn't work. Finally the master of BV pulled the right string. He contacted California Senator Hiram Johnson, whose personal clout with the State Department was renowned. Suddenly Tchelistcheff received a telegram from Johnson assigning him a visa number. On September 15, 1938, BV's new enologist arrived in Northern California to begin a thirty-five year career at that Napa winery. Beaulieu, the Napa Valley, and the entire California premium wine industry would benefit from the work and influence of this tough-minded perfectionist, long after his first retirement from BV in 1973.

Tchelistcheff was enormously impressed by the beautiful Beaulieu estate and by the de

B. V. Winery, 1939.

Latours and their rather aristocratic life in the country. But the wines and the production facilities were another matter. He had been met in New York and was introduced to BV's wines at their agency there. Most of the wine was in barrels. The sweets were in generally acceptable condition. The dry wines definitely were not, except for the Cabernet Sauvignon, which impressed him. He knew all about the Park and Tilford problem of the previous year, but he was not prepared for the rather primitive situation he found at the BV Rutherford plant.

He immediately went to work applying the principles of sound winemaking he had learned over the last dozen years in Czechoslovakia, Hungary, Yugoslavia, and France. Clean, cooler fermentations, carefully measured application of sulfur dioxide, and an end to copper and iron fittings all became the order of the day. In short, Tchelistcheff was putting into effect most of the basic ideas being advocated at UC Davis. He also brought with him a practical know-how that put him in a position to act as a model for others. Historian Ruth Teiser called him a "bridge between early European winemaking techniques and California." Professor Amerine called him "a technician's technician." Tchelistcheff "brought a fresh point of view to the valley and winemaking and he made better wines. He made some of the best wines in the valley."

The Russian worked closely with the professors and learned things from them which he would later advocate to others. And the professors learned from him. He later stated that "the highest title that I hope will be buried with me and put on my grave," was that of "'a permanent student of the University of California.'"

Tchelistcheff was as much a viticulturalist as an enologist at BV. He was obsessed by the tendency to plant grape varieties in the wrong places. To him, Napa had three climates. In the south, near the influence of the Bay, was Burgundy. Mid-Valley was warmer, more like Bordeaux. And above St. Helena, toward Calistoga, the climate was similar to France's Rhône Valley. It was simply écologie, well-appreciated in France, but not here. Later work by Winkler and Amerine helped others finally to understand and accept these views. All it took for Tchelistcheff was a 1939 sip of a 1910 Pinot noir, made from grapes taken from the old Stanly ranch, to convince him that Carneros was Napa's "Burgundy."

Except for the serious technical problems needing his immediate attention, André Tchelistcheff's work at Beaulieu was aimed at carefully calculated long-range improvements. These would take some years before they were reflected in BV's wines. His reputation skyrocketed after the great triumph of BV's Burgundy at the 1939 Golden Gate Exposition and the subsequent release of the 1936 Cabernet Sauvignon. In his own words, Tchelistcheff became "the prophet of Napa Valley Cabernet styling...." Just as Napa Cabernet had been the chief vehicle for the rise of the Valley's great reputation in the 1890s, just so did history seem to repeat itself in the quarter century between 1936 and 1961. André Tchelistcheff was the symbolic prophet in this process; he was the practical scholar who did so much to make it happen.[33]

THE BRANDY PRORATE

A one-shot government program in 1938 made it possible for Beaulieu and other Napa wineries, particularly Beringer, to get rid of some questionable wine in their inventory and profit from the process. The bumper crop of 1937 and the coming deluge of grapes in 1938 prompted the combined forces of the federal government, the California State Department of Agriculture, and the Bank of America to put together the so-called prorate program that would divert about 45 percent of the state's grapes to brandy production. Its purpose was to save the tottering grape and wine industry of the Central Valley, but the government rules applied to almost everyone with a vineyard. Eventually about 10,000 growers and 250 wineries took part, the program operating on the New Deal philosophy of fighting low prices by promoting scarcity. The vineyardists voted 6,302–1,349 to accept the Marketing Order, with most of the opposition coming from North Coast growers. Inglenook, Larkmead, and Louis M. Martini wanted none of it, so far as Napa grapes were concerned. But Martini had a field day at his Kingsburg operation, where his plant distilled over 2,000 barrels of brandy from wine surpluses.[34]

After the 1938 vintage the Beringer still was running twenty-four hours a day. So far as Tchelistcheff was concerned, "it was a life saver. . . . I cleaned out the inventory of Beaulieu. . . . All this junk went out. I think we sold 300,000 gallons for distilling purposes." Later he used the brandy credit to secure top-grade fortifying brandy for the BV sweet wines. The Christian Brothers distilled their material at Beringer, but it didn't amount to much. Nevertheless, the prorate had a greater effect on the Brothers' operation than on any other Napa winery.

The new brandy was barreled up and stored all over the state. To get their money the distillers had to send samples to San Francisco where Professors Amerine and Marsh tasted them and certified the chemically pure and legally acceptable lots.

Meanwhile a thirty-six-year-old German immigrant with good experience in wine and brandy production, was making 65 cents per hour as a distiller at a Central Valley winery. In 1939, when he heard that war had broken out in Europe, Otto Meyer got the idea that all this brandy sitting around in warehouses might become a valuable commodity when European sources dried up. He spent six months tasting through all these warehouses, selecting the best batches. He tried to sell the idea to Schenley, but they were not interested in a product that might compete with whisky. So he turned to the Christian Brothers where his brother-in-law, Alfred Fromm, had recently struck the deal to market their wine. Meyer and Fromm had to negotiate very carefully with the churchmen, since many were not keen on the idea of the La Salle Institute being involved in the sale of distilled spirits. But eventually an agreement was struck, which, in the forties, made Christian Brothers the first popular national brandy.[35]

Two other important industry developments in 1938 and 1939 affected the future of Napa wine. The Wine Institute was instrumental in both. First, a marketing order was approved by wine producers to promote and guide a nationwide wine advertising campaign. In the first three years of the program California table wine sales grew at an annual average of almost 10 percent. In addition, the Federal Alcohol Administration, prompted by the Wine Institute, accepted California's fairly stiff wine-quality standards, a move vigorously supported by Napa producers.[36]

EVENTS OF 1938

The 1938 Napa vintage was huge, the largest since 1891. But grower income, even with the prorate, was down 45 percent from 1937. Another blow was the Bisceglia bankruptcy, which again closed down Greystone. Still, the morale in the Valley was fairly upbeat. Shipments of Napa table wine were up sharply at the end of the year and the entire industry was preparing to put its best foot forward at the upcoming Golden Gate Exposition in 1939, which would have a $50,000 wine temple with Napa wine well represented.

Also in 1938 some independent growers noticed that those who had signed up with the Co-op had not been held to the same strict guidelines in the prorate as they had been. With this in mind a few St. Helena growers decided to start another cooperative operation. They would use the old Laurent Winery (1877), just north of town, operated by the Navone family. There were seventeen original members of this St. Helena Co-operative Winery, soon to be known as the "little co-op." Today it is the site of the Markham Winery.[37]

MODERN INGLENOOK

When Suzanne Niebaum decided to reactivate the Inglenook cellar at Repeal, to manage the winery she chose Carl Bundschu, an organizer and leader with deep roots in the wine industry. His convivial presence and genuine appreciation of hospitality as an important part of public relations secured the

Inglenook name in the vocabulary of the typical Napa visitor who enjoyed fine table wine. He was not, however, a man with technical training.

The Inglenook cellar was in the charge of two technically skilled men, John Gross and George Deuer, production manager and winemaker respectively. Gross retired in 1942 and Deuer ran the cellar until 1965. These two were directly responsible for the quality of Inglenook wines, which, by the 1940s, many declared to be the best in the Valley. Actually, the impetus for this drive to perfection came from the mind of Captain Niebaum himself, through the commands of his widow and her grandnephew, John Daniel, Jr. Only the best wines were to be sold under the Inglenook label. There were to be no compromises in quality. Inglenook was not to operate with profit as the bottom line. The concepts laid down by that Finnish sea captain in the 1890s when he considered Inglenook a sort of hobby were to be the winery's credo a half century later. Bundschu accepted the challenge and young Daniel, born in 1907, seems to have bought into the family tradition long before he took over the reins of management in 1939. André Tchelistcheff later recalled that he envied the situation at Inglenook where "the philosophical position of Captain Niebaum still remained in the mind of the nephew. . . . If a vintage was not corresponding to the quality of Inglenook, it was sold in bulk. . . . Beaulieu never did that; it was too commercial."[38]

The wines made at Inglenook in the 1930s were carefully segregated. A small part was bottled at the winery under the Inglenook label and sold mostly in the Bay Area and Los Angeles markets. Most was sold in bulk, primarily in the New Orleans market, but never under the Inglenook label. Bundschu did buy wine from others and then sold it under the Inglenook label. Only thus could there have been a 1926 Inglenook Cabernet Sauvignon or 1927 Sherry, for the cellar had not operated in the dry years.

There was a stronger emphasis on premium white wine production at Inglenook than at most other Napa wineries in the thirties. Of the four gold medals won by the winery at the State Fair before the war, two were for Riesling and one was for Traminer. But old-timers remember the early Inglenook reds, particular the Cabernet Sauvignon, which won three silvers in these early years. Inglenook Zinfandels also won two silvers, as did their Barbera, later identified as Charbono by Professor Winkler. Bundschu also bought and bottled quite a bit of sweet wine, sold under the diamond label, or the I.V.Y. label, for wines of lesser quality. At the Golden Gate Exposition Inglenook wines won five silver medals, two of them for their sweet wines.

Mrs. Niebaum died in 1936 and, in Leon Adams' words, "Johnny Daniel was ready." The young Stanford graduate had prepared himself to take over the management of the entire Inglenook operation and, when he and his sister inherited the Niebaum estate, a situation developed so Bundschu could leave without it appearing that he had been forced out.[39]

In May 1939 Frank Schoonmaker came west and tasted through many of the wines at premium wineries in Northern California. Like Alfred Fromm he understood the consequences of the coming European war on wine supplies. He had organized an importing company in 1935 and was now putting together a marketing organization whose goal was to sell California table wine that lived up to the potential of the best California winegrowing districts. These wines were to be bottled under their varietal designations; no generic "Burgundy" or "Chablis" would be offered. Schoonmaker and his partner, Alexis Lichine, selected four wineries: Wente, Fountaingrove (Sonoma), Larkmead, and Inglenook. Schoonmaker also bought several wines from Louis M. Martini for his "Schoonmaker" label: a Folle Blanche, a Pinot noir, and two Cabernet Sauvignons (1935 and 1938). In the fall Carl Bundschu resigned his position at Inglenook and became the California sales manager for Frank Schoonmaker.[40] Thirty years after he took over operations at Inglenook, Daniel looked back on Schoonmaker's pioneer effort in varietal designation and wrote that it was a key factor in promoting American public awareness of top quality California table wines.[41]

Far more obvious in 1939 were the results of the wine competition at the Golden Gate Exposition, held on Treasure Island. Many in the industry likened the events to those of 1915 at the PPIE. But it was quite different. The judges at the earlier event had been distinguished and capable, but the torrent of awards had detracted from the significance of the results. At Treasure Island there was a good panel of judges chaired by Maynard Amerine. But this time the medals did not flow so freely. There were but two grand prizes, ten gold, and thirty-three silver medals for the 402 wine and brandy entries. In 1915 there had been twenty grand prizes and more than a hundred golds. Beaulieu won a grand prize for its Burgundy, Wente for its Sauvignon blanc. De Latour was also awarded golds for his Cabernet Sauvignon and Muscat de Frontignan. There were no other Napa golds, but several silver medals went to Beringer, Inglenook, and Larkmead. Four medals in all were awarded to Cabernet Sauvignons, more than to any other single varietal. Of these, three went to Napa wineries (BV, Inglenook, and Larkmead) and one to Sonoma (Fountaingrove). In Professor Amerine's opinion the Golden Gate competition "was probably the best tasting we'd had in California" since Repeal.[42]

Vintage 1939

Napa Vintage 1939 was not quite so happy and reflected the wisdom of having formed the new co-op. Many Napa wineries simply did not buy grapes from independent growers and few outside grapes were crushed at Napa wineries. A terrible heat wave hit in mid-September, with Valley temperatures reaching 108°. The vintage was orderly, the crop size about average, but prices were down from their 1938 levels. Total grower income was half what it had been in 1937. The total value of Napa grapes amounted to about 10 percent of the total agricultural product of Napa County. Poultry products here were twice as valuable as Napa wine grapes.

1940 TRANSACTIONS

Georges de Latour died on February 28, 1940 at his home in San Francisco. Leon Adams thought that his funeral in that city was the greatest of the decade, with four archbishops presiding. The 1936 Cabernet Sauvignon, which Tchelistcheff had been bringing along, was ready for release at the end of the summer, and the family decided that the wine should be named for the winery's founder. This was quite appropriate, for the Frenchman had conceived of the wine himself. For this Tchelistcheff believes that de Latour "should be considered the grandfather of California Cabernet Sauvignon." The label read "Beaulieu Vineyard / Georges de Latour / Private Reserve /

Georges de Latour's first Private Reserve Cabernet – the 1936 vintage.

Napa Valley Cabernet Sauvignon." The neck label read "A Founder's Wine," with the vintage date and de Latour's signature. Almost forty years later French wine expert Alexis Lichine wrote that "the wines of Beaulieu, particularly the Private Reserve Cabernet Sauvignon, have been among the finest wines produced in the United States." Following the founder's death there were continuous rumors that Beaulieu was for sale, but Mrs. de Latour told Horatio Stoll in 1941, "We have turned down a number of good offers because we have no desire to sell."[43]

But 1940 did see important winery property change hands in Napa. Louis Stralla's lease of the Krug place ran out, and he was not willing to pay the asking price. So he bought the Covick Winery in Oakville, moving the production equipment for his Napa Wine Company to that old Brun & Chaix plant. When he set up for the coming vintage he had a capacity of 1,500,000 gallons.

In March Louis Martini sold off his huge Kingsburg winery/distillery, determined to concentrate on premium table wine production from his Napa and Sonoma vineyards, which now totaled 550 acres. Frank Schoonmaker had convinced him that the wines he was producing in Napa should be traveling under their own labels and at the end of the year his first bottles appeared in retail stores with a label that Schoonmaker had helped him design. Years earlier Martini had told Leon Adams that someday he would be producing the greatest wine in California. In Adams' opinion the 1940 releases were "as fine an assortment of wines as the Beaulieus and the Inglenooks. . . they, ranked overnight right with the very finest premium wines of California." Tchelistcheff thought Martini's accomplishments made him an "apostle of the California wine industry." The Beaulieu winemaker loved the Martini wines, but he did not follow the same principles of production. Martini was a great blender. "He believed in a bouquet of flowers." Tchelistcheff "believed in the individual flower."[44]

The Martini Kingsburg plant was purchased by a new and short-lived wine corporation called Central California Wineries. It had been organized by the Bank of America and nineteen wineries in hopes of continuing the stabilizing operations of the 1938 prorate. In the process they gained control of Napa's Greystone Winery, which had been returned to the Bank's control after the Bisceglia bankruptcy. The U.S. Justice Department thought it saw another California Wine Association in the making and decided to come down hard on the consolidation. A young Department lawyer, Joseph Alioto, even had an indictment drawn up. But the war was now on and the government backed off when Schenley moved in and bought the two huge wineries in 1942.[45]

A more important transaction, at least for its historic symbolism, was the purchase in 1940 of the Lombarda Winery from the Forni family by a partnership headed by Albert M. Ahern, a retired businessman from Southern California. His partners' names were Charles Freeman and Mark Foster. Ahern's boyhood nickname was Abbey. Thus, Freemark Abbey became the name of the new wine operation. They bought good lots of available wine and

Albert Ahern,

founder of Freemark

Abbey, 1940.

hired Alsatian Leon Brendel as their winemaker.

The historic significance of this premium wine operation becomes apparent when one reflects on the fact that virtually every bottle of Napa wine made since Repeal and aimed at the premium trade had been produced by men with long tenures in vineyard and cellar. Here we see the beginning of a trend, previously manifest between 1880 and 1900, of men and their families attracted to the Napa Valley wine scene. They had capital to invest in a personal wine venture and a powerful desire to produce great wine. This first Freemark Abbey Winery operated for twenty years, closing after Ahern's death in 1959. During that time the winery produced a wide variety of wines. Their most famous was Pinot noir, which won a gold medal at the State Fair in 1952. A few more like Ahern would come to Napa in the 1940s. The trickle would grow in the fifties and sixties and become a flood in the seventies.[46]

Another feather in the Napa wine cap in 1940 was the filming of the Carole Lombard movie, "They Knew What They Wanted," on the Fagiani ranch (Villa Mt. Eden today). When the film premiered at San Francisco's Golden Gate Theater in October, there was a large display of Napa wines in the lobby. The stars of the movie had been invited to visit the Beringer cellars by manager Fred Abruzzini, and they did. Celebrities at Beringer became a Napa tradition over the next fifteen years. Abruzzini compounded his managerial skills with some effective public relations work, which continuously placed the historic Napa winery in the Sunday rotogravure sections of the nation's newspapers. The Lombard movie was but the first in a long series of photoplays set in the Napa Valley in the next half century.[47]

The 1940 vintage was the last in which Depression prices ruled in the Napa Valley. Prices were up a little, but growers' incomes increased sharply from the large crop. Napa winegrowers had weathered the hazardous years of the thirties and had taken steps to reestablish the Valley's reputation for premium wine production. War had come to Europe; America would be drawn into a world war before the next year ended. As a result, the California wine industry would never be the same. More important, the seeds of a dramatic revolution in Napa wine were being planted.

NOTES FOR CHAPTER TEN

1. San Jose Mercury, 3/15/1933, 3/21/1933; NVWLA III: 83; Star, 3/24/1933; Adams oral history, 53.
2. James Morgan Bray. "The Impact of Prohibition on Napa Valley Viticulture." Research paper in Librarianship, San Jose State University, 1974. A copy is in NVWL.
3. See the annual reports of the County Agricultural Commissioner for complete statistics.
4. Bancroft has a good collection of these pamphlets.
5. Saturday Evening Post (March 21, 1931): 10.
6. Harvey Levenstein. Revolution at the Table (New York 1988): 185-193.
7. NVWLA III: 320.

8. Chronicle, 10/11/1933.

9. Teiser and Harroun, 183, 200.

10. NVWLA II: 12-17; Chronicle, 12/6/1933.

11. Star, 11/3/1934; American Wine Journal (December 1933): 21.

12. American Wine Journal (January 1934): 8-10; L. M. Martini oral history, 29-30.

13. NVWLA II: 138.

14. NVWLA II: 201-210; Wines & Vines (March 1977): 24.

15. NVWLA I: 116-120; II: 69, 284-285; III: 223, 318-320, 359; Redwood Rancher (July 1979): 44; Chronicle, 12/13/1971; Register, 9/19/1969.

16. Vintage (February 1981): 51; American Wine Journal (August 1934): 15; Brother Justin Meyer (Raymond Meyer). "The History of the Christian Brothers Wineries in California." (May 5, 1966), in Bancroft; Star, 2/16/1934; NVWLA I: 246-252; III: 46-49.

17. NVWLA II: 313-334; American Wine Journal (February 1934): 20.

18. Wines & Vines (December 1933), (September 1935); NVWLA I: 61-91; II: 56-59; III: 102-109; American Wine Journal (January 1934): 8-10.

19. American Wine & Liquor Journal (June 1934): 39; Wines & Vines (June 1934), (January 1936), (June 1936), (March 1938); San Jose Mercury, 9/3/1934.

20. Adams oral history, 57, 64-69; Wines & Vines (July 1934), (December 1934); American Wine & Liquor Journal (June 1934): 124.

21. San Jose Mercury, 7/21/1934, 8/10/1934, 8/15/1934; Star, 3/30/1934, 4/6/1934.

22. Irving Marcus. "California's Co-operative Wineries." Wines & Vines (March 1953): 8-12; Star, 8/3/1934, 2/15/1935, 4/30/1937.

23. Author's interview with M. Amerine, 7/23/1984; NVWLA II: 38.

24. L. M. Martini oral history, 40-42; Adams oral history, 40, 60; Star, 4/26/1935, 5/24/1935, 8/9/1935; Wines & Vines (October 1935).

25. Frank Schoonmaker and Tom Marvel. The Complete Wine Book (New York 1934): 27-46.

26. Star, 4/10/1936, 5/1/1936, 8/21/1936; L. M. Martini oral history, 31-33.

27. NVWLA II: 46-47.

28. Ronald Eugene Isetti. Called to the Pacific (Moraga, CA 1975): 345-347, 352-355; Brother Timothy (Anthony Diener). Bancroft Oral History, 1973: 33-40; Justin Meyer manuscript, 6-7; Author's interview with Arthur Fromm, 8/16/1984.

29. Isetti, 357-358; The Wine Review (December 1939): 13-14; Wine Spectator, 6/3/1989.

30. NVWLA III: 198-199; Robert Mondavi. "Creativity in the California Wine Industry." Bancroft Oral History, 1984: 9-11; Star, 6/4/1937.

31. Maynard Amerine. "The University of California and the State's Wine Industry." Bancroft Oral History, 1972: 38; Star, 9/17/1939, 12/17/1937.

32. A. J. Winkler. "Viticultural Research at University of California, Davis, 1921-1971." Bancroft Oral History, 1973: 10; Harold P. Olmo. "Plant Genetics and New Grape Varieties." Bancroft Oral History, 1976: 94; Amerine oral history, 12-13; William V. Cruess. " A Half Century of Food and Wine Technology." Bancroft Oral History, 1967: 33-34; Tchelistcheff oral history, 82-86; NVWLA IV: 144-158; American Wine & Liquor Journal (September 1941): 24.

33. Tchelistcheff oral history, 20-66, 89-90; NVWLA II:5-46; Wine Spectator, 5/16/1986; John N. Hutchison. "André Tchelistcheff." Wines & Vines (March 1990): 24-29; Wine Country Review, 1/10/1986; Examiner,10/15/1972; Los Angeles Times, 12/27/1976, 6/28/1984; Gourmet (October 1990): 92;

A. Tchelistcheff talk to the Society of Wine Educators, Napa, 2/19/1978, from my notes.

34. The origins of the prorate are not clear; the chief actors' stories were not consistent. For a thorough, scholarly discussion see M. H. Watson. "An Analysis of Raisin Marketing under the California Agricultural Prorate Act." Master's thesis, UCB, 1940. Also see Ralph Burton Hutchinson, "The California Wine Industry." Doctoral dissertation in economics, UCLA, 1969 for a useful analysis of sources on the prorate at 200-205. Also see: Fortune, 5/1941, 8/1946; Wines & Vines (December 1962); Teiser and Harroun, 205; Blout, 19.

35. Wines & Vines (August 1938); L. M. Martini oral history, 43; Otto Meyer. "California Premium Wines and Brandies." Bancroft Oral History, 1973: 6-11; Tchelistcheff oral history, 52-53; Amerine oral history, 18-19. Author's interview with Otto Meyer, 12/20/1984; NVWLA I: 250; II: 20-21; III:88.

36. Adams oral history, 83-86.

37. NVWLA II:223; Star, 9/15/1939.

38. Tchelistcheff oral history, 112; NVWLA II: 97-137; Adams, 305-307; No Inglenook Cabernet Sauvignon for Vintages 1945 or 1947 was ever sold as such.

39. Author's interview with Leon D. Adams, 12/20/1982.

40. Wine Review (December 1939): 32; American Wine Merchant (October 1942): 28-29.

41. NVWLA II:235-237.

42. Star, 9/29/1939; Amerine oral history, 38.

43. Adams (1st Edition): 219; Star, 3/1/1940; Wines & Vines (November 1940); Tchelistcheff oral history, 89-90; Alexis Lichine. New Encyclopaedia of Wines & Spirits (New York 1985): 498; American Wine & Liquor Journal (May 1941): 26.

44. L. M. Martini oral history, 10, 48; Adams oral history, 72; Tchelistcheff oral history, 96-98; Teiser and Harroun, 203.

45. Wine Review (March 1940): 42-43; Adams oral history, 114-118.

46. Charles L. Sullivan. "The Other Freemark Abbey." Vintage (February 1981): 51, and "Winegrowing Pioneers, Yesterday and Today." Bulletin of the Medical Friends of Wine (September 1984): 3-4; Star, 7/26/1940.

47. Star, 7/12/1940, 7/19/1940; Sorensen, 140-151.

THE SEEDS OF REVOLUTION

*There are few dabblers or dilettantes among the new group. It is too tough
to produce fine wines; it requires too much skill and patience and
hard, sweaty labor to appeal to the mildly interested.*

—MAYNARD AMERINE
1964

W HEN AMERICA ENTERED THE WAR IN DECEMBER 1941, THE PEOPLE IN THE
Napa Valley went through the whole range of the country's home
front experience: rationing, war bonds, labor shortages, victory
gardens, and drives for almost everything imaginable. In 1942 the St. Helena
school kids collected over thirty tons of unused metal equipment sitting
around in vineyards and orchards for the scrap iron drive. The Beringer
victory garden came close to feeding the entire staff.

The wartime economy had a profound short-term effect on the local wine
industry, for it was not long before every raisin grape in the Central Valley

became a raisin. This situation brought a sharp decline in grapes available for crushing and tremendous profits to Napa vineyardists by the 1943 vintage. But the inflated prices peaked in 1946 and by the next year it looked like more hard times for those with large plantations of standard wine varieties.

Nineteen forty-two brought government prohibition of whisky production. Eastern distillers with capital to spare had a short-lived field day buying up California wine production facilities. This situation did not touch Napa profoundly, since most of the Valley's producers were small-change operations in the eyes of the liquor barons. In 1942 Schenley did acquire Greystone, to go along with its acquisition of Cresta Blanca and Roma, but this did not settle the future of the historic St. Helena property.

The war also modified the marketing of California wine by diminishing the number of tank cars available for shipping bulk wine to eastern bottlers. For Napa this situation only accentuated a developing reality in the Valley's case goods production. All over California it became increasingly necessary to bottle wine at the winery, a given today, but a rarity in 1941. The industry played up the quality aspect of the situation in its advertising and by the end of the war "bottled at the winery" on a California wine label had come to mean "higher quality." Napa's premium wineries benefited from increased public recognition of this variable.

Napa's top producers had already taken many of the technical and marketing steps necessary to introduce their wine to the segment of the American public that wanted high-quality wine to go with their meals. The war served as an almost perfect exclusive tariff on the European wines that had normally found their way to these consumers' tables. From 1940 until 1946 California's premium producers had a chance to sell their products with virtually no competition from France, Germany, or Italy.

It is almost impossible to examine American statistics for table wine consumption during the war to gain an insight into the Napa situation. In 1940 only about 25 percent of the California wine consumed in this country was dry table wine. This figure actually declined during the war years, although total wine consumption increased. Even when we look at Napa figures themselves, we cannot obtain a clear picture of the Valley's wine production in the early forties. Production really depended more

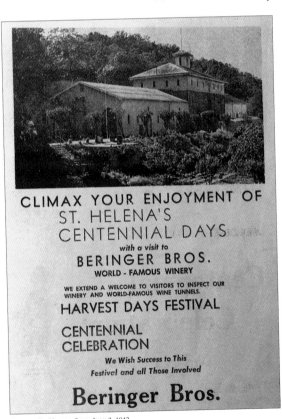

CLIMAX YOUR ENJOYMENT OF
ST. HELENA'S
CENTENNIAL DAYS
with a visit to
BERINGER BROS.
WORLD - FAMOUS WINERY

WE EXTEND A WELCOME TO VISITORS TO INSPECT OUR WINERY AND WORLD-FAMOUS WINE TUNNELS.

HARVEST DAYS FESTIVAL

CENTENNIAL
CELEBRATION
We Wish Success to This
Festival and all Those Involved

Beringer Bros.

SOURCE: ST. HELENA STAR, JULY 3, 1942.

on weather conditions than on the economic environment. In Napa, total acreage in wine grapes actually declined from 1940 to 1948, from about 12,500 to 10,500 acres.

The premium sector of the Valley's production did grow, however stagnant and depressing the overall statistics appear. During the 1940s the reputations and sales of the Big Four (or Big Five, when we start to include Charles Krug under the Mondavis) grew in the California and national markets. When we include the Christian Brothers table wines produced in Napa, the growth is even more remarkable. In 1943 the wine list of New York's Waldorf Astoria Hotel contained twenty-eight table wines from Napa producers, and no less than seventeen of these were labeled as varietals: Sémillon, Gamay, White Pinot, Folle Blanche, Cabernet Sauvignon, White Riesling, Traminer, Sylvaner, Charbono, Pinot noir, and Pinot St. George. All six of Inglenook's wines were varietals.[1] Although Frank Schoonmaker was off serving in the OSS, his varietal campaign at home was showing good results. This was a development that the California wine industry as a whole understood and supported very little. In fact, the industry press and certain officials at the Wine Institute openly resisted the use of varietal designations for many years.[2]

Brother John (at left) greets Christian Brothers workers who commuted on the winery bus during World War II.

Source: Hess Collection.

NAPA WINE PRODUCTION: 1940 — 1950

YEAR	RED TABLE WINE*	WHITE TABLE WINE*	SHERRY/ DESSERT*	TOTAL*	PRICE PER TON
1940	3,999,000	1,068,000	328,000	5,395,000	$17.00
1941	3,766,000	1,074,000	448,000	5,288,000	24.50
1942	3,150,000	878,000	456,000	4,484,000	25.00
1943	3,872,000	1,319,000	355,000	5,546,000	74.50
1944	3,913,000	1,257,000	435,000	5,605,000	104.00
1945	4,637,000	1,455,000	653,000	6,745,000	69.00
1946	4,965,000	2,324,000	752,000	8,041,000	101.00
1947	3,582,000	1,393,000	600,000	5,575,000	36.00
1948	4,599,000	1,578,000	778,000	6,955,000	35.00
1949	3,796,000	1,262,000	469,000	5,527,000	54.00
1950	2,877,000	1,042,000	212,000	4,131,000	91.50

* = In gallons.

The 1941 vintage was almost featureless, except that Napa producers made several great wines. The Inglenook Cabernet and the Martini Zinfandel (from Napa and Sonoma grapes) were both fifty-year wines, which were still drinking well in the late 1980s. The 1942 vintage was as uneventful as the previous year's. But it was clear to all by the 1942–43 dormant season that there was going to be a grand escalation of wine and grape prices during the coming year. Napa vineyardists prepared for the event by leaving monumental numbers of buds on their vines, making 1943 the largest vintage here since 1888, with the exception of 1938, when overcropping was also the rule. Grape prices ballooned to triple the 1942 level. The 1944 crop was even larger, prices even higher. In terms of constant dollars (C$), that is, grape prices corrected for price inflation, the return to growers in 1944 would not be topped until 1970. Even with the huge crop there were several excellent 1944 Napa Cabernets that were still enjoyed in the sixties.

The bud retention program in the Valley was expanded for the 1945 vintage and the growers paid for it. There was a huge state crop, a tremendous statewide dry wine carryover from 1944, and a terrible deluge in the midst of the harvest. Tonnage was up 20 percent and prices were down more than 30 percent. Quality was wrecked. But the relief and joy that came with the end of the war in August softened this economic blow.

Wartime Transactions

Edgar Bergen

visits St. Helena.

The war brought shortages of almost everything except liquid capital for investment. It was next to impossible to acquire materials to build or renovate a wine facility before 1946, but the government's calls for sacrifice did not hamper the buying and selling of buildings and vineyards. Distillers were eager to acquire anything that might produce an alcoholic beverage. The eastern bottlers wanted to acquire West Coast plants to do their bottling "at the winery." And those who could sense the growing potential of premium wine production were also on the lookout for places to settle their dollars. This type of investment would most affect the future of Napa wine.

The large transactions in the industry did not have a great effect on Napa production. Schenley turned Greystone into a bottling plant where

Source: St. Helena Star.

NAPA WINE

the liquor concern bottled much of its Cresta Blanca line. Actually, a large part of the bottled goods leaving Greystone during the war carried the label of that historic Livermore winery.[3] The only purchase of a Napa facility by an eastern bottler was the acquisition of the old Montebello plant in St. Helena by New Jersey's L. M. Renault Company.

A casualty of the war years was the prestigious Larkmead label. Felix Salmina's death in 1940 put the winery in a state of limbo for a while. In 1943 it was purchased by a group of Chicago investors, then by B. C. Solari in 1948. It was a story that would be repeated all too often in the North Coast wine country; a historic premium winery is acquired by outside interests intent on cashing in on the label's prestige, but not willing to invest the capital or energy to maintain the quality on which the image was based.[4]

Louis M. Martini

An important transaction took place in the Carneros in 1942 when Louis M. Martini bought two hundred acres of the Stanly ranch. André Tchelistcheff had joined Martini in this rediscovery and was buying Carneros grapes, particularly Pinot noir, throughout these years. He was not able to get the de Latours to make a real commitment here until 1962, when they bought 142 acres near the Martini vineyards.[5]

North of Napa the Eshcol Winery had not been making wine for several years. When owner J. C. Fawver died in 1940, his widow leased the great wooden edifice and the surrounding vineyards to the Beringers. Fawver's tenure at Eshcol had lasted since 1893.[6]

Further up the Valley, 1943 brought three historic transactions. In Oakville Martin Stelling, Jr. purchased a large part of the historic To Kalon vineyard and set about creating one of the largest premium varietal properties in the world. A wealthy San Francisco real estate tycoon before he was forty, Stelling acquired his first Napa vineyard land in 1935. No one in Napa Valley in these years understood better than he the great change taking place there in terms of premium varietals. When he was killed in a 1950 automobile accident, the Valley lost a pioneer in the coming revolution. But his six-hundred-acre vineyard went on to become a core plantation that helped supply that movement.[7]

Later closely related to the To Kalon situation, another transaction saw the Charles Krug property finally come into the hands of a committed winegrowing family, Cesare Mondavi and his sons, Robert and Peter. The elder Mondavi had shipped Lodi grapes for the past twenty years and also owned a part of the nearby Acampo Winery. Before the war, son Peter handled the enologist's job at the 2,400,000-gallon Acampo operation, while Robert directed the production at Sunny St. Helena. Like so many Central Valley operations, Acampo was an attractive property for eastern bottlers pressed by tank car shortages. Kentucky's Gibson Wine Company bought Acampo in 1943 and Robert encouraged his father to use the money to buy the Krug property from the Moffitt estate. Peter was off to war in the Chemical Corps and mother Rosa Mondavi seems to have been a powerful force in persuading Cesare to borrow the $75,000 needed to buy the Krug place. A year later a family partnership was formed and in 1946 the Mondavis bought the Sunny St. Helena Winery outright. Cesare and Rosa kept their home and business in Lodi, while Robert and Peter produced Napa wine, good quality standard wines at the Sunny St. Helena plant under the CK label, as well as a new line of Charles Krug premium wines, mostly varietals, they hoped would expand the Napa Big Four to the Big Five.[8]

Seven checks for $200 each, made out to Louis M. Martini, comprised the third important transaction of 1943. They were the result of Martini's persuasive and very successful machinations to form an association of Napa vintners. To hear the old-timers talk about the genesis of the Napa Vintners, Martini's arm-twisting was primarily in the form of a great lobster dinner, at his Sonoma property, of all places. The result was a decision to meet regularly to discuss matters important to Napa wine, be they technical, financial, cultural, or gastronomic. The founding fathers were Martini, Tchelistcheff, John Daniel, Fred Abruzzini, Stelling, Stralla, Charles Forni, the Mondavis, and Brother John of the Christian Brothers. Martini was the first president and Daniel was the first vice president.

Martini always liked to make it sound as if having a jolly time was what really brought the organization together. "An eating and drinking association," he called it. Tchelistcheff put it more elegantly. It was "epicurean not administrative." Martini "decided to have a group who enjoyed the products of the local folklore and the cuisine and wines." But there were always serious matters to consider. In 1943, the vintners were most concerned about government price controls on wine and the lack of such controls on grape prices.

Stories of the regular Vintners' meetings at a certain St. Helena restaurant abound. Years later they let a *San Francisco Chronicle* reporter sit in. He called the affair "Lunch with the Brotherhood." Actually, it was very Napalike, particularly when we recall that Charles Krug, Henry Pellet, and Seneca Ewer called together just such a group in 1875, the St. Helena Vinicultural Club, which met regularly for years at Vintners' Hall. In 1983 the Vintners became a formal trade organization, the Napa Valley Vintners Association (NVVA).[9]

Another transaction that took place in 1946 just after the war was the Trinchero family's purchase of the old Sutter Home/John Thomann Winery. John and Mario Trinchero now began putting together a vinous product line that, in a few years, would be the widest in the Valley.

THE ENTHUSIASTIC ENTREPRENEURS

Francis Lewis Gould was an eastern wine merchant who came to California in 1940, became a friend of Frank Schoonmaker, and worked a while at Los Amigos Winery near Mission San Jose. Robert Mayock, who resuscitated that old Grau and Werner property in 1934, was probably the first of a new breed of gentleman vintners who started coming onto the California wine scene after Repeal. The most famous of these was Martin Ray, who bought the Paul Masson Winery in Saratoga in 1936. Chaffee Hall, a corporate lawyer, built his Hallcrest in the Santa Cruz Mountains in 1943. In the same year Frank Bartholomew began reviving Buena Vista in Sonoma. These were men attracted to fine wine, good food, and the pleasant life that seemed to accompany winegrowing, particularly if they had already made a good fortune, or inherited one.

"Paco" Gould, longtime publicist for the Charles Krug Winery.

We have already met Albert Ahern, who in 1940 opened the Freemark Abbey Winery north of St. Helena. Ahern qualifies as the first of these enthusiastic entrepreneurs in the Napa Valley. Others would follow, people who would soon be investing their energy, their capital, and their intellectual resources to produce wines in small quantities. They would serve as models for those who followed in the fifties and sixties.

Gould's second job in the Northern California wine country was at Freemark Abbey, where Ahern lured him to make wine recommendations and to help promote the new premium brand. Ahern may have been the first of Napa's post-Repeal idealistic enophiles, but the new Freemark Abbey was not a great success. Gould did not stay long and in 1949 took a job in the Valley that would make his name something of a legend here. We shall meet him then in charge of public relations at Charles Krug.[10]

A remarkable early wave of enthusiasts

SOURCE: JACK ELLIS.

struck the Valley in 1943 when a triumvirate of friends began casting about in the hills east and west of St. Helena, looking for property, with an eye on potential vineyard land. The result was three winegrowing operations, one on lower Howell Mountain and two on Spring Mountain, right across the Valley.

In 1943 Jerome and Virginia Draper found the old Lemme Vineyards and La Perla Winery on Spring Mountain up for sale. Herman Hummel had been running the famed property since Repeal, buying it outright in 1941. But he could not make a go of it on the old Schilling land. The Drapers loved the 285-acre estate with its eighty acres of vines and bought it. They began replanting the vineyard to top-quality varieties and eventually added the 150-acre Beringer property, downhill from their place. They never brought the Lemme/Schilling La Perla Winery back into production, but the vineyards have become an important source of fine varietals for the Napa region. In 1945 the Drapers also bought a portion of the Stanly ranch in Carneros. In 1970 Hummel sold the upper ranch, formerly the McPike estate, to Fritz Maytag, who, in addition to his acquisition of the Anchor Steam Beer company, began meticulously terracing and planting his York Creek Vineyard, a home today to some of the most prized grapes on the continent.[11]

The Drapers' friends, Fred and Eleanor McCrea, also bought land nearby on Spring Mountain in 1943. He was an advertising executive from San Francisco. They did not start planting vines on the 160-acre Timothy Feeley homestead until 1948, diversifying in whites, Chardonnay, Pinot blanc, White Riesling, and Traminer. They obtained their Chardonnay budwood from the Wente Livermore Valley vineyard. This variety made the name for the tiny Stony Hill Winery, which they built in 1951 for the next year's first real crush. Over the next four decades the thirty-five acres of vineyard at Stony Hill produced grapes that have added a dimension to Napa's reputation for fine white wines. Certain vintages of Stony Hill Chardonnay with some age are treasures, purchased in years past by those lucky enough to make it onto the McCrea mailing list. These wines have shown the potential ageability of some California whites.[12]

J. Leland Stewart and his wife were neighbors of the Drapers in Hillsborough, on the San Francisco Peninsula. They found their way to the other side of the Valley, on about the 1,100-foot level of Howell Mountain, where they bought Peter Stark's property, the 1887 Rossini Winery. Stewart had been a supervisor of export sales for Armour and Company, but was only forty-eight when he retired and settled into the bucolic life of a mountain winegrower. He had yet to acquire a fortune and was destined to keep getting his hands dirty in the vineyard and winery for several years. On the advice of his label printer, Jim Beard, he named his winery Souverain. By the 1950s he was producing a diversified line of fine varietal wines that regularly piled up medals at the State Fair. Many of these wines became the standard for the time.

Stewart had a small vineyard, which he began replanting to better varietals. But he bought grapes all over, particularly from his friends Draper and McCrea. Robert Mondavi, another early Napa friend, helped him sculpt some of his varietals and bought some of Stewart's wines in bulk, until he was ready to release his finished case goods. Another friend was Laurence Stern, a winemaker at Charles Krug, who had a good background making wine in the German style, that is, whites with moderate alcohol, a touch of residual sugar, and a solid acid backbone. Souverain's White Riesling became famous. Perhaps even more famous was Stewart's Green Hungarian, from an ordinary grape of uncertain origin, which Jerome Draper had in abundance on his place. Draper challenged Stewart by contending that Spring Mountain grapes, however poor the variety, could be made into a superior wine. To prove his point he gave the Howell Mountain winemaker several free tons of Green Hungarian. Somehow, Lee Stewart made memorable wines from these grapes year after year, regularly winning medals in the "miscellaneous white table wine" category at the State Fair. It was claimed, but never proved, that Stewart, like Jacob Schram a century before, kicked up the quality of his ordinary grapes with the careful addition of a little muscat.[13]

Stewart thought his best wine was his 1951 Cabernet Sauvignon, which won three gold medals at Sacramento: the one he won himself, and those won by two others to whom he sold small batches when he was strapped for cash. He was also proud of his Petite Sirah, but was always miffed that the Concannons in Livermore beat him by two months in releasing the first post-Repeal varietal from that grape.

Along with Louis M. Martini, Lee Stewart was a pioneer in exploiting the Zinfandel as a fine varietal, capable of producing a wine worthy of extended cellaring when produced from hillside vineyards and fermented into a concentrated style that retained the raspberry fruit associated with that grape. Souverain Mountain Zinfandel produced from Stewart's source in the Atlas Peak area helped break down the post-Repeal low-quality stereotype that had plagued that variety prior to the sixties.

Between 1947 and 1957 tiny Souverain Cellars won thirty-four medals at the State Fair, in ten separate categories of table wine. Stewart won gold medals for Grenache Rosé, Zinfandel, Green Hungarian, Sylvaner, Cabernet Sauvignon, and Burgundy. When Robert Mayock died in 1945, Stewart acquired his Los Amigos label and used it on his popular dry sherry. By the late sixties, when the great wine boom hit the California industry, many lovers of Napa wines had concluded that Lee Stewart's little winery on Howell Mountain had lived up to its name.[14]

Entrepreneurial enophilia was in the air in the upland to the south even earlier than 1943. In fact, Jack and Mary Taylor were struck by the bug in 1936 when they stayed at Lokoya Lodge on Mt. Veeder and she came across a beautiful old winery on one of her walks. In 1941 they were able to buy the building and its 260 acres from Henry Brandlin, who had owned the old Fischer Winery since 1921. They had contacted Professor Winkler, who came up and approved the area for winegrowing.

Jack Taylor was a chemist who had been working for Shell Oil Company. After the war the couple headed back to the Mt. Veeder property with their three children and started putting together Mayacamas Vineyards. They began reconstituting the vines, like the McCreas, placing special emphasis on Chardonnay. Also like the McCreas they got their Chardonnay budwood from Herman Wente. Later they planted Cabernet Sauvignon and took out the old orchard, ending up with sixty acres of vineyard. Until the new vines came into bearing in 1951 they bought wine and sold it under the Lokoya label. In 1958 they did something unheard of, to underpin their financial position; they sold stock in Mayacamas and paid dividends in bottles of Chardonnay. Their annual shareholders' meeting in late summer became a popular attraction for wine lovers all over. Their Chardonnay won a gold medal at Sacramento in 1957. Later their interesting rosés from Gamay, Zinfandel, and Cabernet Sauvignon became quite popular. Their chatty newsletter, one of the first after the Mondavis' effort in 1949, contained recipes by Mary Taylor and news of their vintages and life on Mt. Veeder. By 1968, when they sold the winery to

Vintage time

at Mayacamas in

the early fifties.

Robert Travers, they had developed a mailing list that reached more than 10,000 people. Travers has operated Mayacamas ever since, concentrating on Cabernet Sauvignon, Sauvignon blanc, Chardonnay, and Pinot noir. These long-lived wines of remarkable authority led a noted wine writer to proclaim recently that Mayacamas was "the best winery in the USA."[15]

THE END OF THE WAR

The end of the war in 1945 meant challenge and opportunity for the California wine industry. One of its foremost leaders, Edmund Rossi, looked into the future and predicted that in the next twenty-five years Americans would be drinking more table wine than sweet wine. He foresaw that the North Coast counties would gradually convert their entire vineyard plantation to first-class varietals.

Frank Schoonmaker, back from the war with a bronze star and a French Croix de Guerre, wrote in 1945 that Americans no longer served California wine "with an apologetic smile or shrug. Almost against their will they have been convinced." He now felt that California "produces at least a few wines worthy to rank with the world's best." But he warned that European wines would soon be back on the shelves.

The postwar years were certainly full of promise for Napa producers. Their premium wines had become thoroughly established during the war years. But Rossi's time frame was correct. There were still two decades of hard work ahead.

VINTAGE 1946

Napa vineyardists had a great vintage in 1946; it was huge and grape prices almost reached the record level of 1944. This vintage was, however, the last gasp of the wartime boom in the wine business. For wineries things were not quite so fine. Raisin grapes no longer had to become raisins, and the old oversupply squeeze was soon on them. There was lots of talk about the future of grape prices and the way they were currently hurting wineries. It was widely and correctly predicted that North Coast grapegrowers were killing the goose that was going to have to supply their eggs in the future.

Not only was the 1946 vintage huge, but the quality was excellent as well, particularly for those who did not overcrop their vines. Tchelistcheff made sure that his suppliers made a proper crop and he turned out some BV wines that became famous. Twenty years later his 1946 Pinot noir, what there was left in a few cellars, was proof positive for those who thought that this temperamental grape had a fine future in the Golden State. In 1990 to replenish their wine library the owners of BV paid $1,700 per bottle of this 1946 elixir at a Los Angeles wine auction. They were able to buy some of the 1942 for a mere $550.[16]

Reality came with a thud in 1947 when grape prices in Napa dropped by more than 60 percent. It was an average-size crop, but the wine from it had to trickle into a gigantic state inventory, swelled by the 1946 flood and bloated by the general decline in wine consumption after the war. Again, the quality of the reds was very high, a fact that few noticed until several years later.

From 1947 until the early 1960s the Napa Valley wine industry seemed to be running in place. The number of bearing vines in the county barely changed until the mid-sixties, holding at about 10,500 acres. There had been twice that number in 1891. From 1947 to 1960 the Napa Valley vineyardist averaged just under $60 per ton for his grapes. From 1943 to 1947 he had averaged $87. The general national price inflation that made the dollars he received worth even less than before exacerbated this bad state of affairs.

Nevertheless, many factors would help move Napa wine in the direction Rossi had predicted. The industry itself, in its national advertising campaigns, was pushing the use of table wine with food, and there was some evidence that it was paying off. More important was the fact that Napa's large-scale premium producers were turning a profit. In a national brand name poll Christian Brothers placed first in the country for domestic consumer recognition. Other California premium brands in the top twenty were Beringer, Beaulieu, Simi, and Wente. Louis Martini's sales were growing steadily, as were Inglenook's, although John Daniel rarely turned a profit. The Mondavis were also growing with their premium line and their CK generic line.

During these years, as well, the percentages of Napa's most common grape varieties were gradually shifting. The most ordinary, that is, Palomino, Alicante Bouschet, Grand noir, and Mission, were slowly being replaced by better varieties. By 1961 only about 9 percent of the Valley's vineyards were planted to these very undistinguished vines. On the other hand, the total Cabernet Sauvignon, Pinot noir, and Chardonnay came to just over 6 percent of the total. (In 1991 these three accounted for 66 percent of the Napa plantation.) About half the Napa vines were in good standard red wine varieties, such as Carignane, Zinfandel, Gamay, and Petite Sirah. There was also a good stand of white varieties such as Sylvaner, Sémillon, Sauvignon blanc, and French Colombard, which amounted to about 20 percent of Napa's vines. It should be clear from these statistics, however, that in 1961 there was still no clear focus on the varieties that would best demonstrate Napa's ultimate potential for premium wine production. But when the demand appeared, producers would accelerate the transition. (See the table at the end of this chapter that illustrates the situation.)

High quality did not come simply from better varieties. In Napa André

Tchelistcheff worked to bring winemakers together to pool their findings and their knowledge. In 1947 he set up the Napa Valley Enological Research Laboratory in St. Helena. He did jobs for wineries, testing chemical composition to avoid catastrophes. But more important was his creation of what he called the Napa Valley Technical Group, a no-nonsense, cooperative effort to exchange practical information on the production of high-quality wines. Lee Stewart, the Mondavis, "Louis Martini, son," as André called Louis P. Martini, John Daniel, and others reenacted the technical sessions of the 1880s promoted by Charles Krug's Vinicultural Club. It was very non-European and very much in the tradition of the Napa Valley. Everyone involved understood that individual success promoted the success of their beloved wine valley. The spirit was the same that animated the NVVA. All for all and all for one, and have a good time in the process. It was Krug's "Gemeinschaft," community effort, as opposed to "Gesellschaft," corporate self-interest.[17]

The State Fair revived its wine competition in 1947. Napa won 45 percent of all the medals awarded for table wines. Wente of Livermore and Sonoma's Fountaingrove took top individual honors, but Louis Martini was right in there with five medals. Inglenook had four. With his two silvers Lee Stewart showed that the enthusiasts were coming alive. Even though times in the industry were difficult, the competition at the Fair, supervised by the university professors, gave Napa producers a sense of well-being. Until 1957 the outcome of the competition was a happy part of the Napa wine scene.

The Davis professors still visited the Valley, promoting better varieties, giving technical short courses, helping wherever they could and, in the process, keeping abreast of the practical developments passed along by Tchelistcheff's Technical Group. The professors' technical papers in industry publications gave a solid scholarly underpinning to day-to-day advances being made in Napa cellars and vineyards. In 1950 the American Society of Enologists was formed to give structure to this scholarly work and to bring wine producers into closer contact with the scholars.

1948 — 1953 TRANSACTIONS

Despite some grim statistics there were signs of growth and development for Napa wines in the forties and fifties. In 1948 wine industry consultant Louis Gomberg declared that "Napa wines are in a class by themselves." Others were listening. Visitors to California, particularly in groups, were placing the Napa Valley on their want-to-see list. In 1949 a group of six hundred Harvard graduates toured the Valley's wineries. The Medical Friends of Wine regularly toured the Valley, as did the Bay Area chapters of the International Wine & Food Society. Fred Abruzzini made the great Beringer estate, with its hand-hewn caves and spectacular Rhine House, a must-see for Valley visitors. When the results of the 1949 State Fair wine competition were announced, *Wines & Vines*, "The Voice of the Wine Industry," casually remarked that "as usual Napa County took more awards than any other." In the summer of 1949 BV organized a tasting of their wines in Paris, which was attended by some of the top names in the world of French wines. No scorecards were tallied, but on this side of the Atlantic the outcome was touted as a great triumph for California premium wine.[18] Just outside St. Helena a sign now greeted visitors announcing their entry into the "Table Wine Center of the World."

Napa Vintages 1948 to 1951 have little historical importance, although several wines could later be cited as additional jewels in the Valley's red wine crown. Huge volume and low prices were the features of 1948. Fewer grapes and outstanding Cabernets marked the 1949 vintage. In 1950 there was half a crop and an exhilarating but short-lived jump in grape prices. And then there was 1951, with a big crop and some of the best red wine grapes in local vintners' memory. In a few years the 1951 Cabernets from such as Martini and Beaulieu would send the same kind of messages to connoisseurs and potential investors that the 1946 and 1947 Pinot noirs would deliver in the 1960s.

1950 brought the Christian Brothers' purchase of Greystone. For some years they had been using the huge building as a storage facility. The Institute's profits were now soaring, mostly from their brandy and sweet wine production in the Central Valley, but also from their table wines, which were among the most popular in America.[19]

The year also brought the death of Martin Stelling in a terrible automobile accident. By now his To Kalon Vineyard in Oakville had almost 600 acres of first-class varieties. In 1953 Ivan Schoch, Stelling's foreman, purchased the estate. At first, production went to Beaulieu, later to Charles Krug. Today a large portion of To Kalon is part of the Robert Mondavi vineyards.[20]

Soon after the 1950 vintage

several enthusiastic wine entrepreneurs in Northern California formed the Chateau Winegrowers Association. It was the coming together of some very serious "amateurs" who had started up small premium operations just before or during World War II. The Napa wineries included Souverain, Stony Hill, and Mayacamas. The organization was more symbolic than effective. It is also worth noting that no new small-scale Napa premium vintners had come onto the scene in recent years. In fact, the 1950s saw few such new enthusiasts striking out into the almost uncharted currents of premium winegrowing. In the North Coast the few who did were generally less successful than those of the thirties and forties.

Douglas Pringle tried to revive Schramsberg in 1951 when he organized Mt. Diamond Cellars, with the hope of producing sparkling wine and table wine in Jacob Schram's old caves. He had been preceded there in the 1940s by Joseph Gargano's California Champagne Company. In neither case was the wine good enough to carry the enterprise.[21] Such was not the case with Leon Brendel, Freemark Abbey's first winemaker. In 1949 he bought a plot along Highway 29, south of St. Helena, and planted a small vineyard of Italian Grignolino vines, a seemingly strange choice for the sixty-five-year old Alsatian enologist. The operation was a retirement project for Brendel, but his "Only One" Grignolino became popular enough after its 1955 release to be chosen to carry the Paul Verdier label for the City of Paris department store.

Actually, the only enthusiast to start up in the 1950s and make a lasting mark on Napa premium wine was Hanns Kornell. He bought the old Larkmead Winery in 1958, after the fine Salmina structure had lost its old luster as a cog in the B. C. Solari Italian Swiss Colony/Allied Grape Growers empire. Kornell had a solid background in winemaking. He came from a German winegrowing family, having fled the fatherland at the beginning of the war. In California he made wine at Los Amigos and Fountaingrove before going east to work at two wineries specializing in sparkling wine. When he returned to California in 1952 he started producing his own bottle fermented sparklers at Bonded Winery 870, the old Sonoma Wine Company. To help pay the bills he also made dry wines, dessert wines, and vermouth under several labels. But it was the méthode champenoise sparkling wine that was on Kornell's mind. He and his family have been producing these bottle fermented wines at the Salmina plant ever since. Some have been in a traditional French style, others unusual, from grapes such as White Riesling and muscats.[22]

Kornell and Pringle were not the only Napa folks caught up in the sparkling wine fever of the 1950s. The national market was growing and the Christian Brothers went all out for it in 1955, soon converting Greystone into a Champagne plant for their bulk process sparklers. And in 1954 when

Tchelistcheff took over as BV general manager from J. J. Ponti, the winery took up the production of sparkling wines again. To start off they laid down 16,000 bottles of the 1950 vintage; by 1956 there were 90,000 in their bins. Even Mario and John Trinchero made some bottle fermented sparkling wine at Sutter Home in the fifties. They won an award at the State Fair, but these bottles were a very small part of the almost fifty vinous products to be found on their price list at the modest plant across from the Martini Winery.

In 1952 a truly important Napa transaction took place when the Gallo Winery in Modesto struck a deal with the Napa Co-operative Winery to buy the growers' entire production of red and white wine. The arrangement lasted for thirty-four years and helped bring financial stability to the large number of Napa vineyardists dependent on the Big Co-op as an outlet for their grapes. Next year the Little Co-op also became an exclusive Gallo supplier. Over the years one often heard that an important part of Gallo's popular table wines came from North Coast sources. For the reds, particularly the Hearty Burgundy, Napa Petite Sirah was an essential component. In 1956 the two Napa co-ops sent Gallo the wine from almost 17,000 tons of grapes, about 40 percent of the total Napa Valley crop.[23]

It took a lot of energy and commitment for a high-quality winery to survive in the 1950s. Most did, but some went under. The greatest shock came in 1953 when Sonoma's Fountaingrove announced it was pulling its vines. For that county it was the equivalent of Beaulieu going out of business. Napa's Deer Park Winery on Howell Mountain stopped production in 1958. Freemark Abbey closed its doors in 1959.

Wine industry expert Louis Gomberg was incensed by the fact that the California industry was not more concerned about the fate of its premium producers. "Lose the premium sector and you lose everything." In the same column he attacked the cheap goods then parading as quality items under some California labels. He estimated that 2 percent of adult Americans were drinking premium wine at a rate ten times greater than the rest of the population. This tiny element had to be nurtured and increased.[24]

THE MONDAVI BOYS AT CHARLES KRUG

Irving Marcus, the publisher of *Wines & Vines,* was dazzled by what had been happening at the old Charles Krug place since Cesare Mondavi bought the winery in 1943. After the 1949 State Fair Marcus wrote that "The Mondavi boys at Charles Krug walked off with four gold medals and also established themselves as the leading Rhine wine producers in the state."

Actually, the Mondavi feat at Sacramento was nothing compared to their conquests in the next years at the Fair. In the ten competitions between 1947 and

1956 the brothers won 121 medals for their table wines, forty of them gold. No other California winery came close to this mark. At first they were most successful with white table wine, varietal and generic. They even won a few medals for wines in their Napa Vista line of lower priced generics. From 1948 to 1952 they had an absolute lock on the gold for Traminer. (The term Gewürztraminer was not yet seen on California labels.) They won gold medals for varietals in ten categories: Traminer, Sémillon, Sauvignon blanc, Pinot blanc, Chardonnay, White Riesling, Grey Riesling, Gamay, Cabernet Sauvignon, and Zinfandel. Toward the end of this period their red wines did better and better, their Cabernet winning three golds in the mid-fifties. By the early 1950s it was irrefutable that the Valley's Big Four had been augmented by one.

After Peter Mondavi came home from World War II the Charles Krug Winery became a family corporation on May 3, 1946. But Robert Mondavi had been running the Krug place since 1943, while Sunny St. Helena was still pouring out a steady flow of palatable bulk wine. The 1943 vintage had been so profitable that Cesare Mondavi was almost able to pay off the note he had negotiated to help buy the Krug place, just from the grapes alone.

The family decided to keep the bulk and premium operations separate. The bulk wine was good enough to sell in glass and was introduced to the national market under the CK label. Until the mid-fifties they tried to keep their CK and Krug lines out of the same regional markets. The Charles Krug label was reserved for varietals and certain generics, such as Chablis and Claret. Peter and Robert were not impressed by the lax regulations that allowed a wine with only 51 percent of a variety in its makeup to carry that varietal designation on its label. Many of the Krug wines contained 100 percent of the variety indicated.[25]

After 1946 the division of labor at Charles Krug was fairly well-defined. Robert was the general manager and called the shots. Peter was in charge of production. Robert was in charge of selling Krug wines and was on the road continually in the early years. Matters of wine style were family decisions, but again Robert tended to call the shots. But the brothers' relationship was not always a placid one. The division of labor seemed to fit the two men's characters; Peter was the careful technician, quiet and somewhat introverted. Robert was more outgoing, enthusiastic, charming, and forceful. Each of these Stanford graduates had all the intellectual equipment needed to run his side of the family business.

Both young men had a solid technical background, having worked at UC Berkeley after they had finished at Stanford. Robert's skills were augmented by his practical work at Sunny St. Helena, Peter's at the Acampo Winery before the war. But Peter's UC experience was special. He had worked with Professor William Cruess and had been deeply involved in experiments on cold fermentation of white table wine, a field well-understood in Germany, but almost unheard of in California. The ultimate success of the Krug whites derives from this early work and the brothers' continued devotion to the project in the more practical environment of St. Helena. During these years Peter worked with Tchelistcheff. Questions concerning the perfection of Napa's white table wines were ever on the agenda when the Technical Group had its informal meetings. Later Tchelistcheff thought that he and his "great friend" Peter Mondavi had taken the important steps in this field. The two men's accomplishments were "parallel," he said. But the necessary equipment to take the practical steps involved was first obtained at the Krug plant; BV had to wait until after the big fire there in 1947. Only then would Madame de Latour come up with the requisite financial support for Tchelistcheff.[26]

Peter and Robert also experimented with acid correction, sterile bottling, and vacuum corking. Later their slightly sweet whites were properly stabilized through a system of sterile filtration that helped produce the series of crisp, fruity wines that so mesmerized the State Fair judges. Later their interest concentrated on the improvement of their red wines through experimentation with skin contact and small French oak cooperage. Peter's production team also contributed to his success in the Krug cellar. First came Al Huntsinger and Laurence Stern. The latter thoroughly understood the principles of white wine production in the Germanic style. Later came William Bonetti and Robert Stemmler, both technical masters in the field of red wine production.[27]

Robert Mondavi's energy and commitment made him a roving ambassador for table wine as a part of the good life in America. He was a zealot on this matter and has remained one into the nineties. For the industry he acted as chairman of the Wine Institute Board of Directors. His contributions to the industry have become legendary. Even in the early years he took his message about wine into every medium open to him. He wrote for industrial periodicals on table wine production and promotion. In 1953 he called on the industry to concentrate its effort on the "real wine users," that is, the people who regularly drank table wine with dinner. It was what might have seemed a bootless call in an age when almost 80 percent of all California wine production was concentrated on fortified sherry and dessert wines. Over the next eight years these "real wine users" upped their consumption by 64 percent. In a 1963 radio broadcast Mondavi was so brash as to predict that in ten years Napa's total wine grape acreage would rise 50 percent. (In fact, it doubled.)[28]

Robert Mondavi believed that in wine promotion the image was almost as important as the wine itself. When he traveled he treated clients lavishly, too lavishly to Peter's way of thinking. Robert loved wine tastings and promoted them whenever he had a chance. He was ever ready to set an expensive foreign bottle next to a like bottle of Krug wine, inviting comparisons and suggestions. In 1944 Jim Beard introduced Robert to Francis Lewis Gould, the bon vivant formerly in charge of public relations at Freemark Abbey. "Paco" and Robert liked each other and over the years developed the idea of a winery newsletter that would help carry Robert's message about Krug wine and about wine in general to the consumer.

In 1949 Gould became editor of *Bottles and Bins*, "uncorked and poured from time to time" until 1979 when the beloved Paco died at the age of ninety-five. Gould brought to the publication an elegant wit and erudition, combined with a no-nonsense love of wine. But he understood his job well. He printed recipes, industry chatter, and anecdotes "on wine in general, as may be pleasing to wine lovers, be they drinkers of Charles Krug wines, or be they in the diminishing ranks of those to whom that delectation has yet to be revealed." Jim Beard printed the elegant little folio, illustrated by Malette Dean, a noted graphic artist. By 1952 it was mailed to 7,000 wine lovers.[29]

The next year the Mondavis opened their tasting room, with Paco Gould in charge. There would be wine tastings on the lawn; later came August Moon Concerts at the winery. Robert Mondavi loved to place wine in an environment of high culture— art, ballet, classical music, jazz, folk music—not because wine somehow was enhanced by the juxtaposition, but because it belonged. Good wine, in Mondavi's mind, was an integral part of high culture in the Western World.

The good Krug wines seemed to get better and better in the fifties, and there was increasing variety. In 1954 Peter seemed to bring it all together with a 6,000-gallon batch of Chenin blanc which he sterile filtered, leaving about 2 percent residual sugar. Robert knew the wines of the Loire and particularly liked the semi-sweet wines of Vouvray, produced from the Chenin blanc. In California it often traveled in bottles improperly labeled "Pinot Blanc" or "White Pinot." (The Mondavis actually made a White Pinot of their own for a few years, a blend of Pinot blanc and Chenin blanc.) Robert's wide knowledge of European wines and Peter's technical ability brought this California wine into being. They entered their 1954 Chenin blanc in the 1955 State Fair competition as

Uncorked and poured
from time to time by

Charles Krug Winery
St. Helena, California

BOTTLES AND BINS

VOLUME I   ST. HELENA, CALIFORNIA, JULY, 1949   NUMBER I

"miscellaneous white wine" and won the gold medal, repeating that success in 1956.[30] Looking back in 1986 Peter Mondavi recalled that he and his brother "were a good combination."

In 1959 Cesare Mondavi died. His wife, Rosa, became president of the family corporation. They continued their aggressive varietal approach three years later when they bought Ivan Schoch's 550 acres of To Kalon, 107 of which were in Cabernet Sauvignon. But there were familial storm clouds on the horizon. Without their father's quiet, authoritative, and moderating presence, even though he had been in Lodi most of the time, Robert and Peter's relationship became more strained and eventually ruptured in 1965.[31]

THE AMERICAN CONSUMER

The seeds of the coming revolution were germinating as the decade of the fifties wound down. In 1958 Louis Gomberg, always the champion of high quality, used his column in *Wines & Vines* to point out the continuing profitability of premium wine production. "High priced table wines are going great guns while the old standbys are languishing." In 1956 Inglenook, Krug, Beringer, Beaulieu, and Martini joined others to form the California Premium Wine Association, aimed at working cooperatively to further the cause of wine for "real wine users."

In the same year *Consumer Reports* discovered premium American wine and did their first evaluation of California table wine producers. Fifty-eight percent of the reds and 51 percent of the whites came from Napa producers. Krug led the field with thirteen recommendations, followed by Martini (11), BV (8), Beringer (8), Christian Brothers (6), and Inglenook (4). This report heralded a remarkable change in national consumption patterns. In the fifties Americans increased their consumption of table wine at just a slightly higher rate than population growth. Then between 1960 and 1962 this consumption increased more than it had during the previous eight years. A large part of this growth came in the California market itself. Whereas in 1945 the ratio of dry table wine consumption to sherry/dessert wine consumption in the Golden State had been 1.0:2.5, in 1960 it was 1.0:1.1. Yet the national ratio in 1960 was still 1.0:2.3. California was about six or seven years ahead of the rest of the nation in consumption of dry table wine.

It is difficult to account precisely for this remarkable change, but the factors are fairly clear. Premium producers were working hard to market their wines, putting special emphasis on restaurant sales. The Wine Institute and Wine Advisory Board's advertising campaigns focused on the use of wine with meals. Consumers themselves were changing. Before Prohibition those few who drank premium table wines might have traveled in Europe and seen firsthand the Old World traditions that placed wine on the table of a large part of the French and Italian populations. These Americans were an uncommon few whose perceived aristocratic ways were as likely to draw scorn as emulation. But after World War II millions of Americans traveled in Europe, mostly solid middle-class folks who were being exposed to Western European wine culture and to the relationship between good wine and good food.

At home wine and food clubs became attractive social outlets. American wine writers such as Frank Schoonmaker, Robert Balzer, and Mary Frost Mabon had drawn attention to California's premium table wine producers in the 1940s. In 1955 John Melville's *Guide to California Wines* gave the potential enophile a tour of the California wine country, winery by winery, wine by wine. Three years later Leon Adams produced the first edition of his popular *Commonsense Book of Wine*, which stripped away much of the irrelevant wine pedantry that might intimidate beginners.

Certainly not the least of the contributing factors was the general improvement in the quality of California wine after World War II. Before the forties there was no way that a typical bottle of California table wine could have attracted the interest of anyone who knew and admired good European wine. The minuscule production of Napa's premium producers in the 1930s simply did not find its way onto the shelves of very many quality East Coast wine shops. By the end of the fifties New Yorkers intent on buying bottles from Napa's Big Five could find them. And it was also possible to find bottles of Souverain and Mayacamas here and there. Stony Hill was another matter.

In Napa one could measure the growing interest in wine by the number of people now pouring into the Valley to visit wineries, take a tour, and take advantage of the tasting room's sampling services. In 1960 Charles Krug hosted 50,000, Christian Brothers 85,000.[32] People had also become willing to pay more for good wine, and Napa grape prices rose accordingly. Between 1950 and 1959 vineyardists here earned $184 income per bearing acre. But the period of 1955–1959 saw the figure climb to $201. From 1960 to 1962 the number soared to $267.

These high prices also brought happy faces to growers who supplied grapes to the Valley cooperative wineries. The Napa Co-op had 230 comfortable members in 1960; their two plants now had a total capacity of 2,500,000 gallons. The St. Helena Co-op had upped its capacity to 1,250,000 gallons for its sixty members. Often at the annual meeting of the Big Co-op's members Julio Gallo would drive up from Modesto to review the year's work with the assembled growers. In later years he would fly over by helicopter.[33]

There were also some frowns among the smiles. Many people still grumbled that Napa wineries were crushing too many grapes from outside the Valley. No one complained about Louis Martini's Sonoma Zinfandel. It was the truckloads hauled in from the Central Valley that provoked the same kind of complaints that had been heard since the 1880s.

Another somewhat puzzling complaint came from Napa's premium producers about the State Fair wine competition. Beaulieu had dropped out in 1954, Martini in 1955. Inglenook and Krug widened the boycott in 1957, along with producers from other districts, such as Wente, Almaden, and Paul Masson. In the following years Professor Amerine was in charge of the reformed organization of the judgings, but, except for Christian Brothers, only the smaller producers such as Souverain, Mayacamus, Sutter Home, Stony Hill, and Leon Brendel would compete. To this day the reasons advanced by the larger producers have never shown any sort of central logic or uniformity. Amerine later observed that most of the big producers had all the medals they needed.[34] And what more could they gain, except perhaps defeat at the hands of such enthusiasts as Lee Stewart, the Taylors, or the McCreas?

INGLENOOK — JOHN DANIEL AT THE CONTROLS

If the demands of family loyalty had not placed John Daniel at the helm of Inglenook, he probably would have settled on some vocation that placed him regularly at the controls of an airplane. If his passion for wine had approached his love of flying, could the wines of Inglenook in the fifties have been any better? Daniel christened the little landing strip near the winery "Rutherford International Airport" and in 1951 was appointed Commander of the Napa County Sheriff's Aero Squadron, whatever that meant. But he did give Inglenook his best shot, even in the face of personal and family problems that might have sent another winery into a tailspin.[35]

Daniel and winemaker George Deuer had Inglenook perfectly focused on the coming triumphs of the fifties before the forties were gone. They were both committed to a varietal approach. Daniel decided that any wines not good enough to bear the Inglenook label would be sold in bulk or under a second label, which meant that there was no 1945 or 1947 Inglenook Cabernet Sauvignon. Vintage dating of wines at Inglenook became a tradition before most California wineries were willing to consider the practice. Estate bottling became something of a passion for Daniel.

Most of the Inglenook production then was concentrated on white wines. Daniel won a gold for his Chardonnay at Sacramento in 1949 and 1956. He consistently won medals for his Pinot blanc, Sémillon, and Traminer. But those who look back today on Inglenook's great days commonly emphasize the excellence of Deuer's red wines, which by the early fifties were turning people's heads. He won golds for Pinot noir, Gamay, Charbono, and Red

Pinot, from a variety Californians called Pinot St. George (probably the French Négrette).[36] Deuer also made small batches of Grenache rosé, which Daniel called Navalle, after the little creek which then ran through the Inglenook property. For these he won golds in 1948 and 1955. Daniel also loved sherry and followed the university's work on the use of flor culture in sherry production. Like Louis M. Martini up the road, Daniel turned out a series of consistently fine dry apéritif sherries, which won three golds in the fifties.

Cabernet is the varietal for which Napa Valley can claim world-class status today. In 1987 James Laube claimed that Inglenook Cabs of the forties and fifties are "perhaps the greatest expression of what Napa Valley Cabernet has to offer."[37] Deuer aimed for consistency through blending these wines. He actually had a little of the then rare Merlot and Cabernet franc to add to the Cabernet. But it was the blending of wines from Daniel's three vineyards that was unique. They had the old vineyard in front of the winery, there were the vines around Captain Niebaum's old home next door (now Niebaum-Coppola), and there were the vines from Napanook. In 1947 Daniel had bought this last vineyard, which lay along the western hills near Yountville, from Louis Stralla. It had promising gravelly clay-loam soil and gave the blend tremendous power and wonderful fruit definition. This powerful fruit led André Tchelistcheff to argue that Deuer's represented the quintessence of Napa Cabernets, while BV's were more in the French style. Part of the result came from the blending and part from the long ageing in large oak ovals, never small barrels. The best of these ovals were the "casks," which became a part of Inglenook's marketing strategy for the vintages of 1955 and after.[38]

Most people from these early days, and those who have paid the enormous prices bid up at recent auctions, have their own list of top Inglenook Cabernets. The 1941 and 1943 vintages are usually mentioned but rarely seen. The 1958 seems to be on everyone's list, as is the 1955 Cask Selection. The 1964 Cask Selection is still a favorite.

These great wines were essentially Deuer's handiwork, but what limited financial success Inglenook gained in the late fifties depended on Daniel himself. His high standards cost Inglenook money, but he was always ready to take commercial advantage of these standards. His campaign for recognition of the "Estate Bottled" term on the label is a good example. He combined this effort with a strong Northern California advertising campaign in 1953. He later worked up a series of lighthearted ads on this theme. One showed a little grape looking wistfully over the fence into Inglenook. The ad asked, "Did you hear of the neighbor's poor little grape that tried to crash the crush at Inglenook?" Not a single outside grape went into an estate bottled Inglenook wine.[39] We shall see this concept was badly battered in years to come after Inglenook changed hands.

No one did more than John Daniel to achieve and maintain the high level of quality and the attendant prestige that Napa Valley premium table wine received in the fifties. His high standards were, Tchelistcheff thought, "exquisite." The BV winemaster admired and envied Daniel, "a real vintner-châtelain, with an estate, properly speaking. Now there are many estates, but then his was the only one." Tchelistcheff found Daniel's consistent commitment to quality standards was "unbelievable."[40]

THE VANGUARD OF THE REVOLUTION

We have noted already the short list of enthusiasts who jumped into the rough waters of Napa Valley premium wine production in the fifties. Things would soon be changing. The conversion of the Valley's vineyards to top premium varietals was gradually taking place. People were also beginning to look for additional places here to do the planting. Louis M. Martini and André Tchelistcheff already had the idea. In 1961 Professor Winkler openly expressed it when he called for the re-vineyardization of the Carneros. The year before René de Rosa bought a 400-acre Carneros ranch on which he found the remains of the old Talcoa Winery. He heard Winkler's call and in 1963 became a Carneros vineyardist when he began planting his Winery Lake Vineyard.[41]

Andre Tchelistcheff

and Joseph Heitz

in the BV enology

lab. 1957.

Orchard land was also being converted to grapes where the soil and situation were right. Between 1956 and 1961 Napa prune acreage dropped from 9,000 to 7,651 acres. By 1971 there would be less than 2,000 acres. One such historic conversion took place in 1959 on a forty-two-acre plot of excellent Bale loam. An enthusiastic couple found the place south of Oakville, across from the university's experimental vineyard. Bernard and Belle Rhodes contacted Professor Winkler and were advised to plant the new vineyard to Cabernet budwood taken from rows 34 to 38 on the university plot. About twelve acres went in to Cabernet and fourteen to White Riesling, later budded over to Cabernet. But the Rhodes decided that a Napa commute to his physician's office in the East Bay was a

NAPA WINE

bit much, so they sold the ranch to Tom May. He bought the adjacent property, planted it to Cabernet and named the whole spread after his wife, Martha. There is, of course, more to this story.[42]

A related situation, beginning here in 1961, brought another enthusiastic entrepreneur into the winemaking game. Joseph Heitz was a thorough professional in terms of his winemaking background, having graduated from the Davis enology curriculum in 1948. He worked for Gallo, Guild, and Mission Bell before moving to Beaulieu in 1951, where he served as Tchelistcheff's assistant for seven years. Meanwhile he earned his master's degree at Davis and in 1958 moved to Fresno, where he taught enology and was instrumental in establishing the state college's program there in that discipline. But how many could have worked seven years in the Napa Valley at BV and stay in Fresno?

On Hanns Kornell's suggestion Heitz contacted Leon Brendel and found his "Only One" vineyard and tiny winery below St. Helena for sale. The old Alsatian was seventy-six and in failing health, now willing to part with his retirement hobby and its Grignolino vineyard. Heitz needed to borrow money to buy the place and to purchase start-up equipment, but stirred little interest at the banks. Eventually he was able to round up a few private investors.[43]

Thus began the first of the eight new successful Napa winery enterprises of the sixties. Heitz Cellar, Schramsberg, Robert Mondavi, a revived Freemark Abbey, Chappellet, Spring Mountain, Sterling, Chateau Montelena—these names march across the page like hussars, leading the charge, in the vanguard of the great wine revolution of the sixties and seventies.

NAPA VALLEY VINTAGES, 1951 - 1959				
YEAR	TONS PRODUCED	GALLONS PRODUCED	VALUE	GROWER PRICE
1951	39,109	6,919,000	$2,275,000	$58.17
1952	24,932	5,078,000	1,144,860	45.92
1953	28,504	5,458,000	1,488,479	52.22
1954	34,234	6,505,000	1,797,337	52.50
1955	32,743	7,085,000	1,994,580	60.92
1956	41,504	7,458,000	2,490,240	60.00
1957	30,405	5,242,000	1,581,000	52.00
1958	39,959	7,006,000	2,497,437	62.50
1959	31,512	5,752,000	2,123,145	67.38

1951

In 1964 Maynard Amerine pronounced the 1951s "magnificent wines, full of color and with delicate bouquet." Bernard Rhodes declared that they were what started him collecting California Cabernets.[44] It was a fairly big crop that didn't start coming in until late September. Prices slipped from the heady numbers of last year. Vintage in Napa was 66 percent red and 5 percent sweet.

1952

Spring frosts below 26° cut crop in places. But the short crop did nothing to improve prices. Vintage was long and orderly, lasting into November. Many excellent wines, powerfully concentrated.

1953

A long and rainy spring was interrupted by several bad frosts. Crop was thought very short until grapes started coming in. Another long vintage which lasted into November. Quality was satisfactory. Rising table wine consumption a popular topic.

1954

A big crop severely hurt by an August 28 rain that caused havoc in the Zinfandels. Otherwise a good vintage and a long, orderly harvest. Prices stayed firm. Imported grapes, with a crop this large, very irritating to Napa growers. Co-op profits up. Napa vintage 63 percent red.

1955

There was not enough rain to support what would have been a large crop. More and more growers outside the co-op made long-term contracts with independent wineries for their premium varieties. But of all premium varieties, only Sauvignon blanc, Petite Sirah and Zinfandel were yet listed separately in official statistics. White wines particularly successful this year. Prices rose and table wine consumption figures were even more promising. Napa vintage 67 percent red.

1956

Christian Brothers bought the 250-acre Forni ranch below St. Helena. The Valley was flooded between December and February, but spring was almost perfect. Better prices led to lots of overcropping. Prices remained steady with a huge crop. Grape quality of later ripening varieties very good. Low temperatures and October rain hurt the quality of reds, which had good flavor but did not age well.

1957

Everything pointed to a good vintage, with plenty of rain and fine weather until the September 26 downpour, followed by seven inches in October. Early varieties harvested in great shape and brought high prices. Some Pinot noirs were cellar candidates, but Cabernets were not memorable. Average prices went down and a short crop left growers unhappy.

NAPA VALLEY WINE GRAPE ACREAGE — 1961 VS 1991

BEARING & NONBEARING ACREAGE	1961	1991
Red Wine Varieties		
Alicante Bouschet	228	1
"Burgundy" (includes Early Burgundy,		
Refosco, Mondeuse, and others)	752	10
Cabernet Sauvignon	387	9768
Carignane	819	29
Gamay	554	367
Grand noir de la Calmette	270	0
Grenache	17	6
Malvoisie (Cinsaut)	40	0
Mourvèdre (Mataro)	25	3
Petite Sirah (Duriff)	1748	412
Pinot noir	166	2636
Valdepeñas (probably Tempranillo)	49	0
Zinfandel	949	2179
White Wine Varieties		
Burger (Elbling)	232	10
Chenin blanc		1152
French Colombard	236	43
Green Hungarian	191	2
Palomino (Napa Golden Chasselas)	332	8
Pinot blanc (includes Chenin blanc in 1961)	278	124
Sauvignon blanc (includes large		
Sauvignon vert acreage in 1961)	890	2827
Sauvignon vert	14	
Sémillon	221	352
Sylvaner (includes all Rieslings in 1961)	327	4
White Riesling		388

These data give but a faint hint at the dramatic effects of the coming wine revolution on Napa Valley acreage. Note the small 1961 acreage in Cabernet Sauvignon, however good a few wines from some producers. Compare that to the current acreage. And where is Chardonnay? In 1961, it was still included in "miscellaneous white," which was not even included in the annual report. By 1991 this variety had become Napa's most common white wine variety with 9989 acres planted.

1958

The number of wineries declined from thirty-eight to thirty since 1951. Lots of spring planting, mostly to good white varieties. Total acreage remained stagnant. Vintage was early and orderly. Prices went back up, with national wine consumption rising steadily. Warm weather lasted into November. All varieties seemed to produce good wine. Some Cabernets were great, rivaling the 1951s for later fame. In 1964 Amerine advised people to let them age. Some were still excellent in the nineties.

1959

A dry year with a scorching summer. St. Helena hit 111° on July 10. The vintage started on August 28 and was rapid and fairly orderly. Hot weather cut crop, but yields were satisfactory. A huge September 17 rain frightened growers, but excellent weather followed. Prices remained firm. Lots of grapes were brought in from other districts. Many Cabernets were memorable, despite the heat.

NOTES FOR CHAPTER ELEVEN

1. American Wine Merchant (February 1943): 27. Sonoma had thirteen, Livermore and Santa Clara eleven each.
2. Wines & Vines (January 1943). The Idwal Jones papers in Bancroft contain revealing examples of the opposition within the industry to varietal labeling.
3. Star, 11/301942, 1/29/1943; Wines & Vines (March 1943).
4. American Wine & Liquor Journal (May 1942): 21; Wines & Vines (June 1948).
5. L. P. Martini oral history, 35.
6. Wine Spectator, 6/16/1985.
7. NVWLA III: 136; Wines & Vines (August 1943), (June 1950).
8. R. Mondavi oral history, 12-19; NVWLA III: 197-202; Star, 3/5/1943, 12/22/1944, 2/22/1946, 5/3/1946.
9. Star, 2/1/1962; L. M. Martini oral history, 40-43; Tchelistcheff oral history, 100; San Francisco Examiner/Chronicle, 10/13/1974; The Napa Valley Newsletter (1:1)(1985):5, published by NVVA.
10. Francis Lewis Gould. My Life With Wine (St. Helena 1972): 21-23.
11. NVWLA II: 283-309.
12. NVWLA I: 146; San Francisco Magazine (October 1964): 26; Connoisseur's Guide to California Wine (November 1976): 93.
13. Author's interviews with Jerome C. Draper, Jr., 8/17/1990, and Bernard Rhodes, 2/3/1991.
14. NVWLA III: 223-228; Vintage (February 1977): 20.
15. NVWLA II: 254-279; Vintage (November 1976): 20; Wine & Spirits (February 1990): 22.
16. Star, 1/4/1990.
17. Star, 2/13/1948; Tchelistcheff oral history, 90-92.
18. Wines & Vines (August 1949).
19. Star, 4/27/1950.
20. Star, 5/11/1950; Tchelistcheff oral history, 73-74.
21. Adams oral history, 33; NVWLA IV: 295.
22. Wine Spectator, 11/16/1978; Wine Country (December 1981): 50; Chronicle, 4/15/1982, 1/15/1988; Star, 10/23/1980.
23. Star, 9/25/1952; Register, 9/19/1969; Tchelistcheff oral history, 110-111.
24. Wines & Vines (May and November 1955).
25. NVWLA III: 200-208; Mondavi oral history, 19-35; Cyril Ray. Robert Mondavi of the Napa Valley (London 1984): 60-69.

26. Lindy Lindquist. "A Legacy of Golden Grapes." Vintage (November 1973): 35; Tchelistcheff oral history, 131, 126.

27. Wine Spectator, 6/1/1986.

28. Robert Mondavi. "The Long Memory." Wine West (38:6), 9; Wines & Vines (February 1953).

29. Gould, 27-29; Bottles & Bins, 7/1949; Los Angeles Times, 10/18/1979; Fred Beck. Wine Book (New York 1964): 177-179; John N. Hutchison. "The Remarkable Robert Mondavi." Wines & Vines (March 1986): 20.

30. John Melville. Guide to California Wines (San Carlos, CA. 1955): 21-22, 79-81.

31. Star, 12/3/1959, 1/18/1962; Wine Spectator, 6/1/1983.

32. Star, 10/20/1960.

33. Star, 4/18/1957, 5/2/1957, 8/25/1960.

34. Amerine oral history, 39-46; Star, 8/29/1957; Bottles & Vines, 10/1956.

35. For a lively and controversial story of Daniel's personal life see: James Conaway. Napa, The Story of an American Eden (Boston 1990): 37-44, 53-55, 64-67.

36. Pierre Galet came to this conclusion, but after his ampelography was published, as the result of a visit to California in 1980. See viticultural expert Lucie T. Morton's letter to Wines & Vines (October 1982): 52.

37. Wine Spectator, 4/30/1987.

38. NVWLA II: 122-123; Wine Spectator, 6/1/1985.

39. Wines & Vines (November 1953), (September 1955), (April 1960).

40. Tchelistcheff oral history, 68-69, 112.

41. Practical Winery (November 1984): 46; Wine Spectator, 5/15/1987.

42. San Francisco Examiner/Chronicle, 9/18/1983; Philip E. Hiaring. "Martha's Vineyard." Wines & Vines (May 1979): 70-73.

43. NVWLA III: 236-240; Joseph E. Heitz. "Creating a Winery in the Napa Valley." Bancroft Oral History, 1986; Wine Spectator, 1/31/1990; Robert Benson. The Great Winemakers of California (Santa Barbara 1977): 176-177.

44. Maynard Amerine. "The Anatomy of a Superb Wine." San Francisco Magazine (October 1964): 29; Wine Spectator, 6/1/1985.

REVOLUTION ACHIEVED

The Napa Valley has influence beyond the wines we make here.
The camaraderie that exists, the long term values we share may be more important
than the wine itself. It is still possible for the individual to break new ground,
achieve new things in a decent way.

—JAMIE DAVIES
1984

THE REVOLUTION IN AMERICAN WINE IN THE SIXTIES AND SEVENTIES PROBABLY changed the country's wine drinking habits forever. Napa experienced the revolution as a turbo-boost for table wine consumption. The corporate ownership of old family wineries also became a Napa fact of life in these years, complicated in some cases by foreign ownership of these corporations. The number of new enthusiastic entrepreneurs skyrocketed. The continuous upward surge of California wine quality was no revolution at all, but public perception of California wine, particularly Napa wine, as a real contender in the world of great wine was certainly revolutionary. In this regard the Bastille was stormed at a 1976 blind tasting in Paris. But the grapes that went into the ten Napa wines involved were harvested between 1969 and 1973.

From 1960 to 1973 Napa had a private revolution of its own. The land in the Valley and on its hillsides regained the predominant viticultural character it had possessed in 1890. During these years Napa vineyard acreage almost doubled to more than 20,000 acres. The quality of varieties also improved; by 1973 most of the vines in Napa were of varieties generally associated with the production of world-class wines. Most new wineries were larger than those started since Repeal. These had been small operations, often referred to in the press as "boutique" wineries. Almost all those entrepreneurs in the first wave had taken over old, disused winery facilities. The difference in the capital position of the new operations can be inferred from the sizeable structures that began changing the physical environment of the Valley.

In 1966 the Sutter Home tasting room offered the widest range of wine products in the Napa Valley.

The greatest revolution in the Napa Valley in these years was in the attitude of its inhabitants toward the environmental future of this gem of nature. This movement peaked in 1968 when the County Board of Supervisors acted to save the unincorporated areas of the Valley and its hillsides from the steady incursion of suburbia, which had caused thousands of acres of agricultural land around the Bay Area to be paved over since World War II. But this important issue was not finally resolved in 1968.

The fight began in December 1959 when the *Star* mentioned that a freeway bypass might be built in the Valley, cutting around St. Helena. Next

September the call to arms was sounded when the State Highway Commission unveiled a proposal for just such a bypass. It would take off around Rutherford to north of St. Helena, east of the old highway, and right through the vineyards. The Mondavi family immediately denounced the plan and called for organized resistance.[1]

The upshot was the formation of the Upper Napa Valley Associates (UNVA), a coalition of environmentalists, vineyardists, and some winery people. Their first goal was to head off the freeway and kill the bypass. In 1964 the Commission firmed their plans. A final stretch of freeway from Yountville to Ritchie Creek above St. Helena would be finished in 1974. The *Star* cried out that it was now a question of "Vineyards vs. Freeways." Farm Advisor Lloyd Lider painted a grim picture of Napa's viticultural future. But Supervisor Julius Caiocca answered that there was no question as to the necessity for a freeway. It was "only a question of location." The Napa Valley Vintners Association had warmly endorsed Caiocca for reelection in 1962. His victory by eleven votes was properly credited to that organization's support.[2]

The 1974 date meant that the threat to the Valley was not imminent. In fact, the State Commission eventually made it clear that whether or not Napa had a freeway depended on the people of the Valley and their elected representatives. One state official indicated that "the last thing the people of the Upper Napa Valley have to worry about is a freeway through their vineyards," that is, if their supervisors opposed it. But, he added, if they went ahead and filled up the Valley with homes, a freeway was exactly what they would get.[3]

Anyone concerned about the fate of the Valley's vineyards would have been impressed by their demise near the town of Napa in the early sixties. This conversion south of Salvador Avenue, where mostly prunes and older vines had grown, caused Napans to extrapolate the process into the next two decades and predict what became the watchword of those committed to saving the vineyards—"Santa Clarafication."

By now the great agricultural land that had been the Santa Clara Valley was being transformed into the Silicon Valley. It was a very thorough urban and suburban conversion. For the next two decades the image of what had happened to that South Bay valley and its viticultural industry would act as a meaningful caveat in the rhetoric of those intent on preserving the agricultural environment of the Napa Valley.

Actually, the vineyards around and just north of Napa, mostly on deep silty and adobe clay soils, were not important in the production of first-rate table wine. Vineyards were being pulled up around Napa at the same time as prune orchards above Yountville were being torn up and the old-style vineyards there were being converted to the premium varieties of the future. Between 1960 and 1973 a total of 7,066 acres of Napa prune orchards disappeared, along with 1,000 acres of walnuts. During this time the value of the Napa fruit and nut crop rose more than 500 percent. Meanwhile, the value of wine grapes as a percentage of the fruit and nut crop rose from 43.5 percent to 97.9 percent, partly because of the rise in grape prices and partly because vineyards were increasingly planted to more expensive varieties.[4]

NAPA VALLEY VARIETAL ACREAGE, 1961 - 1973

Red Wine Varieties	BEARING 1961	1964	1968	1973	NONBEARING ACREAGE 1973
Cabernet Sauvignon	387	504	1067	2432	2168
Pinot noir	166	198	506	1013	1339
Zinfandel	949	955	899	747	421
Merlot	3*	5*	5	183	216
Petite Sirah (Duriff)	1748	1791	1577	1153	82
Gamay varieties	554	688	937	1071	448
Carignane	819	811	764	534	3
Alicante Bouschet	228	223	168	58	0
Grand noir de Calmette	270	267	225	144	0
Mondeuse (Refosco)	370	376	373	242	0
Early Burgundy (Abouriou)	382	380	390	268	0
Misc. and mixed	434	560	425	345	46
TOTAL RED ACRES	**6310**	**6758**	**7336**	**8190**	**4723**
White Wine Varieties					
Chardonnay	60	75	246	785	917
Sauvignon blanc	120*	150*	272	298	175
White Riesling	150*	200*	294	517	529
Chenin blanc	150*	317	616	729	301
Sémillon	221	226	267	190	7
Gewürztraminer	40*	40	112	193	66
French Colombard	336	523	670	643	9
Sylvaner	150*	130	230	208	0
Grey Riesling	100	90	151	220	83
Burger (Elbling)	232	243	265	215	0
Green Hungarian	191	191	182	116	0
Palomino	332	330	289	176	0
Pinot blanc	100	100	78	39	0
Misc. and mixed	899	798	822	595	0
TOTAL WHITE ACRES	**3081**	**3561**	**4496**	**5269**	**2090**
TOTAL WINE GRAPE ACRES	**9391**	**10319**	**11832**	**13459**	**6813**

*Prior to 1968 some totals are only approximate. The 1973 nonbearing acreage indicates the immediate future in the early 1970s and the varieties in high demand, since they were recently planted and have vines under four years old. In 1973 the true character of Napa's coming white plantation was still not in focus. Between 1973 and 1990 Chardonnay acreage grew by almost 1000 percent. In 1973 the predominance of red wine varieties is also obvious. Planting in the next few years will close the gap between the two categories.

As if to mirror the concerns for the future of the Valley's vineyards in the sixties, other Napans came together in these years to promote and preserve the history of Napa wine. Many of these also had risen to the challenge of the freeway and suburban development. The origin of the idea for a wine library in the Valley is difficult to discern from the historical data. M. F. K. Fisher mentioned the possibility after an informal dinner discussion in 1961. Maynard Amerine talked to a library support group later in the year, stressing the importance of preserving the primary sources of Napa wine history. Francis Gould did most of the early legwork, collecting money and rounding up a few books to get things started. Later he contended that he, "despite my sex, was midwife for this infant." After Amerine's talk a wine library board was formed, with "our wine bibbing printer" Jim Beard as president. Mrs. Albert Ahern, André Tchelistcheff, Mrs. Stephen Clark, Charles Meadows, and Louis P. Martini were on the first board, as were those already mentioned. After the first meeting the *Star* named Gould the organization's "guardian angel." In July 1963 they began forming the association. The first president was Bernard Rhodes, with the aforementioned as the first board of directors. Amerine and Gould added to the book collection by rounding up duplicates on wine and viticulture in the UC Davis Library.

Next year Beard and Amerine expanded the NVWLA's operations by organizing a series of five St. Helena lectures by the professor on wine and wine history. By 1967 the concept of an Association wine course had been expanded considerably. At first Beard organized a series of weekend wine

The Napa Valley Wine Library's summer courses are taught by experts. Here Hanns Kornell explains sparkling wine production.

classes taught by wine and food people of the Valley. In 1968 these short courses were concentrated in the summer months. By 1971 they had attracted a total of 687 alumni, 77 percent of whom were from the Bay Area. Each received a classy diploma printed by Beard that granted the degree of Journeyman of Wine Appreciation. It conferred on the graduate the right to "voice and defend opinions on vinous matters with confidence, extol wine with conviction, and drive a hard bargain with wine merchants." (My wife and I received our degrees in 1968.)

Meanwhile the growing library became a part of the St. Helena Public Library and collected materials on wine in general and primary source material on the Napa wine industry. Maynard Amerine contributed his collection of lantern slides of the Valley wine scene that Frona Wait had made in the 1880s. In 1963 John Melville contributed his papers.

Certainly the most lively aspect of the NVWLA's activities has been the member's annual tasting of Napa wines. It started in a small way after a showing of "They Knew What They Wanted" in 1963. Starring Charles Laughton and Carole Lombard, the 1940 movie was filmed in the Napa Valley. By 1966 the tasting was an outdoor affair at the Spottswoode mansion in St. Helena. In 1972 the event attracted 870 to the lawn of the Charles Krug Winery. In recent years the tasting has been held at the Silverado Country Club to accommodate the two to three thousand tasters. In 1990, 107 Napa wineries showed off their Chardonnays.[5]

An important contribution to the preservation of Napa wine history was the oral history project that Jim Beard instituted in 1968. In 1974, when Gunther Detert was president of the Association, the first volume of recollections by long-time Valley residents was transcribed. In 1985 Detert's committee released the fourth volume. To date the bound collection contains eighty-five interviews and documentary collections amounting to 1521 typed pages, an essential source for this study.

THE BIG FIVE

The Christian Brothers

In the fifties references to the Big Five Napa Valley wine producers meant Beaulieu, Inglenook, Louis Martini, Charles Krug, and Beringer. One might well ask, what about Christian Brothers?

Certainly that great wine and brandy operation produced good wine. But as public perception in the sixties came to focus on the wineries which might someday bring forth world-class table wines, one rarely heard the Christian Brothers label mentioned. Its size, its profits, its emphasis on fortified wines and brandy from its Central Valley plants, and its large production of bulk process Champagne all worked against a premium image. Its twenty-one State Fair gold medals for table wines from 1960 to 1962 added little to this image, since none of the Big Five was in the competition.

Following Brother John's death in 1962, Brother Timothy was in charge of the Institute's vast cellar operations and became something of a national celebrity. His name and face, not to mention his world famous corkscrew collection, became intimately associated in the public mind with Christian Brothers products. But "Brother Tim" and his production assistant until 1972, Brother Justin Meyer, did more than create public images. They took advantage of the advances in sterile filtration to bring out several extremely popular, slightly sweet table wines. One, a light muscat dubbed Chateau La Salle, was one of the few California table wines that could be purchased almost anywhere in the United States. Leon Adams minced no words in 1972 when he called it "the best-known wine of its type in the world." Wines such as this and the well-received Pinot de la Loire (Chenin blanc) placed the Christian Brothers on the cutting edge of the wine revolution. They could profit from the growing interest in table wines and from the residual American sweet tooth. Through the huge Fromm and Sichel marketing mechanism they could place their products wherever wines in America were sold.

Brother Timothy and his associates bought into the movement toward varietal wines but would not budge on the matter of vintage dating. By the mid-sixties the new breed of American wine connoisseurs regarded this practice as essential when they selected premium wines. The old saying that "all California years are vintage years" had become a scorned symbol of ignorance among collectors of California Cabernets, who well knew the difference between the '56s and the '58s.

Christian Brothers emphasized blending in the traditional fashion of France's Champagne houses. For the moment this approach to production and marketing worked well where consistency of product, rather than vintage variation, was a plus for the novice consumer. The Christian Brothers label, with Brother Timothy's signature, continued to be number one in American consumer recognition in the sixties. But in the seventies the operation's unwillingness to fight for a position among the top varietal producers eventually placed the Institute's products in the category of such mid-premium producers as Almaden, Paul Masson, and Cresta Blanca. This was a position which, by the eighties, would have a deadening effect on the sales growth of the Christian Brothers' varietal table wines.

But nothing deadened the Valley's warm devotion to the Brothers' world-renowned cellarmaster. Brother Timothy served as President of the NVVA and for twenty-eight years sat on the executive committee of the Wine

Institute. In 1977 he won the American Society of Enologists' Merit Award. In that year he was also named *Wines & Vines* man of the year. In 1976, however, he reminded an interviewer that the Christian Brothers constituted a religious congregation devoted to educational work. Wine and brandy production was simply a means to that end.[6]

Beringer Brothers

In the sixties, Beringer Brothers lost its luster in the constellation of the Big Five. Through the fifties the winery was generally thought to be competitive with the best of Napa table wine producers. But an examination of the State Fair medals prior to 1957, for what that may be worth, indicates that the 1876 winery almost never broke into the winner's circle, and was rarely even close. A 1957 silver for Pinot noir was Beringer's nearest thing to a triumph in that decade.

Their product line lacked clear focus. In 1963 Beringer offered no less than eighteen different table wines, including a blend of Grignolino and Pinot noir. The generic wines could be purchased by the gallon, a plus for the consumer but no boon for the Beringer premium image. There were also nine fortified wines, several bulk sparklers, and a brandy. Beringer quality suffered from a shortage of working capital. The *San Francisco Chronicle's* wine critic looked back from his 1977 vantage point on the decaying situation and concluded, as did most industry observers, that "the high and never-ending demands for capital arising out of modern technology and today's competitive marketing could not be met by the private resources of the family. As a consequence, the quality of the wines sadly deteriorated." Roy Raymond, winery general manager, later observed that quality was increasing throughout the premium industry, "and so much of it was dependent on new equipment, and we just didn't have the money."[7]

The Martinis

Nobody was talking about decline in quality at the Martini winery in these years. The family expanded its vineyard holdings in Napa and Sonoma Counties in the sixties and raised production to almost 250,000 cases by the end of the decade. The key to the Martini success and their consumer image was consistent quality coupled with fair value. In addition they offered an interesting variety of specialties that did not detract from the winery's solid reputation for good vintage-dated Cabernet Sauvignon and Zinfandel.

Two of these were holdovers from the Kingsburg days. One, a slightly sweet, low-alcohol Moscato Amabile gained a sort of cult following, obtained only at the winery when available. Another was the Martini sherry, produced from a solera developed in the thirties and brought to Napa in 1936. The founder was also partial to his unique Folle Blanche, produced from vines he found growing on the Monte Rosso property when he bought it. But the centerpiece of Martini production remained Cabernet and Zinfandel, with special selections and reserve bottlings that appealed to collectors.

In 1968 Louis P. Martini took over the direction of the family operation. His influence had been growing for years, a situation difficult for outsiders to comprehend, given the popular image of his father as a rather hard-nosed tyrant. But the family worked well together, whatever others might think. The founder lived until 1974 in total retirement, he would say, but still kept an eye on the working of the business.

In 1968, in what seemed a salute to the Martini philosophy toward wine, Louis P. put together a series of five Cabernet Sauvignons from that excellent vintage, stressing blending and varietal definition. There were lots from Napa and Sonoma, two lots were blended with Merlot and Malbec, and some wines were held in large containers, some in small oak barrels. The new boss has always insisted that the family was making wine "for people to drink, not to sip and spit out." When these five wines were released in 1975, along with a regular 1968 as a Private Reserve, they set off an explosion of sipping at blind tastings by collectors of California Cabernet Sauvignon. It is doubtful if there was much spitting.[8]

As the wine revolution advanced, the Martini family refused to be caught up in what they considered the romantic side of it. A quarter of a century ago Louis P. Martini contended that making wine was hard work and that the end result should be good, consistent wines with clear varietal definition, red to the extent that the market would permit, and fairly priced. This was still his position in the nineties.[9]

Beaulieu

Down the road at Rutherford, Beaulieu struggled through the sixties in a similar fashion to Beringer, at least so far as finances were concerned. What many considered the flagship of the Big Five was able to maintain its position primarily due to the tenacity of the production crew, headed by André Tchelistcheff. Mrs. de Latour had died in 1951 and the winery came under the management of her daughter, Hélène de Pins. She saw BV as a capital resource whose purpose was to maintain the comfortable life-style of the family. But the same economic forces at work on Beringer and Martini were coming down hard on the historic Rutherford operation.

Madame de Pins was a good businesswoman so far as details were concerned, but she never understood the capital requirements that were squeezing the winery. Tchelistcheff understood matters all too well and more than once thought that his days were numbered there. But he held on and made sure that the Private Reserve Cabernet Sauvignon, in particular, did not suffer from Madame's penny-pinching approach to business. Toward the end of the decade, as Louis P. Martini was complaining that their winery was making money as never before, and never before had they had so little money to live on, Tchelistcheff had to age BV white wine in large redwood tanks. What was happening? The Martinis were reinvesting every possible dollar in the business. At Beaulieu the profits maintained an affluent family life-style.

Whatever the difficult conditions under which Tchelistcheff had to work, the image of BV quality was maintained during the sixties. No one was more particular than the Russian winemaster in making the consumer aware of what was in the bottle. Even generics like Chablis (Chenin blanc, Melon, and Colombard) and Burgundy (Pinot noir, Petite Sirah, Gamay, and Mondeuse) carried their precise varietal message. The small output of bottle fermented sparkling wines was continued, as were the sweet wines, which maintained a high degree of popularity among wine enthusiasts for whom such wines really were no longer in style. In all, BV was producing about 150,000 cases per year at the end of the decade.

In 1967 Tchelistcheff contacted Richard Peterson, a research chemist for Gallo, and asked him if he would like to take his place at BV. The master of the Beaulieu cellar was now sixty-six and wanted a change. His son Dmitri knew Peterson from their days at UC Davis and from a mutual interest in acquiring Schramsberg some years earlier. In Peterson's words, when such an opportunity comes in your life "you run, you don't walk; you jump at it."

Beaulieu Vineyard's Carneros planting as it looked when first acres were staked in 1963.

He went to work at BV on April 1, 1968 and soon came to know the strengths and weaknesses of the winery. For the next year he and Tchelistcheff were inseparable.

One of Peterson's first questions related to the white wines—why no stainless steel tanks? Tchelistcheff replied, "After you know Madame de Pins a little better you will understand that she does not, of her own free will, put money into the winery." But when she asked Peterson why BV whites were not keeping up with the competition, he told her. She replied that she thought that stainless steel might be part of the answer. Peterson recalled her comment. "If I'm not mistaken, André mentioned that once or twice to me."

The winemakers got their stainless steel and the surge in the quality of Beaulieu white wines was attributed to Peterson's arrival, a fact he has always considered an embarrassment. The purchase of those stainless steel tanks seemed to spark a change at BV that was part of a new stage in Napa wine history, a change that had begun in 1964 and would be accelerated by BV the following year.[10]

Charles Krug

At Charles Krug in the sixties the Mondavis played out a scenario that would become fairly common at family-owned California wineries in years to come. There was no real problem with the wine. Sales were growing; the perception of high quality established in the fifties was still strong in the public mind. In 1956 the Mondavis began releasing their Vintage Select Cabernets, starting with the 1950 and 1951 vintages. Before long people were speaking of Krug Cabernets in the same breath as those of Inglenook, Martini, and BV.

The problem at Krug was between the brothers. Plain and simple, Robert and Peter could not get along. In 1965 the acrimony exploded into a physical confrontation that split the brothers for the next twenty years and changed the history of Napa wine.

Cesare had left the family corporation in the hands of his widow, Rosa, who controlled 40 percent of the stock. The brothers had 40 percent between them and sisters Helen and Mary had 20 percent. Rosa sided with Peter in the conflict, and Robert was given a six month leave of absence, with the understanding that his son Michael would not have a place in the family business when he graduated that year from Santa Clara University.

Robert kept his Krug stock but he was pushed out of any position of power inside the family organization. To help pay his bills he became an industry consultant, working for Guild and Mirassou. But by the spring of 1966 Robert Mondavi had determined to set out on his own and establish his own winery. Money would be a serious problem, but he had the means to get the project moving. In fact, there would be a crush at the new winery that year.[11]

Meanwhile Peter Mondavi moved ahead vigorously to keep the Krug facility at a high level of technical efficiency. He bought another hundred acres of land in Yountville. The winery's capacity was increased and stainless steel gallonage was upped to 450,000 gallons. He underscored his commitment to small oak cooperage when he bought 540 new French oak barrels in the next few years. Peter Mondavi clearly understood what was necessary now in terms of capital investment to maintain the Krug position in the Big Five.

Inglenook

On April 11, 1964, when the word broke that John Daniel was going to sell Inglenook to United Vintners, a shudder of disbelief reverberated through the Napa Valley. Everyone knew that the historic winery's profits had been marginal since World War II. But the Niebaum estate had been able to keep Daniel and his family afloat in fine style and to cover the losses that had accompanied the obvious successes of Inglenook wines in the fifties.

Several factors moved him to sell, similar to those faced by all the Big Five. Chief of these, of course, were the ageing plant and the growing demands for capital investment, just to maintain the facility. There was also the question of his family. Neither of his two daughters was going to take over the winery after he was gone, and his family situation itself acted as a continuing drain on his psychological reserves. There was talk that George Deuer was thinking about retirement. When Daniel sold the winery, the family explained the sale by referring to Deuer's retirement.

United Vintners was a giant operation organized by Louis Petri. It now acted as the production and marketing vehicle for Allied Grape Growers, a huge viticultural cooperative he had organized in 1951. It supplied grapes to several Central Valley wineries and to the Italian Swiss Colony plant in Asti. The company's president was B. C. Solari, who had presided over the earlier demise of the great Larkmead label.

George Deuer was dumbfounded by Daniel's decision to sell. He had never had a hint, but he now agreed to stay on. So did Daniel, as a consultant. Deuer got them through the 1964 vintage but, at age sixty-five, he decided to retire next year. Daniel stayed on until 1966.

Solari knew that to maintain the Inglenook image he had to guarantee a solid line of quality continuity with the past. He promised just that, announcing after the 1964 vintage that Inglenook would continue its tradition of varietal production and estate bottling. To mollify the anxiety that the Bay Area press was expressing concerning the old winery, Solari announced that "we did not buy Inglenook for volume."

In 1965 the production equipment at the old winery was transferred to the Oakville plant that United Vintners had bought from the Cella family in 1960. Within two years the production of Inglenook "generic vintage dated wines" was announced. But in no way did this imply any change in United Vintners' commitment to Inglenook quality, or so stated the corporate press release. During the next decade, wines shipped under the Inglenook label flowed out at the rate of about 4,000,000 cases per year.

Through all this Daniel refused to raise his voice against the way United Vintners was diluting his historic label. As a matter of fact, the Inglenook estate varietals maintained good quality, measured primarily by the success of the Cabernet Sauvignon. In the eighties the 1966 Estate, the 1968 Cask H-12, and the 1970 Cask were still getting good press and being knocked down for high prices at national wine auctions. In the mid-1970s, at the San Francisco Vintners Club, evaluation of Inglenook varietals from vintages of the late 1960s and early 1970s received positive enough ratings.

Then in 1969, Heublein, the giant Hartford, Connecticut, food conglomerate, bought 82 percent of Inglenook from United Vintners for $32,000,000. Daniel had received $640,000 in his 1964 sale, but there had been huge capital investments in the subsequent five years. From now on profit became the key to promoting the Inglenook label. In 1970 a line of half-gallon jug wines came out under the Inglenook Navalle label, named for the little creek that used to run through the Niebaum estate. Little of that wine was grown anywhere near Navalle Creek. It was produced at the huge Italian Swiss plant at Asti. Before long any grapes produced by any of the hundreds of Allied growers were now considered part of the Inglenook estate. Tens of thousands of cases of "estate bottled" Inglenook wine flooded the national market, taking advantage of the soaring demand for cheap white jug wine, for the moment the darling of the industry. A San Francisco wine writer later wrote that in 1970 "Inglenook jumped from prestige to plonk." John Daniel's death in 1970 seemed an unhappy coda to the demise of a great Napa institution. A person viewing this situation in the late sixties, with the imminent threat of freeways and "Santa Clarafication," might have despaired for the future of Napa wine.[12]

THE SECOND WAVE

The Heitz Family

But such fears were not confirmed. The very magnet that began attracting corporate investment in the Napa wine industry was also attracting more enthusiastic entrepreneurs. These usually had a lot more capital backing than in the previous wave, but no less enthusiasm.

We have already examined the crest of the previous comber, the coming of Joseph Heitz. To look at Heitz's fortunes in 1962–63, one would have written off the new enterprise at the Brendel place. Hepatitis hit the winemaker during the 1962 vintage, and the next spring he was almost killed in an automobile accident. But he and the family made wine and acquired some very important wine from Sonoma's Hanzell Vineyards after founder J. D. Zellerbach died in 1963. These included Pinot noirs from Vintages 1959–1962, Chardonnays of 1961 and 1962, and a bit of Cabernet Sauvignon. Heitz also purchased some of Hanzell's French oak barrels, which helped make these wines quite distinctive in the California market.

Next year Heitz bought the Holt ranch on Taplin Road above Spring Valley on the east side near the Silverado Trail. On this land was the 1898 Rossi Winery. He kept the Brendel place, for its special Grignolino vineyard and for its strategic position on Highway 29, where it has served these many years as the Heitz tasting room. Heitz was able to swing the deal with financial help from the Rhodes and May families and others, who became stockholders in the operation.

Heitz met Tom and Martha May through Bernard and Belle Rhodes and in 1965 bought some of the Cabernet from their young vines. The wine went into the regular Cabernet release, but the quality of this wine from Martha's Vineyard, as Tom May called it, moved Heitz next year to keep it separate and to market it under its special vineyard designation. Such a practice was not unique in modern California wine history, but it was rare. Thus began a string of Cabernet Sauvignon releases that helped establish the Napa Valley in the 1970s as one of the world's great sources of red wine from Bordeaux grapes. Heitz contends that he does not attempt to make his Cabernets French in style. And there are few who have claimed that the powerful, sometimes minty, sometimes herbaceous, long-lived Cabernets from Martha's Vineyard are Bordeaux-like in character. (Some say that the wines derive this herbaceous taste from the eucalyptus trees near the vineyards. All who know better have declared apocryphal the suggestion that Martha May occasionally tosses a few handfuls of their leaves into Heitz's fermentation tank.) When the San Francisco Vintners Club began tasting the Martha's vintages in 1974, they won a series of blind tasting victories never matched in club history. From 1968 to 1974, they took five firsts, two seconds, and a third. (No 1971 Martha's Vineyard was released as such.)[13]

Joseph and Alice Heitz announced their offerings in a newsletter that gave the consumer valuable technical information about the wines. The prices rose steadily as the wines' popularity and national price inflation took off in the coming years. The 1966 Martha's was released in 1971 at $7.50 (about $24.00

C$ 1990). The 1970 came out at $12.75 ($29.00 C$). But plenty of their lower-priced wines also won critical praise. There was a Grignolino and its rosé, White Riesling, a Pinot blanc made from Stony Hill grapes, Barbera, Zinfandel, Pinot noir, and a few dessert wines. There were also bottle fermented sparkling wines, and two made by the Millerway process, developed by Napa's F. Justin Miller, from Malvasia bianca and Grignolino. These two didn't fly because government regulations forbade the term "sparkling" on their labels. It is difficult to sell wines labeled "carbonated."

There were also some curiosities. The Chablis was a blend that was produced from a kind of solera process that put part of the wine through French oak barrels, producing a moderately-priced generic with remarkable elegance. In 1970 there were 260 bottles of "Alicia," a dessert wine from *botrytis*-infected Chardonnay and Gewürztraminer grapes. The price, $27.50 ($91.00 C$), was probably a Napa record. But the Chablis was only $1.85. As high in price as some of Heitz's wines have been, he still contends that you must be fair and offer good value. He says, "You can cut a man's hair many times, but you can scalp him only once."

Heitz considers himself a winemaker, not a grapegrower, although he does own vineyards. He esteems his sources. In his words, "The vineyardists I work with are as proud of their product as I am of mine." If he spent too much time in the vineyard he might be a "half-assed winemaker." So he bought grapes, he bought wine to blend and/or age, or to bottle straightway, and he made wine from his own grapes. He thinks well of his accomplishments, once offering in his now famous, somewhat tongue-in-cheek acerbity, that his wine tasted different because his sweat "went into the bottle instead of the hired help's."

His son David became a part of the winemaking team in 1974 after graduating from Fresno State, appropriately enough in enology. Two years earlier the Taplin Road facility needed expansion, so a modern winery was built to complement the old stone structure. This addition brought their capacity to about 175,000 gallons and a sales level of about 20,000 cases. By 1990 sales were up to 40,000 cases, about 5,000 of which were the 1985 Martha's Vineyard Cabernet, released at $50 ($16 in 1971 C$). Controversial as its maker, the wine was called "truly magnificent" by *Wine Spectator*, but judged "disappointing" by *Connoisseur's Guide*, a wine for "those with unlimited optimism and budgets."[14]

The Davies
Resuscitation of Jacob's Schram's hand-carved Mt. Diamond cellars in previous years had been unsuccessful. Both attempts had aimed at producing

sparkling wine, which had not been a part of Schram's operation. The third attempt was a great success, although the first years were shaky. But these were good times for enthusiastic enterprises, if capital were sufficient and technical expertise substantial. Napa winegrowing camaraderie also helped Jack and Jamie Davies make Schramsberg one of Napa's success stories in the sixties.

They had gained experience in winegrowing with Martin Ray at his Mt. Eden venture in the Santa Cruz Mountains in 1961. They soon pulled out of that combination and in 1964 began looking for a place in Napa, where a buyers' market had put many old properties up for sale. They looked at Chateau Montelena, Chateau Chevalier, and the moribund Freemark Abbey. But when Jerome Draper, Sr. introduced them to Schramsberg they became determined to make wine on that property. They put together a group of investors and bought a rundown vineyard, soon to be pulled up, a fine old home in disrepair, and a set of five tunnels, perfect for ageing sparkling wine. They "liked the idea of starting a new business, something with a heritage that we could build on and pass on to the family."

They moved onto the property on August 28, 1965 and began looking for some Chardonnay grapes for their first Blanc de Blanc cuvée. They ended up obtaining White Riesling from Draper, which they traded to Robert Mondavi for five tons of Chardonnay. Meanwhile, Robert and Peter had split up, and when Davies approached Peter on the subject, the Krug winemaster owned that he knew nothing of the deal, but would honor it. In fact, Peter made up the little lot exactly to Davies' specifications, for Champagne not table wine. When they picked it up later in the year it seemed that everyone at the Krug Winery was on hand to insure proper delivery. Jack Davies said, "it was as if they were delivering the crown jewels to someone in an armored truck."

Next year the crush was on the mountain, something of a historic event, since the number of wineries in California producing sparkling wine by the traditional French process had fallen to three. They asked a few people to

When the crusher motor wouldn't start for the first vintage at Schramsberg in 1966, Jamie Davies and friends jumped right in.

SOURCE: SCHRAMSBERG VINEYARDS.

drop over to watch, including the press. But they couldn't get the crusher to work. André Tchelistcheff called out from the crowd to Jamie Davies, "My dear, your duty is clear." She kicked off her shoes and did her duty. In a few minutes a few more jumped in to help. It all seemed too clever to be true. Jamie Davies noted that "We have been accused of a setup ever since."

They planted Chardonnay and Pinot noir in the old Schram vineyard, twenty acres at first, then twenty more. They were soon turning out their well-received line of California sparklers. There was the Blanc de Blanc (Chardonnay and Pinot noir), a Cuvée de Gamay (from Napa Gamay, later Cuvée de Pinot as the percentage of Pinot noir grew), and a Blanc de Noir, which was traditional in France but not part of California wine since the days of Paul Masson. In 1974 they produced a semi-sweet Cremánt from the UC Davis Flora grape (Sémillon x Gewürztraminer) and a Reserve Champagne. In retrospect it almost seems a miracle that these wines were so well-made. But Davies thinks it was no miracle at all. André Tchelistcheff and his enologist son Dmitri were always ready to help, as were the McCreas and Drapers. Louis M. Martini gave special encouragement for their use of Pinot noir in their cuvées. William Fuller, the Martini enologist, gave Jack Davies a rapid fire series of short courses in wine chemistry, which the Harvard MBA/ former businessman passed summa cum laude.

It is said that "a good wine needs no bush," but a solid dose of positive publicity is always useful, however good the wine. In January 1972 Davies received a call from the White House. They wanted some Schramsberg Champagne and there was none in the Capital. So Jack Davies hauled thirteen cases down to Travis Air Force Base near Fairfield. When the news broke that President Nixon loved the wines and was taking them to China to serve at his banquet for Premier Chou En-Lai, the winery was overcome with orders.

From then on Schramsberg has flourished. By 1975 *Forbes* was calling Jack Davies a "Champagne superman," ticking off the many offers he had had to sell his winery and label. From a 1970 production of a little more than 1,000 cases, production grew to more than 20,000 by the end of the decade, and 50,000 by the mid-1980s. The capacity of the cellars was tripled by Santa Rosa's Alf Burtleson, whose giant British Alpine Miner machine in years to come would go on to dig passages at many wineries to hold millions of bottles of North Coast wine.[15]

Robert Mondavi

Robert Mondavi knew he had to move fast after he made the decision to break with Charles Krug and his brother. He knew that the movement into the premium wine field was just beginning to accelerate. He could not afford to let a vintage slip by before he began establishing a new brand. Thus, at age fifty-four, he cast around for the financial backing he would need to start a winery from scratch. Ivan Schoch and Fred Holmes came up with a good part of the seed money, and Mondavi bought a piece of land in Oakville on which to build a 15,000-case winery that could expand in the future. The style was hybrid Spanish colonial-mission, with a large arch and tower, today known to anyone even casually familiar with California premium wine labels. The structure was the first new Napa winery since well before World War II, if one doesn't count the little structure at Stony Hill.

Mondavi raced to get ready for the 1966 vintage, crushing several batches of grapes that added up to a total of 497 tons. They didn't even have a roof on the place when the grapes went into the crusher. But everyone involved agreed that equipment and facilities were to be aimed at making world-class wine. When the first of the 1966 grapes were crushed, Mondavi organized a little ceremony in which a local clergyman said a few encouraging words over the crusher. It would become a tradition at the winery in years to come. John Daniel ordered the first five cases of the 1966 vintage, which Mondavi delivered to him personally after the wine was bottled.

Next year Mondavi was able to spend a little more time lining up the grapes and planning the crush schedule. He also began crafting certain wines that he hoped would be specifically identified with his label. In 1967 he tried to do something a little different with his Sauvignon blanc grapes, looking for a style somewhat like that of the French wines made from that grape along the upper Loire Valley. The first vintage didn't turn the heads of many wine critics, but he put everything together in 1968 when he had better grapes. The result was a remarkable wine. He had decided that one of the problems in selling Sauvignon blanc was its name, so he brought out the new wine labeled Fumé Blanc. The growing white wine drinking public lapped it up in the wake of overwhelming critical acclaim. Hurst Hannum and Robert Blumberg called it "among the two or three best dry Bordeaux-type white wines we have ever tasted . . . one of the best California white wines on the market today." Harry Waugh, the noted English wine expert, stated that, "Unless I could taste a blanc

The new winery under construction in 1966. Robert Mondavi and architect Cliff May (center) check it out.

fumé from the Loire alongside, I doubt whether I would discern the difference."[16]

Mondavi was concentrating at first on wines he could get onto the retail shelf right now. The approach fit nicely with the pattern he had developed at Krug: establish the whites, then move in with the big reds. Mostly these new whites harked back to twenty years earlier when Irving Marcus had marveled at the wonderful wines the Mondavi boys were bringing out. There was Chenin blanc, White Riesling, Traminer, and a Riesling blend of White Riesling and Sylvaner. Onto the shelves quickly came his Gamay Rosé, and a light, fruity Burgundy style Gamay that got the best notices from his short list of 1966 wines. Some of the reds, Zinfandel and Pinot noir, produced in the early years were also light and fruity. The first two Cabernets were on the light

Robert Mondavi

at the new winery

with lab samples of

Sauvignon blanc.

side as well, but from 1968 Mondavi developed this varietal as the flagship of his wine fleet. Robert Mondavi Cabernet Sauvignon tended to be rich, elegant, and powerful, emphasizing varietal character. It was definitely meant for the cellar. The 1969 Cabernet did for Mondavi what the call from Washington did for Jack Davies. In 1972 a group of ten wine industry technical people got together at Buena Vista Winery and evaluated thirty-three California Cabernets currently on the market.

The tasters included André Tchelistcheff, Louis P. Martini, Joseph Heitz, Brother Timothy, and Myron Nightingale from Napa. Mondavi's 1969 won the palm and the subsequent public accolades. In 1971 he brought out his Reserve Cabernet, produced mostly from To Kalon grapes. He had acquired 250 acres of that old property in 1969.[17]

By 1968 it had become evident that additional capital was necessary to keep the Mondavi winery growing at the speed of its potential market. The source was Emil Sick's Rainier Brewing Company in Seattle. They bought out the Schoch and Holmes shares in the business and also pumped in a huge infusion of dollars through the purchase of non-voting stock. The Rainier money made the To Kalon purchase possible. Mondavi and his immediate family retained overall control of the operation. Robert kept his part of the ownership in the Krug company, even though he was excluded from the management of the winery. But Peter, his mother, and their lawyers worked out a deliberate plan to restructure the family corporation to keep Robert from getting his full share of the Krug profits.

The upshot was Robert's 1976 lawsuit against Peter, Rosa, and the rest of the family. The suit aimed to dissolve Charles Krug so that Robert could get his share of the family corporation set up by his father. The trial lasted 103 days and the result was a resounding victory for and vindication of Robert Mondavi. Superior Court Judge Robert Carter ordered that Robert be paid $538,885 in compensatory damages. Charles Krug was to be sold and Robert was to get his share from the sale. The key to Robert's victory lay in the judge's finding that Peter's peripheral partnership had siphoned off $1,500,000 between 1974 and 1975. Judge Carter also ruled that Peter's "fraudulent activities" had made him the father of two millionaire sons.

Eventually the whole thing was worked out in a way that kept Charles Krug in Peter's hands and supplied Robert with the money owed him. This left Peter with a gigantic debt and Robert with the means to buy out Rainier and gain complete control of his winery. It took two years to bring it off, but in August of 1978 it was announced that Robert and his family had bought back the 1.1 million Rainier shares. The total bill for the financial independence of his winery came to $19,960,000, but Robert Mondavi appeared satisfied and ready for new enterprise.[18]

He brought back another aspect of wine production he had known in the old days at Krug and Sunny St. Helena. The Cherokee Co-op Winery at Woodbridge, near Lodi, had been modernized in 1972 by Southern California interests that eventually went under. The place was then purchased by the Santa Clara Valley's Filice family, who had recently sold their San Martin Winery. Further modernization did not bring success and in 1979 Robert Mondavi was able to acquire the 6,000,000-gallon plant for the production of a line of red and white table wines that harked back to the old CK brand. By the mid-eighties this facility was turning out over a million cases of popular jugs, often referred to as "Bob White" and "Bob Red" by the crew at Woodbridge.[19]

A New Freemark Abbey

When we look back on the wine revolution, the number of new Napa wineries then seems small indeed when we compare the last four years of the sixties to the 1978–1981 explosion, when forty-six new operations started up here. There weren't even forty-six wineries in the Napa Valley until 1973.

The lights at Freemark Abbey came back on in 1967 when a partnership headed by Charles Carpy bought the old Lombarda place, part of which was being used as a candle shop and a restaurant. So dim was the memory of the Ahern and earlier Forni operations that Charles Carpy wondered at first what kind of religious institution had been housed here.

Between them three of the partners owned several hundred acres of grapes. A fourth partner, R. Bradford Webb, was formerly winemaker at Hanzell. He possessed a solid academic background as well as many years of practical experience. He set the tone for the style of Freemark Abbey wines in the years to come, although Jerry Luper took over the working winemaker's job in 1970.

These wines came in a slow trickle at first, only 1,500 cases by 1970. Chardonnay and Petite Sirah got rave notices. White Rieslings were also well-received, particularly a late harvest "Edelwein" in 1973, which helped promote an interest in this style of dessert wine that had been growing since the late sixties. But, as with most Napa premium producers, the Cabernet Sauvignon made the Freemark Abbey reputation, specifically the wines made from John Bosché's twenty acres in Rutherford. He had sent his grapes to Beaulieu until 1967, where they had become part of the Private Reserve Cabernet.[20]

In 1968 Bosché and Carpy got together and established a grower/producer relationship similar to that of May/Heitz. Webb made up separate batches from Bosché's 1968 grapes, one with 10 percent Merlot. The result was an international success. In 1974 when the International Wine & Food Society held its convention in San Francisco, three 1966 Napa Cabernets were served at the final dinner. Next year they decided to duplicate the affair in London, but member Harry Waugh, wine writer and a director of Château Latour, threw in the 1968 Bosché. The consensus was that the Freemark Abbey was the best of the four. Waugh thought the wine was "up to first growth standard." For Society editor H. W. Yoxhall the tasting showed that with some Merlot in the Cabernet "Napa notions would move closer to Bordeaux. . . ." Leon Adams wrote in 1978 that this Bosché was the first California wine that he might have mistaken for a Château Margaux of a good vintage. Today Freemark Abbey produces 12,000–15,000 cases of Cabernet Sauvignon per year, of which 3,000–4,000 come from the Bosché vineyard, which is now planted to about 14 percent Merlot.[21]

The partners' winery has long since outgrown the confines of the old

Lombarda structure. Later additions have brought the operation's capacity to about 400,000 gallons. In fact, as we shall see, their holdings have expanded substantially to another venture that today produces five times as much Napa wine as Freemark Abbey.

Donn Chappellet

The Valley's second new full-sized winery since World War II went up in 1967. It was a spectacular pyramid-shaped structure in the eastern highlands on Pritchard Hill above Sage Canyon and Lake Hennessey. Donn Chappellet, like Jack Davies, left a successful Southern California business career to do what he wanted. In 1971 he said, "I think that I have subconsciously wanted to become a wine maker for years." Unlike Davies, however, his financial situation as the founder of the country's third largest food service company made it fairly easy to do what he wanted.

The winery was finished by 1969 and the vineyards were planted on about 110 acres of the 600-acre ranch. A substantial stand of Chenin blanc had been planted there in 1964. Wine from this grape has been a fairly hard sell since the 1970s, but not for Chappellet. Davis Professor Harold Berg declared that the Chappellet dry wine from that grape in 1968 was the best California Chenin blanc he'd ever tasted. But it was actually the early Cabernets that put Chappellet on the Napa wine map. Nevertheless, he has had four different winemakers over the years and critics have complained of a lack of stylistic and qualitative consistency, at least until the eighties after Cathy Corison took over the winemaking.

Since the mid-seventies Chappellet has held his production to a comfortable 25,000 cases, about a third of which is Cabernet Sauvignon. He and his family have kept a low profile in the Valley wine scene. They follow what son Cyril, the sales director, calls a "European ethic," avoiding heavy-duty marketing, and pricing their wines each year according to their perceived quality.[22]

Spring Mountain Vineyards

Michael Robbins was another Southern California businessman who tried to escape to Napa in the sixties. He had been an early investor and director of Mayacamus in 1960. In 1962 on a visit to the Valley he found a beautiful 1876 Victorian just north of St. Helena for sale. Owner Fritz Rosenbaum called the property, with its surrounding vineyard, "Johannaberg." Robbins bought the home, and began restoring the place. In 1964 he announced to the press his intention of developing a small chateau-style winery there. Robbins called it Spring Mountain Vineyards and got his bond in 1968. Because of the close quarters in the little cellar at the house, he did his crushing elsewhere. For this reason some of Robbins' early wines could not legally be vintage-dated. Nevertheless, the label often told the careful consumer all he needed to know. His first Cabernet Sauvignon was a blend of 1968 and 1969 wine made from grapes grown on Robert Adamson's vineyard, with a small amount from Martha's Vineyard. (Adamson and Bernard Rhodes had grown the Merlot that went into the 1968 Freemark Abbey Bosché Cabernet.) Robbins aged the wine in Limousin and Nevers oak barrels, after fermentation at Joseph Heitz's little winery. Thus, the label designated this wine "Lot 68-69 LN." This wine and the early releases of Robbins' Sauvignon blanc and Chardonnay were critical and financial successes.

In 1971 he hired Charles Ortman as his winemaker. This former commercial artist had just finished a three-year apprenticeship with Joseph Heitz. Years later he would be acknowledged as one of the industry's most sought-after consulting enologists. Before this Robbins had pulled through in typical Napa fashion, with plenty of help from Heitz, Webb, and Robert Mondavi.[23]

Robbins' Spring Mountain did not become truly historic because of the early wines. His real estate business kept him on a leash back and forth between Napa and Los Angeles. But in 1974 his eye for real property helped him to pick up Tiburcio Parrott's old Miravalle estate on Spring Mountain. It had something over a hundred plantable acres in its total of 265. The great house became a celebrity showcase, not for the wine that Robbins produced at his 1976 winery nearby, but because the estate was the venue for the Falcon Crest television series. In 1982 Robbins brought out a few wines under the Falcon Crest label.[24]

Chateau Montelena

Another great Napa property was brought back to life in 1968 when wine enthusiast Leland Paschich purchased the old Tubbs estate in Calistoga. Built in 1882, the winery had operated some after Repeal, but after World War II, in the hands of a new owner, the estate was transformed into something of a Far Eastern paradise. There was a five-acre lake with islands, arched bridges, and a real Chinese junk in the center of it.

Paschich understood the nature of the wine revolution and found partners with capital to bring back the old winery and replant the vineyards. James L. Barrett, a Southern California lawyer was chief of these. The result was a crush in 1969 that propelled Chateau Montelena into the Napa wine world in a way that it had never experienced under the Tubbs family.

Barrett believed that the winemaker could make such an enterprise a world-class operation. In 1972 he hired Miljenko (Mike) Grgich, a Croatian with a solid Old World academic background and winemaking experience that included an apprenticeship with Lee Stewart at Souverain, nine years at Beaulieu, and four years with Robert Mondavi. Grgich's philosophy was simple: "Make it right; then leave it alone." The Chardonnay that he produced from 1973 grapes gave Chateau Montelena an international reputation. Actually, he always thought that his 1975 was better. His Cabernets helped make the winery a "First Growth" in the view of Cabernet specialist James Laube.

When Grgich left after the 1977 vintage, Jerry Luper took over the cellar and continued his successes. Since 1982 James P. (Bo) Barrett, assistant winemaker since 1972 and son of the general partner, has run the cellar. The wines he has produced at the 30,000-case facility continue to reap praise for their depth, concentration, and powerful varietal character.[25]

Sterling Vineyards

The first crush on the hill at Sterling Vineyards was in 1972. The first three vintages took place down below.

Another new winery appeared in 1969 between Calistoga and Larkmead on a hilltop with a commanding view of the surrounding vineyards and mountains. At first it was to be Mt. Sterling Vineyards, then Sterling Vineyards. The name came from the San Francisco paper products company of that name. Peter Newton and Michael Stone had made money in that venture and began buying vineyard land in the area in 1964. Then in 1967, when the owner of the little mountain died, the partners jumped at the opportunity to buy it from the Charles Rockstroh estate as the site of their winery. It would be the most expensive of the new Napa Valley enterprises to date.

The end result was an imposing structure, blazing white, in a style

reminiscent of an Orthodox monastery on an Aegean island. To Leon Adams it was the "most spectacular in America and quite possibly in the world." But before the winery could be built it had to be planned, with the future winemaker in on the planning. The new owners selected one of the Davis star master's candidates. He had just the right background: a B.S. in chemistry, a vintage at Stony Hill, and one with Robert Mondavi. This was a person who should be able to make lots of good wine. Richard (Ric) Forman was twenty-four years old when they hired him in 1968; they wanted Sterling to have a 1969 vintage.

The first grapes were fermented in a ware-house structure at the bottom of the hill, but before this could happen Forman was off to France to observe cellar operations in Bordeaux and Burgundy. To him "it was the most significant thing that happened in my career." The upshot was that the new winemaker would be modifying some of the Davis precepts. Chardonnays would be fermented in oak barrels, not steel tanks. Cabernets would be given extended fermentation time to soften tannins. The first crush at the winery itself was in 1972, but the first three vintages down the hill produced wines that set a pattern of perceived excellence in these early years.

The winery was opened to the public in 1973. The building was designed to produce fine wines efficiently and to cater to the visitor. Tourists bought an English halfpenny at the bottom of the hill for $2.00, which they could turn in for credit on a wine purchase. The coin was their ticket to ride up to the winery on a funicular tramway built by a Swiss ski lift company. There was nothing else like it in the California wine country.

Sterling now owned over 400 acres of bearing vines, with experimental sections, some planted on close centers in the French style. In 1976 they started planting Cabernet on their new vineyard on Mt. Diamond. Production was steady at about 40,000 cases. The next year the owners sold the whole operation to Coca-Cola for about $8,000,000. In 1983 Sterling was sold again, to Seagram.[26]

THE HEIGHT OF THE REVOLUTION

By 1990 the eight new enterprises begun in the Napa Valley between 1960 and 1969 were producing over 600,000 cases of Napa wine, almost 30 percent of it Cabernet Sauvignon. All but Sterling were still independent producers.

The wine revolution, which these enthusiasts had perceived in the years before their investment, took off in 1968, although analyst Louis Gomberg considers 1968 the last normal year. He says, "The explosion came in 1969." From that year to 1972 American wine consumption increased at 12 percent per annum, compared to a 2.8 percent average for the preceding twenty years.

Actually, shipments of California table wine increased even more dramatically. In 1967 shipments jumped 11.4 percent. The acceleration peaked

Napa Vintages, 1960 - 1974

YEAR	TONS PRODUCED	VALUE	GROWER PRICE PER TON
1960	23,776	$2,211,168	$ 93
1961	16,845	2,358,300	140
1962	39,516	3,951,000	100
1963	32,382	3,076,290	95
1964	22,081	2,904,720	132
1965	40,063	4,807,560	120
1966	37,286	4,288,000	115
1967	39,456	5,822,000	148
1968	38,276	6,078,000	159
1969	43,673	8,055,000	184
1970	24,212	7,100,000	293
1971	42,153	16,920,000	401
1972	42,153	19,467,000	462
1973	55,659	33,916,000	609
1974	55,317	18,565,000	336

in 1970 with an almost unbelievable increase of 26.8 percent. Things calmed down by 1973 when growth in this category was a mere 5.8 percent.

In the early sixties Napa wine grape acreage grew very little. From 1963 to 1969 the total jumped from about 10,000 to 14,000 acres. By 1973 there were more than 20,000. The Napa vintages from 1960 to 1973 also supply insights to the revolution, not so much for the great amount of Napa wine being made, but for the great value of the grapes that made it. Figures for 1974 are included above to suggest why this chapter closes with the 1973 vintage.

CORPORATE WINE

At the end of the 1968 vintage *Forbes* told its readers that several California wineries were targets for acquisition. In an article on the wine industry titled, "California Wine: Everybody Wants It," this leading financial periodical stated that "the potential for growth is breathtaking," and listed Beringer, Beaulieu, Krug, and Martini as likely candidates.

After Inglenook the next to fall to corporate interests was Beaulieu. Madame de Pins was seeing the light and understood that the way to maintain the family's lifestyle, without allowing her father's great enterprise to run down completely, was to sell the place and bank the money. Richard

Peterson's announcement in April 1969 that BV needed a $500,000 infusion of new equipment probably sealed the deal in advance. The actual agreement was worked out between Madame's son-in-law, Walter Sullivan, and a young Heublein executive, Andrew Beckstoffer. In June it cost Heublein $8,400,000 to make the venerable Beaulieu Vineyard its second Napa jewel, after Inglenook.

The shock from the Inglenook sale in 1964 and the subsequent denigration of the old winery's label by United Vintners/Heublein caused the most negative suspicions and forecasts to radiate from the Valley and the Bay Area press. But the corporate executives in Hartford knew that Beaulieu would be useless to them if a sense of continuity was not maintained here in a way it had not been at Inglenook. Actually neither Peterson nor Tchelistcheff were displeased at the sale. At least now they probably wouldn't have to fight tooth and nail to get a new stainless steel tank.

Heublein decided to keep Legh Knowles on as general manager. He had come to BV in 1962 from Gallo, like Peterson. As much as anyone Knowles was able to work with the corporate hierarchy at Heublein to avoid the destruction of the Beaulieu label. BV's sales would grow to 450,000 cases in the 1980s, of which about 200,000 were Cabernet Sauvignon. But the winery did not go through the trying process suffered at Inglenook in the eighties, when the parent company had to strain mightily, and at great cost, to rekindle a glow of prestige for Gustav Niebaum's old label.

Tchelistcheff finally retired in 1970, but kept on working at BV as a consultant until 1973. In that year Peterson left to take charge of the Monterey Vineyard near Salinas. Knowles stayed on, promoting the BV image and wines, and defending its reputation against corporate policies often apparently conceived with little in mind save short-term profit. He retired in 1989, making a point with the press at the time that he wished for once they would pay more attention to his twenty years of maintaining BV's reputation than his three years playing trumpet for Glenn Miller in the thirties.[27]

The third member of the Big Five fell in 1970, this time to foreign capital. The Swiss Nestlé Company added to its diversified international food operations when it culminated the deal with the Beringer family on January 11, 1971. The Nestlé managers in charge of the new venture into wine took a long and patient view toward the eventual success of the enterprise. They understood that the luster on the Beringer label had been tarnished, but that the situation was not irreversible.

They hired Myron Nightingale to run the Napa operation. Eighteen years earlier this former star pupil of Professor William Cruess and a graduate of the famed 1940 "winemakers class" at Berkeley had taken over the chores of winemaster at Livermore's Cresta Blanca. There he made winemaking history by producing America's first authentic Sauternes-style wine from *botrytis*-infected grapes. In Napa he had a virtual blank check to resuscitate the Beringer wines. In his words, the Nestlé people asked him, "What do you need? Whatever it is, we'll do it."

Beringer had always maintained a good reputation for its hospitality, with the picturesque ambience of the Rhine House and the hand-carved cellars. These artifacts from the past were maintained and upgraded, but winemaking was shifted to a huge plant across the highway, finished in 1975. A corporate restructuring was needed to keep Nestlé out of the legal position of producing alcoholic beverages and running a string of restaurants. Thus a company titled Wine World was created to operate Beringer and the many other wine properties that would be acquired in years to come.

In the mid-seventies Nightingale worked to produce well-crafted varietals with grapes from the old Napa vineyards and Knight's Valley. A jug line under the Los Hermanos label was also part of the operation, but was kept separate from the Beringer brand, so far as marketing and promotion were concerned. The new Beringer approach was to reestablish the old brand with good wines at reasonable prices. When Nightingale retired in 1984 the brand had been revived. In the words of wine critic Anthony Dias Blue, Beringer had been "miraculously converted from a lackluster producer of undistinguished wines to one of America's best and most prestigious wineries." To solidify that prestige, so far as Napa wine is concerned, great Cabernet Sauvignon is today a historic necessity. Beringer produces 50,000–60,000 cases, led by its Private Reserve, introduced in 1977. James Laube calls these wines "First Growth" for California today, a category shared by twelve other California producers, eleven of them from Napa.[28]

Corporations attracted by skyrocketing profits were not guaranteed success if they bought into Napa wine. The Pillsbury story became a bête noire for future investors here; the story illustrated the evils of ignorance and greed in the corporate rush to take over California wine properties in the seventies.

In 1970, after twenty-seven years on Howell Mountain, Lee Stewart decided to reap the rewards for the excellence of his Souverain wines and their great reputation. He didn't quite want to retire, but at age sixty-five he was tired of the routine. A group of investors headed by Ivan Schoch and Fred Holmes agreed to buy the 100,000-gallon winery and its thirty acres of vines. It seemed like the perfect move for the investors, who hoped to expand production in the booming market. They acquired new property east of the Silverado Trail and began building a winery with a wonderful view of the Valley. There was enough land to expand later, perhaps a restaurant, even an inn. The winery was a picturesque structure that looked something like a huge nineteenth-century California barn.

In 1972 Pillsbury of Minneapolis decided to dabble in California wine. Meanwhile the Souverain partners sold Stewart's Howell Mountain winery to former Air Force pilot Thomas Burgess. That property became Burgess Cellars; the new winery west of Rutherford became Souverain. Then the partners sold Souverain to Pillsbury, which had hired Frank Schoonmaker to guide the company into the California world of wine. In Sonoma Pillsbury began building a huge facility between Healdsburg and Geyserville that they decided to call Ville Fontaine. Lee Stewart became a consultant for the whole Pillsbury operation and they began making wine at the Napa place with the 1972 vintage.

It took just three years for the folks in Minnesota to discover that it took more than good wine to make a go in the current world of premium wine. They were spending too much money to sell the wine. By 1975 they were losing $6,000,000 per year and wanted out. They told the press they couldn't continue to operate Burger King and produce wine. Wall Street's Lehmann Brothers, which had to peddle this disingenuous story, was embarrassed by the prospectus put out under their name. Months passed and the sale wouldn't go. By now the Sonoma winery had to change its name since the Ville Fontaine label was already owned. Now they decided to call it Souverain of Alexander Valley, while the Napa winery would be Souverain of Rutherford.

Finally a group of investors headed by William Jaeger and Charles Carpy of Freemark Abbey bought the Napa winery. An association of North Coast vineyardists bought the one in Sonoma. They continued to operate the beautiful Sonoma facility at little profit until 1986, when Nestlé/Wine World/Beringer bought it to expand their production capacity.

Lee Stewart's great Souverain label was now fastened onto the Sonoma winery. His Los Amigos Dry Sherry label was also transported to Sonoma and used to sell Zinfandel in Texas and New Mexico. It had a label embellished with cowboys, obviously good friends. It didn't work.

The new Napa combination took the name Rutherford Hill and became an important factor in premium wine production here. In 1986 Jerry Luper became winemaker; he'd come full circle, again working for his previous employers of Freemark Abbey. By the end of the eighties Rutherford Hill was producing 150,000 cases. They also had made the decision to concentrate on Merlot, a seemingly brave move in this land of Cabernet Sauvignon.[29]

It was inevitable that there would be other false starts and failures at the end of this period of dynamic expansion. When the little Lyncrest Winery on Spring Mountain went under in 1976, soon after the Pillsbury debacle, some industry observers logically predicted a storm of failures as growth in consumption leveled off, interest rates soared, and price inflation continued its steady climb. It became increasingly obvious that making good wine simply wasn't enough to insure entrepreneurial success. Marketing skill and organized distribution were becoming sine qua non.

Undercapitalization was also a serious problem for some. Many wineries survived these dangerous years, but had to go through reorganization, infusion of new capital, and changes in management. But in most of these instances the label, land, and physical equipment were the actual survivors. Many original owners had to give up their stake in the operation, or a large part of it, to someone else with a longer line of credit or deeper pockets. The slaughter was far less painful in Napa than in some other districts.

The greatest entrepreneurial failure in Napa in these years was that of Oakville Vineyards. It was an operation of grand design that produced excellent wine. Founding partner Wilfred E. Van Loben Sels began putting the deal together in 1969. He was able to attract almost 400 small investors into the limited partnership, which went into operation in 1971 when he purchased the Bartolucci Brothers Winery in Oakville. He hired Almaden winemaker Peter Becker to run the cellar and acquired vineyard land in the area. From the John Daniel estate he bought the old Niebaum mansion and its vines.

Van Loben Sels also bought the old John Sehabiague home across the highway from the winery. The pretty Victorian provided offices and reception facilities. The trees for which the Palm Row Winery (1898) there had been named still stood but the winery was gone.

Oakville wines were very well-received by the press and the public, particularly Becker's whites, to which he brought his German experience. The Oakville red and white generics, labeled "Our House Wine," were skillfully blended bargains.

Years later Van Loben Sels gave perhaps too simple an explanation of what brought the multimillion dollar operation to its knees— undercapitalization and "14 percent money." A midwestern bank cut their credit line in early 1975 and by the end of the year it was over. In the spring of 1976 Oakville was selling off its equipment. The Bartoluccis got their winery back, which they quickly sold to neighbor Inglenook. Another creditor, Robert Mondavi, got the inventory of wine and the Oakville label. Francis Ford Coppola bought the Niebaum mansion and the adjacent vineyard. The great American wine boom had flattened out by 1974. For future investors in Napa wine the Pillsbury and Oakville stories would be sobering education.[30]

The received wisdom in the world of business and finance holds that in times of contraction following a boom there is little tendency for business to invest. In this light, the incorporation of M & H Vineyards on March 26, 1973 might appear to be an act of courage.

The company's initials stood for Moët-Hennessy, the producers of Moët & Chandon and Dom Perignon Champagnes. The French company's officers had prepared for this event for the last five years. Their purpose was to plant vineyards, build a winery, and produce sparkling wine from Napa grapes, employing the classic method of Champagne. They wanted a facility that would produce 200,000 cases per year for the American market at a price about two to three dollars higher than that of other California producers who employed the classic method, such as Hanns Kornell and Sonoma's Korbel.

The timing of this French action was directly related to the fact that vineyard acreage in Champagne could grow very little and that the growth in the world market for premium sparkling wine seemed almost limitless. The American market for these wines looked very good.

The French businessmen chose a management consultant to run the Napa operation who, with Louis Gomberg in 1972, had put together a gigantic analysis of the future of wine in America. John Wright had a degree in chemistry from Wesleyan University and, while in Connecticut in the sixties, had planted a vineyard of French hybrid wine grapes. He came to California in 1969 and next year bought a piece of land on the side of Mt. Veeder, where he started planting a vineyard in 1971. With the experience of starting his Pickle Canyon Vineyard under his belt he began the huge market study, which his bosses eventually sold to eight European companies for $20,000 each.

Four years earlier, in 1968, Robert-Jean de Vogüé, chairman of the board of Moët-Hennessy, had visited California, tasted California wine, talked to California wine men, and decided that his firm's next big move would be to the Golden State. It was not until 1972 that the Frenchmen were ready for this, but when they were,

John Wright

surveying vineyard

land in the Carneros.

everything came in a rush. By December Wright was putting together samples of young California still wines for Renaud Poirier, the Moët chef des caves. He rejected most of the wines, but there were enough he liked and most of these were from Napa.

They quickly started to buy land and began making plans for the 1973 crush. Wright found a good 200 acres on Mt. Veeder, and then purchased a 550-acre ranch in the Carneros. A nursery was laid out on Mt. Veeder with vineyard planting to begin the following spring. Later in the year he found 350 acres in Yountville, right next to the Veterans' Home on the highway. There were a few dilapidated vineyards, but it was just the place for a winery. They bought it for about $1,100 per acre, since the owners' hopes to develop the land for purposes other than agriculture had been dashed, as we shall soon see.

The first crush took place on August 18 at Michael Bernstein's little Mt. Veeder Winery, a small load of Sémillon from Pope Valley. There were a large number of experimental lots from a wide range of varieties and vineyard locations. Most of the winemaking took place at the historic Eshcol/Trefethen Winery south of Yountville. The winemaking was supervised by Edmond Maudière, who had replaced the now-retired Renaud Poirier. (Maudière has been flying back and forth between France and California ever since.) They crushed a total of 162 tons and in November tasted the results.

Rene di Rosa

at his Winery

Lake Vineyard

in the Carneros.

Chardonnay, Pinot noir, and Pinot blanc were, not surprisingly, the best candidates for Champagne cuvées. Later they would include some Pinot Meunier, a grape employed in Champagne. The 1973 wines they liked and kept would be employed as a reserve stock to add depth and flavor to later vintages, since Moët and Wright had decided not to produce vintage-dated wines. Maudière was particularly impressed by the Pinot noir, even though it was difficult to get the juice into the tanks before it had picked up some color. Through experimentation he was able to hold down the color with machine harvesting in the cool of night. But the attractiveness of this blush wine led them to produce a sort of *oeil de perdrix,* as Paul Masson had done fifty years earlier. It would be their Blanc de Noir.

The 1974 crush produced their first truly commercial cuvée. The Brut would be two parts Pinot noir, one part Chardonnay, with a touch of Pinot blanc and Ugni blanc. There would be about 150,000 bottles, 40,000 of them Blanc de Noir. They were released in December 1976 for the holidays. Meanwhile, in December 1975 work began on the 80,000-square-foot winery at Yountville. The wine was made in the leased Trefethen premises through the 1977 harvest.

Now they had to decide what to call the operation and what to call the wine in the bottles. The French thought "M & H" was just fine, but Wright convinced them that it sounded more like a plumbing firm than a sparkling wine brand. When someone came up with Domaine Chandon the people on both sides of the Atlantic went for the idea. They held their breath to see if the Treasury Department would accept the brand name, with Almaden's Le Domaine sparkling wine on the market. The wine was labeled and into distribution well before Christmas. Next spring, April 25, 1977, the huge winery was opened to the public.

The term "Champagne" did not appear on the label of the new wine. To have used it would have flown in the face of all the French had been saying for years about what was and what was not Champagne. The label read Chandon Brut and Chandon Blanc de Noir. Later there would be a Chandon Réserve. For a while there was also a tart and very dry Chardonnay in the style of Côteaux de Champenois, labeled "Fred's Friends" after Moët's president, Frédéric de Brialles. Maudière also showed them how to produce a traditional apéritif of Champagne called there Ratafia, made by blending Pinot noir press juice with neutral spirits. They called it Panache.

The Chandon wines received critical applause and were a financial success. The first twentieth-century French wine operation in California was a triumph. This historic investment of foreign capital was certainly not unique, but it confirmed the possibilities already perceived in the Beringer turnaround. Domaine Chandon easily reached the goal of 200,000 cases in 1983. By 1988 the company had more than doubled that sales record.[31]

Today if a person looks at a map of the San Francisco Bay Area so that population growth in the last two decades is graphically represented, Napa County stands out in remarkable contrast to the other counties. An analysis of nine Napa population growth predictions made in the 1960s shows that on average their extrapolation for year 1980 was 38 percent high. Predictions for Sonoma County are about 20 percent low. The dreaded and predicted "Santa Clarafication" of the Napa Valley has not taken place.[32]

The agricultural integrity of the Napa Valley was saved by a concerted movement between 1966 and 1968, triggered by the state's plan to build a freeway through the Valley. We have seen that the state had no interest in extending the freeway beyond Yountville, if population growth there did not warrant it. This two-year movement made a legal reality of the hopes of the Valley's residents to hold growth to a reasonable level and to save the vineyards.

It began in 1966 when conservationist leader William Bronson called for the creation of a national vineyard to save the Napa Valley from the bulldozer. He and others met in June at a statewide conference of conservationists in Calistoga. There was little chance of making the Valley's vineyards part of the National Park System, but the dramatic proposal caught the news media's attention and helped spark the movement to change the basic zoning regulations for the county's unincorporated land.[33] At that moment a proposal to convert a portion of the To Kalon vineyard land to a complex of cluster homes galvanized the Upper Napa Valley Associates (UNVA). They now realized in concrete terms what could happen to the region if a pro-agriculture public policy were not adopted.

Next year the County Planning Commission began holding hearings on whether to change the minimum zoning in unincorporated areas from the current one acre to forty acres. The meetings were stormy, and opponents, mostly developers and owners of farmland, with an eye on development, called the idea absolutely unacceptable, probably unconstitutional, and said it would cause "intolerable hardship" to Napa property owners. It was argued that California's Williamson Act (1965) would save the Valley. But it was obvious that farmers who did not want to remove their land from the growing tax burden for ten years by green-belting could do whatever they wanted with their property. The result would have been a checkerboard pattern, eventually leading to solid development. The Williamson Act certainly did little to save the Santa Clara Valley.

The San Francisco press came down in favor of the zoning regulations finally recommended by the Planning Commission. (In a spirit of compromise the limit had been lowered to twenty acres.) The *Chronicle* warned that "the freeway and the subdivision are now aiming their bulldozers at the vineyards of the Napa Valley." Environmental expert Harold Gilliam wrote that the projected freeway was the "fuse that will ignite the population explosion of the Napa Valley." Schramsberg's Jack Davies and both Louis Martinis led a strong but far from unanimous body of vintners in support of the measure. In opposition stood an organization called Napa Valley United Farmers, led by John Daniel and Louis Stralla. They argued that this new agricultural preserve deprived them of their constitutional right to dispose of their property as they saw fit. Their argument was basically the same as Cornelius Vanderbilt's in opposing government regulation—"It's my railroad, isn't it?"

Great pressure was placed on the supervisors to reject the preserve. Julius Caiocca, who had earlier accepted the inevitability of the freeway, was threatened with policy cancellations by his insurance clients if he cast a YES vote. But he and the rest of the Board did just that, and in doing so made California environmental history. For Gilliam it was a "historic turning point in the struggle to halt the degradation of the American environment." Looking back on it ten years later he called it "an ingenious way to combine controlled growth with preservation of the natural and agricultural landscape." The amendment to Ordinance 186 went into effect on November 11, 1968, rezoning about 24,000 acres of agricultural land north of Napa to the head of the Valley. With some exceptions, parcels could be cut no smaller than twenty acres. In 1979 the size was raised to forty acres, the original proposal.[34]

Daniel and Stralla did not give up their spirited opposition and mounted a suit challenging the constitutionality of the preserve. First they unsuccessfully applied for an injunction to block implementation. Then they filed a suit that eventually went to the State Supreme Court, which held in August 1970 that California law and the state legislature certainly did allow such regulation. (Daniel died a few days before the ruling was handed down.)

For now the conservationists' battle was won, but all concerned with the fragile character of the Valley's natural and agricultural environment also knew how fragile the ordinance was. All it would take were the votes of three supervisors and the preserve would be dead. Speaking to the UNVA two years later, Maynard Amerine called for vigilance and warned that "what we do now will have a lot to do with what the valley will be in 2072."[35]

There would be more skirmishes and pitched battles in years to come. Those concerned for this fragile environment understood that unless the principles on which the agricultural preserve was based were set in some kind of legal concrete, the vineyards that produced Napa wine eventually could have the same fate as those of the Santa Clara Valley.

1960

A 5/22 freeze in the Valley dipped to 28°. Then came a hot June and July. Harvest began in late August with a fairly short crop, especially for Zinfandel. Sugars were good. Prices were steady and rising, the best since the war. Despite a short crop, grower income rose. Wines were noted for their concentrated flavors. Cabernets were delicious. Large amounts of grapes were brought from other areas into the Napa Valley for crushing.

1961

A cool, damp spring also brought two severe April frosts. Then a mid-June heat wave cut the crop even more. Harvest started in early September and was very orderly. Sugars were good. Prices soared, particularly for top-grade whites, which produced outstanding wines. Zins were also outstanding in another year of very flavorful wines. Yields were again quite low, the shortest crop in recent history. Another year of very flavorful wines. Again, many imported grapes crushed here.

1962

Good winter rain was followed by substantial planting, mostly to top varieties. A cool summer brought a late vintage that lasted until early November. The large crop ripened slowly. A cool October and far too much fall rain almost ruined the vintage. Downpour on 10/12 of 5.58 inches brought the month's total to almost twelve inches. Vineyards were quagmires. Clear skies in late October and wind from helicopters saved some late varieties. Most soft-skinned varieties were harvested before rains hit, but late-ripening reds were mediocre at best. Prices were excellent again and growers were happy with a crop that averaged over four tons per acre.

1963

It was a record year for California wine production, but Napa had problems. A very wet rainy season was followed by lots of frost and a cool summer. September was cool and foggy. The early October rain hit with 50 percent of the crop unharvested. There was a race to get grapes in, and pickers were scarce. Prices were again very good, super for top varieties. Some good wines were made from hillside grapes, but overall quality was poor.

1964

Rainy season was almost a drought except for 2.5 lonely inches in March. Bad 4/24 frost. Hot days in September accelerated the vintage, which lasted until November after October cooled off. Yields were low and prices high. Chardonnay growers were very happy with profits and overall quality, which was excellent, particularly for Cabernets.

1965

Another record state crop; big in Napa too, but no record. Vintage stats reflected recent planting of better varieties. Wet and almost frostless spring. August was cool with drizzles. Sugars were slow coming up. After a freak September frost, temperatures returned to normal. Vintage lasted into November with good sugars and balanced musts. Prices fell off some, but crop's value was the highest since World War II's halcyon days. Quality was better than average. Much competition for grapes not already contracted. Reds are 65 percent of vintage.

1966

A good spring and nice berry set were followed by a hot summer. For a while vintage looked early, but cool weather slowed things down. Vintage was finally under way by mid-September. Then hot winds pushed up sugars and dehydrated many grapes. Then came another unseasonal fall frost. Overall quality was good. Cabernets were excellent and long-lived. Demand and prices remained solid. White grape acreage was now growing faster than red.

1967

Abundant winter rain. April and May cool and rainy. April had twenty-seven overcast or rainy days. Then came a moderate summer. Reds were late to show color. Vintage was late. Early whites dribbled in through September. Then 10/12 rain stalls harvest. October turned warm and grapes came in a rush, varieties often out of normal order. That and variable sugars made for a disorderly harvest. Zins were in poor condition. Everything finally was in before November rains hit. Growers who stuck it out with Cabernets did very well and made good money. Chardonnay prices skyrocketed. Reds 63 percent of vintage.

1968

A warm and dry February and March set up vines for sharp April frosts that cut tonnage. Then came a great summer. August rains hurt soft-skinned whites. Vintage moved slowly but it was orderly. Sugars slowed with some raisining in red varieties. Napa received two inches of rain on 10/13, then perfect weather until 10/27. Cabernets came in with great chemistry before heavens opened up again on 10/29. Demand for top varieties was frantic. A nerve-shattering vintage ended with great quality and high prices. Yield was ordinary but crop value was a record. Almost 2,000 acres were now nonbearing as the boom began to take off. Cabernets of 1968 would make California wine history in years to come. Locals said it was the best vintage since 1947.

1969

Still lots of planting this year. Rainy season was very good and spring was luxuriant. Summer was hot with some mildew problems. Vintage started slowly in late August and proceeded slowly into September. Then it was a stampede.

Varieties came in too close to one another and often out of normal order. Yields of red grapes were lighter than expected. October rains caused anxiety. Vintage ended in early November. Everyone was surprised by excellent quality after it is over. Musts were balanced. Prices remained high. Good yields made this the best crop since World War II in C$. The boom was on.

1970

Planting continued to expand Valley vineyards to areas not planted to vines since Prohibition. Over 2,300 acres were nonbearing. Early fall frosts in 1969 hurt vines' starch reserves. Dry spring and warm March pushed vines to leaf early, setting them up for devastating 4/27–28 frosts. In all, thirty-six nights during normal growing season had temperatures under 33°, including 23° in Calistoga on 4/27. Then came a very hot summer that further cut crop. Many days were over 100°. The vintage started slowly in late August. Very selective picking was needed because so much second- and third-crop fruit had developed on the frosted vines. Crop was extremely light with great competition for available grapes. Vintage lasted into November with generally benign weather. Prices soared again. Crop was barely half-normal size; lots of grapes were imported. Quality of Napa grapes was wonderful. Merlot had become a noticeable part of the claret vintage. Many Cabernets were still developing in the nineties.

1971

The planting binge continued; over 3,000 acres were now nonbearing. Only 61 percent of vines were red wine varieties. Spring was cool and the vines bloomed late in hot weather, which caused shatter and poor berry set. But crop was not overly short. Vintage started slowly in late August. Hot weather moved things along quickly in September. Sugar development was irregular from variety to variety. There had been some overcropping. Cold weather halted vintage on 10/1. Days were cold, with a frost so bad that growers turned on overhead sprinklers to save rest of crop. Then on 10/28 frost fried many grapes still on vines. Vintage dragged into November, mostly on growers' hopes. Some Cabernets made it. But average Cab Brix (sugar) was only 21.6°. Crop was large, yields good, and prices up 30 percent from 1970. The value of the crop was more than those of 1969 and 1970 combined. Quality, though, set no records.

1972

Planting didn't let up. Nonbearing acreage was now about 4,000. Winter rain was not ample and spring frosts cut crop. Several torrid July days also lowered yields. Vintage started 8/20 but sugars were slow coming up. Late September rains halted harvest. Sugars were still not satisfactory when nine days of rain started on 10/9. When rain ended, Cabernet, Petite Sirah, and Colombard were hanging in vineyards so muddy that they were virtually inaccessible. Sugars had collapsed. Rest of vintage was a cleanup operation that left many whites unpicked. Light crop brought good prices. Cabernet sugar averaged only 21.1°. Chardonnay prices soared to $850/ton. For all the horrible conditions and shortness of crop, the value of the crop was even greater than the larger 1971 vintage. Reds comprised 56 percent of crop. There were now forty-four wineries in the valley; in 1967 there were just twenty-nine.

1973

Over 3,000 acres were planted this spring, over 1,000 Cabernet. Dormant season was cold and wet, followed by a mild spring. Conditions during bloom were excellent with a huge berry set. Summer conditions were almost ideal. Slow vintage started 8/25. Size of crop astonished all. South county grapes ripened slowly. Two October rains slowed harvest; then warm weather. Most late varieties were uneven in quality, but Cabernets were very good. Value of the crop was double the record harvest of 1971. Yields were over four tons per acre. Nonbearing acreage now topped 6,000. Suddenly there was concern about overplanting. Many of the better 1973 reds were not appreciated at first. Napa wine quality ended up well above average for entire vintage. For California the boom had peaked; for Napa next year would be reckoning time.

Notes For Chapter Twelve

1. Star, 12/24/1959, 9/29/1960.
2. Star, 11/1/1962, 11/8/1962, 10/29/1964, 11/26/1964.
3. Star, 11/26/1962, 1/19/1967, 12/19/1968.
4. In 1966 the reports of the Napa County Agricultural Commissioner start containing varietal statistics. Before this date one must depend on the imprecise annual reports of the California Department of Agriculture's California Grape Acreage or on anecdotal information from newspapers and industry sources.
5. Star, 12/24/1961, 4/25/1963, 7/11/1963, 10/31/1963, 9/1/1966, 4/13/1967; Bottles & Bins, 4/1962, 4/1963.
6. Adams (1st Edition), 209-211; Benson, 217-224; Brother Timothy oral history, 40-51; Los Angeles Times, 11/6/1975; NVWLA II: 213-214; California Living, 11/12/1978; Wines & Vines (April 1960), (March 1977).
7. Chronicle, 7/6/1977; Los Angeles Times, 6/25/1981; Sorensen, 163.
8. The overwhelming favorite of the forty-seven tasters at the San Francisco Vintners Club (11/20/1975) was Lot 4, from Sonoma grapes and aged in small American oak barrels. Also see: Connoisseur's Guide to California Wines (5:1): 72-74.
9. L. P. Martini oral history, 61-77; L. M. Martini oral history, 44-56; Benson, 207-215; Adams (1st Edition), 221-224; Julius L. Jacobs. "In the Shadow. . . ." Vintage (July 1981): 21; Star, 6/2/1983; Chronicle, 6/8/1974; Wine Spectator, 1/16/1979.
10. NVWLA II: 168-177; Tchelistcheff oral history, 120-122; Conaway, 103-116, 117,118, 126-128; Wine Spectator, 1/16/1979.
11. NVWLA II: 197-212; Mondavi oral history, 36-41; Conaway, 22-34; Jay Stuller and Glen Martin. Through the Grapevine (New York 1989): 242-245; Wine Spectator, 6/1/1985, 7/16/1985.
12. Ruth Teiser. "Louis Petri. . . ." Wines & Vines (August 1983); NVWLA II: 133; Conaway, 39-55, 74-77; Chronicle, 3/16/1979; San Jose Mercury, 9/18/1984.
13. Mary-Ellen McNeil Draper, ed. Vintners Club (San Francisco 1988) traces the club's tastings from

1973-1987. A good collection of Cabernet Sauvignon evaluations can be found in James Laube's California's Great Cabernets (San Francisco 1989), which covers the seventy-seven modern Napa producers Laube thinks have made great Cabernets.

14. NVWLA III: 238-248; Star, 4/23/1964; Benson, 176-187; Wine Spectator, 3/1/1981, 2/16/1984, 1/31/1990; Mark Allen Gill. "Fun with Joe and Alice." Wine World (May 1977): 18.

15. NVWLA IV: 282-313; Register, 6/19/1969; Philip Hiaring. " The Look to the Future. . . ." Wines & Vines (June 1969): 37; Julius Jacobs. "The Continuing Renaissance. . . ." Vintage (February 1981): 29; Wine Spectator, 9/15/1985; Oakland Tribune, 1/24/1988.

16. The Fine Wines of California (New York 1971): 179; Harry Waugh. Pick of the Bunch (London 1970): 15.

17. Redwood Rancher (September 1972): 49.

18. Chronicle, 8/14/1976, 6/13/1977, 7/2/1978, 3/31/1978, 8/11/1978; Moira Johnson. "A Magnificent Obsession." New West (August 1981): 67-70; Stuller and Martin, 243-245; Conaway, 169-174;   Wines & Vines (May 1978): 18.

19. Wines & Vines (August 1972): 21; (October 1974): 38; (October 1975): 17; (November 1980): 56.

20. Wines & Vines (October 1967): 7; (September 1969): 19; Vintage (October 1969): 13; Benson, 168-174.

21. Laube. Cabernets, 173-186; Harry Waugh. Winetaster's Choice (New York 1973): 92-95; The Journal of the International Wine & Food Society (August 1975): 43-44: Adams (2nd Edition): 327.

22. San Jose News, 9/6/1971; Author's interview with Donn Chappellet, 11/19/1971; Connoisseur's Guide to California Wines (May 1975): 94; Wine Spectator, 4/1/1983, 11/15/1986; Star, 10/11/1990; Laube. Cabernets, 117-120.

23. "Spring Mountain in Transition." Wine World (January 1976): 16-18; Conaway, 263-266; Benson, 143-150; Wine Spectator, 6/15/1983; Author's interview with Michael Robbins, 11/19/1971.

24. Star, 12/4/1975; Wine Spectator, 5/1/1982, 9/1/1983; Chronicle, 3/18/1982, 3/24/1986.

25. Adams (3rd Edition), 333-334; Laube. Cabernets, 121-124; Blumberg and Hannum (3rd Edition), 244-245; Benson, 152-159.

26. Star, 7/17/1969; Chronicle, 8/9/1977; Adams (2nd Edition), 332; Benson, 189-197.

27. NVWLA I: 177-191; Tchelistcheff oral history, 116-119; Conaway, 130-146, 156-160; John N. Hutchison. "An Interview with Legh Knowles." Wines & Vines (July 1982):66; Los Angeles Times, 4/8/1979; San Jose Mercury, 10/31/1988.

28. Norman S. Roby. ". . .An Ode to a Nightingale." Vintage (October 1979): 35; Julius L. Jacobs. "A Salute to Myron Nightingale." Wines & Vines (March 1985): 38; Richard Paul Hinkle. "Nightingale." Wine West (40:5): 17; Anthony Dias Blue. American Wine (New York 1985): 34; Laube. Cabernets, 94.

29. Wines & Vines (September 1970): 7; (March 1973):27; Register, 12/1/1972; Wine Spectator, 5/1/1986; Chronicle, 2/1/1989.

30. Redwood Rancher (September 1971): 27; Wines & Vines (March 1970): 15; (December 1976): 19; Chronicle, 11/24/1976; Star, 3/15/1976; Richard Paul Hinkle. "The Great Shakeout." Wine Country (September 1982): 22; Author's interview with W. E. Van Loben Sels, 4/16/1973.

31. Philip Hiaring. ". . .A French Connection." Wines & Vines (June 1973): 24-26; John Wright. ". . .How Moët Made the Decision." Wines & Vines (June 1967):54; Conaway, 185-190; Wine Country (December 1981): 14; Wine Spectator, 10/1/1982, 3/31/1988; Practical Winery (March 1986): 29; Chronicle, 10/1/1973, 9/6/1988; Los Angeles Times, 5/15/1975, 8/19/1976, 2/23/1978; Jamie Laughridge. Rising Star (New York 1983) is a good history of Domaine Chandon's early years.

32. Donald Joseph de la Peña. "Preservation of Vineyards and Wineries in the San Francisco Bay Area." Master's thesis in city planning, UCB (1962): 50; Irving Hoch and Nicholas Tryphonopoulas. A Study of the Economy of Napa County, California. CAES, UC Giannini Foundation Research Report No. 303 (August 1969): 57-64, 85; E. R. Horner, ed. California Cities, Towns and Counties (Palo Alto 1987): 71-78;
Ralph B. Hutchinson and Sidney M. Blumer. "The Williamson Act and Wine Growing in the Napa Valley." California State Polytechnic College (Pomona 1972): 1-8.

33. Star, 5/12/1966, 6/9/1966; Examiner, 6/8/1966.

34. Register, 10/9/1968; Star, 11/7/1968; Chronicle, 3/19/1968, 4/11/1968, 4/3/1977; Examiner, 3/17/1968, 4/7/1968.

35. Star, 8/27/1970, 12/4/1972; Conaway 82-92 gives details of the infighting during the struggle for the preserve.

THERMIDORS

There is over anticipation and over speculation in the whole industry. The day of reckoning will come.

—ALFRED FROMM
1973

THE MOMENT OF TRUTH SEEMED TO COME FOR THE CALIFORNIA WINE INDUSTRY in 1974. It has been said that revolutions have in them the seeds for reaction against their own tendencies, sometimes referred to by historians as Thermidor, after the eleventh month in the French revolutionary calendar when Robespierre and the Terror were put down. But the reaction to overplanting and oversupply was statistically mild. California wine sales rose from 1973 to 1976 by an average of only 4 percent, but they rose. Shipments of table wine averaged a 7 percent increase in these years.

For Napa the blow of Thermidor, for a moment, came crashing down like a guillotine's blade. The total value of the Napa wine grape crop in 1974 was down 45 percent from 1973. But Napa grape prices in 1973 had been ridiculously high. In constant dollars (C$) the value of 1973's crop would not be surpassed until 1982, when bearing acreage was 84 percent higher. The value (C$) of the 1973 crop, in terms of income per bearing acre, has never been surpassed.

The economic shakeout had a sobering effect on the entire industry. Planting was cut to almost nothing after 1973, growing very slowly until 1981, when the numbers took off again. Few nonbearing Napa vines were pulled as a result of the panic, however. In 1974 young, nonbearing vines accounted for almost 40 percent of the Napa acreage, presaging a continued rise in production. But by 1979 this number had dropped to less than 8 percent. In general, Napa wine grape crops continued to grow in size and the market was able to handle the amount of wine that these grapes produced. From 1971 to 1973, crops averaged 44,000 tons. From 1974 to 1979, the average rose to 57,000. By the early eighties the average was well over 80,000 tons.

Certainly there was no abatement in the quality revolution that had already taken place in Napa vineyards. In 1973 the great red and white wine grapes of Bordeaux and Burgundy were planted in 30.2 percent of the Napa vineyards. Ten years later the percentage had doubled. Growers and wineries also gradually transformed Napa vineyards from the predominant production of red wine grapes to white. In 1974 the Napa red plantation accounted for 62.7 percent of the total. By the early eighties it was less than half. After 1979 the total value of the white wine grapes was almost always higher than that of the red. This was part of the growing dominance of white table wine in the industry's growth figures, often referred to into the eighties as the "white wine craze."

THREE NEW WINERIES

Three new Napa wineries in these years illustrate many of the factors affecting a premium winery startup in these turbulent times. Albert Brounstein began planting his Diamond Creek vineyards to Cabernet in 1967. He had about twenty plantable acres on Mt. Diamond and noticed that the soils were quite variable on the small property. When his 1972s were harvested he kept two lots separate, one from a sloping eight-acre plot of gray, volcanic material, the other from a steeper slope, ruddy in ferric oxide. In 1974 he asked a group of local wine writers to taste them blind and tell him whether they thought they were as different from each other, and as well-flavored, as he believed. They said YES. When he sold his sixty-five cases of 1972 Cabernet Sauvignon he labeled the two lots separately, Volcanic Hill and Red Rock Terrace. Later he added another wine from the rocky five-acre vineyard he called Gravelly Meadow.

Brounstein's wines were greeted with cheers. The 1972 Volcanic Hill was the only wine from that generally mediocre vintage in the April 1975 Vintners Club Cabernet tasting, and it won easily. A year later his three 1974 wines finished one-two-three at the club tasting of that excellent vintage. Contrary to received American academic opinion, Brounstein contends that "the soil is the important thing. It's all right there in the dirt."[1]

Of much vaster proportions was the winery Joseph Phelps built in 1974 in Spring Valley near the Heitz Winery. A Colorado builder involved in constructing the new Souverain wineries two years earlier, Phelps first thought to go public as Stonebridge Cellars. His first wine was a White Riesling made by German-trained Walter Schug, who stayed on until 1982 as winemaker. By then Phelps' Cabernets, particularly his proprietary "Insignia," had brought the most attention to his label. Even more noteworthy to some were the Cabernets made from Milton Eisele's Calistoga vineyard since 1975. Phelps' vineyards cover about 300 acres and produce far more than Cabernet. When he began planting the true French Syrah in 1973 he qualified as a charter member of California's "Rhone Rangers." Since 1990 his wines in the spirit of the south of France have been released under the "Vin du Mistral" label.[2]

Bernard Portet established Clos du Val in the southern part of the Stag's Leap area in 1971 on behalf of a group of French and American investors who also owned winegrowing properties in South America and Australia. Portet was a 1968 graduate in the enology curriculum at the School of Agronomy at Montpellier, in Southern France. But his roots were in Bordeaux, where his father had been the technical director at Château Lafite. His goal was to make Napa varietal red wine in an elegant and complex style, reminiscent of the best Bordeaux clarets, and without so much of the muscle that he found in California Cabernets and Zinfandels. The winery's first vintage came from the generally mediocre grapes of 1972. But these

Diamond Creek

vineyards with

their diverse soils

and microclimates.

SOURCE: WINE SPECTATOR.

Stag's Leap grapes from the nearby Steltzner Vineyard were good enough for the wine to compete in the 1976 Paris tasting that helped fix Napa's world-class image on the international wine scene. Portet's 1972 and 1973 Zinfandels both took first places at the Vintners Club. In 1979 the Paris Figaro crowned Portet, "le roi du vin californien." By the nineties Clos du Val Cabernets were totaling more than 25,000 cases. Meanwhile the owners had acquired the St. Andrew's Winery, a few miles south, where Chardonnay was to be the primary concentration.[3]

VINTAGE 1974

Where this vintage stands in quality in relationship to the best five since Repeal is still a matter of debate. It was special in several ways. Planting was continuing frantically, with just under 4,000 acres going in during the dormant season. A May 19 frost cut the crop, but some thought it a boon with so many new vines coming into production. Then a mild summer brought up sugars slowly. The harvest began on September 1 with cool nights and warm days. The vintage slowed with a few light October showers. Then hot, smoggy weather brought in the rest of the grapes in a rush, but most of the fruit was in excellent condition. Cabernets and White Rieslings were historic in their quality. Chardonnays were excellent. But grape prices collapsed in the face of a large crop and huge inventories carried over from 1973. It was a sobering year for growers, but a great year for wineries and consumers. A crop about the same size as 1973 brought growers only 55 percent as much money. In James Laube's words it was the vintage which "put California Cabernet on the map." When the wines came onto the market in 1977–78, the 1976 "Judgment of Paris" had already taken place and had focused the interest of Cabernet collectors on this great vintage.

New Wineries: Villa Mt. Eden (Oakville), Stags' Leap Winery (Stag's Leap), Ritchie Creek (Spring Mountain), Conn Creek (Silverado), Raymond (St. Helena).

1975 TRANSACTIONS

There was no sign of frantic planting in the dormant season of 1974–75. The vines that went in this year were just about balanced by pullups.

Napa acreage continued to change hands. In 1975 independent growers owned about 60 percent of the Valley's acres. But winery and corporate ownership grew steadily for the next fifteen years. The formal organization of the Napa Valley Grape Growers Association (NVGGA) in 1975 was aimed at promoting the interests of this important but dwindling group.

The events at Franciscan Vineyards illustrate the hard times some experienced in Napa. Founded in 1972, its winery building south of St. Helena was built the next year, its first crush was in 1974, and its third set of owners took over in 1975. The new principals were Justin Meyer and Raymond Duncan, the latter a Colorado oilman. We have already met Meyer at Christian Brothers in the sixties. In 1972 these partners had started their own Silver Oak Cellars on the Oakville Cross Road. They intended to concentrate on producing first-class Cabernet Sauvignon and were highly successful, mostly with grapes grown in Sonoma's Alexander Valley.

The new owners helped save Franciscan, but the winery was still not a great success. In 1979 they sold it to the German Eckes Corporation, with Meyer staying on for two years. Still Franciscan's profits lagged, however well-received the wines. The actual process of resuscitation did not really begin until 1985 when Chilean-born Augustin Huneeus became a part owner and the winery's president. By 1990 Franciscan had a capacity of 900,000 gallons, owned 470 acres of Napa vineyard, had recently purchased Mt. Veeder Winery, and was successfully marketing other wines under the Estancia label. Huneeus' turnaround of Franciscan Vineyards shows that individual leadership can determine the success of a struggling winery.[4]

The old Chateau Chevalier winery on Spring Mountain was revived and owner Greg Bissonette's wines were first released under the Mountainside label in 1975. His estate wine would bear the Chateau label. Stockbroker Bissonette and his family had started putting the estate back together in 1969, replanting fifty-seven acres on terraced vineyards. But the operation was a mixed success. In 1984, 100 years after Fortune Chevalier had founded the winery, it was sold to the Nickel family, which had already brought Far Niente back to life. Nevertheless, within a year the winery was again up for sale; it was still for sale six years later.[5]

Another important 1975 transaction was Francis Ford Coppola's purchase of the old Niebaum home estate. There were about 85 acres of vines, mostly Cabernet Sauvignon, on the property next to Inglenook. Coppola's

Francis Ford Coppola and his original Tucker automobile. In the background the old Niebaum Mansion, which he now owns.

Italian background guaranteed an interest in hearty red wine. He called his powerful homemade concoction "Vinoforte." The bottles had his grandfather's picture on the label with the slogan, "One glass is worth two." In 1978, with counsel from Robert Mondavi and André Tchelistcheff, Coppola made his first Rubicon, a concentrated Cabernet blend of red Bordeaux grapes. Rubicon means "red river," but the flow of this wine from the old carriage house, now winery, was more like the flow of the tiny Italian creek which bears that famous name. As years went by, more wine was made. The first three vintages were bottled and in 1985 they were still lying in their bins, unreleased. Coppola's first winemaker commented on the filmmaker's financial problems in these years and thought they caused him to treat the winery more as a hobby than a business. (Niebaum would have understood.) But when the flow of the Niebaum-Coppola Estate wine began, more than ten years after he had acquired the property, his Cabernet took its place with the other high-priced wines of the mid-eighties that helped Napa develop its image as a latter-day Médoc. No wonder—these Cabernets were produced on soil that had helped bring forth some of the great Inglenook Cabernets of the forties and fifties.[6]

The crew at Caymus celebrates the great 1975 vintage.

(Left to right: Randy Dunn, Charles Wagner, Sr. Charles Wagner, Jr.

While Rubicon sprang from great soil and the wealth of its producer, Caymus sprang from the son of the Napa soil, his son, and their winemaker. Charles F. Wagner's Alsatian family had come to Napa in 1906. In 1941, he bought seventy acres of prunes and walnuts. On the property stood the old Liberty School where he and his wife had learned to read, write, and cipher. When the old building fell down some years later, they used part of the wood to build a portion of their current home. The Wagners started producing wine in 1972, but hired Randall Dunn to be their winemaker in 1975. But they did not hire the University of California doctoral candidate because they were having trouble with their wines; the 1972 Cabernet just released was well-received, and their 1973 won a first at the Vintners Club and later won a taste-off there against all comers. Dunn's first Caymus Cabernet, the 1975, also took a first, but was second in the 1978 taste-off to the Phelps 1975. In fact, Caymus Cabernets have taken more Vintners Club firsts than those of any other winery.

In 1987 the *Wine Spectator* dubbed Charles Wagner, Sr. "Napa Valley's Unlikely King of Cabernet." James Laube contends that "perhaps the most consistently excellent California Cabernet Sauvignon is grown by a crusty old prune farmer who first sold wine as a bootlegger." Winemaker Dunn left Caymus in 1986 to concentrate on his own winery on Howell Mountain, but the *Wine Spectator* judged his valedictory 1985 Caymus Special Selection Cabernet to be the best in California for that very great Cabernet year. Since then father and son, Charles F. and Charles J., have handled the winemaking chores. The Wagners make a lot of other wines and buy some from other producers to sell at bargain prices under their Liberty School label.[7]

VINTAGE 1975

A cool spring held back the vines, but there was plenty of rain. July was very hot; one day in St. Helena hit 110°. August weather was a "roller coaster ride." There was even a heavy shower on August 18. Then cool temperatures and morning fog persisted until September 10. Grape deliveries were shockingly short, coming in about 20 percent under predictions. Rain on October 9 and 10 slowed the harvest. Then it was clear and mild into November, saving many vineyards. But low sugars were common in the south Valley. More than 1,000 tons there were never harvested. Hillside Cabernets were quite good, even though overall average Brix (sugar percentage) was only 22.0°. Prices were down again, averaging less than half the 1973 level, which was a blow to growers and a boon to wineries. Overall quality was good, with many excellent Chardonnays and Sauvignon blancs. The crop was 36 percent white.

New wineries; Tulocay (Napa), Napa Wine Cellars (Oakville), V. Sattui (St. Helena).

THE JUDGMENT OF PARIS

The four inches of rain that dropped on the Napa Valley in October of 1975 would be the area's largest downpour for the next twenty-six months. The most severe extended drought of the twentieth century, so far, was under way. But whatever the pluvial situation in the Valley, 1976 was a great year for Napa wine.

In Greek legend Aphrodite won the Judgment of Paris. In 1976 Napa wines won the judgment of Paris for the same reason the goddess had triumphed—their beauty.

The year marked the bicentennial of the American Republic, and Paris wine merchant Steven Spurrier decided to put on a blind tasting, matching good California reds and whites against French Cabernets and Chardonnays. The tasters were French and represented all levels of the French wine establishment, from journalist to producer.

In May André Tchelistcheff had brought in the California wine to Paris, or better, the people in his tour group had brought in the bottles. The tasting was public, held on the patio of the Hotel Inter-Continental. When the results were broadcast to the world, one of the great wine controversies of all time exploded. But the outcome was clear. No whining French apologists or cleverly dodging Francophile East Coast wine writers could obscure the fact that the winners, red and white, were both Californians, both from the Napa Valley.

Actually, the French reds did better than the Californians, when the same ranking formula was used to rate the countries as was used to rate the wines. The white wine numbers show an absolute statistical dead heat. But the wine world heard that Stag's Leap Wine Cellars 1973 Cabernet Sauvignon had beaten the

Miljenko Grgich

likes of 1970 Château Mouton-Rothschild and Château Haut-Brion, and that the Chateau Montelena 1973 Chardonnay had beaten a Meursault-Charmes. A 1974 Chalone and a 1973 Spring Mountain took third and fourth place. When the Vintners Club duplicated the Spurrier tasting in January 1978, the 197 participants in the blind tasting again ranked the Stag's Leap first. But this time the Chalone nosed out the Chateau Montelena in the Chardonnay competition.

Warren Winiarski, whose Cabernet Sauvignon won the Paris tasting, came to Napa in the sixties with an interest in winemaking. He landed a job with Lee Stewart at Souverain. After two years he went to work for Robert Mondavi and started looking for vineyard property. He eventually found forty-five acres east of the Silverado Trail, just below the Yountville Crossroad. In the hills to the east was a dramatic outcropping of stone long referred to as Stag's Leap, a name he gave the little winery he built in 1972. Nearby was the old Stag's Leap Manor and the ruins of Horace Chase's Stag's Leap Winery, which Carl Doumani had bought in 1970. When he named his 1974 operation Stags' Leap Winery, he and Winiarski became entangled in a complicated legal battle, which we shall examine in the last chapter.[8]

Chateau Montelena's Miljenko Grgich had made the Chardonnay that triumphed at Paris. He too had worked for Lee Stewart and Robert Mondavi. He was interested in creating his own winery and in 1976 met Austin Hills, of the Hills Bros. coffee family. He had the money to help get the new winery going and also owned Napa vineyard acreage. The first Grgich-Hills Chardonnay was actually made at Montelena in 1976, before they broke ground next year for their new winery just north of Beaulieu. For many wine lovers this winery was to become "the House of Chardonnay." Grgich's vintages from 1978 to 1981 received nothing less than a second place in Vintners Club tastings. *Wine Spectator* felt that this winery's Chardonnays were of the most consistently high quality in California. Grgich's Cabernets and Zinfandels also won fairly consistent critical praise, particularly in the eighties. Still, his Chardonnay production is three times his Cabernet output of about 10,000 cases.[9]

THE STEVEN SPURRIER TASTING

Hotel Inter-Continental, Paris, 1976

White Wine

1. Chateau Montelena, 1973 Chardonnay
2. Domaine Roulot, 1973 Meursault-Charmes
3. Chalone Vineyard, 1974 Chardonnay
4. Spring Mountain Vineyards, 1973 Chardonnay
5. Joseph Drouhin, 1973 Beaune, Clos des Mouches
6. Freemark Abbey, 1972 Chardonnay
7. Ramonet-Prudhon, 1973 Bâtard-Montrachet
8. Domaine Leflaive, 1972 Puligny-Montrachet, Les Pucelles
9. Veedercrest Vineyards, 1972 Chardonnay
10. David Bruce, 1973 Chardonnay

Red Wine

1. Stag's Leap Wine Cellars, 1973 Cabernet Sauvignon
2. 1970 Château Mouton Rothschild (Pauillac)
3. 1970 Château Haut-Brion (Graves)
4. 1970 Château Montrose (Saint-Estèphe)
5. Ridge Vineyards, 1971 Monte Bello Cabernet Sauvignon
6. 1971 Château Léoville-Las-Cases (Saint-Julien)
7. Mayacamas Vineyards, 1971 Cabernet Sauvignon
8. Clos du Val, 1972 Cabernet Sauvignon
9. Heitz Cellars, 1970 Martha's Vineyard Cabernet Sauvignon
10. Freemark Abbey, 1969 Cabernet Sauvignon

Another business that opened in 1976 was named after the owner of a nineteenth-century San Francisco winery, Vittorino Sattui. His great-grandson, Daryl, decided in 1972 that he wanted to start a winery, but he didn't have any money. Also, he really didn't know very much about wine production. He worked for a while at Carneros Creek and Christian Brothers and in 1974 started getting serious after he found a piece of property on the main highway just below St. Helena. At the outset the little business was more a cheese shop and delicatessen with picnic tables out front.

Sattui later said, "at first we were in the recreation business, but it worked." The historic significance of the Sattui Winery in those days comes from the questions raised about it, since next to no wine was made there at first. "Just what is a winery?" some neighbors asked.

But with the help of neighbor Bob Trinchero of Sutter Home, Sattui began making more wine than he bought in bulk. In 1985 he built a real winery on the property, also over the objections of some neighbors. In 1991 Sattui's friendly ambience attracted 267,000 visitors. Nevertheless, the question, "What is a winery?" would continue to arise for others and eventually would rend the Valley in the late eighties.

VINTAGE 1976

The dry winter and spring were hard on the vines and the berry set was poor. Shatter was a real problem for Cabernet. Crop estimators caused a ruckus by overestimating the Valley crop. Bunch and berry size were both small. Table wine harvest began on September 1. Grapes poured in too fast and out of order. Harvest weather was good and fruit quality very good. Five days of September rain caused some mold problems. Prices went up 43 percent from last year's poor showing. But yields were less than two tons per acre. Cabernets were intense and highly concentrated, but few would describe them as "balanced" and "charming." Chardonnays were rather coarse and unbalanced. Sauvignon blanc took top notices. The crush was 22 percent Cabernet Sauvignon.

New Wineries: William Hill (Napa), Rutherford Vintners (Rutherford), Rutherford Hill (Silverado), Round Hill (Silverado), St. Clement (St. Helena; formerly Spring Mountain Vineyards).

1977 TRANSACTIONS

1977 was charged with historically important events for many of the Valley's wineries. The Trefethen family released their first wines from their historic wooden winery. The owners of Freemark Abbey released their first Rutherford Hill wines. Bernard Skoda, longtime sales manager at Louis

Martini's, had his first crush at his own Rutherford Vintners winery across from Franciscan. And two old winery properties that Louis M. Martini bought in the 1930s were sold to Jerome Komes and his family to develop their Flora Spring Winery at the end of Zinfandel Lane. The Martinis had used these two old winery buildings (Brockhoff–1885 and Rennie Brothers–1883) for storage.[10]

In 1977 the Roy Raymond family released their first estate bottled wine, a botrytis-infected White Riesling, from vines planted on their ninety-acre estate beginning in 1971. In 1970 Raymond had left his position as general manager at Beringer, where he began work in 1933. He had married Martha Jane Beringer, Jacob's great-granddaughter. Their sons, Walter and Roy, Jr., planted the vineyard on Zinfandel Lane and made the wine, starting in 1974. It is certainly arguable that the Raymond-Beringer family is the oldest in the Valley continuously involved in wine production.[11]

Probably the most important transaction of 1977 was the sale of Sterling Vineyards to Coca-Cola of Atlanta. The giant soft drink company had decided to take a flyer in the American wine business, with the Sterling operation just one of many in the Wine Spectrum division of the Corporation. Sterling's founders, Peter Newton, Michael Stone, and Richard Forman, stayed on with

La Perla vineyards on Spring Mt. Original site of the Lemme Winery and the Schilling estate.

Coke for a short time. Newton took his piece of the $8,000,000-plus deal and built his own winery on Spring Mountain, with Forman as winemaker and partner. That relationship ended with an acrimonious lawsuit in 1983. Forman now has his own winery on the lower slopes of Howell Mountain in the old Remi Chabot building (1881).

The new management team at Sterling first cut the number of wines produced from seven to four. Then in 1977 they acquired an important 320-acre property on Mt. Diamond from viticultural entrepreneur William Hill. Eventually about 120 acres of vineyard

land were developed there, which began producing in 1982, mostly Cabernets and Chardonnays. Under Coke and the next owners, the vineyards here have been used as a sort of mountain experimental station. Soil erosion, water stress, and training systems have been but three of the matters studied.

But the directors in Atlanta were used to getting more return on invested capital and Sterling again changed hands in 1984 when they sold it and other properties to Seagram.[12]

Vintage 1977

This drought year was not so cruel as the last, but it was very dry. Tractors were able to work the vineyards right through the winter. The Napa River stopped flowing. The spring was cool with early leafing. Many young vines died from the drought. There was a mild summer and a harmless mid-August shower. The vintage was on time but had to stop after September 20's downpour, which hurt Chardonnays. Then good weather extended the vintage into November. This year's grapes were juicier than last year's. The overall quality was good and the chemistry was excellent. The yield was close to three tons per acre. Nonbearing acreage was cut in two this year. The shock of overplanted reds hurt other California districts, but not Napa, where Cabs reached $603 per ton and Merlot $627. The crush was 24 percent Cabernet, 8 percent Chardonnay.

New Wineries: Green and Red (Chiles Valley), Cakebread (Oakville), Grgich-Hills (Rutherford), Keenan (Spring Mountain), Smith-Madrone (Spring Mountain).

1978 Transactions

There were several important beginnings for Napa in 1978. Robert Keenan, at the revived Conradi Winery (1904), released his first wine. William Hill made his first Cabernet Sauvignon from his vines on Mt. Veeder. The St. Helena Wine Company, headed by Daniel Duckhorn, had its first crush. He marketed his wine with his name on the label and later dubbed the winery's second label "Decoy." Sonoma's ZD Winery (1969) moved to Napa and set up shop on the Silverado Trail. And in the Stag's Leap area Gary Andrus and his associates began planting their fifty-acre vineyard, soon to be the Pine Ridge Winery.

Sutter Home and Zinfandel

There was nothing really very new going on at the Sutter Home Winery in 1978, but it was in this year that Bob Trinchero began taking a very serious interest in a new aspect of his winery's Zinfandel sales. We last looked at this winery in the sixties, with its gigantic line of products, ranging from Marsala to sparkling Moselle, including even a quinine-flavored vermouth.

Later in the sixties some changes were made. The winery had always bought its grapes and the Trincheros were ever on the lookout for something special. One such discovery came in 1968 when Bob Trinchero found some Zinfandel grapes in Amador County's Shenandoah Valley. It was at this moment in the wine revolution that this variety was achieving a real premium status, responding to the pioneer work done by Louis M. Martini, Ridge Vineyards, and David Bruce. The Deaver Vineyard in the Sierra Foothills gave Trinchero grapes that produced rich and concentrated wines that would last for years. The wine was well-received and Sutter Home narrowed its product line exponentially.

In 1972 Trinchero made a small batch of white, or blush, Zinfandel. There was nothing new about such a wine, first made by George West in the 1860s near Stockton. The first Sutter Home "white" Zinfandel was dry and oak-aged. But in 1975 a slightly stuck fermentation left a touch of residual sugar which Trinchero liked. So did his customers, so he made a little more next year. By 1978 production had passed the 10,000 case mark.

This was the time when white wine was the rage of the industry, and white Zinfandel fit nicely into this active market. In 1982 they were producing 40,000 cases of red and 85,000 cases of white Zin. In 1986 Trinchero bought the old Lambert Egg Ranch and began building "Zinfandel Ranch" about a mile east of the winery. It would be a 3,500,000-gallon facility to help meet the 2,000,000-case demand for Sutter Home White Zinfandel in 1987. The grapes were coming now from the Central Valley, but the wine was the product of a Napa winery. Some looked at this flood and could easily tell the difference between this phenomenon and the few imported grapes brought into the Valley regularly by such as Louis Martini and Silver Oak. But using Central Valley grapes was an old Napa tradition.

This situation helped fuel the coming debate on what was Napa wine and what was a Napa winery. It also helped to save red Zinfandel as a quality table wine. The concentrated red Zinfandels of the seventies had become less popular and many wineries had simply given up on the variety. A red Zinfandel producer could get his white Zin onto the market within a few months after the grapes were crushed. By the mid-eighties it seemed that almost every serious red Zinfandel producer left was helping his winery's cash flow by producing the hugely popular white Zinfandel. Even Louis P. Martini joined the crowd. Such a strategy helped a smaller winery stay in the red Zin business, even if it were not greatly profitable at the moment.

In 1986 Sutter Home was still selling 100,000 cases of red Zinfandel. Two years later Trinchero emphasized his family's Zinfandel commitment by purchasing Amador's Monteviña Winery, long a red Zinfandel specialist. That same year Trinchero hosted a very serious industry symposium on Zinfandel, stressing the proud history of California's own varietal and its future in many forms.[13]

A far smaller Napa Valley Zinfandel specialist bought land near Calistoga in 1976, where brothers Jacob and Adam Grimm had begun digging their cellars and building their winery in 1888. J. Bernard Seps was intent on planting Zinfandel on the red clay and loam soil in the area and eventually had almost forty acres on the somewhat isolated spot near the Sonoma County line. This idyllic isolation and the name "Grimm" suggested the name for the new winery, Storybook Mountain Vineyards. Seps began selling his wine in 1981, even though Zinfandel was becoming something of the Rodney Dangerfield of California's premium varietals. But Seps and others, such as Bob Trinchero, have made a strong commitment to bring more respect to California's own.[14]

VINTAGE 1978

There was some planting this season, mostly top white varieties. Finally, there was rain, torrents in January. It was also the most frost-free spring in forty-three years. There was good berry set and a large harvest that came in a rush in late August. Crushing continued into the warmest November here in decades. White wine grapes brought excellent prices, averaging almost $300 more per acre than red. The crush was 28 percent Cabernet. This was more than the wineries really wanted, but quality was excellent. The press and wine writers were later writing about "a vintage of the century" with virtually no knowledge of the century's great vintages. Chardonnays were full of flavor but not long-lived.

New Wineries: Mont St. John (Carneros), Pine Ridge (Stag's Leap), Long (Sage Canyon), Buehler (Conn Valley), Niebaum-Coppola Estate (Rutherford), Quail Ridge (Silverado), ZD (Silverado), Duckhorn (Silverado), Markham (St. Helena), Charles Shaw (Larkmead), La Jota (Howell Mountain), Robert Pecota (Calistoga).

1979 TRANSACTIONS

Transactions in Napa during the 1979 season showed an increased foreign influence in the Valley. We have already noted the sale of Franciscan to German interests. This year the Swiss Schmidheiny family purchased Cuvaison Winery.

The winery's turnaround really didn't come until the mid-eighties under the management of John Thatcher and Manfred Esser. They eventually acquired over 400 Napa acres, including valuable Carneros property.

Far more conspicuous was the 1979 announcement that Robert Mondavi and Bordeaux's Philippe de Rothschild were combining forces to produce a "first growth" Cabernet blend from Napa grapes. They made the first wine this year, about 5,000 gallons from four Napa vineyards. The deal was not finalized at the time, but the *Los Angeles Times* reported that the negotiations were "in the hands of attorneys for the final dotting of the i's." The cornerstone for the arrangement had been laid in 1978 when Mondavi and daughter Marcia made an August visit to the French aristocrat in Bordeaux. The final details were discussed in the spring of 1979, but as yet they didn't know what to call the wine.[15]

The Valley felt foreign influence in a different way during the 1979 gasoline crunch. Motorists were again lining up at the pumps and staying home instead of hitting the road for the wine country. This became particularly obvious in the spring, when tourists stayed away from Napa in droves. The same thing had happened during the 1973–74 gasoline crisis, but the effect had not been so obvious.

Robert Mondavi and Phillipe de Rothschild combined forces in 1979 to produce Opus One.

VINTAGE 1979

There was some planting this year, particularly of Chardonnay. Growing conditions were good except for a windy May and June that reduced Cabernet berry set. The vintage began September 1 with lots of hot weather that hurt fruit quality and forced in varieties out of order. Some producers crushed Chardonnay and Cabernet on the same day. Then cloudy and drizzly October days caused rot. Much Cabernet went begging after last year's heavy supply, but some elegant and complex Cabs were made from grapes picked before October 18. Some aged well. Chardonnays and Sauvignon blancs were both excellent. The overall vintage quality was mixed, but the best wines were very good. Prices were steady, but national price inflation was on the rise.

New Wineries: Acacia (Carneros), Sky (Mt. Veeder), Shafer (Stag's Leap), S. Anderson (Stag's Leap), Chateau Chevre (Yountville), Evansen (Oakville), Johnson-Turnbull (Oakville), Far Niente (Oakville), Shown & Sons (Rutherford), Silverado Hills (Silverado), Flora Springs (St. Helena), Prager (St. Helena), Whitehall Lane (St. Helena), Calafia (St. Helena), Tudal (Larkmead), Newton (Spring Mountain), Deer Park (Howell Mountain), Storybook (Calistoga).

A NEW BREED

The explosion in the number of new wineries in the Napa Valley between 1977 and 1981, rising from fifty-one to one hundred ten, was the result of numerous long-term decisions made earlier in the seventies by people who had the reserve capital to be relatively unhurt by the current energy crisis, the downturn in the business cycle, and the double-digit price inflation. Old-timers in the Valley were talking about a new breed of moneyed entrepreneurs who seemed to be dipping into large fortunes to buy a mildly bucolic life-style, close to the heart of Northern California society and not much more than an hour's drive from international airports. The character of the development was nothing new in Napa history; the same kind of attractive magnet had produced fairly similar results here between 1883 and 1895.

By the late 1970s the idea of a farm family buying Napa vineyard land was virtually unheard of. There were no Charles Wagners coming onto the scene to create new Caymuses. Andrew Beckstoffer, who first came to Napa for Heublein, had now settled into a very lucrative business of managing vineyard land for people who were not farmers. His Napa Valley Vineyard Company was handling about 2,500 acres for such accounts. In 1982 he remarked on the situation. "Now they don't want to have anything to do with the vineyard. They just want a weekend place." Robert Dwyer, executive director of the Napa Valley Grape Growers Association, was a bit more caustic. "This is no longer just a farming area. It's a label, like Calvin Klein." Rennick Harris of the NVGGA guessed in 1982 that "there are only 100 to 150 real farmers left." But in all the negative comments there was no suggestion that such new arrangements of land ownership and management were hurting the quality of Napa wine.

An economist for the Bank of America put forth a view that was as sound in 1885 as it was in 1980. "The Napa Valley is a unique commodity that demands a premium, like buying a unique painting. It's a unique socioeconomic environment that takes a certain clientele." In truth, what was happening in Napa was also happening in such places as Pauillac, in the heart of Bordeaux's greatest winegrowing district. There vineyard land was climbing to $50,000 per acre, for the same reason that Napa vineyard land had reached the $25,000 level.

An analysis of Napa grape and wine prices and yields per acre in these years shows that the cost of potential vineyard land of more than $13,000 per acre could not be justified on economic grounds. Obviously, the people planting the vineyards, or better, having them planted, had other goals in mind than simply the profit to be made from the final investment. As Beckstoffer put it, "These aren't speculative investments. They are way-of-life investments."

The flood of tourists that was now pouring into the Valley was also giving a new look to the cultural environment. Boutiques in Calistoga and St. Helena replaced hardware and yardage stores. There were few motels being built in the upper Valley. Now there were country inns. Elegant bed and breakfast facilities were beginning to dot the Valley. In 1960 one had to know just where to look to get a really good meal in the Napa Valley. Now visitors had a long list to choose from. They could be found listed in free, fat, weekly periodicals full of maps, winery stories, and loaded with invitations to visit them, to tour, to taste, and to buy at the gift shop that often acted as an adjunct to the tasting room. In Dwyer's words, "We're watching the Carmelization of the Napa Valley. We get cuter and cuter." Louis P. Martini wondered at the "cloud nine" approach to the operation of wineries.

At the end of the eighties the *San Francisco Chronicle* took a special look at what it called "The Napa Valley: Second Home Heaven." The story was that if you wanted to stay in the Valley in the lap of luxury it would probably cost you about $200 to $250 per night. But the really wonderful way to do it was to have a place of your own. Building sites with a vineyard view were going for half a million. To rent a summer place with all the amenities was going to cost $6,000 per month. An end of the decade summer analysis of the real estate section of the *St. Helena Star* reveals seventeen homes for sale in the Napa Valley for a million dollars or more, not counting the vineyard land that might be included.[16]

Far Niente's first wine release was in the new spirit of the times. In September of 1980 their 1979 Chardonnay was introduced to Northern California wine writers aboard the owner's motor yacht *Lycon*, sailing out of Sausalito. The wine had been made from grapes crushed at the Markham Winery in St. Helena. The first crush at Far Niente in the rehabilitated 1885 stone edifice took place in 1981. Meanwhile the new wine was to go for $15, a dollar more than Chalone's 1979, two dollars more than Freemark Abbey's. Years later James Laube would rate Far Niente a first growth for California Chardonnay, calling the 1979 and 1980 the best made by the winery. They had been produced before the operation moved into its permanent home.[17]

Francis Mahoney

of Carneros Creek

Winery welcoming

the late afternoon

fog to the Carneros.

Other 1980 events included the first vintage at Acacia, in the Carneros. Financial problems would bring this winery into the Chalone group in 1986. Work on another Carneros winery, Chateau Bouchaine, began this year. Built around the shell of the old Garetto Winery, Bouchaine acquired winemaker Jerry Luper from Chateau Montelena. Like Acacia its goal was Burgundian, primarily Chardonnay and Pinot noir from the cool Carneros climate and the hospitable loamy soils. Bouchaine Vineyards, as it is now called, improved its cash flow in the early years by doing a large amount of custom crushing for others. In 1981 Saintsbury Winery would go into production and by 1987 its 14,000 cases of Pinot noir would make it the number one Carneros winery for that varietal.

Perhaps more important to the history of Napa wine was what was happening at nearby Carneros Creek Winery. Built in 1973 by Francis V. Mahoney and San Francisco wine importer Balfour Gibson, Carneros Creek made a good name for itself in the seventies for Zinfandel, Cabernet Sauvignon, and Pinot noir, with grapes from vineyards all over Northern California. But Mahoney had settled in the Carneros because he believed that Pinot noir would do well there. In 1977 he served notice that he could make a Pinot noir from Carneros grapes that could satisfy the most demanding California-Burgundian tastes. His Pinot noir won its Vintners Club tasting easily and was named the best of vintage, along with Joseph Swan's, by *Connoisseur's Guide*.

In 1980 Mahoney started bottling wines made from grapes grown on his 1.75-acre experimental vineyard plot, planted in 1975. It was a joint venture supported by Davis Professor C. J. Alley. Its purpose was to test nineteen Pinot noir clones, some from various historic California vineyards, such as Louis Martini, Hanzell, BV #5, and Joseph Swan, and others from Burgundy, Switzerland, and Germany. He and research assistant Melissa Moravec found that there were remarkable and predictable differences between wines made from different clones planted next to one another and whose fruit had been vinted identically. They cut the useful number to five and planted a ten-acre vineyard near the winery. In 1990 Carneros Creek released its 1987 Signature

Reserve Pinot Noir, a wine that finally brought together the results of Mahoney's research. For the good of Napa and California wine, other wineries will be getting the benefit of Carneros Creek's findings. Bouchaine and Beaulieu have been planting and budding over clones Mahoney has found particularly useful. One, the Swiss Wädenswil, may change the taste of Napa Pinot noir.[18]

VINTAGE 1980

The country found itself in a serious recession. Shipments of table wines were still strong, but collapse was imminent. In Napa the national white wine craze was still evident with 1,000 new acres of white varieties planted and 500 of red budded over.

The winter was mild, the spring cool and damp. There was a good berry set. A cool August delayed maturity. There were great variations in maturity from vineyard to vineyard. A winery strike from September 15 to the 21st was actually a boon with such slowly developing sugars. Then a heat wave came in early October. After rain on October 13 and 14, beautiful weather for three weeks brought in many good Cabs. The end result was a very uneven mix of wine quality. Yields were excellent, 3.6 tons per acre overall. The crop size was a record, as was its value, but only if uncorrected for the volatile price inflation sweeping the country. True grower return per acre of Chardonnay was almost double that for Cabernet. Many whites were rich and grapey and very popular.

New Wineries: Monticello (Napa), Lakespring (Yountville), Schug (Yountville, later to Sonoma), Vichon (Oakville), Sequoia Grove (Oakville), St. Andrew's (Silverado), Girard (Silverado), Napa Creek (Silverado), Casa Nuestra (Silverado).

1981 TRANSACTIONS

The first Napa Wine Auction was the big social event here in 1981. At first glance one might think that the auction was the idea of the "new breed" of Valley resident, but actually Robin Daniel Lail and Robert Mondavi were its chief promoters, the NVVA its sponsors. It was meant to add to the public awareness of Napa as a world-class wine region and to raise money for local hospitals. No less than 260 wine enthusiasts paid $100 each for their bidding paddles, and spent $324,142 on some very expensive Napa wine.

The most expensive lot was the first case of the then unnamed Mondavi/Rothschild joint venture Cabernet, named "Napamedoc" at the auction. A businessman from Syracuse paid $24,000 for the case. If he had waited for the second case he might have had it for $2,601.

By 1989 the total take reached $850,000, the top sale being $55,000 for a lot of nine 18-liter bottles of Stag's Leap Wine Cellars Cabernet. In 1990 the total bidding cooled some to $700,000, the top bid this time being $38,000 for ten eighteen-liter bottles of Caymus Cabernet.

After a decade of these events it was clear that there was more to the auction than wine. *Star* editor Marilee Talley thought that winery hospitality and the great food events that accompanied the auction throughout the week had developed into a magnificent experience for visitors. "The real reason many bidders pay good money to visit our fair valley is that while here they are treated like royalty. . . all our visitors leave with smiles."

The day after the 1981 auction the eastern hills were scorched by a terrible arson fire that threatened several wineries in the Stag's Leap area and destroyed fifty-two homes near the Silverado Country Club. The barrel facility at the Napa Cooperage Company was burned out. By the third day flames were threatening the Chappellet and Long Wineries on Pritchard Hill. The inferno charred more than 23,000 acres.

It was a close call for the Shafer Winery. If it had gone up John Shafer might have had little left of his 1978 Cabernet, his first release. It had just won the final tasteoff at the Vintners Club. Second place in this year-long competition went to William Hill's 1978 Cabernet from his Mt. Veeder vineyard. This year Hill sold off 200 acres of Mt. Veeder land to Donald Hess, who would be starting his own wine operation there soon.

In 1981 forty-eight cases of 1978 Caymus Cabernet Sauvignon were released under the Grace Family Vineyard designation. In 1976 Richard and Ann Grace had planted an acre of Cabernet at their home vineyard in St. Helena from cuttings taken from the Bosché Vineyard. They brought out their own label in 1983. With almost three acres now in production, the winery can count on about 400 cases of wine that go to a select mailing list. In 1989 a case of Grace Family wine brought $42,000 at the annual auction.[19]

For all the upscale activity in the Napa Valley wine industry, the state wine industry was having problems that were seriously affecting Napa wine. Growth in table wine shipments dropped off to almost nothing in the coming year. National wine consumption per capita peaked in 1982 and has dropped ever since. Another perceived problem for California producers was the competition from foreign table wines, whose importation had risen from 24,000,000 to 88,000,000 gallons since 1970. But for now Napa acreage was still on the rise and most Napa wine was selling well. Certainly the top line Cabernets seemed totally immune to any kind of red wine oversupply. Merlot was also on the rise here, as a blender with Cabernet, and on its own as a varietal. But there were weaknesses. Pinot noir was becoming a difficult sell. So were premium Zinfandels and the once hot premium Petite Sirahs.

For the California wine industry as a whole there seemed to be a chance for a second Thermidor in the near future. For the top end of the quality market the future appeared far less bleak.[20]

Vintage 1981

Planting was still going strong in Napa, mostly to white varieties, which accounted for more than 80 percent of the nonbearing acreage. Growing conditions this season were without feature until a summer hot streak hit with many days over 100°. Calistoga was 111° on July 27. Ripening was very irregular, with varieties developing out of normal order. The vintage for still wine grapes started about August 15, cutting short many summer vacations. Lots of Cab and Zin were ready to pick at unbelievably early dates. Acids suffered. Lots of must correction occurred in the cellar. Pickers were scarce.

The quality of resulting wines was very mixed, defying generalization. Many were amazed at how delicious some of the wines were, given the difficult growing conditions. But most were not wines for long ageing. Only Caymus and Raymond made 1981 Napa Cabernets that won an initial tasting round at the Vintners Club.

The vintage was over by October 26. Only 55 percent of the harvest was to red varieties. White wine prices went through the roof, with Chardonnay averaging $1364 per ton. Cabernet brought only $799. Yields were very good. The crop's value set another record, but price inflation cut profits.

New Wineries: Bouchaine (Carneros), Saintsbury (Carneros), Silverado Vineyards (Stag's Leap), Sage Canyon, Newlan (Yountville), Robert Pepi (Oakville), Folie à Deux (St. Helena), Frog's Leap (Larkmead).

Appelation Napa Valley

Since the early seventies the Bureau of Alcohol, Tobacco and Firearms (BATF) of the Department of the Treasury had been concerned about the information on wine labels indicating the origin of the grapes going into the wine. In 1977 the Bureau issued guidelines to establish viticultural areas, or "appellations of origin," that would appear on wine labels. The objectives of the proposal were to improve consumer information and to obtain better credibility for American export wines.

Unlike similar regulations in European countries, the Bureau did not mean that such terms would imply any level of quality, nor which grape varieties had been used. There were to be two types of appellations. One was established by the political boundaries of the state or county, and implied nothing more or less. But for an area to acquire the designation of a viticultural district, the applicants had to show that there was geographical evidence, such as climate and soil, that set it off from surrounding areas. Thus, any wine produced from grapes grown in Napa County could be labeled "Napa County" without the growers or producers going through an application process. But after January 1, 1983 no wine could be labeled "Napa Valley" unless a petition for that term had been submitted to the Bureau and accepted by it.[21]

Napa winegrowers had been aware of this impending process for some time. In fact, a committee of vintners and growers had been at work on the idea since 1972. For Napa the matter was complicated. Would "Napa Valley" simply refer to grapes from the valley floor? Historically the surrounding hillsides had been considered part of the Valley's wine production since the 1860s when Jacob Schram cleared his land on Mt. Diamond. And what about Carneros? By no stretch of the imagination could the rolling lands southwest of the town of Napa be considered a geographical part of the valley proper. But Carneros wine had always been called Napa wine. And what of the eastern valleys, Pope, Chiles, Wooden, Foss, and Capell? Historically their grapes had been intermingled with those of the valley floor as Napa grapes for Napa wine.

After the BATF laid down the time frame for application, the Napa committee was ready to go. But they had to delineate the area for the district as something other than the county itself. Finally the idea was put forth to define Napa Valley as the area that was part of the direct watershed for the valley. The problem with that idea was that 2,000 acres of traditionally Napa grapes would be excluded, since some of the eastern valleys' streams didn't drain to Napa.

In the summer of 1978 the question was put to a vote of the membership of

The champagnerie of

Domaine Carneros.

the Vintners and Growers Associations. The result called for the exclusion of such as Pope and Capell Valleys from the Napa Valley Appellation. Before the vote there had been many who opposed this idea, among them Robert Mondavi, Louis P. Martini, Roy Raymond, and Brother Timothy. Others such as Joseph Heitz indicated they didn't care.

In April 1980 a hearing was held on the application that would exclude these eastern valleys. Next February the bureau handed down its decision. The eastern valleys were to be included in the Napa Valley appellation. The decision was accepted without rancor. It was clear that the bureau was not going to exclude areas from an appellation that had a sound historical basis for inclusion, whatever direction the streams happened to run.[22]

Another battle was fought over the North Coast appellation. This term had been applied historically to all winegrowing portions of the San Francisco Bay Area, including the Santa Clara and Livermore Valleys. Winegrowers from Sonoma and Mendocino Counties led the drive for a petition that excluded all winegrowing areas outside these counties and Napa, even those of Lake and Solano Counties. *Wines & Vines* had earlier editorialized against a limited district that would exclude "many historic producers in the necklace of counties around San Francisco Bay. . . ." Napa winegrowers had no real interest in the matter. Napa grapes would go into bottles labeled "Napa Valley," not "North Coast." But for Sonoma and Mendocino growers, a narrow limitation on the size of the North Coast region would be to their economic advantage. Again, the BATF rejected such an exclusive proposition. After a heated 1981 hearing on the matter a new application was submitted that included parts of Lake and Solano Counties.[23]

The question of Carneros was more complicated, if less controversial. While the crest of the Mayacamus Range separates Napa from Sonoma County as an obvious geographic limit, no such height of land exists between the two counties in the rolling hills of the Carneros. ZD Winery had first used the Carneros appellation informally in 1970 when it was still located in Sonoma. Then in 1972 Napa's Veedercrest used it. But long before that the area had begun acquiring a distinct reputation. Its shallow, loamy soils did not give high yields, rarely over three tons per acre. But the cooler temperatures regularly resulted in Chardonnay and Pinot noir fruit of superior and distinctive character.

The Carneros appellation accepted by BATF in 1983 was unique, cutting across two counties and taking in parts of the Napa Valley and Sonoma Valley appellations. The Napa side had about twice as many plantable acres. By 1987 about half the district's plantable land (ca. 15,000 acres) was in vines, about 90 percent to Chardonnay and Pinot noir.[24]

The national recession became a depression by 1982 as unemployment rates surged above the 10 percent level. History has shown, however, that sales of high-quality Champagne can ride out such downturns. And certainly producers of California sparkling wine who used the traditional Champagne method were not feeling much of the economic pinch. Between 1975 and 1983 such California production rose from about 240,000 to 1,100,000 cases, about a quarter of the latter figure from Napa producers. Well over half of that came from Domaine Chandon. Between 1977 and 1981 Hanns Kornell's sales had increased by 40 percent. Schramsberg had doubled its case count in the same period.

In 1982 Jack Davies struck out in another direction by concluding a deal with France's Remy-Martin, the Cognac producers. It would put Schramsberg into the brandy production business. The product was to carry the RMS label. Production of this California alambic brandy would take place on a thirty-acre site in the Carneros. The brandy would be a pot-still product in the Cognac tradition. Jack and Jamie Davies had been interested in such a project for many years and had actually imported Cognac under the "Eclipse" label, named for the historic nineteenth-century California Champagne of Arpad Haraszthy.[25]

But the rest of the wine industry was feeling the depression. Between 1982 and 1983 many producers, including Napa wineries, lowered the prices on some wines. Robert Mondavi cut the price of his 1981 Fumé Blanc by $3.00 per bottle.

For some enterprising wine people high winery inventories were a boon. Ernest Van Asperen had taken advantage of the oversupply of some quality wines in the North Coast during the first Thermidor of 1973–74, bottling them under his own "Ernie's" label. They were sold in the string of liquor stores that bore his first name. Some also were bottled under the Round Hill label. In 1977 he sold this label to his engineer friend, Charles A. Abela and several of his partners. Soon Round Hill was actually a little winery on Lodi Lane above St. Helena.

For a while Van Asperen could not take a direct hand in the wine production because of his position in the retail side of the industry, but Virginia Van Asperen, his wife, was a Round Hill partner. As the years passed, more and more of the wine Abela sold was actually made in-house, for a while under the eye of Charles Ortman. Part of this production began appearing under the Rutherford Ranch Brand label, mostly powerfully flavored reds, such as the 1976 Zinfandel that won the Vintners Club tasteoff in 1978. By 1982 the little winery was producing 65,000 cases, but the *negociant* aspect of the business was still important. In 1987–88 the partners built a 600,000-gallon winery on Silverado Trail.[26]

For all the problems in the industry in 1982 there was still lots of entrepreneurial activity in Napa. Silver Oak was building its new winery. So was Louis "Bill" Honig, California's soon to be elected Superintendent of Public Instruction.[27] Monticello Cellars (1980) and S. Anderson Vineyard (1979) both released their first wines. Far Niente was now fully restored. Up in Pope Valley French businessman Robert Skalli was purchasing the 1,500-acre Dollarhide Ranch and was soon planting vines that would eventually total 425 acres. In 1986 he acquired the old home of Joseph Atkinson (Ewer & Atkinson–1885) and built a winery behind it which he called St. Supéry, after the Frenchman who owned the home after 1899.

Probably the most historic enterprise of 1982 brought together two traditions in wine production and eventually produced wines that would add to Napa's stature for world-class red wine. When John Daniel sold Inglenook in 1964, he did not include in the sale his 120-acre property just north of what is today Domaine Chandon. He had acquired it from Louis Stralla in 1946 and called it Napanook. For many years it was the source for some of the grapes that had gone into the great Inglenook Cask Cabernets. Before he died in 1970 Daniel told daughter Robin that she and her sister Marcia should not sell the land, "no matter what happens to me," and they didn't.

Over the years the grapes went to various Napa wineries, particularly Robert Mondavi's. He had long nursed the notion that Napanook's production should have a special identity. In 1981 he introduced the sisters to Christian Moueix, the general manager of Château Pétrus, the first-growth estate of Pomerol (Bordeaux). Next year Robin Lail and Marcia Smith formed a partnership with Moueix, establishing the John Daniel Society, aimed at producing a Napa Valley wine from the classic red varieties of Bordeaux. In 1983 the first grapes were crushed for the new Dominus brand, under the care of Moueix and his enologist, Jean-Claude Berrouet. The wine was not intended to be a California Pomerol. The gravelly clay loam of Napanook was nothing like the heavy clay and gravel atop an impenetrable subsoil of iron oxide at Pétrus. And the French vineyard was planted almost entirely to Merlot, while Napanook had about 75 percent Cabernet Sauvignon, with some Merlot and Cabernet franc, and just a touch of Petite Verdot.

The wine was made at the Rombauer Winery and not released until 1988. Then the 1984 was released before the harder 1983, but only by a few months. The reaction of wine critics to these wines was as positive as if they had been drinking the great first growth itself. The $40 price tag on the 1983 would have bought about eight ounces of the 1983 Pétrus.[28]

Vintage 1982

There was heavy planting in the dormant season, mostly Cabernet Sauvignon and Chardonnay. A good spring ended in excellent berry set. It was clear very early that a huge crop was coming. Many thinned their crops and those who didn't paid dearly in the fall. The vintage began September 1, but storms hit on the fifteenth, followed by the northern portion of Hurricane Olivia. October saw better weather but the vintage was frantic, particularly from October 7 through 13. The harvesting was quite selective with vast quantities of grapes never harvested. A hard rain hit again on October 22 and it was all over.

Zinfandel and White Riesling suffered huge losses, but the overall yield per acre was high, over four tons. The crush was only 53 percent red. Prices were very strong. The overall income per bearing acre was not topped until 1989. The overall quality was well below average, but a few very good Cabernets were produced. Given the growing conditions, some wines were a pleasant surprise. Quality ultimately depended on the growers' care and foresight.

New Wineries: Marston (Spring Mountain), Cain (Spring Mountain), Cosentino (Yountville), Groth (Oakville), Honig (Rutherford), Chateau Boswell (Silverado), Rombauer (Silverado), Spottswoode (St. Helena), Dunn (Howell Mountain).

1983 Transactions

The national economic climate in 1983 was a salutary turnaround from the three previous years. But an examination of the California wine industry does not project a very healthy picture. Few realized that 1982 would be the high point for national per capita table wine consumption, nor that figures would decline every year thereafter into the nineties. The white wine boom also peaked in 1983. But again, Napa did not feel the general hurt that the industry was to suffer.

Close analysis of industry figures was soon bringing forth a special inference which favored Napa wine. The wine drinking public continued to be eager consumers of higher-priced table wine; Napa's best wines were still selling very well. But their producers would have to compete for shelf space and consumer attention. Some didn't come through. Pope Valley, Pannonia,

A gondola of grapes passes through St. Helena during one of the downpours of the 1982 vintage.

NAPA WINE

and Veedercrest went under during these months. But ten new wineries got their bonds in 1983, bringing the Napa total to 118.

The most important transaction of the year was Coca-Cola's sale of Sterling Vineyards to Seagram in October. The Mondavi/Rothschild wine also received a name—Opus One. The wine would debut next year. Whitehall Lane, Cain Cellars, and Vichon released their first wines. Stanley Anderson brought out his first champagne.

Napa had weathered its second Thermidor in ten years. The number of Napa wineries would continue to grow, the tourist figures would continue to rise, and the flow of Napa wine would continue to increase. But this growth would soon force the people of the Napa Valley and their elected officials to face up to the outcomes of seemingly never-ending expansion.

VINTAGE 1983

The Napa vineyard approached the 30,000-acre level. There was lots of budding over of red varieties to Chardonnay and Sauvignon blanc. Spring was mild, but the summer heat hurt overall quality. The still wine vintage began about September 5. Cool, damp weather slowed the harvest between September 22 and October 2. Then came warm weather, but sugars were slow to rise. Grapes had a below-average juice content. Bunch rot forced selective harvesting. Growers sat and watched Cabs into late October, waiting for sugars to rise. Then heavy rains accelerated the harvest. Much Zinfandel and Chenin blanc went unplaced. The overall quality was uneven. Cabernet quality was very spotty, but some producers made excellent wine with grapes from patient or lucky growers. The crush was just 50.1 percent red; the corner on white wine production was almost turned. The yield was satisfactory. Prices came down some, as did the total value of the crop. Napans were generally content with the outcome. Such unsettled conditions in former years could have brought economic havoc.

NOTES FOR CHAPTER THIRTEEN

1. Wine Spectator, 10/16/1981, 12/1/1985; Wines & Vines (June 1974): 49; Wine World (May 1981): 17.
2. Practical Winery, (September 1984): 33; Chronicle, 3/14/1984.
3. New York Times, 5/15/1975; Vintage (July 1976); 47; (August 1976): 25; Wines & Vines (July 1979): 47; Wine Spectator, 5/15/1988; Conaway, 182-183.
4. Stuller and Martin, 185, 188-191; Chronicle, 8/12/1983, 9/10/1990; Wine Spectator, 7/31/1990.
5. Wines & Vines (August 1970): 23; (May 1983): 68; Wine Spectator, 12/16/1985; Star, 11/30/1989.
6. San Jose Mercury, 7/10/1985, 2/26/1986; Wine Spectator, 2/16/1985, 2/28/1987; Star, 8/17/1989.
7. Redwood Rancher (July 1975): 15; Wines & Vines (June 1976): 54;Wine World (September 1979): 10; Wine Spectator, 2/15/1987.

8. Redwood Rancher (1976 Vintage Issue): 14; Wine Spectator, 11/15/1987.

9. James Laube. California's Great Chardonnays (San Francisco 1990): 181-183.

10. Haynes, 56-57.

11. Wine World (May 1982): 14; Los Angeles Times, 10/17/1985.

12. Practical Winery (November 1985): 28; Conaway, 212-217; San Jose News, 8/26/1981; Laube. Cabernets, 169-170, 252-276, 358-361; Wine Spectator, 6/15/1988.

13. Star, 10/7/1982; California Grape Grower (December 1979): 26; Stuller and Martin, 103-107; Conaway, 266-270; Wine Spectator, 5/16/1984, 2/16/1986; Wines & Vines (November 1987): 13.

14. Wine Country (June 1984): 44; Wine Spectator, 9/16/1982; Adams (3rd Edition), 334.

15. Cyril Ray, 114-117; Conaway, 231; San Jose News, 9/27/1979; Los Angeles Times and Chronicle, 4/17/1980.

16. Jane Carroll. "Valley of the Dollars." San Francisco Examiner & Chronicle, 3/14/1982; Chronicle, 7/12/1990; Star, 6/7/1990.

17. Wines & Vines (November 1980): 92; Laube. Chardonnays, 153-155.

18. Star, 10/8/1987, 2/15/1990; Wines & Vines (April 1977):31; Wine Spectator, 5/16/1984, 6/15/1990; Practical Winery (January 1988): 17; Connoisseur's Guide to California Wine (5:3): 49.

19. San Jose Mercury, 7/20/1988; Wine Spectator, 7/31/1989.

20. Wines & Vines (January 1981): 42; (July 1990): 21.

21. Treasury Decision (ATF) #53 on Notice #304, amended 6/9/1977.

22. Star, 11/30/1978; Wines & Vines (February 1980): 43; (June 1980): 28; BATF. Viticultural Areas. October 1983. There are two boxes of manuscript material in NVWL that deal with both sides of this appellation controversy.

23. Wines & Vines (April 1974): 14; (June 1974): 74; (May 1976): 22; (February 1980): 20; Wine Spectator, 2/16/1981, 12/16/1981; San Jose News, 8/30/1976; American Bar Association Journal (June 1976): 791; (October 1978): 1595. I prepared the historical research supporting the Lake County grape growers' attack on the exclusive petition and testified at the BATF hearing on their behalf.

24. Treasury Decision (ATF) #142, 9/9/1983.

25. NVWLA IV: 316; Wines & Vines (November 1982): 102; (January 1983): 36.

26. Wines & Vines (May 1976): 23; (December 1977): 14; (September 1978): 24; Wine Spectator, 5/1/1983; California Visitors' Review, 9/11/1987, 2/24/1989.

27. Jim Gordon. "Readin', Writin', and Viticulture." Wine Spectator, 10/16/1985.

28. NVWLA IV: 441; Fine Wine Review (July 1987): 6; Laube. Cabernets, 154.

WHAT IS THIS VALLEY?

*Foreign investors understand and appreciate the dramatic
edge the Napa Valley name and image give their wine.
The Valley is a national treasure that deserves
to be protected—at any cost.*

—JAMES LAUBE
1990

THE MOST WONDERFUL THING THAT HAPPENED TO NAPA WINE FROM 1984 TO THE end of the decade was a series of excellent vintages. There had never been anything like it before in the Valley's vinous history. The same thing was happening in Bordeaux. It seemed that Bacchus, and whichever subdeity was in charge of claret vintages, was casting a special smile on the Médoc and the Napa Valley. But whichever gods were in charge of delivering the Valley its share of rain after the spring of 1986 were obviously involved elsewhere. By the spring of 1991 a water shortage had developed into a parching drought, which was threatening the life of California agriculture.

More important for the long-term future of Napa wine was the growing concern in these years for the environment. There was a new, broader, almost holistic focus that transcended the simple concern for keeping the developers out of the vineyards. It became clear that the great success of the Napa wine industry during the boom years of the wine revolution was threatening paradise as much as the bulldozer.

We have already seen the decline in national wine consumption in the early eighties. To a great extent this decline was the result of a growing national concern about alcohol in American life. Fine Cabernet and Chardonnay were not really seen as part of that problem, but some within the new temperance movement were unwilling to recognize the difference between a glass of table wine with dinner and a swig from a fortified wine concoction on skid row. In the late eighties Napa wine leaders, particularly Robert Mondavi, would mount a campaign to make the difference manifestly clear.

The late eighties also saw a continued flurry of land and winery transactions that placed ownership of the Napa Valley in a constant state of flux. It was an interesting story but the changes did not place the image of Napa wine quality in jeopardy. Another set of transactions involved the continuing interest in establishing appellations of origin. The process continued unabated and produced one of the liveliest controversies in recent Valley history.

HOWELL MOUNTAIN, 1984

We have already seen the rise of Howell Mountain as one of Napa's great viticultural regions in the 1880s. The decline after the turn of the century was a reflection of the difficulties of transport and the economic realities of winegrowing. The coming of the Seventh Day Adventist community to Angwin compounded the tendency against winegrowing here well through World War II. Some vines survived and a few were planted in the fifties and sixties.

In 1983 Howell Mountain winegrowers applied for an appellation and received it the next year without contest. From this we can see that wine from the mountain had started making the same kind of impression it had made eighty years earlier. We have already seen the work of Lee Stewart at Souverain, today Burgess Cellars. Technically this winery is not within the appellation, because it lies below the 1,400-foot contour line delineating the district, as does nearby Deer Park Winery, revived by David and Kinta Clark in 1979. But both are certainly on Howell Mountain.

In the seventies Ridge Vineyards in the Santa Cruz Mountains bought Howell Mountain Zinfandel and bottled the wine under that appellation. Randall Dunn, formerly the Caymus winemaker, produced his first Howell Mountain Cabernet in 1979. Since then Dunn's Cabernets from the mountain and from other Napa vineyards have attained an almost unbelievable success. In 1990 a Southern California wine dealer had the 1979 for sale at $3240 per case. The 1982 could be had for $2400. In 1990 *Wine Spectator* named two Howell Mountain Cabernets among the top twenty wines in the world for that year. One was from Dunn (1986), the other from La Jota (1987), the old Hess Winery that William Smith had revived in the seventies.

In 1981 the historic Brun & Chaix Winery came back to life on the mountain, when former owners of Château La Mission Haut-Brion purchased the property and began planting Chardonnay. These new owners, Francis and Francoise Dewavrin-Woltner, invested more than $6,000,000 in the project, planting fifty-five acres that produced about 2,000 cases in 1985, sold under the Chateau Woltner label. The property is divided into four separate vineyards, the four-acre Titus Vineyard, named for the family dog, being the source of grapes that went into a 1986 Chardonnay marketed for $54. The Woltner operation illustrates an important part of the transition being made on the mountain. Their neighbors at the nearby religious community made strong objections to the expansion, complaining of the possibility that this very dry group might be subjected to convivial tourists seeking out the winery's tasting room. But the expansion was allowed. This transition, of course, was along parallel lines to the area's historical development eighty years earlier.

The mountain has two main areas of viticulture, both with shallow, low-yielding volcanic soils that stress their vines and give crops about half as large as those from vineyards on the valley floor. Most of the older vines are in the northwestern area, above and below Angwin. Here on ruddy, rock-strewn soil are the old vines on Michael Beatty's ranch and in the Park-Muscatine Vineyard, both of which have supplied Ridge Vineyards with powerful Zinfandel grapes. Nearby Robert and Susan Brakeman produce mostly

Zinfandel for their Summit Lake label. Robert Lamborn and his family also concentrate on Zinfandel, which they bottle under the Family label. Also near at hand are Randall Dunn's six Cabernet acres, planted in 1973.

La Jota and other vineyards stand to the south and east on soil loaded with gray volcanic ash. Just up the road are the remains of W. S. Keyes' Liparita Winery with new vineyards planted in the eighties. These and the nearby Bancroft Vineyard supply grapes to some of the Valley's most famous wineries. But in all, there are barely 400 acres of vines on the mountain, less than half the number growing here in 1900 when Keyes won the gold at the Paris Exposition for his Cabernet.[1]

1984 TRANSACTIONS

At the same time that Howell Mountain was receiving its appellation, William Hill was planting vineyards in the Foss Valley, twelve miles to the southeast, underneath 2,660-foot Atlas Peak. He had bought the land after he sold his Diamond Mountain vineyards to Sterling. The first vines went in here in 1981, mostly red Bordeaux varieties. Five years later he sold the partially developed (170 acres) 1,100-acre tract to a foreign combination from Britain/France/Italy with corporate names Whitbread/Bollinger/Antinori. They intended to expand Hill's vineyards, dig massive caves, and eventually build a winery. They were able to get Richard Peterson, formerly of Beaulieu, to come back from Monterey Vineyard. By 1990 there were about 450 acres of vines, even

Wine lovers line up at the Heitz Cellar tasting room to buy their allotment of the 1985 Martha's Vineyard Cabernet Sauvignon.

some Tuscan Sangiovese. In February of that year Whitbread sold its 85 percent interest in the enterprise to another British conglomerate, Allied-Lyons, which had already acquired Hiram Walker in this country. Then in July the plans for the winery were shelved and Peterson resigned his presidency. Nevertheless, the next year Atlas Peak Vineyards released its first bottle of Sangiovese and announced that the area would soon be receiving its appellation. In 1992 Allied-Lyons, now owner of Sonoma's Clos du Bois, Callaway Vineyard in Southern California, and Atlas Peak, bought out William Hill and acquired his new Napa winery. Allied was now operating as The Wine Alliance.[2]

In 1984 there was building activity on the grounds of Sterling as the new owners joined France's G. H. Mumm to build a temporary sparkling wine facility at the bottom of the hill. The Chandon success was now perfectly clear to other French Champagne producers. The formation of this combination was facilitated by the fact that Seagram owned a large piece of Mumm. Eventually Domaine Mumm was integrated into the Seagram Classic Wine Company under Samuel Bronfman II. For the first years their big task was to search out good vineyards. Eventually the raw material for the Cuvée Napa would come from about thirty different growers. In 1987 a high-tech winery was built next to the Silverado Trail with an eventual capacity of 125,000 cases. In 1988 Domaine Mumm produced a vineyard-designated sparkling wine from Winery Lake grapes; Seagram had bought that famed Carneros property in 1986.

The local chronicles of the Napa Valley wine industry were loaded with history in 1984. Greystone had to close down for structural repairs; for more than two years visitors to the Christian Brothers tasting room had to do their tasting in a great tent. The Mondavi/Rothschild Cabernet, Opus One, was released, the 1979 and 1980 both in the same six-bottle wooden box. Remy-Martin and Jack Davies showed off their remarkable brandy facility in the Carneros (RMS). (Three years later these two would dissolve this relationship, Remy-Martin continuing the operation as Carneros Alambic.) The Nickel family (Far Niente) bought Chateau Chevalier. A Belgian family (Deschepper) bought Napa Cellars, renaming the Oakville operation De Moor Winery. And Myron Nightingale stepped down as winemaster at Beringer after helping to revive the quality of Beringer wine. But perhaps the best thing about 1984 was the vintage.

Vintage 1984

A very wet winter was followed by a dry spring and early leafing. The good crop moved along briskly through the warm summer. The growing season was actually of normal length but it started so early that the still wine grapes were pouring into wineries in mid-August. A very hot September made the vintage somewhat disorderly, causing overloaded fermenters and more than the usual panic in the wineries. It was over before the end of October. The image of an early start and a hectic harvest did not fit the excellent overall wine quality. Next spring the NVVA actually held a special luncheon for Bay Area wine writers to show off the excellence of the final products. This was to override the bothersome anecdotal vintage snips in the press that gave an impression of a problem vintage.

The yield was excellent, over four tons per acre. The crush was only 44.4 percent red; Chardonnay exceeded Cabernet Sauvignon for the first time. Prices were solid. The vintage set a record for tons and total value. The Cabernets were rich and supple, seductive even when young. The Chardonnays were rich and extremely fruity.

1985

By the end of 1985 there were more than 150 wineries in the Napa Valley. The the size of the crop was a record and the quality perhaps better than 1984. For the industry as a whole it was a time for White Zinfandel and wine coolers, a time when a powerful dollar made it possible to buy great red Bordeaux cheaply. For Napa it was a time to concentrate on high quality. The Valley vineyard didn't grow, but the percentage of top varieties did. There was lots of planting, but mostly on land where older, less profitable varieties had been rooted out, replaced by Cabernet, Merlot, Chardonnay, and Sauvignon blanc. In the Carneros, growers and producers organized the Carneros Quality Alliance, better to advertise the new appellation and its Pinot noirs and Chardonnays. Next year, appropriately, Francis Mahoney was elected president.

The Mondavi family made history this year, not so much for Robert Mondavi's purchase of the troubled Vichon Winery, as for the event that brought the two branches of the family together, twenty years after their dramatic split. It was an event that emphasized Napa wine as much as the family itself. The reunion was part of a retrospective tasting of Charles Krug and Mondavi Cabernets, organized by Napa's Bernard Rhodes and wine collector Tawfiq Khoury. On June 13, in the Vintage Room at Robert's winery, wine collectors, industry leaders, retailers, and restaurateurs met, having paid $1,000 per seat to benefit the enology scholarship program at Davis. Rhodes and Khoury had assembled Charles Krug Cabernets from 1944 to 1965 and Robert Mondavi vintages from 1966 to the 1984 barrel sample. Michael Broadbent of Christie's Auction House in London led the tasters through the wines. They also tasted Opus One vintages 1979–1984. As they sampled the wines Robert and Peter Mondavi became more and more animated in their exchanges of vintage memories. When it was over they stood up, shook hands, and then embraced. Cheers and applause filled the room.[3]

VINTAGE 1985

Spring weather was mild and fairly dry. Growing conditions were excellent through the warm summer. The still wine vintage was early again, starting August 20. But it was far less hectic than in 1984. Early fruit arrived in excellent condition. Then a rainstorm from September 6 through the 9th hurt the Zinfandel, Sauvignon blanc, and White Riesling. Warm days and cool nights drew on into October for an ideal Indian summer. Prices fell some, but tonnage surpassed 100,000, first time ever. Chardonnay was too plentiful, as over 1,300 tons were crushed to growers' accounts. The crop was 53 percent white. Chardonnays were rich and well-structured, Cabernets elegant and concentrated. Both have aged well.

The architectural style of Clos Pegase caused extended controversy when the plans were first released.

1986

The first crush at Clos Pegase took place in 1986, but not until a symbolic controversy had been fought in the Bay Area press and before the Napa County Planning Commission. Today the winery stands across the way from the entrance to Sterling on Dunaweal Lane. No visitor needs to examine the address to see if he has found his way to this winery. The edifice sends the clear message.

This winery sprang from the mind of art book publisher Jan Shrem, whose cosmopolitan background stretches from Columbia to Israel to Japan and to Paris. His original concept in 1984 was a marriage of art and wine in an appropriate structure of classic proportions. The plans derive from the winning submission in an international competition.

When details of the original design hit the Valley, a storm of opposition voiced concern for what many thought was a Disneyland approach to wine production. Construction work employing a toned-down set of plans was held up almost a year in the ensuing squabble. The first crush actually took place at the nearby Rombauer Winery in 1984. The new winery was opened to the public in 1987.

Clos Pegase is named for the winged horse of Greek legend that broke the ground with its hooves to release the spring that watered the vineyard of Bacchus. The painting of the steed, by French symbolist Odilon Redon, dominates Shrem's label. Some have said that the winery's structure evokes the architectural spirit of Tuscany. I think that the form and spirit have a more obvious relationship to the early Aegean style of Middle Minoan III. Whatever the style, all seem to agree that placing such a structure in the agricultural environment of the Napa Valley is startling. It remains to be seen, when a mature landscape has grown up, whether such a building is appropriate here.

The Shrems have made the place into something of a museum for their large art collection. Jan Shrem's wife, Mitsuko, is a talented ceramist. By 1989 the winery's 20,000 square feet of caves had been finished, with carved niches throughout, filled with objects of art related to wine and viticulture. Shrem has commissioned bronze copies of Renaissance Bacchuses by Michelangelo, Donatello, and Sansovino from an Italian foundry.[4]

The construction of Clos Pegase, the controversy surrounding it, and the economic and psychological stimulus behind such a scheme mark a development in Napa Valley winemaking in the eighties that is as artistic as it is vinous. Jan Shrem's winery was the center of an imbroglio because of its stark central situation on the Valley floor. But such statements have become an established part of the winery scene.

Donald Hess started out simply to make good wine when he bought his first block of Mt. Veeder land from William Hill in 1978. He ended up creating a winery and a 13,000-square-foot art museum. Called The Hess Collection, the operation is housed in the old Theodore Gier Winery, long a part of the Christian Brothers' holdings. From the outside, the museum is rather ordinary, but inside the visitor finds himself in an impressive combination of rooms full of paintings and sculpture, much of it truly avant-garde. The wine side of the business has been successful to date. The Hess Collection and Hess Select bottles have won much praise. The Swiss businessman now controls about 900 acres on Mt. Veeder, about half of it in vines. Production stresses Cabernet and Chardonnay.

Up the road from Hess's winery is Villa Zapu, built in 1984 by Swedish millionaire Thomas Lindström. *Wine Spectator* called the home a "zany Shangri-La," built on a 130-acre plot in the English Palladian style of the 1930s, designed by a "British architect with his roots in the punk movement." Vineyards have been planted but a winery has yet to come, even though a 1986 Chardonnay was the first wine released under the Zapu label. That label is as zany as the Villa. From a painting by a protegé of Andy Warhol, it depicts the estate's stark white tower, actually the guest house, festooned with huge banners. Whirling around it in the black sky Kandinskiesque objects seemingly come to life. The first wines were made at the Monticello Winery.[5]

Monticello Cellars also deserves some mention in the Valley's recent architectural evolution. Owner Jay Corley from Virginia wanted to make his estate "a living monument to Thomas Jefferson," whom he considers the father of American wine. Corley has built a small replica of Jefferson's Virginia mansion, housing offices, a hospitality center, and a modern kitchen.

Corley's heart is in Burgundy and he concentrates on Chardonnay and Pinot noir from the cooler, southern end of the Valley. He has also acquired land in the Carneros. But Monticello's Cabernets have a good reputation, as well. Alan Philips, the winemaker, has also produced a Napa Valley Marilyn Merlot, which has sold well in Japan and in this country. Philips insists the wine "is no gimmick." Another Monticello operation is Domaine Montreaux, a separate facility down the road that began producing Napa sparkling wine in 1987. Actually, production dates from 1983, when it was made at Monticello itself. Philips produces about 3,500 cases a year.

Monticello Winery offers a miniature rendition of Thomas Jefferson's Virginia estate.

The most extraordinary piece of new architecture in the Stag's Leap district, except for Robert Mondavi's 14,000-square-foot, one bedroom mansion,[6] is Chimney Rock Winery. In 1980 Sheldon S. Wilson bought the eighteen-hole Chimney Rock Golf Course just above Clos du Val and promptly reduced it to nine holes plus vineyards. These eventually amounted to seventy-five acres of mostly Cabernet Sauvignon, Chardonnay, and Sauvignon blanc. The buildings at Chimney Rock, and the Wilsons' home in the hills above, are in the design of Cape-Dutch architecture, the style of the historic winery buildings in the old Cape Colony of South Africa. They were the hallmark of the old Union's viticultural landscape.[7]

Not all the start-up activity in 1986 was at new

operations. Two resuscitated wineries in St. Helena reflect the recurring tension between many of the old town's residents and those wanting winery growth. The Sunny St. Helena Winery had gone through many ownerships after its birth at the dawn of Repeal. Since 1971 the Christian Brothers had owned it and used it for storage. Now a group of investors, including Robin Daniel Lail, decided to buy the old plant. In the next years the winery was refurbished and made particularly attractive to the tourist trade, which had to pass its door to get into town from the south. The owners brought out wines under two labels, Sunny St. Helena and the higher-priced Merryvale. In St. Helena most of the interest regarding this revival centered on a continuous fight between the owners and the City Council and Planning Commission. The battle raged over matters such as a gravel driveway and a pedestrian walkway across Sulphur Creek.[8]

On the west side of town, the Spottswoode Winery also needed to go through an obstacle course of restrictions and limitations before it was finally in operation. This was George Schoenewald's estate, which he called Lyndenhurst. Nearby were the remains of his Esmeralda Winery. Jack and Mary Novak bought the place in 1970 and began replanting the old forty-acre vineyard. But they were unable to get a permit to use the Esmeralda as a winery. It was finally bulldozed in 1977. When wine was first produced here in the eighties, the grapes had to be crushed elsewhere, but the wine was aged in the great home's cellar. The Spottswoode Cabernet Sauvignons of 1983 and after have been of such high quality that the zoning battles might have been worth the trouble. In 1990, Mary Novak, widowed since 1977, acquired the 1884 Frank Kraft Winery across the road from her vineyard to serve as a real production facility for Spottswoode wines.[9]

The big story of 1986 was the flood, one of the worst in Napa history. The downpour in February was greater than the total average annual rainfall here for the next five years. It

Flooding along the

Yountville Crossroad

during the 1986 flood.

SOURCE: STEVE GIRARD.

NAPA WINE

started violently on the 14th and kept up incessantly for the next five days. On the 17th the levies on parts of the Napa River disappeared; by the 19th 13,000 acres of Valley land were under water. Some wineries stood like half-exposed islands in the flood. Duckhorn, Monticello, Silver Oak, Steltzner, and others on the east side

went under. February 1986 was the wettest Napa month since January 1909. The final cleanup and reconstruction bill came to about $15,000,000.

Winery transactions in the Valley came fast and furious in 1986. U.S. Tobacco Company bought the Villa Mount Eden and Conn Creek operations. The old Villa Mount Eden Winery (1881) had been brought back to life in 1974 by the J. J. McWilliams family. Winemaker Nils Venge made the winery name synonymous with fine Cabernet Sauvignon. After the sale he went to Groth Vineyards (1982) in Oakville, where he continued to work a kind of magic with Cabernet grapes.

A Carneros transaction that turned heads was the Seagram purchase of René di Rosa's Winery Lake Vineyard as an additional grape supply for Sterling. The concern expressed at the sale was twofold. Winery Lake's grapes had previously gone to many producers who were usually happy to pay a premium to get them. Now they were in the hands of one producer. And that producer was controlled by the company that had launched its so-called "equivalency" campaign in 1985 to convince the public that the effects of a shot of whisky were no different from those of a glass of table wine. The purpose had been to promote a federal alcohol tariff that taxed a bottle of table wine for its alcohol content, or to bring the tax on whisky and vodka down to the level of the wine tax. The campaign failed in its purpose.

Samuel Bronfman II now headed the Seagram Classics Wine Company's western division, which controlled Sterling, Domaine Mumm, and other West Coast operations. In 1990 he moved the Classics headquarters from the San Francisco Peninsula to Sterling. People who know Bronfman consider him firmly committed to Napa wine. But it was the profits from whisky and vodka that paid for Winery Lake.[10]

Groth Winery combines the styles of the California Mission and the Dutch Cape Colony.

Right across the highway from Winery Lake was a ninety-three-acre vineyard planted in 1982–83. In 1986 the owners made an arrangement to unite with the Taittinger Champagne firm in France to build a great champagnery there, to be called Domaine Carneros. The huge four-story structure was finished in 1989, modeled after the Château de Marquetterie in Champagne. Again some Napans reacted quite negatively to so grand a structure in the wine country.[11]

Another important transaction was the Beringer-Nestlé purchase of the 3,000,000-gallon Chateau Souverain in Sonoma County. In a manner of speaking Lee Stewart's old Souverain name had come home to Napa, since Nestlé's Wine World subsidiary was centered in the Valley. Beringer's revival was complete, verified by the Cabernet Sauvignon winemaster Ed Sbragia made in 1986. In 1990 *Wine Spectator* proclaimed it the best wine on the retail market, partly for its price of $30, which was modest compared to many other extravagantly priced super-premium Napa Cabernets.[12]

For all the satisfaction at Beringer's revival, some Napa wine folk had wrinkled brows concerning one aspect of the Nestlé operation. In 1986 the company introduced the Napa Ridge label on a line of inexpensively priced "fighting varietals." Here was a Napa-based operation, making wine in the Napa Valley, 100,000 cases the first year and 400,000 by 1989, without having to use Napa grapes. (Actually, a good part of the first production did come from Napa grapes, but this soon ended.) There was nothing illegal about it, but many Napa growers were indignant at the possible implications. Chiles Valley's Völker Eisele asserted, "It's legal, but it's a hoax." One could envision

Codorníu – Napa's

massive underground

champagnerie in the

Carneros sits in

marked contrast to

much of the modern

winery architecture

in the Napa Valley.

the floor of the Napa Valley covered with huge wine factories, which produced millions of gallons of inexpensive wine from Central Valley grapes at their Napa addresses. Then they could be shipped out as Napa Glen, Napa Summit, or Napa Crest. Certainly the White Zinfandel explosion at Sutter Home seemed to fit this view of the future. The battle over this issue would soon be joined with passion.[13]

VINTAGE 1986

The great flood was a bother but it didn't hurt the quality of the Napa grape crop. The flood water and a mild spring caused early bud break. Thereafter growers could hardly have defined a better set of growing and harvest conditions. The vintage began very early, with large tonnage coming from the outside for sparkling wine and White Zinfandel. Cool nights and morning fogs slowed sugar in early September, with signs of mildew here and there. An October Indian summer guaranteed good Cabernet and Merlot. Cab yields were very high. The whites' chemistry was excellent. The huge crop brought down prices for most varieties, but Cabernet and Merlot profits soared from the high yield per acre, Merlot being the Valley's most profitable variety per acre. The crush was 56 percent white. This season produced many great wines.

WHAT IS A WINERY?

Napa Valley had grown increasingly attractive to tourists since the 1960s, but in the 1980s this growth left the charts. With this rise came a sizeable investment in facilities to accommodate the influx. In 1980 Napa County had 1,036 hotel and motel rooms; by 1985 there were 7,164. A 1983 survey counted 2,448,665 visitors to the Valley's ten largest wineries. (For comparison, the San Diego Zoo had about 3,000,000 visitors that year.) The congestion of the Valley's main arteries had become a serious problem for wineries and residents. The same survey estimated that on a typical summer day, at the height of the tourist season, Highway 29 handled 17,000 vehicles. Whether tourist vehicles have caused a large part of this clogging is still a matter for debate in the Valley.[14]

Part of the attraction was the growing number of wineries, about 150 and rising in 1984; ten years earlier there had been a third as many. Another set of attractions were the numerous nonwinery activities, such as concerts, cooking classes, and art exhibits, which had become an integral part of some wineries' overall marketing approach. To these factors was added what some were calling the "tourist winery," an establishment that rang up gift shop sales on anything and everything that might or might not have some connection to wine and food. Soon people were talking about "wineries" that didn't produce wine, but operated a sales room and gift shop before there was a grape crushed on the property. There was also the matter of the great production facilities that might only incidentally use Napa grapes. Nevertheless, their trucks and employees were helping to clog the Valley's roads, and their wines were doing little for the Napa quality image. Finally there was a related question: what if such facilities, now or in the future, didn't even process grapes from the outside? What if they became nothing but blending and bottling plants for wine shipped up from the Central Valley? What exactly was the legal definition of a winery in the Napa Valley? It was clear that the great successes of the sixties and seventies might actually have been a Pyrrhic victory. One could almost hear the shade of Charles Krug muttering, "Wir haben uns totesgesiegt."

When he retired from the County Planning Commission in 1985, Monticello's Jay Corley called on the Board of Supervisors to develop a proper definition of a winery here. "We're not in the picnic business," he said at the time. The board then asked Corley and the NVVA to identify the proper activities of a winery and to indicate the effect of these activities on the future of the Agricultural Preserve. The *Star*'s Marilee Talley followed up with a three-part series of articles examining the entire question. The implication was that some study, some hard work, and some good will would yield a logical and satisfying answer. There would be more than four years of hard work and plenty of ill will before the matter was settled.[15]

James Hickey was the head of the County Planning Department and had been wondering aloud about what wineries should be allowed to do long before matters came to a head in 1985. He was concerned over the possibility of a "broad and permissive definition of a winery that would allow individual wineries to expand their operations in almost any direction with little or no direct relationship to the wine making process." At the outset the Grape Growers leadership favored a fairly restrictive approach. The Vintners wanted to allow a broad range of winery activities. A leader of that group stated that "efforts to curtail some of these marketing techniques would put the entire industry at a competitive disadvantage." Working together in 1987 the two organizations were unable to devise a definition they could both live with. Finally in April the Growers and the Farm Bureau submitted one proposal, the Vintners another. At this point the wineries were willing to compromise only to the point where they agreed that a winery was a place where grapes were converted into wine. Up until now they had insisted that a purely blending and bottling plant should qualify.

Later in the year the Growers came up with their 75 percent plan, which became the main fighting point in the months to come. They proposed that

75 percent of all the grapes processed by new wineries in the future had to be from the Napa Valley. And they called for this formula to apply to expansions at existing wineries. The NVVA branded the suggestion as extremist. But Andrew Beckstoffer for the growers countered that, "We don't see how you can preserve Napa County's agriculture by setting up processing plants for other than Napa County grapes." The Vintners replied that this was simply a ploy to boost the price they would have to pay the growers for their crop.[16]

In 1988 the battle was complicated by another issue. By mid-year, with the definition issue yet unresolved, Hickey and the Planning Commission began pressing the question of winery density. Everyone knew that at some point there had to be a limit on the number of wineries. At the current pace there would soon be two hundred. Before this, in the spring, there had been a rush of new winery applications, as observers predicted correctly that Hickey meant to place a moratorium on new wineries. In July the commission reported that a number of wineries in the Valley were nothing but retail stores. Supervisor Varrelman stated that the density question was as critical as the creation of the Agricultural Preserve. In August the board made its move and placed a seventeen-month moratorium on new winery applications. The *Chronicle* headlined: "Valley Ferments Over Winery Glut." Three weeks later the hard feelings between the Vintners and Growers were manifested by the cancellation of the 150th anniversary celebration of the beginning of viticulture in the Valley. All were girded for the fight; by January 1990 some kind of decision was going to be made. The question "What is a winery in this valley?" had to be answered.[17]

A bitter election campaign in the fall of 1988 pitted slow-growth against pro-growth candidates for the County Board of Supervisors. The fight further polarized the Growers and Vintners. The tension became white-hot when the Vintners actually endorsed the two pro-growth candidates. The close victories by the pro-growth candidates seemed to mean that the new board would probably allow established wineries to continue their nonwinery activities and that the larger wineries would be allowed to continue processing outside grapes without limit.[18]

But the Growers kept up the attack, pushing for the 75 percent rule. The audacity of their public campaign infuriated some of the Vintners leadership. But after the election the outlines of a workable compromise became clear. Many of the Vintners seemed ready to accept the 75 percent rule, so long as established wineries were exempt from many of the new restrictions. This was an important concession, which rankled some of the corporate executives of the large wineries. But it made sense from the Growers' point of view, since their argument looked to potential abuses down the line, not to the impossibility of the current situation. Growers also accepted the continuation of special activities at wineries, so long as they did not cause expansion into the Ag Preserve.

When the outlines of the draft ordinance became generally known in November, those who had chafed at the unseemliness of the public squabble breathed a sigh of relief. But there was still the question of the new, pro-growth board. They were not compelled to accept the compromise hammered out by the combatants and the Planning Commission. There was still corporate pressure to reject the agreement.

On December 28 the *Star* called on the board to "switch their focus to the recommendations of the electorate and the expertise of planners and environmentalists." In other words, corporate interests should not have the final say on the future of the Valley.[19] When the commission finally released the draft ordinance, the newspaper praised the result as a good balance between the needs of industry and the need to keep the Valley rural and in open space. On January 16, 1990, the final board hearing saw a marathon of winery, grower, and environmentalist advocates state their cases. The ordinance was passed the next day. The 75 percent rule would be in effect at all new wineries and at expansions of established ones. New wineries were not permitted to offer open house tours and tastings. Appointments would be necessary. Generally, the activities that had been part of an established winery's cultural and culinary programs could continue.

The result was a Growers' victory. But it was a true compromise, which, resting on the vote of the Board of Supervisors, was no more secure in the long run than the Ag Preserve. The future of Napa wine seemed to hang on a tenuous thread of public policy. And yet the small start-up wineries would be cut off from the tasting room approach that had helped establish the wineries, which now had a monopoly on them. But the statistics indicated a clear trend. There would soon be 200 wineries here. In 1980 there had been half that number.[20]

1987

1987 brought several significant changes. Foreign capital, specifically Japanese capital, became a special factor in winery ownership this year. First the Markham Winery, formerly the Little Co-op, went to Sanraku, Inc. Then down the road St. Clement was purchased by Sapporo. Next year the troubled Mihaly Winery on Silverado Trail was sold to Minami Kyushu and its name changed to Silverado Hills Cellars. Then Whitehall Lane went to Hideaki Ando.[21] Another 1988 surprise was the sale of the Raymond Winery to Kirin Brewery.

Also of historic proportions were the events taking place at the Napa Co-operative Winery. We left that post-Repeal savior for Napa growers firmly in the financial arms of the Gallo brothers, who began taking the facility's complete production in the mid-fifties. In the early eighties the relationship between the growers and the Gallos began to unravel. Between 1985 and 1987 the operations of the Co-op underwent a revolution. First Gallo dropped the white wine contract, then the red. Meanwhile membership and crush numbers were declining. By 1984 only about 9,000 tons were crushed at the winery, about 9 percent of the Valley's total.

The upshot was a new board of directors and by 1987 a new premium direction. The new leaders looked at the winery's history and discovered that it had been the William Peterson Winery from the late 1870s to 1894, when it was purchased by Robert Bergfeld. Later Theodore Gier had owned it. They took the Bergfeld name and in 1987 Bergfeld Cellars went into operation with a hospitality center and a line of premium varietals. The year before, the Co-op had begun producing varietal wine for Hiram Walker's Julius Wile & Sons label. In 1990 Bergfeld bought the 70,000-case brand and added it to its expanding product line.

Since 1982 the number of member growers had dropped from 217 to little more than a hundred, but their outlook was hopeful. They owned the only really premium wine co-operative in the country. There were still many negatives in the wine industry, but Napa wine and premium wine were holding their own. And the Big Co-op had them both now.[22]

VINTAGE 1987

There was some planting, with red acreage increasing, white declining. The spring was mild but dry. The first year of California's great water shortage had begun, but for Napa it was no drought; there was half again as much rain as in 1976–77. A May heat wave hurt berry set, particularly Cabernet Sauvignon. The crush would be lighter, but quality was excellent. Fall conditions were excellent, with an early harvest peaking in mid-September. Almost everything was in before the first real rain hit on October 23. The grape chemistry was excellent. But Cabernet averaged under two tons per acre. Chardonnay yielded almost four tons. The crush was 58 percent white, with 27 percent Chardonnay, a record high for the variety. A short Cabernet crop helped create concentrated flavors and an excellent ageing potential.

FOCUSING ON THE ENVIRONMENT

We have already noted the fragile political character of the Agricultural Preserve. It must ever rest, it seemed, on the whim of three of the five members of the Board of Supervisors. Exceptions to the preserve had been voted from time to time, but in the seventies the acreage limit was raised from twenty to forty and the hillsides of the Valley were incorporated into an environmental pattern similar to that in the 1968 ordinance. These lands were now part of the Agricultural Watershed.

A formidable test of the underlying concept had come in 1981 when developers proposed to create a community of twenty-seven "ranchettes." Each would have forty acres on a 1,200-acre stretch of Carneros land right next to Winery Lake. The idea seemed bucolic enough at first glance, but solid opposition soon formed, led by Carneros growers René di Rosa and Ira Lee. They were joined by the Napa Valley Foundation under grower Milton Eisele. They raised the cry to "Keep Carneros Green," and brought the fight to the board chambers. The result was a 5–0 vote rejecting the idea.[23]

The board that had rejected the Carneros plan in 1981 had been moderately pro-growth. But by 1988 the board definitely favored slow growth. In that year two of the slow-growth members were challenged by pro-growth opponents and the latter were supported by the NVVA. Going to war often brings results that the combatants never dream of at the outset. A modern Thucydides would have been sorely taxed to predict the long-term outcome of this fight.

First, the Vintners' leadership decided to endorse pro-growth candidates. This alienated many of the active members of the NVVA with strong environmental convictions. Then the leadership withdrew the endorsement. But there was still powerful support for the the pro-growth candidates, Fred Negri and John Mikolajcik. These two stressed the economic benefits of growth and tried to convince the workers in the Valley's larger wineries and in support industries that by voting pro-growth they were protecting their jobs. The result was a close victory for the pro-growth candidates, but we have seen that this victory did not mean a Vintners' victory on the winery definition issue.

St. Helena

traffic waits

for the light

to change.

The next step in the fight occurred on June 29, 1989, when the new board forced James Hickey to resign his position with the County's Planning Department. This officer had long been a thorn in the side of local developers and others supporting county growth. Hickey had always been a friend of the environmentalist element in the Grape Growers Association and these, led by Völker Eisele, decided to enter the political arena themselves. Next year Bob White, who was the third vote in ousting Hickey, was up for reelection. They targeted him and also decided to make the Ag Preserve immune to tampering by the Board of Supervisors.[24]

At this point one might ask whether the slow-growth approach in Napa had been working in the eighties. The county started off the least populous in the Bay Area and then grew only 10.1 percent during the decade. Adjoining Napa on the west, winegrowing Sonoma had grown 27.8 percent. Solano on the east had grown 41.2 percent. The city of Napa had grown 21 percent. Meanwhile the area south of the city was growing much as any of the other Bay Area satellite regions. In the *Chronicle*'s words, "the southern end of the wine country is becoming a burgeoning commercial and industrial zone." In 1989 Sutter Home had even built a huge 150,000-square-foot warehouse facility south of the airport. This was the kind of growth that Napa growers like Völker Eisele were glad to see, because it helped hold down the distribution traffic on the upper county roads. Napa was clearly growing, but slowly, and not at the expense of the agricultural environment.[25]

Following Hickey's removal, a group headed by Napa lawyer Victor Fershko, Supervisor Mel Varrelman, and orchardist Ruth von Uhlit went to work putting together an organization to defeat Supervisor Bob White and to prepare a proposition for the June 1990 ballot that would remove modification of the Ag Preserve and Watershed from the hands of the board. The legislation finally drafted would allow no such modification without approval of the voters for the next thirty years; if passed in 1990 it could last until the year 2020. Thus, "20/20 Vision" became the watchword of this slow-growth campaign. It had the support of the Growers and several winery owners. Warren Winiarski, Thomas Burgess, and Daniel Duckhorn were active in forming the Napa Agricultural Preservation Action Committee, which supported the proposition.

Former Napa City Councilman Harold Kelly expressed the campaign's chief concern: "We think the majority of the Board will slowly eat away the Agricultural Watershed." Von Uhlit thought the new rules were "a wonderful gift to pass to our children." She predicted it would win by a two-to-one vote. The response of the Board's newly appointed head of the Planning Commission: "It's stupid."

A technicality voided the signatures placing the proposition on the June ballot. So its supporters went out and collected them all over again. There was no problem getting them and Proposition J was certified to the November ballot.

California voters faced a bewildering array of ballot propositions in the fall of 1990 and the mood of the electorate was NO on just about everything put to them. Of particular interest in the wine country was the so-called "nickel-a-drink" initiative that would have taxed wine heavily. Napa voters outdid the rest of the state when 71 percent said NO to this idea. Bond issues that normally cruise past California voters were knocked down like duckpins. But the 20/20 initiative won easily. Ruth von Uhlit had been close in her prediction; it received 63 percent support from Napa voters. The results stood out from those on the rest of the ballot like a gutter ball. Unless the proposition were successfully challenged in the courts, the Ag Preserve and Watershed were now virtually closed to development. In the board election Vincent Ferriole ousted Bob White from his seat, to reverse the 3–2 lineup established in 1988. Predictably a legal challenge to the constitutionality of Measure J was mounted by developers and landowners in the spring of 1992. But in July Napa Superior Court Judge Wes Walker ruled that voters have as much right as elected officials to legislate such issues of local concern.[26]

Amid all these alarms and skirmishes, another environmental issue came tooting into the Valley. It was the Wine Train. The issues involved were clearly environmental, but they were only indirectly related to Napa wine.

In April 1984 the Southern Pacific took steps to abandon the old Napa Valley right-of-way, from the Kaiser Steel plant south of Napa up to the Charles Krug Winery. In November 1985 a group of investors bought the right-of-way, with the intention of running tourist trains through the Valley with stops along the way at several wineries.

It would be four years before the Wine Train started its three-a-day runs, without stops at wineries. Those four years were full of bitter controversy. In this matter the Vintners and Grape Growers were in concert in their opposition to the train. Andrew Beckstoffer called it "a moving car wreck." The Upper Napa Valley Association termed it "merely a restaurant on wheels." For Louis Martini it was "a damn nuisance."

The first run was a freight delivery in February 1988, appropriately a load of large tanks for a Valley winery. The first passenger run went out on a rainy September 16, 1989, and was met by crowds of placard carrying protesters. Diners aboard the train raised their glasses of Napa wine in salute to the hardy, rain-drenched opponents of their pleasure. Later an emeritus president of the Napa Valley Wine Library Association was slapped with a citizen's arrest for blocking the right-of-way in his protest. The charges, of course, were dropped.

From outside the Valley the reaction was almost universally positive. Journalists from every major newspaper in the Bay Area took a run on the Wine Train and came back full of praise for the experience. The *Chronicle*'s Herb Caen called it "an all-out plus." Even the *Star*'s David Turin loved his ride and his plate of Sonoma free-range chicken. The *Register* called it "a heavenly movable feast." In 1992 the opposition to the train was holding its ground, but for now the railroad was a part of Valley life—again.[27]

Recent developments indicate that Napa's environmental battlefield in the nineties may be on the undeveloped hillsides suitable for new vineyards. After the deluge of rain in 1986, there was talk in the Valley about the terrible erosion that had taken place on some of the newly planted hillside vineyards. By the 1988–89 season county officials knew that there were some real problems in a few places, particularly above Bell Canyon Reservoir and on Mt. Veeder. In November 1989 the *Star* called for measures to save Napa hillsides and their topsoil. The editorial pointed out that Napa's vineyards were not the county's great natural resource; it was the soil. In March 1990 the Napa County Resource Conservation District released its report. Since 1985 there had been 3,810 acres of vineyards planted here on sloping land subject to heavy erosion. The district staff had measured the loss of topsoil in several vineyards and found that some were giving up as much as fourteen tons per acre each year from runoff. Napa's vineyardists began taking special notice of the problem that year when the District Attorney charged two vineyard owners above Bell Canyon with violation of state codes against the creation of siltation hazards.

In 1990 there was virtually no valley land left for vineyard planting. The 75 percent rule would put even greater pressure to plant more Napa vineyards. After a great land rush in 1988 to buy what potential vineyard land was left in the Carneros, the hillsides were just about all that remained. In May 1990 the county issued a one-year moratorium on hillside

Despite the popularity of the Wine Train, some locals are forthright in their opposition.

planting on slopes steeper than 15 percent. As Marilee Talley pointed out in the *Star*, since the Neolithic revolution, man has needed six inches of topsoil and some rain to survive. If more Napa wines were to come from the Valley's hillsides, the "vineyardization" of those hillsides, as one Spring Mountain resident put it, would have to include rules for saving those six inches.[28]

THE APPELLATION GAME

When we last discussed the appellation question, the North Coast controversy had been resolved and the broad Napa Valley appellation had been approved with some heat but little fire generated in the process. The Carneros question was complicated but resolved without conflict. Howell Mountain went through easily. The BATF seemed willing to grant applications so long as they did not exclude areas with reasonable grounds for inclusion.

The granting of the Stags Leap District application marks a historic watershed in the appellation game. This was a real battle. The press from the Bay Area to Los Angeles picked up on the story and made the most of it. The combatants roared and gesticulated as if the future of the Valley depended on the outcome. When it was over everyone shook hands and went back to work making good wine.

The whole thing started in 1961 when Nathan Fay began planting a few acres of Cabernet Sauvignon among the fruit trees on the property he had bought in 1953. Richard Steltzner joined him in 1967. Then came Warren Winiarski, John Shafer, Carl Doumani, Gary Andrus, and others. Mostly they planted Cabernet where before they found prunes, walnuts, or the old rustic reds from post-Repeal days—Carignane, Zinfandel, and Petite Sirah.

They planted these vines on land that was sort of a valley within the Valley. It was along the Silverado Trail, mostly east of it, several hundred feet beneath the remarkable geologic outcropping that had been called Stag's Leap since the 1880s. Horace Chase had built his winery

The rocks which give Stags Leap it name. Below are John Shafer's Cabernet vineyards.

SOURCE: JOHN SHAFER.

NAPA WINE

and home here in 1888, the latter functioning as a country inn from 1917–1953. The soil in this vale was mostly volcanic alluvium, washed down for millions of years from the slopes of the Vaca Range from which Stag's Leap protruded. The best of this was a Rhyolite classified as Bale clay loam. The area had never developed any kind of reputation for fine wine, as prunes and dairy operations had taken up a large part of the agricultural activity here since the turn of the century. The old Occidental Winery still stood back from the Trail, but no wine had been made there since before Prohibition.

People liked Nathan Fay's Cabernet grapes. Robert Mondavi and Charles Krug bought them in the early years. Even the little Woodside Winery came up to haul a few down to the home of the famous old La Questa Cabernet. Winiarski knew that there was something special about the Cabs that came from this volcanic soil when he decided to settle here. In 1976 the world suddenly learned that there was something special here when his Cabernet won the Spurrier tasting in Paris. Afterward he said, "I don't think that people would give two hoots about the name Stag's Leap were it not for the events in Paris."[29]

Carl Doumani bought the Chase estate in 1970 and began reviving the old Petite Sirah vines on the place. Eventually he and Winiarski became entangled in a legal battle over the use of the term "Stag's Leap" on their labels. Doumani's read Stags' Leap Vineyard; Winiarski's read Stag's Leap Wine Cellars. (Note the apostrophes.) Before this contest was finally adjudicated, Gary Andrus, just west of the Trail, brought out a "Stag's Leap Cuvée" Chardonnay under his Pine Ridge label. Later when he used the term for Cabernet Sauvignon, Winiarski and Doumani joined forces in a suit to claim the Stag's Leap term as their own. In 1985 Andrus won his judgment. Stag's Leap was a geographical term and belonged to no one.

Meanwhile, other growers in the area had undertaken to secure a Stag's Leap appellation from the BATF. Capitalizing on the perceived quality of the Cabernets grown in this little area, no more than 500 acres in size, seemed natural. Stag's Leap as a winegrowing district was gaining a distinct place in the consumer's mind. John Shafer and Richard Steltzner both won Vintners Club tasteoffs, in 1981 and 1983, for their Stag's Leap Cabernets.

At first Winiarski would have nothing to do with a Stag's Leap appellation. In 1984, before Andrus had won his legal fight, Winiarski had stated that "the whole idea of a Stag's Leap appellation would dilute the name." But he decided to rethink his opposition now that the courts had held that he and Doumani did not own the name of the rocks standing above the area.

By now Winiarski and Doumani had buried the hatchet. In fact, they produced a 1985 Cabernet together, which they named "Accord." And they decided now to support the application for the appellation. But first it was agreed that the famed apostrophe would be eliminated and that the term "District" would be added. Thus, the Stags Leap District was the name on the application to the BATF.

Then things got sticky. The Robert Mondavi family and the Disney family of Silverado Vineyards owned almost 500 acres of vineyard land on the west side of the Silverado Trail, and more could be planted. They were able to persuade the original group to take them in and expand the application to include these lands, which extended all the way out to the Napa River. Suddenly the Stag's Leap appellation would apply to land totaling more than 2,000 acres, most of which had had nothing to do with the reputation of the great Stag's Leap Cabernets developed here since the 1960s.

It was argued correctly that there was lots of the very same Rhyolite soil in these lands to the west of the Trail. But there were also large stretches of Cole silt loam and young alluvial Yolo loam out there. Such soils were nothing special and could be found all over the center of the valley floor. The southern end of the proposed district would be below Clos de Val, marked by what was termed an intermittent creek. The northern limit would be a line running through the low hills just north of the Disney property, but well south of the Yountville Crossroad.

Stanley B. Anderson had a vineyard on the Crossroad, planted predominantly to Chardonnay. He also had a pair of caves carved into the hills just north of the proposed border. He had developed a good reputation for his Chardonnay and sparkling wines since he had founded his winery in 1979. From his vineyard he looked right up at the rocks of Stag's Leap and he wondered why his vineyard had been excluded. His soils were the same as those from that little area across the Trail where those great Cabernets had been grown. And he didn't think his climate was different. So he attacked the amended application and asked that he

d the few growers along the Crossroad be included. It amounted to another 150 acres. The expansion from the original area with the Mondavi and Disney land had added almost ten times that amount.

The hearings were held in Yountville, December 1–2, 1987. A parade of witnesses argued for the applicants and for the inclusion of Anderson and his neighbors. After all the historical, geological, and climatological evidence was submitted, it all seemed to boil down to whether Anderson should be kept out if the Mondavi and Disney lands were allowed in. At the end of the hearings on the second day, a grower, whose vineyard lay just south of the proposed boundary, asked to speak. He noted that the southern boundary line wasn't a little creek but a drainage ditch his father had dug. What kind of natural boundary was that? And he wondered how the breezes passing over his land, which had the same soil as north of the ditch, were changed as they crossed over the proposed appellation. The Treasury officials shook their heads and headed back to Washington.

Many thought the bureau would kick the application back to the original petitioners and ask them to draw boundaries that included the vineyard land that had made the Stag's Leap reputation. It took over a year for the BATF to make its ruling. It came down January 27, 1989. They ruled that everyone was in. Stags Leap would include the original area, the Mondavi and Disney lands, and Anderson and his neighbors along the Yountville Crossroad. Tens of thousands of dollars in lawyers' fees and research time had been spent to effect an outcome that might have been predicted in advance from the Bureau's previous inclusive decisions. Many now questioned the process. Others were becoming concerned that the Napa Valley appellation might soon be sliced up into sub-units that drew attention to themselves, without reference to the larger appellation.[30]

While the Stag's Leap question was being resolved, the Vintners in 1988 requested the BATF to place a moratorium on new Napa applications. Already in the works, however, was the request for a Mt. Veeder appellation, put together by the Hess Collection winery. No one was offended by the proposed boundaries and the application was granted in February 1990. In 1989 a Wild Horse Valley appellation had been granted in Solano County from which two tiny portions protruded into Napa Valley about four miles west of the city of Napa. Also in the works in 1989 was an application for a Chiles Valley appellation. For a while nothing was heard from Spring Mountain where some winegrowers had opposed appellations for "fractionalizing Napa Valley." In 1991, however, a move was made to establish a Spring Mountain viticultural district, led by York Creek's Fritz Maytag. The petition was granted in June 1993.[31]

Back in 1981, during the North Coast hearing, Leon Adams had remarked that the appellation process "had become a comedy." The laughter level went up a notch in 1989. For some time there had been talk of dividing the valley floor into wine districts on the basis of the little towns that extended north above the city of Napa—Yountville, Oakville, Rutherford, St. Helena, and Calistoga. In March 1989 it was learned that proposals for an Oakville and a Rutherford appellation had been put together, which caused no laughs. But they included a suggestion for sub-appellations west of the Napa River to be named Rutherford Bench and Oakville Bench. Not surprisingly, growers and wineries inside the "bench" areas supported the idea. Those outside expressed various levels of disgust. Caymus' Charles Wagner, Sr. stated that "the public will be fooled." Joseph Heitz referred to the authors of the bench idea as "clowns." He pointed out that "there is no geological evidence of bench land in the Napa Valley." In truth, it would be difficult to find here the normal terracing associated with bench lands. André Tchelistcheff left no question as to where he stood. "I think whoever invented the appellation should be hung." Some wags set up a bus stop arrangement near the highway with a "Rutherford Bench" sign attached. Hearings on the Oakville and Rutherford petitions were held in Napa December 9-10, 1992, without reference to the "bench" idea, which has been dropped by the petitioners. Meanwhile a petition was being prepared for a St. Helena district just north of Rutherford, extending above the town to Bale Lane.[32]

Meanwhile, on January 1, 1990, an act of the California State Legislature quietly became law (SB 771). Supported by the Vintners and Growers, work on the measure had begun in 1986. It required that labels on Napa wine from appellations located within the Napa Valley must carry the "Napa Valley" appellation, whatever the sub-appellation. This law should end the concern over the fractionalization of the Valley's image.

VINTAGE 1988

The nonbearing acreage exceeded the 2,500 mark, 73 percent of it red, mostly Bordeaux varieties. There was a rush to buy Carneros land. Purchasers included R. Mondavi, Grgich-Hills, Silverado Vineyards, Shafer, and S. Anderson.

The late spring was a roller coaster of weather conditions on the heels of a fairly dry rainy season. March was dry and mild. April started out hot, followed by heavy storms. Half of May was either stormy or cloud-covered, with heavy winds late in the month. June began cool with more rain. The result was a disastrous berry set for red and white Bordeaux varieties. July was extremely hot, stressing many vines. The vintage started in mid-August, but mild conditions made for an orderly harvest. Cabernet and Merlot yields were worse than predicted and Sauvignon blanc yields were the lowest since the 1976–77 drought years. Musts showed intense fruit flavors. The overall red Bordeaux quality ranged from good to outstanding, but the 1988s will not be the cellar treasures that the 1987s were. Chardonnay was a very bright spot, with good yields and excellent fruit. Prices were good. A short crop still brought a record value.

1988 - 1990 TRANSACTIONS

Many of the transactions in this recent period have already been discussed as part of individual winery stories. In general, most transactions of importance pointed to industrial consolidation or the influx of outside capital, much of it foreign. But the reverse was also true; those who had capital centered in the

Napa Valley acquired assets outside the area to extend operations in the face of the very finite possibilities of expansion here.

In 1988 Domaine Chandon bought the Shadow Creek label from Corbett Canyon Vineyards in the Central Coast. Now Chandon could expand production and marketing without affecting the style of the regular Chandon sparkling wines. A historic property changed hands in 1988 when the Christian Brothers purchased the old Hedgeside Winery, built by Morris Estee in 1885. It had been revived as Quail Ridge Winery in 1978. Perhaps the most interesting transaction of this year was a transfer. In 1981 Mitch Cosentino had started his winery, Crystal Valley Cellars, in Modesto. Now, like Louis M. Martini years earlier, he was making the move from the Central Valley to Napa, building the winery north of Yountville on Highway 29.

In 1989 Robert Mondavi started work on his joint venture Opus One Winery, eventually to handle about 20,000 cases of that elixir. The Mondavi family continued to extend their holdings in the Central Coast. At the end of the year they acquired the 60,000-gallon Byron Winery in Santa Barbara County, where they had previously acquired about 1,000 acres of land. (Their continued expansion and success could be measured with some accuracy in 1993 when the family corporation filed a registration statement with the Securities Exchange Commission. The purpose was to make a public offering of Mondavi stock valued at something between $48 million and $60 million. The proceeds of the offering would go to reduce rising bank debt and to help fund the replanting of vineyards under attack from phylloxera. The filing papers revealed that the family's net worth rose from $35 million in 1987 to $56 million in 1992. They also showed that fiscal-year profits in 1992 were $7.1 million compared to $7.3 million in 1988. Nevertheless, sales during that five year period rose from $93.8 million to $145.6 million.)[33]

Beringer-Nestlé (Wine World) was also expanding in the Central Coast with its purchase this year of the Estrella River Winery, renamed Meridian Vineyards and under the guidance of Chardonnay master Charles Ortman. They also owned a one-third interest in the Maison Deutz sparkling wine venture in Santa Barbara County. In all, Napa-based Wine World controlled over 6,000 acres of land with sales of about $100,000,000 per year. By the end of the eighties the Beringer label itself was worth about 1,000,000 cases per year. And Wine World also had the Napa Ridge line and the Los Hermanos jug brand.

Certainly the most startling transaction of 1989 was the sale of Christian Brothers to Heublein. Since 1984 the quality of the Brothers' table wine had gone straight up, after having been "left in the dust" in the seventies, in the words of *Wine Spectator*. But it had taken an investment of about $25,000,000 to effect the turnaround. The Heublein purchase, for about $125,000,000, actually placed the Christian Brothers operation in the hands of a giant British conglomerate, Grand Metropolitan, which had bought Heublein in 1987. The great attraction was the Brothers' annual sales of about 1,300,000 cases of brandy. The table wine side of the deal amounted to about 950,000 cases.

Heublein's purchase gave them another 1,200 acres of Napa grape vines, bringing their total control close to 4,600, about one acre in every seven in the Valley total. Heublein now owned Beaulieu, Inglenook, the Gustave Niebaum line, Quail Ridge, and Christian Brothers. Later in the year Richard Maher, formerly in charge at Christian Brothers and now in charge of the Heublein Fine Wine Group, announced a consolidation of the wineries' operations but insisted that "each winery will maintain its separate personality." In the spring of 1991 the "for sale" sign went up at historic Greystone. Later in the year it was sold to a New York culinary school. In 1993 the Christian Brothers tasting room in the grand old building was finally closed.

The most obvious personnel change at Christian Brothers was the departure of Brother Timothy after fifty-four years of service. "When the winery is bought I don't go with the winery. I'm a member of a religious order. . . . I'll move up to Mont La Salle and do something else."[34]

In 1990 another sale of historic Napa property took place when Andrew Beckstoffer purchased the 225-acre Beaulieu Vineyard #3. One of the most famous producers of Cabernet Sauvignon in the Valley, BV#3 was going to be "a vineyard for the '90s," according to the new owner. According to the Associated Press, Beckstoffer was now the largest independent grapegrower in the North Coast. His holdings included 500 acres of Napa vines and about 1,000 acres in Mendocino County. Since 1987 he had been producing medium-priced varietals under the Fremont Creek label, using rented space at several wineries in the area.[35]

No transaction in 1990 did more to cement Napa's historical continuity than the reorganization of the 1890 Nichelini Winery, now the site of Napa's oldest family-run winegrowing operation. When James Nichelini died in 1985, four of founder Anton's grandchildren came together to operate the place and to save the property from sale. One of these cousins is Greg Boeger, founder of the 1973 winery in El Dorado County that bears his name. He is now the Nichelini winemaker and produced a 1989 Napa Zinfandel under the Boeger label.[36]

WHO OWNS THIS LAND?

One way of looking at vineyard ownership is to separate the acreage of independent growers from what the wineries themselves own. One looks in vain for such figures in the public record. In the 1960s, industry estimates suggested that wineries owned about 25 percent of the Valley's vines. By the seventies educated guesses placed the number at around 35 percent. By the nineties there was much concern about the decline of the independent grower here, but the data available on this situation are by no means clear.

The 1990 *Wines & Vines* industry directory shows the number of acres reported by each winery. These data derive from the wineries' own reported figures. When the obviously fanciful exaggerations are culled from the total, the wineries claim about 20,000 of Napa's 31,000 acres, or about 64 percent. But another statistic makes this figure highly suspect. The report of the 1989 crush of Napa grapes shows that fully 63.7 percent were purchased by wineries. The 1991 figure dropped to 57.8 percent. Some wineries, such as Trefethen, do sell grapes to other wineries, but one must conclude that a preponderance of the Napa grapes that wineries purchase are from Napa growers.

The membership of the Growers Association accounts for something over 25 percent of the total Valley acreage. Also, the members of the Napa Co-op own about 1,500 acres. One must understand, of course, that the term "independent grower" today no longer necessarily carries the connotation of the "yeoman" proprietor that it did in the sixties. Some independent growers are corporations that own and farm huge tracts of vineyard land. A good example is the Butte Resources Company of Houston, Texas, whose vines cover 830 acres on 4,700 acres in Pope Valley. It seems clear that wineries do not actually own a large part of the acreage that they claimed in the 1990 directory. Perhaps they included a large amount of leased land. I would guess that about 55 percent of Napa's vines are not yet owned by wineries. And in 1990, more than 100 wineries were small-scale vineyard owners, with holdings of less than 100 acres.

Another way of looking at vineyard ownership is to examine the holdings of the large wineries. A 1988 *Wine Spectator* analysis showed that about

Several of the important vineyards of the Oakville viticultural district.

SOURCE: VINE HILL RANCH, ROBERT PEPI WINERY.

40 percent of Napa wine came from seven producers (R. Mondavi, Beaulieu, Beringer, Sterling, Christian Brothers, Charles Krug, and Domaine Chandon). These operations owned 6,132 acres and controlled through leases and long-term contracts another 4,125, totaling about one-third of the Valley's vineyards.

Another analysis gives a picture of the size of Napa's wineries. In 1987 two UC Davis researchers looked at wineries by capacity and related these figures to their share of total Napa wine production. The statistics from the 82 percent responding wineries showed that about 20 percent of Napa's wineries had a capacity of 10,000 gallons or less. "Small" wineries, or those with 11,000–50,000 gallons, amounted to 38 percent of those reporting. Wineries that could hold from 51,000–999,000 gallons added up to 35 percent. There were ten wineries with capacities of a million gallons or more.

The picture that emerges from these sets of data shows that there are a few wineries with a powerful position in Napa vineyard ownership and wine production. Wineries in general probably *control* more than half of Napa's vineyards. But a large portion of this ownership is in medium- and small vineyard plantations. Thus, independent vineyardists, whatever their size, and small- and medium-sized wineries, still control a very important part of the Valley's total wine production and vineyard acreage. This situation does not validate the gloomy observations that see Napa today locked in the grip of giant corporate control.

Another important factor in both corporate and private ownership here is the foreign component. The huge Heublein/Grand Metropolitan stake is obvious. Seagram, technically a Canadian corporation, Beringer/Nestlé, and Domaine Chandon all have large vineyard holdings. Less obvious are those of Clos du Val, Franciscan, Markham, Hess, Skalli, and Cuvaison. Whatever the public's visceral response to these foreign acquisitions, it is by no means clear that such ownership has had anything but an upgrading effect on the quality of Napa wine. More often than not, foreign capital has been the vehicle for quality resuscitation. One need look no further than Beringer, Franciscan, and Cuvaison to support this hypothesis. In recent years the tendency of foreign capital to take the long and patient view has meant better Napa wine.[37]

Vintage 1989

There has never been such a vintage as 1989. The year began with a rush to plant and graft to red Bordeaux varieties. The nonbearing acreage almost doubled. For the first time since 1985 the red acreage edged ahead of the white. There would soon be over 2,000 acres of Merlot, and there would be more Cabernet franc next season than Petite Sirah or White Riesling.

The winter months were not wet enough, but a great March saved the day, dumping over ten inches of rain on the Valley. But from that month on for the next two years people would be using the "D" word with more and more regularity. The rest of the year, through mid-September, was a textbook series of excellent weather situations. May and June, finally, allowed for an almost perfect berry set and a huge crop.

The sparkling wine harvest began in mid-August. Early ripening varieties came in slowly but with regularity until September 16. Then the tail end of a fall storm swept up from the south and blasted the vineyards for three days. The mild weather that followed was humid. Grape maturity came on too slowly and rot struck the Chardonnay left unpicked, in a bafflingly unpredictable pattern. Some vineyards were spared; in others the crops were virtually destroyed. Selective harvesting was necessary. Another storm hit on September 28.

Some later called it "the vintage from hell." October warmed up some and the rest of the harvest became orderly. Red Bordeaux varieties produced an excellent crop, in size and quality. The total Valley tonnage was enormous, a record. The total yield was close to five tons per acre. Cabernet Sauvignon was almost four tons. Merlot was more than five tons. Prices went through the roof. The total value of the crop was up 57 percent from 1988. Grower income per acre was up 69 percent. Cabernets and their blends appeared early to be excellent wines. Chardonnay prices were excellent. When these appeared on shelves there was surprise at the generally satisfactory level of their quality.

On October 12 the weather became very mild. This lasted until October 17, when the temperature suddenly jumped from the mid-70s to 88°. Shortly after five o'clock in the afternoon the Bay Area was ripped by an earthquake, the likes of which had not been felt here since 1906. But in Napa the experience was very much like that of 1906. People felt the heavy shock, but noted only a bit of damage here and there.

EVENTS OF 1989

1989 was the year when the health warning labels went on wine bottles. It was also the year when the California wine industry thoroughly awoke to a combined threat from declining consumption and the aroused concern over the negative effects of alcohol in American life. The consumption problem did not hurt Napa wineries as much as did the large inventories created by the gigantic vintage. In general the premium sector of the table wine market ended the eighties in excellent shape. Industry consultant Jon Fredrikson commented on the concluding decade: "The silver lining is the incredible growth in premium table wines." A statistic definitely in Napa's favor was the national rise in the consumption of California red table wine since 1985, which would be 11 percent by 1991. But he also warned of a situation that could affect Napa producers. In 1989 growth in sales of the higher-priced premiums began to slow. He warned that producers at the high end of the price scale were starting to feel negative consumer reaction to the price jumps of the previous two years. And economists' predictions of a recession in 1990 also cast a cloud on the future.[38]

The idea that fine wine should be lumped with beer, spirits, and illegal drugs by anti-alcohol groups was an infuriating circumstance for California wine producers. But many thought that the industry, particularly the Wine Institute, had not done enough to promote the positive aspects of moderate table wine consumption. No one was more infuriated than Robert Mondavi, who, in 1987, had begun what he termed a "mission to educate people about what wine really is by telling the truth." He charged that anti-alcohol groups were telling half-truths, or less, about wine's benefits. In 1987 Mondavi began placing the following statement on his wine labels:

Wine has been with us since the beginning of civilization.
It is the temperate, civilized, romantic, mealtime beverage
recommended by the Bible. Wine has been praised for
centuries by statesmen, philosophers, poets, and scholars.
Wine in moderation is an integral part of our culture,
heritage, and gracious way of life.

Other wineries took his lead. But in November 1990 the BATF indicated that it would probably outlaw such expressions on labels, since they might be considered encouragement to consume more alcoholic beverages. A month later Mondavi handed over the reins of his wineries to his sons. "At 77, the time has come for me to pursue my interests in wine and culture." Then in April 1991 the BATF accepted Mondavi's "mission" statement, so long as it did not make reference to the Bible or "our culture." Nevertheless, Mondavi had cleared his calendar to pursue his mission.[39]

Vintage 1990

There was not enough rain, but storms in January and February of 1990 kept Napa above the drought level. There were twenty-eight rainy days between the end of the 1989 vintage and the next summer. Unfortunately for Napa wine, particularly for Bordeaux varieties, eight of those days came between May 19 and May 29. Then came a summer full of warm and hot days, but never in long stretches that might hurt the crop. A rush of days over 100° in early August set off the harvest for sparkling wine grapes. Schramsberg began picking Pinot noir on August 9. Then a fine period of warm weather settled on the Valley, with only a harmless squirt of rain on September 22. Harvest conditions then continued to be just about perfect into November.

It was the second largest vintage in Napa history. Overall prices declined some, but Cabernet Sauvignon shot up to $1,600 per ton. But red Bordeaux varieties were down 7,000 tons from their potential. The Chardonnay crop was a whopper, just below the 1989 record.

At the end of the vintage a complex combination of industry and national conditions made Napa producers and growers wonder at their immediate future. They breathed a sigh of relief when the "nickel-a-drink" Proposition 134 bit the dust in November. Another good sign was the rainy season in February and March of 1991, which brought a series of storms that raised the Napa River to flood stage. But again, just as in the drought years of the 1890s, phylloxera was raising its ugly head. This time, the discovery of a new biotype made it more difficult to combat. Compounding the threat was the awful realization that the resistant rootstock so long promoted by UC Davis, the AxR-1, on which so much of the Valley's vineyards were planted, was by no means resistant. The press jumped at the idea that the Valley would have to be replanted, but it was thought that the process would be a gradual one. California's phylloxera were still just about as lazy as they were a hundred years before. In 1990 a new bug was discovered in Napa, the grape leaf skeletonizer, heretofore a problem only in other areas. The next year a

Opus One

Winery, Oakville

vineyard in Carneros and one in Rutherford were found to be infested and a campaign against the pest was mounted. The business cycle was again a matter for concern. The predicted recession had arrived by the end of the year. A general decline in demand for table wine would now be exacerbated by a general downturn in demand for most consumer products. Napa producers who had felt themselves immune to such cyclical conditions in past years were faced with large inventories, particularly Chardonnay. Most established brands with good marketing programs appeared secure for now. Premium producers might have to cut prices in the face of consumer resistance, but there were no signs that the general demand for premium wines was going anywhere but up in the long run. Nevertheless, Hanns Kornell and Charles F. Shaw sought bankruptcy protection in November 1991, and in 1992 Spring Mountain Vineyards was in the hands of its creditors, clear signs that individual premium producers were not immune to the bad times facing the California wine industry.

NAPA VINTAGES, 1984 - 1992

Year	Tons Produced	Value	Grower Price per Ton
1984	99,996	$ 76,836,000	$ 768
1985	101,407	78,332,000	772
1986	113,220	85,676,000	757
1987	100,180	82,162,000	820
1988	99,774	97,943,000	982
1989	132,849	153,688,000	1,157
1990	114,314	140,484,000	1,229
1991	138,322	174,275,000	1,257
1992	136,255	167,682,000	1,218

VINTAGE 1991

The first few weeks of this vintage year in November and December gave the Valley little rain but by mid-December there were eighteen consecutive freezing nights. On December 21-22 St. Helena had lows of 14-16° F. However, there was little serious damage in the vineyards. Then came virtually no rain until the heavens began opening up on February 26. From then until March 31 Napa Valley had twenty days of good rain, over seventeen inches. Some of the local reservoirs went over the top. Much of the rest of California would continue to talk about drought, but Napa was safe for another year.

The rest of the spring and early summer was quite cool. June highs in St. Helena averaged 5° lower than in 1990. North of Yountville the rest of the summer was fairly warm. St. Helena had 21 days of 85° or more in July. August's average high was 86°. But the lower Valley and Carneros experienced lots of cool weather and morning fog, as did many other winegrowing areas in Northern California, particularly Sonoma. All this added up to a huge crop which matured too slowly in the southern portion of the Valley. Above Yountville the grapes were late in relationship to recent years, but about on schedule for the long run of history. Careful vineyardists thinned heavily, but the crop still averaged well over four tons per acre.

As August went by there was much talk of a coming disaster. A tenth of an inch of rain on August 9 added to the apprehension. Grapes for sparkling wine did not start coming in until after September 1. The *Chronicle* warned that the vintage might be "ugly." But September was warm and dry. So was October. In fact St. Helena had nineteen October days 85° or over. Nighttime September temperatures dipped into the thirties in some areas, which tended to shut down vines and cut short grape maturity. But not in the upper Napa Valley. St. Helena did not have a night under 40° until October 21. Finally, a large storm on October 25 brought an end to almost all grape harvesting.

Vineyardists were happy. Yields were huge and prices remained high, over $1200/ton . Wineries ended the vintage in a sort of euphoric shock. What might have been a disaster now seemed to provide another healthy vintage. At this writing "good" and "excellent" seem to be the words most often applied to the wines just finishing their fermentation. But many winemakers were quietly thinking "great." In the spring of 1992 The California Cabernet Society hosted a huge barrel tasting of 1991 Cabs in San Francisco. This is an organization of 41 producers, 33 of which are from Napa. Although I am more a consumer than an expert in such matters, I think the Napa Cabernets from this vintage are among the best in the last dozen years.

Vintage 1991 was certainly a success. But the economic and social forces at work in the nation continued to point to declining wine consumption. For the state the vintage was just short of the 1982 record, a fact that increased inventories in the face of declining consumption. And this in the face of an all out recession that had already struck a blow to consumer confidence and buying power. Meanwhile, the phylloxera in the Napa Valley was moving at a faster pace than had been predicted. More and more vineyardists were now considering the costly necessity of ripping up vines grafted to the discredited AXR-1 rootstock. But a possible alternative to uprooting was being tested at Napa's Monticello Cellars, where vineyard manager Walt Chavoor was experimenting with an "in-arch" or "approach graft" system of hooking AxR-1 vines to truly resistant rootstock, a technique recently developed at Fresno State University. If ultimately successful this technique could cut conversion costs by more than 75%.

VINTAGE 1992

The 1992 vintage in the Napa Valley was early and fairly orderly, even though some grape varieties ripened in a rush in late August. The size of the crop was satisfying for most growers, though it was no record. The totals were high enough to cover the fact that about 10% of the Valley's vines had been torn out during the last three years. The reason, of course, was the phylloxera, which was still gradually spreading through the Valley and was now appearing in the hills and smaller valleys to the east and west.

The California water shortage continued to hurt the state as a whole, but Napa and the North Coast in general were again saved from drought conditions, this time by five weeks of rainy weather between February 9 and March 15 which brought over 15 inches of rain to the Valley.

The season was moderate through early spring with no late frosts to threaten the grape crop. Then everything was accelerated by a scorching May whose daily temperatures reached into the high 80s and low 90s for more than half of the month. May was actually hotter than June, which had a freak storm at the end of the month which increased the concern over mildew here.

July and August continued hot, perhaps too hot, as half of August's mid-Valley highs exceeded 95 degrees. The sparkling wine harvest was well under way before August 10 and the Valley's fermenters were all bubbling well before the end of the month. By the end of October almost every winery had finished crushing. Few grapes were still unharvested when the Valley was doused October 28-31 with 3.5 inches of welcome rain.

The heat that accelerated grape maturity did not insure the grape quality which might have resulted from fewer sizzling days. But the 1992 fruit was good enough to make Valley winemakers smile and predict another excellent vintage. There was some talk that the wines, though well flavored, might be softer and earlier maturing than those from other recent vintages. Barrel samples of Cabernet Sauvignon displayed in San Francisco in March certainly impressed me for their excellent varietal definition and solid chemistry.

VINTAGE 1993

After the grapes were in, Michael Martini said "the 1993 vintage has taken more patience than any other vintage I've ever crushed." If he had been able to consult the weather charts for Napa valley over the last hundred years he would have confirmed his impression. There has never been another vintage like it this century.

The 1992-93 winter rain was plentiful. No one was talking drought anymore. From December through February there were 43 rainy days, dropping 39 inches of rain. But it kept raining off and on through the spring, much of it coming down in May and early June. In fact, from May 23 to June 5 there were nine days of rain. June 4 brought a gully washer. The result was poor flower set on many varieties and a shorter crop overall.

The summer was hot with several real heat waves. From July 31 to August 5 the average high in St. Helena was 101°. At that point grapes for sparkling wines began pouring in; the harvest had begun. Better, the harvests had begun. Silverado Vineyard's John Stewart remarked that "People would ask me how the harvest was going and I'd have to say, 'which one?'" It was go-stop-go from August through the end of October.

A large part of the Napa Valley grape crop was in the fermenters by the end of September. But the Cabernet Sauvignon crop was largely still unharvested at the end of the month. Everything was ready to go for that last rush of ripeness, but on October 3 the clouds rolled in. The fog, then rain, then more clouds, fog and rain. On October 15 much of the Northern California Cab crop was still hanging under 22° Brix. From October 3 to 17 the valley's average high was only 72°. In 1992 it had been 91°, and in 1992 it had been 94°. Thousands of tons of grapes all over Northern California remained unharvested. Fall seemed over.

And then temperatures began to rise and clear days prevailed. From October 19 to 30 the average high at St. Helena was almost 83°. The Indian summer continued until broken by a storm on November 10. In fact the average high for the first week in November was almost 80°.

The Napa crop was about 15-20% short. Certain varieties were hit even harder. Pinot noir may have been been more than 30% short. But this was no tragedy; there was far too much unsold wine on retail shelves and short crops often meant more highly concentrated flavors.

At this early writing (November 28, 1993) little can be said for sure about Napa wine quality for Vintage 1993. But conditions this year, bizarre as they were, should produce rich fruit and concentrated flavors. For all their frazzled nerves, Napa producers were smiling after the conclusion of this dramatic vintage.

PARALLELS WITH THE PAST

One cannot help but notice the parallels between the modern wine revolution in America and that which the California industry experienced just over one hundred years ago. When we look at the growth in Napa wine production and the development of high-quality standards between 1880 and 1895 and we consider the sad days that eventually followed, we must ask whether historical variables of previous years could combine today to produce a similar threat to the future.

The most important question concerns the basis for the two revolutions. The boom of the 1880s was no revolution in tastes or consumption patterns. The growth of the California and Napa wine industries came primarily from a change in the American population. Immigration was the stimulus for growth in the previous dynamic era. But the great change in recent years has come from a true revolution in consumption. The average American consumer is still not a wine drinker. But for a small and significant percentage of the American population, the consumption of table wine has become an important part of life since the 1960s. For the wine industry as a whole this revolution might be tenuous. Consumption per capita has been declining and even fads in this consumption—white wine, coolers, blush wine—have not altered the general decline in the consumption of the inexpensive wines that led the boom of the seventies. But no such gloomy future appears on the horizon so far as the premium segment of the industry is concerned.

What of the prohibition movement of previous years and today's serious concerns about alcohol abuse? Could the current anti-alcohol drive to alter public policy cause Americans to relive the years preceding Prohibition? Historical analysis cannot provide an answer to this question, but it certainly can point to the important differences in the historical situations.

The drive to national prohibition was a cleverly contrived electoral program whose ultimate success at the national level depended on the lucky convergence of a national dry campaign with the public spirit engendered by a national war effort. That the wine industry was a casualty of this convergence depended on the fact that Americans then had no concern for wine. The typical wine drinker was seen as an aristocrat or as a member of an immigrant class, which, many thought, was threatening the social fabric of the nation.

Today's neo-temperance movement aims to curb consumption primarily through pressure on regulatory bodies to mandate such things as warning labels and restrictions on advertising. There is also pressure on legislatures to raise taxes. The wine industry has chosen to brand such pressure as "neo-prohibitionist." Such hyperbole aside, there is little evidence that such measures are prohibitionist in the least, or that the American public has any interest in prohibition, certainly not in the prohibition of wine. Although a small portion of the adult population regularly drinks wine with meals, the image of wine in America today is quite antithetical to that of the years before World War I. About four in five Americans today believe that there is nothing wrong with a glass of wine with dinner. The Americans today who think that alcohol is a problem in our national life do not seem concerned with Napa wine.

It would also be useful to consider the organization of wine production and winery and vineyard ownership today compared with the situation shortly after the turn of the century. Then, as now, the dynamic core of fine wine production was the enthusiastic entrepreneur, attracted by the goal of such production and the life that accompanied it. But in the years between 1900 and 1915, so far as entrepreneurial enthusiasm went, the zeal for wine and wine production, so obvious in the years after 1880, had collapsed. To own a winery in 1910 was to be involved in the liquor traffic. Such is not the case today.

From 1900 to 1915, industrial consolidation was the name of the game in California wine. So too is it today. But now consolidation has a rich multilevel character that provides keen competition. Eighty years ago such competition did not exist. Today, consolidation, so far as premium wine is concerned, is a positive factor in the growth of quality Napa wine. Eighty years ago consolidation meant movement of land and capital into the hands of one great monopoly, the California Wine Association. The result was good wine, but one looked almost in vain in 1915 for such great Napa wines as could be bought between 1890 and 1900. By 1915 the production of fine wine in Napa was a homogenized operation, with virtually no stimulus for improvement, save the instincts and egos of the industrial monarchs who commanded the industry before Prohibition. Today the competition for a place on a wine critic's approved list is frantic. Giant Beringer-Nestlé competes in deadly earnest with tiny Caymus for a place among Robert Parker's recommendations.

The idea that one can make fine wine, and lots of wine, but not lots of fine wine, has finally been laid to rest. Industrial consolidation and foreign ownership have done nothing to hurt the prestige of Napa wine today. The number of enthusiastic entrepreneurs continues to grow. Technical improvements in vineyard and cellar seem never-ending. The people of the Napa Valley have a genuine concern for the agricultural environment of this "national treasure." I cannot predict the future. But I certainly look with enthusiasm and optimism upon the future of Napa wine.

ENVOY

Reflections on Darkness

Ten years ago I wrote a history of winegrowing in the Santa Clara Valley, a story with dramatic origins and with achievements and triumphs equal to those of Napa at the turn of the century. Ultimately, however, it was a story with an ending. Little remains today to remind us of what was once a great industry there.

Today you can still stand above Silicon Valley in vineyards along Monte Bello Ridge that, like one on Howell Mountain, supplied Cabernet grapes for a wine that won a gold medal at the Paris Exposition in 1900. But if you stand in the dark of night on the Ridge and look down at the valley below, you will be dazzled by a sea of blazing light from an urban civilization that has replaced what was once a modern Eden of vineyards and orchards.

When you stand today on the heights of the Oakville Grade and look down on the Napa Valley and toward the hills around it, darkness still surrounds you. True, there is more light today than thirty years ago when I first stood there. But thirty years from now, around the year 2020, there is good reason to believe that the people of the Valley will have preserved the agricultural environment symbolized by this darkness. Such preservation is essential for the future of Napa wine.

1. Star, 1/12/1984, 6/20/1985; Chronicle, 11/29/1989; Los Angeles Times, 6/23/1985; Gerald Asher. "Howell Mountain." Gourmet (March 1989): 44; Wine Spectator, 2/16/1983. I prepared the historical research to support the Howell Mountain application to the BATF.

2. Wines & Vines (May 1986): 19; Wine Spectator, 7/31/1990, 11/15/1991, 7/15/1992; Conaway, 360-364.

3. Stuller and Martin, 244-245. For a complete evaluation of the wines see: James Laube. "A Tasteful Reunion." Wine Spectator, 7/16/1985.

4. Michalene Busico. "Vintage Discord." San Jose Mercury, 7/11/1987, 1/3/1992; Tessa De Carlo. "Winery or Tourist Trap?" Chronicle, 6/4/1987; House and Garden (September 1987): 156; Progressive Architecture (February 1988): New York Times, 8/20/1987; Star, 1/31/1985, 8/15/1985.

5. Wine Spectator, 12/31/1988.

6. Wine Spectator, 6/1/1983.

7. Harm Jan De Blij. Wine Regions of the Southern Hemisphere (Totowa [NJ] 1985): 124-147 has many good photos of the Cape Colony counterparts to Chimney Rock.

8. Star, 11/9/1986, 11/26/1987; Wine Spectator, 2/28/1987.

9. Star, 10/27/1977; Laube. Cabernets, 340-341; Haynes, 8.

10. Conaway, 364-368; Stuller and Martin, 281-287; Wine Spectator, 7/1/1985, 11/16/1985, 2/16/1986; Wines & Vines (March 1986): 18; Chronicle, 4/30/1985; San Jose Mercury, 6/17/1985; California Visitors' Review, 11/16/1990.

11. San Jose Mercury, 7/1/1989, 9/12/1990.

12. Wine Spectator, 12/31/1990. Five of the top ten were Napa Cabernets. #2 was 1985 Caymus Special Selection ($50), #5 was 1985 Heitz Martha's Vineyard ($60), #6 was 1987 Opus One ($68), #9 was 1987 Spottswoode ($36). Other Napa Cabernets in the top twenty were Duckhorn, William Hill, Silverado Cellars, La Jota, Dunn, and Groth. The red Bordeaux on most retail shelves this year was Vintage 1987, a good but below average year there.

13. Wine Spectator, 4/15/1987; Practical Winery (January 1990): 13; Chronicle, 12/26/1983; Wine & Spirits (June 1989): 46; San Jose Mercury, 1/31/1990.

14. Napa Valley Foundation. Napa Valley Tourism Project (November 1984); Chronicle, 12/26/1983; 10/20/1986; Los Angeles Times, 6/23/1982.

15. Star, 8/15, 8/22, and 8/29/1985.

16. Star, 2/26/1987, 4/9/1987, 7/23/1987, 11/19/1987, 11/26/1987; Chronicle, 11/9/1987; Conaway, 320-328.

17. Chronicle, 6/6/1988, 9/4/1988, 9/15/1988; Star, 9/15/1988.

18. Moira Johnson. "A Very Civil War." California Magazine (January 1989): 54; Chronicle, 10/28/1988; Star, 10/27/1988.

19. Chronicle, 12/18/1989.

20. Larry Walker. "A New, Improved Napa Valley?" Wine Times (May 1990): 33-35; Star, 1/4/1990, 1/25/1990; Chronicle, 1/18/1990, 1/24/1990.

21. The later downturn in the Japanese economy in the 1990s brought a sale of Whitehall Lane to an American buyer in 1993. Star, 2/25/1993.

22. Star, 10/7/1982, 10/10/1987, 12/20/1990; Chronicle, 2/8/1986; Wines & Vines (March 1986): 18.

23. Wines & Vines, (December 1981): 23.

24. Conaway, 491-495; Star, 7/27/1989. The 8/24/1989 issue has Negri's defense of Hickey's dismissal.

25. Chronicle, 1/22/1990, 8/29/1990; Star, 5/3/1990, 9/7/1990.

26. Star, 9/7/1990, 11/8/1990, 6/10/1992.

27. Examiner, 2/4/1990; San Jose Mercury, 8/6/1990, 10/21/1990; Chronicle, 8/24/1989, 9/11/1989, 4/24/1990; Star, 9/21/1989.

28. Star, 11/9/1989, 3/15/1990, 5/17/1990, 7/19/1990, 10/11/1990.

29. Wine Spectator, 1/1/1985, 7/1/1985, 9/16/1985; Vintage (September 1981): 19.

30. Chronicle, 6/23/1986, 12/9/1987, 5/24/1988, 1/18/1989; Los Angeles Times, 5/20/1988; San Jose Mercury , 2/22/1989; Star, 10/5/1989; Wine Spectator, 2/1/1986, 5/1/1986, 12/31/1987, 2/28/1989. I was the last scheduled witness to testify at the BATF hearing on 12/1/1987. I argued that the appellation should be confirmed and limited to that small area that had gained a special reputation for its Cabernets. I stated that if the Disney and Mondavi land were included, so

should Anderson's and his neighbors'. The final holding was in line with this recommendation. Author to William Drake (BATF), 1/10/1988.

31. Star, 10/5/1989, 3/15/1990, 10/11/1990. I prepared the historic research for the Chiles Valley application.

32. Chronicle, 3/11/1989, 3/15/1990; Star, 3/16/1989 Wine Spectator, 7/15/1987 has good maps of the proposed district, as does Star, 10/31/1991.

33. Chronicle, 4/24/93.

34. Wines & Vines (November 1989): 18; Wine Spectator, 6/30/1989, 9/30/1989; Star, 7/13/1989, 11/23/1989; Los Angeles Times, 8/3/1989; David Beck. "Farewell, Brother Tim." San Jose Mercury-News, 6/28/1989 provides a good overview of Brother Timothy's contributions to California wine. For a remarkable analysis of the Grand Metropolitan phenomenon see: P. Unwin. Wine and the Vine (London 1991): 332-343.

35. Wines & Vines (August 1988): 22; (January 1990): 15; San Jose Mercury, 5/12/1990. For an extended and controversial view of Beckstoffer's activities since his arrival in 1969 see Conaway, passim.

36. Author's interview with Greg Boeger, 3/1/1992.

37. California Agricultural Statistics Service. California Grape Acreage 1989 and 1990; California Department of Food and Agriculture. Final Grape Crush Report, 1989 Crop and 1990 Crop; James Laube. "Who Owns Napa Valley?" Wine Spectator, 11/15/1988; Per-Henrick Mansson. "How Foreign Money Is Improving U. S. Wine." Wine Spectator, 9/30/1989; George Cook and Edward P. Vilas. "California Wineries. . . ." California Agriculture (43:2) (March-April 1989): 4-6.

38. Jon Fredrikson. "The '80s Didn't Deliver As Forecast." Wines & Vines (June 1990): 32-36.

39. Wines & Vines (January 1991): 30; San Jose Mercury, 12/21/1990; Star, 12/27/1990; Robert Mondavi. "The Mission." The Wine Educator (1:1): 16-17.

40. Wine Spectator, 2/28/1991 reviews recent American opinion surveys on wine.

APPENDIXES

I. NAPA VALLEY WINE STYLES, 1870 - 1920

The following tables indicate the varieties that went into wines usually included in a generic category. They also provide information about their reputation and uses. I have not included many varieties popular today, such as the Chenin blanc, because there is very little evidence of their early use. Nor have I included the Mission variety , although its use in Napa table wine production, here and there, continued until the turn of the century. The tables answer these questions:

1. What grapes were used to make Napa table wines before Prohibition?

2. How were Napa table wines categorized and what grapes were used in these generic categories?

3. What grapes were commonly found in Napa wines (+) and which only occasionally (0)?

4. What grapes went into wines shown by Napa producers at the State Viticultural Conventions at the end of the first wine boom (+)? Which were grown here but not entered? Which grapes went into wines from other districts (#)?

5. What was the University of California (1944) evaluation of these varieties (0-100)? Did the University recommend the variety in 1963?

6. Which varieties employed in early days are still considered useful today for producing quality table wines? What has been the pattern of acreage planting here since 1974?

7. Which early Napa producers received awards or special commendations for these wines?

TABLE DESIGNATIONS

Each table has six columns. These are the data and symbols for each:

I. Varieties common (+) to Napa or occasional (0).

II. Varieties shown at state conventions (+), not shown (0) or shown by other districts (#).

III. 1944 University of California rating (0-100).

IV. Recommended (+) or not (0) by University in 1963.

V. Considered useful by Napa producers today for high-quality table wine(+).

VI. Acreage planted in Napa in 1974 and 1990. (1974/1990)

CLARET WINE

VARIETIES	I	II	III	IV	V	VI
Zinfandel	+	+	67	+	+	1315/1993
Cabernet Sauvignon	+	+	98	+	+	5209/9131
Malbec	+	#	—	0	+	7/33
Cabernet franc	0	+	—	0	+	?/636
Merlot	0	0	—	+	+	680/2148
Verdot (Petite)	0	0	—	0	+	?/55
Tannat	0	+	69	0	0	—
Malvoisie (Cinsaut)	+	+	—	—	0	—

AWARDS

"Claret" : Beringer, C. Carpy, Brun & Chaix, R. Delafield (Calistoga), Inglenook, Napa Valley Wine Co. (NVWCo), Schramsberg, To Kalon.

Zinfandel: Beringer, Courtois & Co. (Larkmead), Ewer & Atkinson, Eshcol, C. Krug, Migliavacca, G. Groezinger, To Kalon, J. Stanly (Carneros), F. Salmina, R. Wheeler, L. Zierngibl, NVWCo.

Cabernet Sauvignon (Medoc style): C. Carpy, O. Norman (Howell Mt.), Hedgeside (Estee), J. Stanly, Eshcol, T. Parrott (Spring Mt.), C. Krug, NVWCo, Inglenook, F. Salmina, Beringer.

Tannat: J. Stanly

Malvoisie: Courtois & Co.

RED BURGUNDY

VARIETIES	I	II	III	IV	V	VI
Mourvèdre (Mataro)	+	+	47	0	+	12/3
Duriff (Calif. Petite Sirah)	+	0	71	+	+	1137/452
Carignane	0	+	57	+	?	494/36
Grenache	0	+	82	+	?	48/6
Ste. Macaire	0	#	65	0	0	—
Pinot noir	0	+	92	+	+	2526/2719
Syrah (French)	0	+	—	+	+	?/25
Aramon	0	+	—	—	0	—
Beclan	0	+	—	—	0	—
Refosco (Crabb's Black Burgundy)	+	+	65	+	0	231/0
Charbono	0	+	59	—	0	8/81 (in 1978)
Mondeuse	0	+	67	—	0	—
Valdepeñas	0	+	58	0	0	29/0
(Pinot) Meunier (sparkling wine)	0	0	—	—	+	0/147

Red Burgundy: To Kalon, R. Delafield, T. Parrott, NVWCo, L. Zierngibl, Beringer, Schramsberg, S. P. Connor (Larkmead), F. Salmina, Inglenook.

Carignane: R. Wheeler, NVWCo, L. Zierngibl.

Grenache: R. Delafield.

Pinot Noir: T. Parrott ("Chambertin").

Beclan: To Kalon.

Refosco: To Kalon.

Charbono: Hedgeside, Ewer & Atkinson.

Valdepenas: J. Stanly.

(Pinot) Meunier: Edge Hill.

GERMAN STYLE WINES

VARIETIES	I	II	III	IV	V	VI
White Riesling	+	+	88	+	+	1141/442
Sylvaner	+	+	85	+	0	194/9
Traminer (Gewürztraminer)	0	+	81	+	+	300/119
Burger	+	+	61	0	0	204/16
Gutedel	+	+	—	—	0	8/0
Palomino	+	+	48	0	0	180/12
Grey Riesling (White Trousseau)	+	0	47	—	0	348/55
Green Hungarian	0	0	51	—	0	104/4
Chauché gris	0	+	—	—	0	—

AWARDS

Rhine Wine Type: Schramsberg, To Kalon, Ewer & Atkinson, O. Norman, F. Salmina J. Grimm (Calistoga), NVWCo.

White Riesling (Johannisberg Riesling): Schramsberg, R. Wheeler, NVWCo, Beringer, To Kalon, Eshcol, O. Norman, T. Parrott, Inglenook, C. Carpy, California Wine Assn. (Vinecliff), C. Schilling (Spring Mt.)

Sylvaner (Franken Riesling): Ewer & Atkinson, R. Delafield.

Burger (Elbling): Inglenook.

Gutedel (Chasselas Doré): Inglenook, R. Wheeler, Hedgeside, O. Norman, NVWCo.

Palomino (Napa Golden Chasselas): Ewer & Atkinson.

WHITE BURGUNDY

VARIETIES	I	II	III	IV	V	VI
Palomino	+	+	48	0	0	180/12
Chardonnay	0	+	92	+	+	2249/9639
Folle Blanche (Sprklg wine)	0	#	69	—	0	0/39
Chauché gris	0	+	67	—	0	—
(French) Colombard	0	0	67	+	0	641/60
Pinot gris	0	#	—	—	0	—

AWARDS

Chablis : To Kalon

Palomino: C. Krug

White Pinot (?): R. Wheeler

Chardonnay (Montrachet): T. Parrott

SAUTERNE

VARIETIES	I	II	III	IV	V	VI
Sauvignon blanc	+	+	78	+	+	534/2873
Sémillon	0	+	85	+	+	197/345
Sauvignon vert	+	+	48	0	0	342/14
Palomino	+	+	48	0	0	180/12

AWARDS

Sauterne: Eschol, To Kalon, Courtois & Co, C. Carpy, Inglenook, J. Grimm, C. Schilling.

Sauvignon Blanc: To Kalon, Inglenook.

Semillon: Brun & Chaix.

Sauvignon Vert (Sauvignonasse): To Kalon, C. Krug, Schramsberg.

THE 1ST WINE REVOLUTION, 1881 - 1887
NAPA VALLEY ACRES

District	BEARING ACRES 1881	1887	RIESLING TYPES	GUTEDEL & PALOMINO	SAUTERNE TYPES[1]	MÉDOC[2] VARIETIES	MISC.[3] REDS	ZINFANDEL	MALVOISIE & MISSION	ON RESISTANT ROOTSTOCK
Conn Valley	223	657	32	112	3	5	60	390	53	—
Spring Mt.	55	355	11	58	5	10	20	216	32	—
Pope Valley	20	165	2	29	—	1	1	36	85	—
Berryessa	18	33	—	5	—	—	—	12	16	—
Chiles Valley	13	129	15	16	8	5	10	55	20	10
Howell Mt.	100	690	85	110	20	65	150	215	45	20
Calistoga	250	1,710	254	243	25	119	160	522	275	72
St. Helena	1,611	5,246	963	797	83	255	551	1,831	694	49
Rutherford	721	1,527	260	213	55	45	191	452	94	20
Oakville	429	1,085	317	144	33	54	89	433	99	30
Yountville	585	1,674	264	339	43	28	117	582	195	25
Napa and Carneros	1,260	3,340	433	531	137	192	259	1,000	423	425
TOTALS	5,285	16,611	2,636	2,597	412	779	1,608	5,744	2,031	651

1 Mostly Sauvignon vert, with some Sémillon and Sauvignon blanc.
2 Cabernet Sauvignon, Cabernet franc, Merlot, Verdot and Malbec.
3 Pinots, Refosco, Syrah, Carignane, Alicante and others.

A Statistical Picture of the Fresh Grape Deal, by Variety (1929)

CARLOAD SHIPMENTS SELECTED COUNTIES	"JUICE" GRAPES									RAISIN AND TABLE GRAPES				
North Coast	AB	ZIN	CAR	MVD	MSS	PS	GR	MXB	TOTAL	MUSCATS	TS	MAL	TOK	EMP
Napa	326	135	101	3	1	245	1	560	1372	7	—	—	—	—
Sonoma	240	209	56	10	15	113	2	685	1330	—	—	—	—	—
Mendocino	86	179	138	1	7	7	2	556	976	1	—	—	1	1
SF Bay Area														
Contra Costa	70	47	141	68	—	—	1	71	398	1	—	—	1	—
Alameda	14	6	5	—	—	1	—	46	72	—	—	—	1	—
Santa Clara	60	43	60	6	7	12	—	203	397	—	1	7	—	27
Central Valley-north														
Sacramento	40	30	22	1	13	6	—	129	241	4	5	5	1220	23
San Joaquin	1603	2280	1109	11	290	73	4	447	5817	20	10	25	4130	83
Central Valley-south														
Stanislaus	1165	385	825	6	57	2	24	209	2673	29	370	313	41	63
Fresno	1840	705	212	13	176	46	96	142	3230	4930	2153	3263	14	895
Kern	792	36	184	—	2	5	1	157	1172	36	36	784	745	339

AB=Alicante Bouschet, Zin=Zinfandel, Car=Carignane, Mvd=Mourvèdre, Mss=Mission, PS=Petite Sirah, TS=Thompson Seedless, Gr=Grenache, MxB=Red wine grapes shipped without specific variety indicated, e.g. mixed. Mal=Malaga, Tok=Tokay (Flame), Emp=Emperor.

These data for one year show carload shipments, by selected county, of important varieties. They show the relative importance of these varieties. Unfortunately USDA did not start making these detailed surveys until the late twenties. These data give a fairly accurate picture of the portion of vineyard land devoted to each variety in a given county.

Virtually all red wine grapes went to home winemakers, as did a large portion of the muscats. It is impossible to determine the extent to which table and raisin grapes were thus used. But it is sure that many a lug box of such as Thompson Seedless went into the home barrel to cut the coarse Alicante Bouschet, when the price was right.

LEADING NAPA VALLEY BULK WINERIES IN THE 1940S

WINERY (HISTORIC CONNECTION)	SINCE	LOCATION	PROPRIETOR	STORAGE CAPACITY	BONDED WINERY #
Garetto Winery	1935	Carneros	John Garetto	300,000	4263
Gagetta Winery	1933	Rutherford	Dennis Gagetta	**	3652
Garibaldi Winery	1933	Rutherford	Gussie Garibaldi	**	3802
Jackse Winery	1909	St.Helena Library Lane	Stephen Jackse	60,000	604
Larkmead Co-op (Salmina Bros.)	1947	Larkmead	Co-op (Jerome Draper, pres.)	900,000	605
Montebello Winery (G. Schoenewald)	1894	St. Helena, Spring & Hudson	Renault Co. (New Jersey)	525,000	955
Muther Wine Co. (J. Lewelling)	1933	St. Helena, 1621 Spring St.	Fred Muther	200,000	958
Napa Valley Co-op (Bergfeld/Gier)	1934	St. Helena	Co-op (H.R.Pace, pres.)	2,000,000	3565
Napa Wine Co. (Brun & Chaix/ L. Stralla)	1933	Oakville	J. B. Cella	1,500,000	9
Old St. Helena Winery (F. Sciaroni)	1933	St. Helena, Main & Charter Oak	M. Paganini	185,000	4120
L. Pocai & Sons	1912	Calistoga	Libero Pocai	90,000	115
Rossi Winery	1907	St. Helena, Zinfandel Lane	Rachel Rossi	40,000	934
St. Helena Co-op (J. Laurent)	1939	St. Helena	Steven Navone	392,000	957
Sunny St. Helena	1933	St. Helena	Chas. Forni, Cesare Mondavi, Jack Riorda	800,000	4072
Bartolucci Winery	1932	Oakville	Louis Bartolucci	300,000	3179

CALIFORNIA STATE FAIR, 1947-1959

Except for Larkmead, which went through a complicated series of ownerships after 1943, and Deer Park, all important Napa Valley retail wine brands and premium producers were represented at the State Fair competitions through 1954. By 1957 Inglenook, Charles Krug, BV and Louis Martini had stopped entering their wines. Beringer joined this group in 1958. This was a move made by many old-line premium producers throughout Northern California. Thus, after 1956 the State Fair awards give a far less accurate picture of the top end of the product line of California's fine wine brands.

The following chart shows Napa Valley medal winners from 1947 to 1959. Results are given only for those six varietals with categories for competition then on the State Fair premium list whose varietal names were still commonly seen on bottles of Napa wine in the 1990s.

	1947	1948	1949	1950	1951	1952	1953	1954	1955	1956	1957	1958	1959
Cabernet Sauvignon													
Beaulieu	—	—	B	S	G	S	S	—	—	—	—	—	—
Christian Bros.	—	—	—	—	—	—	—	—	—	S	—	B	S
Charles Krug	—	—	—	—	S	B	G	G	G	—	—	—	—
Inglenook	—	G	G	G	—	G	—	G	S	B	—	—	—
L.M.Martini	S	—	—	—	—	—	—	G	—	—	—	—	—
Souverain	—	—	—	—	—	—	S	—	—	G	—	—	G
Pinot Noir													
Beaulieu	B	G	G	G	G	G	G	—	—	—	—	—	—
Christian Bros.	—	—	—	—	—	—	—	—	—	B	B	—	G
Freemark Abbey	—	—	—	—	—	G	—	—	—	—	—	—	—
Inglenook	—	S	G	S	—	B	S	S	G	S	—	—	—
Charles Krug	—	—	—	—	—	B	B	S	—	—	—	—	—
L.M.Martini	—	B	—	—	—	—	—	—	—	—	—	—	—
Souverain	S	—	—	—	—	—	—	—	—	—	S	—	—
Zinfandel													
Christian Bros.	—	—	—	—	—	—	—	—	—	B	—	—	—
Freemark Abbey	—	—	—	—	—	—	—	B	—	—	—	—	—
Charles Krug	—	—	—	—	—	S	S	—	G	—	—	—	—
L.M.Martini	—	G	—	S	—	—	—	—	—	—	—	—	—
Souverain	S	S	—	—	—	—	B	S	G	—	—	—	—
L. Pocai & Sons	B	—	—	—	—	—	—	—	—	—	—	—	—
Chardonnay													
Beaulieu	—	—	S	G	S	B	—	—	—	—	—	—	—
Christian Brothers	—	—	—	—	—	—	—	—	S	S	B	G	—
Inglenook	S	B	G	B	—	—	—	S	S	G	—	—	—
Charles Krug	—	—	—	—	—	—	—	—	G	—	—	—	—
Mayacamus	—	—	—	—	—	—	—	—	—	—	G	—	—
Souverain	—	—	—	—	—	—	—	—	—	—	S	—	—
Stony Hill	—	—	—	—	—	—	—	—	—	S	—	—	S

Sauvignon Blanc (Sweet and dry)

Beaulieu	—	—	S	G	G	B	—	—	—	—	—	—	—
Christian Bros.	—	—	—	—	—	—	—	B	G	G	G	G	G
Charles Krug	—	—	—	—	—	—	S	—	—	S	—	—	—
L. M. Martini	—	—	S	G	G	B	—	—	—	—	—	—	—

White Riesling (Johannisberg Riesling)

Beaulieu	—	G	S	—	G	G	G	—	—	—	—	—	—
Christian Bros.	—	—	—	—	—	—	—	—	—	G	B	—	B
Charles Krug	—	—	—	—	—	—	—	B	—	G	—	—	—
L. M. Martini	S	B	—	—	S	B	B	—	—	—	—	—	—
Souverain	—	—	—	—	—	—	—	—	S	—	—	—	S

These data give the broad picture of awards in these years. But there are some additional results that deserve to be part of the record.

— L. Pocai continued in the competition for several years. Basically a small bulk producer, he won a gold for his Gamay in 1954 and for his Claret in 1951.

— Sutter Home won awards for sweet vermouth and for bottle fermented champagne in the 1950s, a gold in 1953.

— Leon Brendel took a silver for his "Only One" Grignolino in 1956.

— Mayacamas won a gold for Pinot blanc in 1953.

— Hanns Kornell won a bronze for his sparkling burgundy in 1956. Two years later he moved from his Sonoma location to Larkmead. He won a gold for his brut in 1955.

— More often than not Charles Krug won a gold for Traminer in the 1950s.

— Christian Brothers won more gold medals for dessert/sherry wines than any other Napa winery. Inglenook was second.

— In 1959 Hanns Kornell's Brut Champagne from his Napa winery won the only State Fair gold in the bottle fermented category. The Christian Brothers won a gold for their bulk process Champagne.

G = Gold medal, S = Silver medal, B = Bronze medal, HM = Honorable Mention, * = Varietal wine, ( ) = Cases produced

PRODUCER	1948	1949	1950	SPECIAL LABEL
Beaulieu Vineyard				
Chablis	G (416)	G (375)	HM (215)	
*Chardonnay	—	S (1000)	G (705)	
*Pinot blanc	—	—	G (865)	
Riesling	G (450)	S (55)	—	
*White Riesling	G (440)	S (1000)	—	Beauclair
Dry Sauterne	—	S (80)	G (115)	
Medium Sauterne	—	G (1200)	G (115)	Chateau Beaulieu
Sweet Sauterne	G (425)	—	—	Chateau Beaulieu
*Sweet				
Sauvignon blanc	—	—	B (2300)	
Burgundy	S (4200)	—	S (875)	
*Pinot Noir	S (260)	G (485)	G (350)	Beaumont
*Cabernet Sauvignon	—	B (2500)	S (90)	Private Reserve
Rosé	S (1600)	S (3625)	S (1500)	Beaurose
Angelica	S (1000)	—	—	B.V.
*Muscat de Frontignan	B (3750)	HM (2500)	B (500)	B.V.
Beringer Brothers				
Rhine	HM (185)	—	—	Moselle
Riesling	—	—	HM (825)	
Medium Sauterne	—	—	HM (265)	
Sweet Sauterne	G (425)	—	—	Haut Sauterne
Claret	G (425)	—	—	
*Pinot noir	—	HM (150)	—	
Angelica	HM (4600)	—	—	
Port	HM (3000)	HM (26,800)	G (2500)	
Medium Sherry	—	B (5750)	—	
Christian Brothers (Mont La Salle)				
Chablis	—	B (1400)	—	
Rhine	—	HM (1500)	—	
Claret	B (1320)	—	—	
Tokay S (4200)		S (50)	—	
Angelica	HM (50)	—	—	
Port	S (50)	—	—	
Medium SherryHM (4200)		—	—	
Souverain (J. Leland Stewart)				
*Sylvaner	—	—	B (50)	
*Pinot noir	—	—	HM (175)	
*Zinfandel	S (200)	—	—	
*Rosé	—	G (50)	G (165)	
Inglenook				
*ChardonnayB (150)	G (165)	S (100)		
*Pinot blanc	S (1500)	G (1200)	S (2250)	
Riesling	HM (1600)	HM (1275)	B(685)	
*Sweet Sémillon	S (370)	—	—	

*Traminer	B (90)	S (400)	S (165)	
Burgundy	—	HM (2750)	—	Red Pinot (Pinot St. George)
*Gamay	—	G (1900)	G (1325)	
*Charbono	—	HM (1500)	S (435)	
*Pinot noir	S (64)	G (385)	S (260)	
*Cabernet Sauvignon	G (1630)	G (1000)	G (880)	
Rosé	G (475)	HM (1000)	HM (1875)	Navalle
Dry Sherry	B (715)	—	—	
Flor Sherry	S (190)	—	—	Palomino
Port	—	—S (1250)		

Charles Krug (C. Mondavi & Sons)

Chablis	B (1375)	B (100)	S (415)	
*Pinot blanc	—	—	B (110)	
Rhine	S (1550)	G (2500)	G (500)	
Riesling	S (1375)	G (315)	G (500)	
*Grey Riesling	—	—	S (500)	
*Traminer	G (1000)	G (85)	G (500)	
Dry Sauterne B (500	—	—		
Burgundy	—	B (2000)	S (700)	
Chianti	—	HM (1100)	B (580)	Napa Vista
*Gamay	—	G (265)	S (225)	
Claret	—	—	HM (275)	
*Cabernet Sauvignon	—	—	HM (275)	
*Zinfandel	—	HM (100)	—	
Red Table Wine	—	—	B (675)	
Rosé	S (2200)	HM (1200)	—	

Louis M. Martini

Chablis	HM (250)	—	—	
*Pinot blanc	S (1125)	—	—	
Riesling	—	—	HM (1150)	
*White Riesling	B (660)	—	S (1000)	
*Sylvaner	—	—	S (1000)	
*Dry Sauvignon blanc	—	S (475)	G (100)	
*Dry Sémillon	—	B (720)	—	
*Folle blanche	S (440)	—	S (315)	
White Table Wine	—	—	S (3700)	Napa White
*Pinot noir	B (1100)	—	—	
Claret	B (80)	G (150)	—	
*Cabernet Sauvignon	—	—	HM (85)	
Chianti	HM (125)	—	—	Monte Rosso
*Zinfandel	G (3000)	HM (4000)	S (7050)	
Red Table Wine	—	—	B (1075)	
Napa red				
Rosé	—	S (1500)	B (1300)	
Port	—	B (1750)	S (3000)	
Tawney Port	—	S (650)	G (1000)	
Muscatel	—	—	HM (1500)	

Mayacamas

White Table Wine	—	—	S (65)
Lokoya			
*Zinfandel	—	HM (75)	—

Napa Valley Brand Name/Premium Wineries, 1940 - 1975

The Old Timers

WINERY	BONDED WINERY #	PROPRIETOR	OPERATIONAL DATE	LOCATION	STORAGE CAPACITY
Beaulieu Vineyard	71/4456	de Latour Family	1900	Rutherford	1,500,000
Beringer Brothers	403/4263	Beringer Family	1876	St. Helena	800,000
Deer Park Winery	3595	John J. Ballantine	1890	Howell Mt.	50,000
Inglenook Vineyards	69	John Daniel, Jr. and Suzanne Daniel Hawkins	1879	Rutherford	350,000
Charles Krug Winery (1861)	3110	C. Mondavi & Sons	1943	St. Helena	1,400,000
Larkmead Winery	605∞	Felix and Elmer Salmina	1894	Larkmead	450,000
Louis M. Martini	3596	Louis M. Martini	1933	St. Helena	1,600,000
Christian Brothers	1721	La Salle Institute	1882	Mt. Veeder	1,500,000
	12	St. Helena			
Nichelini Vineyards	843	Wm. Anton Nichelini	1890	Chiles Valley	30,000

The Enthusiastic Entrepreneurs

WINERY	BONDED WINERY #	PROPRIETOR	OPERATIONAL DATE	LOCATION	STORAGE CAPACITY
Freemark Abbey (Lombarda-1894)	960+	Albert Ahern	1940	St. Helena	150,000
Souverain Cellars (Rossini-1885)	945†	J. Leland Stewart	1943	Howell Mt.	50,000
Mayacamus Vineyards (Fischer-1889)	4417	J. F. M. Taylor	1947	Mt. Veeder	5,602
Sutter Home Winery (Thomann-1874)	1007	The Trinchero Family	1947	St. Helena	45,000
Mt. Diamond Cellars (Schram-1862)	4329*	Douglas Pringle and Harry Slocum	1951	Mt. Diamond	200,000(?)
Stony Hill Vineyard	4461	Fred and Eleanor McCrea	1953	Spring Mt.	2,500
"Only One"	4454∆	Leon Brendel	1953	St. Helena	6,000
Hanns Kornell CellarsBWC (Larkmead-1894)	605∞	Hanns J. Kornell1958		Larkmead	30,000cases
Heitz Wine Cellars	4454∆	Joseph E. Heitz	1961	St. Helena	40,000
Schramsberg Vineyards (Schram-1862)	4329*	Jack L. Davies	1965	Mt. Diamond	5,000
F. J. Miller & Co.	BWC 4483	F. Justin Miller	1966	Rutherford	1,000
Robert Mondavi Winery	4511	Robert Mondavi	1966	Oakville	600,000
Freemark Abbey	4514+	Charles Carpy et al	1967	St. Helena	40,000
Martin's Spring Mt. (Conradi-1891)	4523	Arthur Martin	1967	Spring Mt.	8,000
Oakville Vineyards	3989	W. E. Van Loben Sels	1967	Oakville	600,000
Chappellet Winery	4537	Donn Chappellet	1967	Sage Canyon	40,000
Spring Mt. Vineyards	4521	Michael Robbins	1968	St. Helena	4,000
Mt. Sterling Vineyards	4533	Peter L. Newton	1968	Calistoga	155,000
Chateau Montelena (Tubbs-1882)	4525	Leland J. Paschich	1969	Calistoga	100,000

Lyncrest Vineyards	4601	Richard Lynn	1969	Spring Mt.	15,000
Cuvaison	4550	Thomas Cottrell	1970	Silverado (north)	47,000
Yverdon Vineyards	4561	Fred J. Aves	1970	Spring Mt.	50,000
(new)Souverain Cellars	4591	Ivan Schoch et al	1971	Silverado	220,000
Burgess Cellars	945†	Thomas E. Burgess	1972	Howell Mt.	37,000
Mt. Veeder Vineyards	4578	A. W. Baxter	1972	Mt. Veeder	2,000
Pope Valley Winery (Sam Haus-1909)	4586	James W. Devitt	1972	Pope Valley	17,000
Caymus Vineyards	4598	Charles Wagner	1972	Rutherford	8,000
Diamond Crk. Vineyards	4606	Al Brounstein	1972	Mt. Diamond	5,000
Stag's Leap Wine Cellars	4609	Warren Winiarski	1972	Stag's Leap	70,000
Carneros Crk. Vineyards	4645	Francis Mahoney	1972	Carneros	6,000
Franciscan Vineyards	4594	Raymond Hanson	1973	St. Helena	275,000
Silver Oak Cellars	4624	Justin Meyer	1973	Oakville	20,000
Chateau Chevalier (F. Chevalier-1887)	4627	C. G. Bissonette	1973	Spring Mt.	25,000
Trefethen Vineyards (Eshcol-1886)	4635	Eugene Trefethen	1973	Napa	80,000
Clos du Val	4638	John Goelet	1973	Stag's Leap	90,000
Stonegate Winery	4640	James C. Spaulding	1973	Calistoga	40,000
Joseph Phelps Vineyards	4647	Joseph E. Phelps	1973	Silverado	157,000
Domaine Chandon	4755	Moët-Hennessy	1973	Yountville	370,000
Stags' Leap Winery (Chase-1888)	4614	Carl Doumani	1974	Stag's Leap	7,500
Villa Mt. Eden Winery	4677	J. K. McWilliams	1974	Oakville	15,000
Ritchie Creek Vineyards	4681	R. P. Minor	1974	Spring Mt.	4,000
Conn Creek Vineyard	4769	William D. Collins	1974	Silverado	26,550
Raymond Winery	4672	Roy Raymond, Sr.	1974	Rutherford	60,000
Tulocay Winery	4696	William C. Cadman	1975	Napa	10,000
Napa Wine Cellars	4737	Charles Wood	1975	Oakville	20,000
V. Sattui Winery	4726	Daryl Sattui	1975	St. Helena	15,000

EXPLANATION OF TERMS

Winery: Historic cross reference in parenthesis. Pairs of symbols (e.g. +) draw attention to historic relationships.

Proprietor: In most cases the person who started the operation, or had the strongest hand in it.

Operational Date: Fairly arbitrary in some cases. Usually indicates when bond was granted or when first grapes were crushed.

Storage Capacity: Data from various sources, mostly industry directories, which often print whatever numbers are supplied by the winery. Capacity usually relates to cooperage, but may relate to space capacity, particularly for new winery buildings. Number given is meant to imply the approximate size of the operation in its early years. Some never divulge such data.

Location: Where winery is located, sometimes with a term that implies a viticultural district, or a proposed one. But Burgess and Deer Park are on Howell Mountain, yet not within that appellation.

Napa Valley Wineries Founded 1976 - 1988

BONDED WINERY #	WINERY	OPERATIONAL DATE	PROPRIETOR (1992)
Carneros			
4928	Mont St. John Cellars	1978	Louis Bartolucci
5067	Acacia Winery	1979	Chalone, Inc.
4263	Bouchaine Vineyards (Garetto Winery- 1899)	1981	Garret Copeland
5114	Saintsbury	1981	Richard A. Ward and David W. Graves
5336	Kent Rasmussen Winery	1986	Kent A. Rasmussen
5443	Domaine Carneros	1988	Claude Taittinger
Napa			
4901	William Hill Winery	1976	William H. Hill
5102	Monticello Cellars	1980	Jay Corley
5109	Costello Vineyards	1981	John Costello
5164	Whitford Cellars	1983	Duncan & Pat Haynes
5212	Chanter Winery	1984	D. & V. Johnson
5259	Napa Valley Port Cellars	1984	Shawn Denkler
5269	Farella-Park Vineyards	1985	Frank E. Farella
5280	Revere Winery	1985	John J.Kirlin
5351	Merlion Winery	1985	George Vierra
5364	Frisinger Cellars	1986	James E. Frisinger
5399	Domaine Montreaux	1986	Monticello Cellars
5485	Star Hill Wines	1986	Jacob & Sally Goldenberg
5401	Caporale Winery	1987	Mark L. Caporale
5423	White Rock Vineyards (J. A. Pettingill, 1870)	1988	Henri & Claire Vandendriessche
Mt. Veeder			
4934	Sky Vineyards	1979	Lore Olds & Linn Briner
5311	Hess Collection Winery (T. Gier-1903; Christian Bros.-1930)	1983	Donald Hess
4833	Chateau Potelle	1983	Jean Noel Fourmeaux (acquired nearby Vose Vineyards[BW 4833] in1989)
Stags Leap			
5012	Pine Ridge Winery	1978	Gary Andrus
4897	Shafer Vineyards	1979	John R. Shafer
4917	S. Anderson Vineyard	1979	Stanley B. Anderson
5064	Silverado Vineyards	1981	Lillian Disney
5175	Steltzner Vineyards	1983	Richard Steltzner
5400	Chimney Rock Winery	1987	Sheldon S. Wilson
5452	Robert Sinsky Vineyards	1988	Robert M. Sinsky
Capell Valley			
5420	Moss Creek Winery	1987	Harold Moskowite
Foss Valley			
5410	Atlas Peak Vineyards	1987	Allied-Lyons

Sage Canyon

4861	Long Vineyards	1978	Robert & Zelma Long
5079	Sage Canyon Winery	1981	Gordon & Eugenia Miller
5322	David Arthur Vineyards	1985	David Long

Conn Valley

4841	Buehler Vineyards	1978	John P. Buehler
5221	Amizetta Vineyards	1984	Spencer Clark
5406	Conn Valley Vineyards	1987	Gustaf A. Anderson

Chiles Valley

4818	Green & Red Vineyard	1977	Jay Heminway
5252	Rustridge Vineyard	1985	Grant C. Meyer

Pope Valley

5352	Aetna Springs Wine Ranch	1986	Paul & Sally Kimsey

Yountville

4933	Chateau Chevre	1979	G. P. Hazen & R. Mueller
5002	Lakespring Winery	1980	Frank Battat
5061	Newlan Vineyards	1981	Bruce M. Newlan
5105	Pina Cellars	1982	Davie Pina
5127	Cosentino Wine Co.	1982	Mitch Cosentino (here in 1987 from Modesto)
5077	Plam Vineyards	1984	Kenneth Plam
5264	Bernard Pradel Cellars	1984	Bernard Pradel
5397	Joanna Vineyard	1984	Richard & John Ryno
5428	Goosecross Cellars	1985	Ray & Patt Gorsuch
5458	Kate's Vineyard	1988	William & Sally Bryant

Oakville

4732	Cakebread Cellars	1977	Jack & Dolores Cakebread
4909	Evansen Vineyards	1979	Richard & Sharon Evansen
4915	Johnson Turnbull Vineyards	1979	Reverdy Johnson
5072	Far Niente Winery	1975 (1885)	H. Gilliland Nickel
4989	Vichon Winery	1980	Robert Mondavi Family
5000	Sequoia Grove Vineyards	1980	James Allen
5052	Robert Pepi Winery	1981	Robert A. Pepi
5178	Groth Vineyards	1982	Dennis & Judy Groth
5183	Saddleback Cellars	1983	Robert Call & Nils Venge

Rutherford

4805	Rutherford Vintners	1976	Bernard L. Skoda
4813	Grgich Hills Cellar	1977	Austin Hills & Miljenko Grgich
4856	Niebaum -Coppola Estate	1978	Francis Ford Coppola
4974	Whitehall Lane Winery	1979	Hideaki Ando, since 1988
5134	Louis Honig Cellars	1982	Louis "Bill" Honig
5230	Peju Province	1983	Anthony Peju
5292	Louis Corthay Winery	1985	Harold Hilker
5431	Domaine Napa	1985	Michel A Perret
4820	Swanson Vineyards & Winery (Cassayre-Forni in 1977)	1987	W. Clarke Swanson, Jr.
5391	Chateau Napa Beaucanon	1987	Jacques De Coninck

5427	St. Supéry Vineyards	1987	Robert Skalli

Silverado South

4782	Quail Ridge Cellars (Hedgeside-1885)	1978	Heublein
4939	Silverado Hill Cellars	1979	Minami Kyushu Co. (from Louis Mihaly in 1988)
4957	St. Andrew's Winery	1980	Bernard Portet
5220	Van der Heyden Vineyards	1984	André & Sandra Van der Heyden
5288	Altamura Winery	1985	Frank C. Altamura
5461	Signorello Vineyards	1985	Raymond E. Signorello

Silverado Central

4524	ZD Wines	1969	Norman & Rosa Lee de Leuze (moved here from Sonoma in 1978)
4591	Rutherford Hill Winery (formerly Souverain-Rutherford)	1976	Wm. P. Jaeger & Charles Carpy
4828	Round Hill Winery	1976	Ernie and Virginia Van Asperen & Charles A. Abela
4999	Girard Winery	1980	Stephen A. Girard, Sr.
5008	Napa Creek Winery	1980	Jack Schulze
5228	Forman Vineyards (Villa Remi, 1881)	1983	R. W. Forman
5431	Mumm Napa Valley (Domaine Mumm)	1984	Seagram Classics
5344	Dalla Valle Vineyards	1986	Gustav & Naoko Dalla Valle
5437	Mario Perelli-Minetti Winery	1988	Mario Perelli-Minetti
5454	Limur Winery	1988	Charles & Eleanor de Limur

Silverado North

4857	Duckhorn Vineyards	1976	Daniel Duckhorn
4990	Casa Nuestra	1980	Eugene Kirkham
5086	Chateau Boswell	1982	R. T. Boswell
5113	Rombauer Vineyards	1982	Joan & Koerner Rombauer

St. Helena

4745	St. Clement Vineyards (Spring Mt. Vineyards before 1976)	1976	Sapporo, USA since 1987
957	Markham Winery (St. Helena Co-op; J. Laurent, 1877)	1978	Sanraku, Inc. since 1987
4853	Flora Springs Wine Co. (Rennie Bros., 1884)	1979	J. W. Komes
4944	Prager Winery & Port Works	1979	James L. Prager
5113	Calafia Cellars	1979	Randle Johnson
5038	Folie à Deux Winery	1981	Larry & Evie Dizmang
5148	Spottswoode Winery	1982	Mary Weber Novak
4072	Merryvale Vineyards (also Sunny St. Helena)	1983	H. Wm. Harlan et al
5191	Jaeger Family Wine Co.	1984	William P. Jaeger
5204	Macauley Vineyard	1984	The Watson Family
5210	Villa Helena	1984	Donald W. McGrath
5224	Shadow Brook Winery	1984	Emil Hoffman

5357	Milat Vineyards	1986	The Milat Family
5404	Grace Family Vineyards	1987	Richard Grace Family
5434	Sullivan Vineyards	1987	James O. Sullivan
5438	El Molino Winery (W. W. Lyman, 1871)	1988	Reginald & Marie Oliver

Larkmead

4930	Charles F. Shaw Vineyards	1978	Charles F. Shaw, Jr.
4891	Tudal Winery	1979	Arnold & Alma Tudal
5075	Frog's Leap Winery	1981	Larry Turley & John Williams

Spring Mountain

4747	Robert Keenan Winery (P. Conradi, 1891)	1977	Ann & Robert Keenan
4825	Smith-Madrone Vineyards	1977	Stuart Smith
4918	Newton Vineyard	1979	Peter & Su Hua Newton
5132	Marston Vineyards (formerly Lyncrest)	1982	Michael & Alexandra Marston
5135	Cain Cellars	1982	Jim & Nancy Meadlock
5172	La Vielle Montagne	1983	John & Shawn Guilliams
5328	Domaine Karakesh also Domaine Charbay)	1983	Miles Karakasevic
5271	Streblow Vineyards	1985	Jack & Patricia Streblow
5290	Philip Togni Vineyard	1985	Birgitta & Philip Togni

Mt. Diamond

| 5279 | Richard L . Graeser Winery | 1985 | Richard L. Graeser |

Howell Mountain

4931	Deer Park Winery (the original Sutter Home [1891] and J. J. Ballantine [1922])	1979	David & Kinta Clark
5094	La Jota Vineyard Co. (F. Hess-1898)	1978	William & Joan Smith
5124	Dunn Vineyards	1982	Randall & Lori Dunn
5255	Summit Lake Vineyards	1985	Robert & Susan Brakesman
5286	Chateau Woltner	1985	Francis & Françoise Dewavrin Woltner
5389	Lamborn Family Vineyards	1987	Robert Lamborn

Calistoga

4845	Robert Pecota Winery	1978	Robert Pecota
4946	Storybook Mountain Vineyards (J. Grimm Winery-1888)	1979	J. Bernard Seps
5181	San Pierro Vara Vineyard	1983	Albert & Norma Giordano
5206	Vincent Arroyo Winery	1984	Vincent Arroyo
5343	Clos Pegase	1986	Jan I. Shrem

These data provide a comparison between the production of the 1990 and 1980 vintages, by variety. Price comparisons with Sonoma County are also given for these two vintages.

VARIETY	TONS PRODUCED		% OF NAPA CROP		1990 PRICE		1980 PRICE	
White	**1990**	**1980**	**1990**	**1980**	NAPA	SONOMA	NAPA	SONOMA
Chardonnay	37,822	9,060	33.1%	11.3%	$1507	$1284	$1005	$835
Sauvignon blanc	10,270	3,204	9.0%	4.0%	794	755	730	737
Chenin blanc	6,641	8,020	5.8%	10.0%	508	412	534	527
White Riesling	1,485	5,115	1.3%	6.4%	750	543	647	601
Sémillon	1,490	441	1.3%	.6%	819	667	472	403

These varieties as a % of the Napa white wine grape crop = 97.0% in 1990.

Red								
Bordeaux Varieties								
Cabernet Sauvignon	21,658	16,817	18.9%	21.0%	$1606	$1275	$558	$416
Merlot	6,143	2,538	5.4%	3.2%	1554	1284	536	405
Cabernet franc	1,943	180	1.7%	.2%	1466	1305	897	—
Malbec	66	15	—	—	1543	1385	—	—
Petite Verdot	51	—	—	—	1580	1378	—	—
Total	29,861	19,550	26.1%	24.4%				
Others								
Pinot noir	10,794	7,550	9.4%	9.4%	$1012	$810	$490	$360
Zinfandel	9,145	6,706	8.0%	8.4%	683	727	486	452
Napa Gamay	1,598	5,619	1.4%	7.0%	601	539	323	—
Petite Sirah	1,228	2,926	1.1%	3.7%	824	708	411	401

These varieties as a % of the Napa red wine crop in 1990 = 96.1%

Other varieties in the 1990 Napa vintage (tons): **White:** Pinot blanc=588, Gewürztraminer=458, Grey Riesling=218, Muscat blanc=199, French Colombard=178, Pinot gris=32, Sylvaner=25, Viognier=16; **Red:** Gamay Beaujolais=952, Meunier=629, Charbono=123, Carignane=95, Grenache=83, Syrah=51, Sangiovese=51, Grignolino=28, Mourvèdre=11

Napa Valley Wine Grape Acreage — 1856 - 1990

The following data are derived from official statistics, published reports and educated guesses. The figures are for total acreage, bearing and non-bearing, for selected years.

WINE REVOLUTION	POST REPEAL	"INNOCENT" YEARS	PIONEER DAYS
1990=32,715	1963=10,025	1917=11,500	1879=3,635
1988=31,781	1958=10,116	1914=13,500	1877=3,360
1986=30,843	1955=10,601	1910=16,110	1874=2,900
1983=28,379	1950=11,850	1906=9,300	1871=2,200
1980=25,215	1945=12,170	1903=5,900	1868=1,000
1977=24,167	1940=12,466		1863= 700
1974=23,350	1935=11,351		1860= 400
1972=17,505	1933=11,500	PHYLLOXERA	1856= 120
1970=14,597		1900=4,730	
1968=13,836	PROHIBITION	1896=11,000	
1966=11,738	1930=11,428	1892=16,651	
	1927=10,890		
	1923=12,200	WINE BOOM	
	1920=9,420	1890=20,763	
		1888=16,500	
		1885=14,000	
		1883=12,278	
		1881=11,733	

Napa Valley Wine Grape Production, 1856 - 1990

TONS PRODUCED

WINE REVOLUTION	POST REPEAL	"INNOCENT" YEARS	PIONEER DAYS
1990=114,304	1963=32,382	1917=24,000	1879= 11,600
1988=99,777	1958=39,959	1914=21,000	1877=13,000
1986=113,220	1955=32,743	1910=20,300	1874=4,800
1983=89,084	1950=22,742	1906=14,200	1871=2,600
1980=80,112	1945=39,328	1903=15,100	1868=1,100
1977=57,630	1940=32,483		1863=1,000
1974=55,318	1935=33,000	PHYLLOXERA	1860= 800
1972=36,653	1933=18,000	1900= 7,300	1856= 400
1970=24,202		1896= 6,700	
1968=38,276	PROHIBITION	1892=27,100	
1966=37,286	1930=19,000		
	1927=22,500	WINE BOOM	
	1923=25,250	1890=30,000	
	1920=18,000	1888=51,000	
	1885=18,200		
	1883=20,100		
	1881=14,000		

Napa Valley Grapes and Prunes

Income for Selected Years: 1922-1990

YEAR	GRAPES	PRUNES
1922	$1,750,000	$1,250,000
1925	1,260,000	836,000
1929	812,000	477,000
1933	480,000	1,089,000
1938	478,250	847,000
1942	965,000	1,646,000
1945	2,600,000	3,622,000
1950	2,075,685	2,486,300
1955	1,994,580	1,349,000
1960	2,211,000	2,264,000
1965	4,807,560	1,451,688
1969	8,055,000	1,012,000
1972	19,467,000	327,000
1976	13,985,000	96,000
1980	49,863,000	37,200
1985	78,332,000	—
1990	144,484,000	—

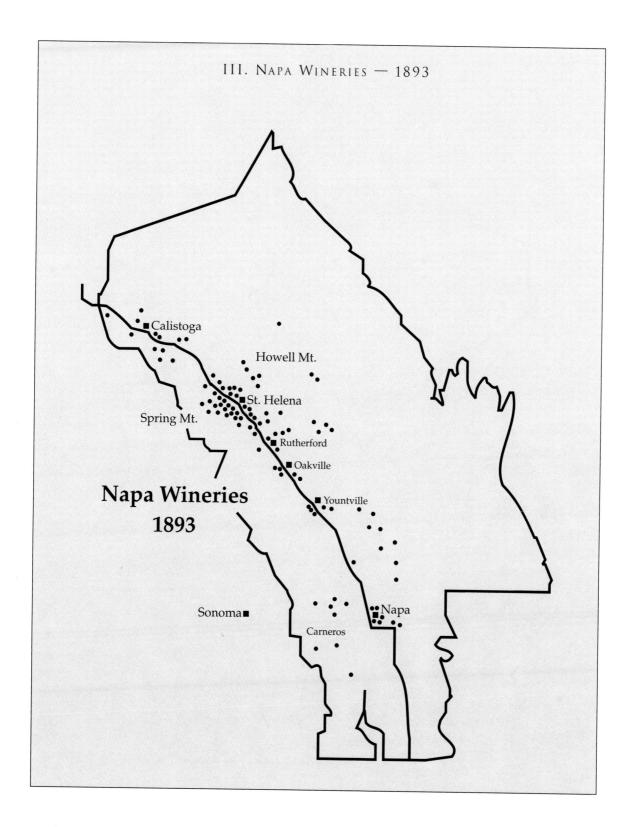

Calistoga

Howell Mt.

St. Helena

Spring Mt.

Rutherford

Oakville

**Napa Wineries
1893**

Yountville

Sonoma■

Napa

Carneros

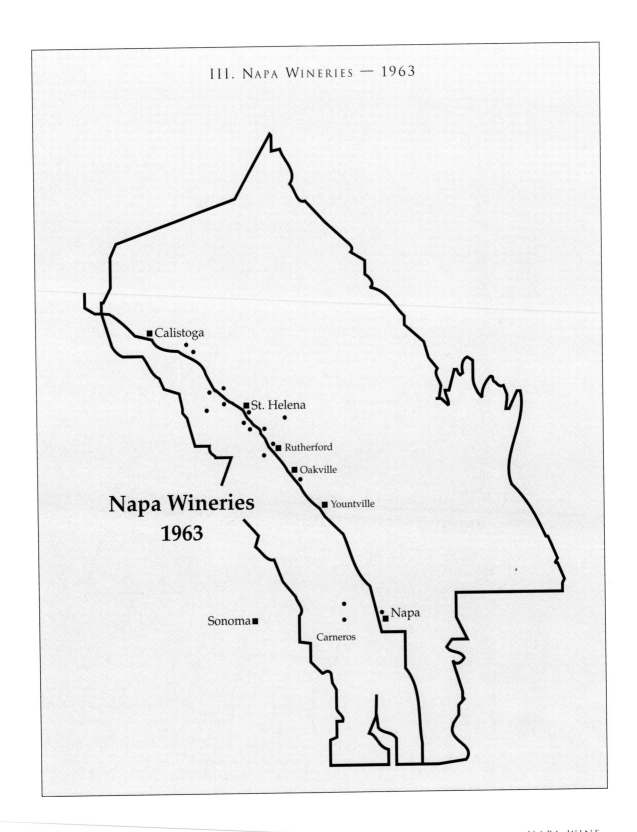

■ Calistoga

St. Helena■

Rutherford■

Oakville■

Yountville■

**Napa Wineries
1963**

Sonoma■

■ Napa

Carneros

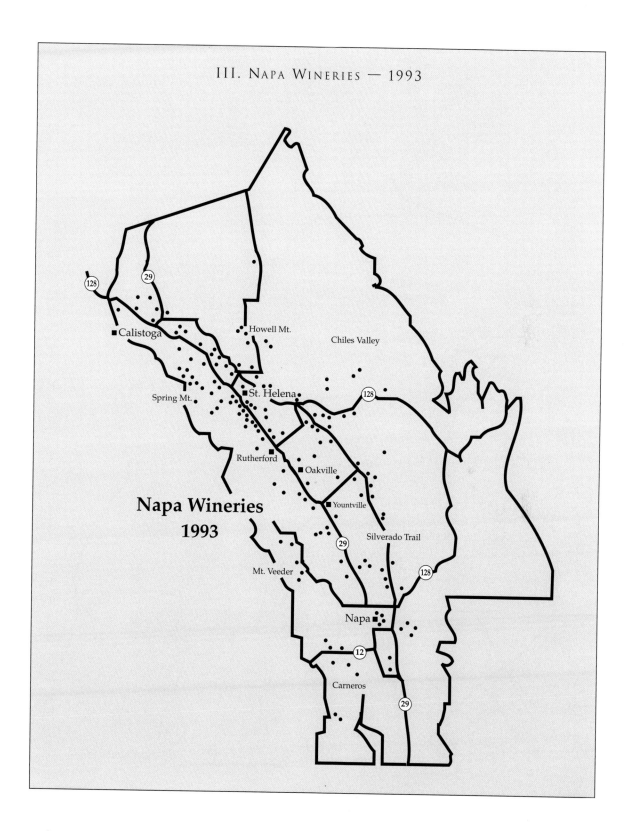

Calistoga

Howell Mt.

Chiles Valley

Spring Mt.

St. Helena

Rutherford

Oakville

**Napa Wineries
1993**

Yountville

Silverado Trail

Mt. Veeder

Napa

Carneros

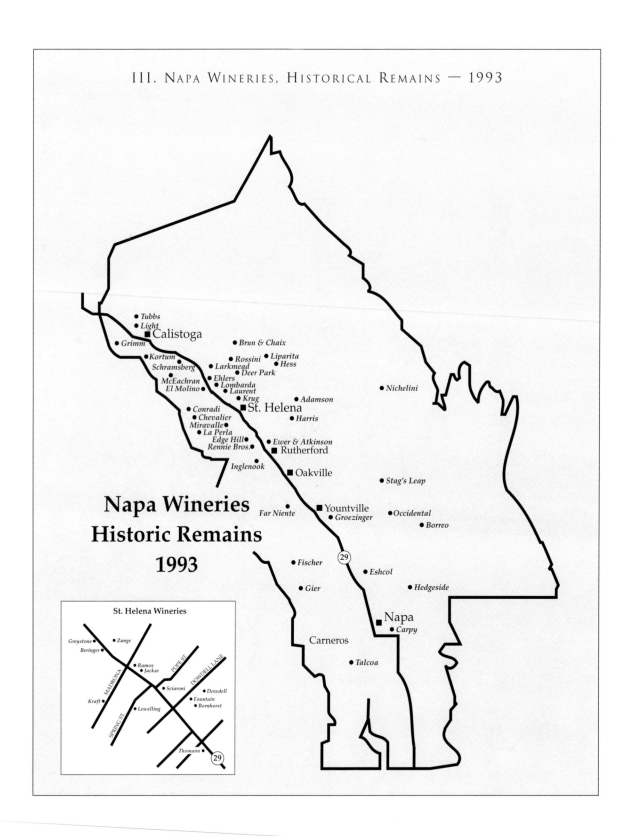

Napa Wineries
Historic Remains
1993

De Gustibus

One of the chief goals of this study has been to trace the development of the quality image of Napa Valley wines. I have examined this reputation by focusing on the opinions of persons considered to be experts by their peers in the wine industry. I have also discussed price as another means of measuring this perception.

To a certain extent a wine region's or a single producer's history of high quality can perpetuate that reputation, whatever the present quality of the product. Thus, it is difficult to get around the fact that people making quality judgments are usually looking at the label of the wine they are evaluating. I have partly been able to avoid this situation by employing statistics derived from tastings held at the San Francisco Vintners Club.Since 1973 the Club has held Thursday afternoon tastings of wines from California and the rest of the world. These tastings are always conducted blind, but, of course, the results are just as subjective as those of any other tasting, except for the fact that the tasters here don't know what they are tasting until after they have turned in their rankings. The founders of the Club nicely represent the North Coast premium wine dichotomy of Napa/Sonoma which figures heavily in my analysis. Jerome C. Draper, Jr. owns the historic La Perla Vineyard on Spring Mountain; W. Reed Foster is one of the founding owners of Sonoma's Ravenswood Winery.

When I began working with the statistics from these tastings I had no idea where the investigation would lead me. I hoped that it would have some meaningful relationship to the other quantifiable evaluations I was planning to examine. I have been happily surprised by the consistency of the final results.

Since Sonoma's Arpad Haraszthy declared in the 1870s that Napa was claret country, the production of dry red table wine somewhat in the style of Bordeaux has been an essential part of the Valley's claim to fame. Zinfandel was the grape that launched this reputation in the 1880s, but Cabernet Sauvignon and other red Bordeaux varieties had given a world class status to Napa "Medocs" by 1900. Just so has Cabernet led Napa's post-Repeal surge to world class status. I have already traced the elements of that surge, but can the perception be quantified, beyond the "Judgment of Paris"?

One fact that leaps out of the numbers in this analysis is that Sonoma County is the only California competitor to Napa in terms of the number of high quality Cabernet producers. and the amount of Cabernet produced. The two counties produced 36,791 tons of Cabernet in 1990, while the rest of the coastal counties from Mendocino to Ventura totaled but 26,906 tons. Napa harvested 6,525 more Cabernet tons than Sonoma, a total that would produce about a million gallons of wine. Together they dominated the production of such red Bordeaux varieties as Merlot and Cabernet franc in an even more pronounced way.

The Vintners Club usually holds six Cabernet tastings each year, twelve wines each, with the top twelve meeting in the Tasteoff. From 1977 to 1988 the Club evaluated about 720 Cabs, of which 66% were produced from Napa grapes. About 20% were Sonoma wines. At the eleven tasteoffs,80% of the wines making the cutoff were from Napa. In the preliminary tastings Napa wines had an average place in twelve of 5.41. (If pure chance had determined the outcome, the expected score would have been 6.50.) Sonoma wines averaged 6.72. This is a significant difference in quality perception, although certainly not overwhelming.(I have been a member of the Club since 1975 and sat at most of these tastings. My averages were Napa 5.91 and Sonoma 6.79.)

Now let us look at some evaluations by wine writers and wine publications to see whether this objectively calculated perception carries through in the published media.

Wine Spectator has made systematic and comprehensive evaluations of California wines since 1988. The results derive from blind tastings and are expressed on a 100 point scale, which is becoming increasingly popular, since the numbers remind us of school days when everyone understood the difference between an 87 (not quite a B+) and a 93 (no minus on that A).

From 1988 to 1990 the magazine evaluated almost 400 Napa Cabernets and almost 200 from Sonoma. Each year the average Napa wine received a slightly higher average rating than that of Sonoma. For the three years combined the average Napa score was 87.68, Sonoma 84.85. If we expand our analysis of the Wine Spectator evaluations, to include vintages since 1975, there is no significant change in averages (Napa= 87.78, Sonoma=84.23) Close, like the Vintners Club results, but a clear Napa win.(I have used only one wine per producer per vintage. When there was more than one bottling I used the wine with the higher score.)

Robert Parker and Claude Kolm publish respected newsletters that regularly evaluate California wines. Both taste their wines blind, unless otherwise noted, and both employ the 100 point rating scale. From 1986 to 1988 Parker gave Napa Cabernets a close nod, 84.70-83.39. Kolm leaned toward Napa a bit more, 84.25-82.92.

The publishers of *Connoisseur's Guide to California Wine* have been rating wine much longer than the other publications. But they do not use the 100 point scale. They depend on written evaluations, but single out superior wines by giving them one, two, or three stars for: fine examples, highly distinctive examples, and exceptional examples. I sat on the publication's red wine panels for ten years and can attest to the blindness of their tastings. For the California vintages 1977-1986 they gave stars to sixty Napa and twenty-six Sonoma producers of Cabernet Sauvignon. The average number of stars granted Napa wines was 1.46, to Sonoma wines 1.27. Close again, but Napa clearly on top.

James Laube is an editor of *Wine Spectator* and in 1989 brought out his 450-page evaluation of California's post-Repeal Cabernets. Seventy-four of the ninety-five "great" producers listed are from Napa, seventeen from Sonoma, and four from the Central Coast region. For vintages 1980-1986 his average scores for the best wine evaluated by producer from each vintage were:Napa=87.73,Sonoma=86.08. For the great vintages 1984, 1985, and 1986 the averages were: Napa=90.50,Sonoma=89.47. Close again, but Napa wins again. (It might be thought that Laube's evaluations would mirror those of *Wine Spectator*. Such is not always the case. For example, he rates the 1985 Phelps-Eisele a 94, while the publication gives it an 81. We all remember the difference between a B- and a straight A.)

I find these evaluations puzzling, not for the closeness but for the consistency. It is true that many parts of Sonoma's winegrowing areas have trouble ripening Cabernet, but there is not much Cab planted in these areas. There is also a lot more Napa Cabernet planted on soil derived from volcanic sources than in Sonoma. We wait in vain for any scientific explanation for such a relationship.

We must ask, of course, whether grape prices confirm these data. The answer is a definite YES. In 1990 Napa Cabernet Sauvignon sold for an average of 26% more than that from Sonoma.

Now let us look at Chardonnay, the variety usually paired in winelovers' minds with Cabernet Sauvignon. By reversing my data path, but following the same line of logic, it would seem that I could look at Chardonnay prices in 1990 and guess correctly the perceived quality comparison between Napa and Sonoma wines in this category. Napa Chardonnay grapes sold for an average 17.4% higher than those from Sonoma, 28.7% higher than those of the Central Coast region.

Does the perception of quality support this price relationship? Since 1977 the Vintners Club evaluated well over 900 Chardonnays, about 750 of them from Napa, Sonoma and the Central Coast. In these blind tastings Napa wines averaged 5.86, Sonoma 5.73 and Central Coast 5.57. All three areas had very good scores, indicating that rarely did a wine from any other region place high. The scores are very close, but Napa placed third.

The *Wine Spectator*'s evaluations yield almost identical results for ratings published between 1988 and spring 1991. Napa scored 83.66, Sonoma 83.79, and Central Coast 84.08. Laube's evaluations of "great" Chardonnays appear in a 370-page volume published in 1990. Again, Napa had the lion's share of producers, a whopping 64%. His average scores for Vintages 1984-1988 closely follow the pattern already indicated for Chardonnay. Sonoma averaged 88.87, Central Coast 88.50 and Napa 87.76. Very close, but Napa again third.

Parker and Kolm follow the same pattern. From 1986-1988 Parker gave Napa Chardonnays 83.54, Sonoma 85.54, and Central Coast 85.58. For 1987-1988 Kolm's scores are close but the pattern is the same: Napa 83.94, Sonoma 84.28, Central Coast 84.19.

I thought that the *Connoisseur's Guide's* awards of stars would show a deviation from this pattern, but I was wrong. For California vintages 1985-1988 the Central Coast Chardonnays singled out for special recognition had the highest average number of stars, 1.39. Then came Sonoma with 1.33 and Napa with 1.25. Again very close, but again Napa in third place.

The data for Cabernets partially clarify the Napa image as the home of the Western Hemisphere's greatest wines from red Bordeaux varieties. But the numbers are too close to those of other regions to explain the overwhelming nature of this perception. I believe the power of this image derives from the historical status given such wines as BV's Private Reserve, Inglenook's Cask wines, and Heitz's Martha's Vineyard. The recent introduction of several highly priced, internationally publicized bottlings, such as Opus One, Dominus and Rubicon have reinforced this reputation. The superstructure of this powerful image was constructed in the last quarter century by the consistently world-class performance by producers such as Caymus, Dunn, Diamond Creek, Phelps, Robert Mondavi, Stag's Leap and Chateau Montelena. (It is difficult to stop adding to this illustrative and illustrious list, when so many other Napa producers who started work in the sixties and seventies so clearly deserve mention.)

The Chardonnay data are more difficult to interpret. It appears that Napa's image boosts its grape prices overall, even when there is no clearly perceived or measurable quality differential in Napa's favor. We have seen that the quality perception scales tilt slightly in favor of Sonoma and the Central Coast for this varietal, even though Napa Chardonnay grape prices are considerably higher than those of the other regions.

It would be interesting and instructive to examine the ratings for other varietal wines, but I think we learn enough from the numbers for Cabernet and Chardonnay. There is, however, one other variety that no California wine lover can overlook in this comparative analysis. We have to look at Zinfandel, the grape that made Napa "claret country" between 1880 and 1895.

For all major grape varieties Napa prices in 1990 exceeded those of Sonoma by an overall 27%. Napa's red wine grapes were 35.4% more costly than those of Sonoma. But hidden in these statistics is a tantalizing pair of numbers. They show that for their Zinfandel grapes Sonoma growers received $44.00 per ton more than their fellows to the east. Napa received top dollar for all other important varieties.

Sonoma has twice as many Zinfandel vines as Napa and far more producers. This helps explain why in the last three years *Wine Spectator* has evaluated half again as many Sonoma as Napa Zins. It doesn't explain the slightly better *Spectator* scores in favor of Sonoma, 83.24 to 82.93.

For the longer term Sonoma Zinfandels have run up a very impressive record at the Vintners Club, with an average place of 5.14 to Napa's 6.04. The Sierra Foothills are a close third at 6.13. But in the annual Zinfandel Tasteoffs Sonoma Zinfandels have clearly triumphed, doubling the number of Napa wines making the finals, with a place differential of 5.80 to 6.88. (I drive a car with a ZINFDL license plate and have a cellar full of Zin dating back to the 1960s. After I finished crunching these numbers I added up the bottle totals by region and found that I had just a few more Napa Zins than Sonoma or Sierra Foothills, but it was close.)

I should be happy to be able to draw weighty conclusions from these data. But I wouldn't think of it. I hope that their significance and my methodology provoke many arguments. I delight in the fact that wine, like music, has a powerful intellectual appeal, that heightens the sensual nature of both these pleasures.

Sources

The chapter notes actually serve as a bibliography for this study. What follows is a highly selective list of works and materials which deal directly with Napa Valley and its wine history or with the broader picture of California wine history.

Some materials are rarely seen in standard collections. A good source is indicated, using the following abbreviations.

BnL= Bancroft Library, University of California, Berkeley
UCB= Main Library, University of California, Berkeley
UCB-BSc= Bio-Science Library, U.C. Berkeley
NVWL= Napa Valley Wine Library, St. Helena
NPL= Napa Public Library
UCD= Shields Library, U.C. Davis
SF= San Francisco Public Library

Selected Newspapers And Periodicals

Alta California (Alta) San Francisco
American Journal of Enology and Viticulture, U.C. Davis
American Wine and Liquor Journal
American Wine Journal, Los Angeles. Also Wine Review
American Wine Merchant
American Wine Press and Mineral Spirits Review (AWP), New York (UCB-BSc)
American Wine Society Journal (UCD)
Bonfort's Wine and Spirit Circular , New York (UCB-BSc)
Bottles and Bins (author)
California Agriculture, University of California
California Farmer and Journal of Useful Sciences (Farmer) San Francisco (UCB-BSc)
California Grape Grower, Fresno
California Historical Society Quarterly (CHSQ), San Francisco. Also California History, since 1978.
California Visitors Review (CVR), Windsor (CA)
California Winelands, Lakeport (CA)
Connoisseur's Guide to California Wine, Alameda (CA)
Gourmet, New York
Hilgardia, University of California
Livermore Herald
Los Angeles Times (LAT)
Napa County Reporter (Reporter)
Napa Register (Register)
New West, Los Angeles. Also California Magazine.
New York Times (NYT)
Pacific Wine and Spirit Review (PWSR), San Francisco. (SF) Several titles.
Practical Winery, San Rafael (CA). Title varies.
St. Helena Star (SHS) (NVWL)
San Francisco Bulletin
San Francisco Call
San Francisco Chronicle (SFC)
San Francisco Examiner (SFEx)

San Francisco News
San Francisco Post
San Jose Herald
San Jose Mercury (SJM)
San Jose News
San Jose Times
Sonoma Democrat
Sunset, Menlo Park (CA)
Vinifera Wine Growers Journal (VWGJ), Virginia
Vintage, New York
Wine Advocate, Maryland
Wine Country, Benecia (CA)
Wine Spectator (WS), San Diego and San Francisco
Wine West, Geyserville (CA). Also Redwood Rancher.
Wine World, Van Nuys (CA)
Wines & Vines (WV), San Francisco. Several titles. (UCB-BSc)

Other Printed Sources

Adams, Leon D. *Commonsense Book of Wine*. New York, 1958. Several later editions.
Adams, Leon D. *The Wines of America*. Boston, 1973; New York, 1979, 1985 and 1990.
 The earlier editions tend to have more detailed historical information.
The American Winery Directory. Published by Wine Review, 1935.
Amerine, Maynard A. "Hilgard and California Viticulture." *Hilgardia*, 33:1 (July 1962) 1-23.
Amerine, Maynard A. "An Introduction to the Pre-Repeal History of Grapes and Wines in
 California." *Agricultural History*, 49:2 (April 1969) 259-268.
Amerine, Maynard A., et al. *The Technology of Winemaking*. Westport (CT) 1967.
Amerine, Maynard A. and Vernon L. Singleton. *Wine, an Introduction for Americans*.
 Berkeley, 1965.
Amerine, Maynard A. and A. J. Winkler. *California Wine Grapes. . . . California Agricultural
 Experiment Station Bulletin 794*, 1963.
Amerine, Maynard A. "Composition and Quality of Musts and Wines of California Grapes."
 Hilgardia, 15:6 (February 1944) 493-673.
Archibald, Robert. *The Economic Aspects of the California Missions*. Washington DC, 1978.
Archuleta, Kay. *The Brannan Saga*. San Jose, 1977.
Asher, Gerald. "Napa Valley Cabernet Sauvignon," *Gourmet* (June 1993): 38.
Bailey, Paul. *Sam Brannan and the California Mormons*. Los Angeles, 1959.
Balzer, Robert Lawrence. *California's Best Wines*. Los Angeles, 1948.
Balzer, Robert Lawrence. *The Pleasures of Wine*. Indianapolis, 1964.
Bancroft, Hubert Howe. *History of California*. 7 vols. San Francisco, 1886-1890.
Bancroft Library, University of California. "Bancroft Scraps." 113 volumes of clippings, mostly
 from California newspapers. Vols. 2 (Napa) and 18-19 (Agriculture) are particularly rich in
 articles on Napa winegrowing, 1865-1880.
Bazin, Jean-Francois. *Le Vin de California*. Dijon, 1984. A lively history and analysis by frequent
 Burgundian visitor to California.
Benson, Robert W. *Great Winemakers of California*. Santa Barbara, 1977.
Benson, Robert W. "Regulation of American Wine Labeling; In Vino Veritas?" *University of
 California, Davis, Law Review*.. 11:2 (November 1978) 115-199. (UCD)
Berger, Dan and Richard Paul Hinkle. *Beyond the Grapes; An Inside Look at Napa Valley*.
 Wilmington, 1991.
Blout, Jessie Schilling. "A Brief Economic History of the California Wine Growing Industry."
 Wine Institute mimeo, 1943. (NVWL)
Bowman, Jacob N. "The Vineyards in Provincial California." *Wine Review* (April-July 1943).
Bray, James Morgan. "The Impact of Prohibition on Napa Viticulture, 1919-1933." Unpublished
 research paper, Department of Librarianship, California State University, San Jose, 1974. (NVWL)
Bucknall, Mary E. Early Days. Privately printed memories from the 1850s by George Yount's
 granddaughter. (BnL)

California. *Annual Report of the Board of State Viticultural Commissioners.* Sacramento, 1881-1894.

California, Board of State Viticultural Commissioners. *Annual Report of the Chief Viticultural Officer.* Sacramento, 1882-1884.

California, Board of State Viticultural Commissioners. *Directory of the Grape Growers, Wine Makers and Distillers of California.* Sacramento, 1891.

California, Board of State Viticultural Commissioners. *The Vineyards of Napa County.* Sacramento, 1893.

California. *Journals of the Senate and Assembly.* Sacramento, 1856-1913.

California. *Transactions of the California State Agricultural Society.* Sacramento, 1859-1911.

California, University of California Experiment Station. *Report of the Viticultural Work. . .* (1883-1895). Sacramento, 1886-1896. Hilgard's work.

California Agricultural Statistics Service. *California Grape Acreage.* Sacramento, 1961-1991.

California Agricultural Statistics Service. *Final Grape Crush Report.* Sacramento, 1954-1991.

California Wine History. The California Wine Industry Series of oral histories, 1969-1990, is an ongoing project conducted by the Bancroft Library. Interviews are personally conducted by Ruth Teiser. These are transcribed and illustrated by the Library. Transcripts of particular interest for the study of Napa Valley wine history include:

    Leon D. Adams. 1972 and 1990.
    Maynard A Amerine. 1969 and 1971 (University of California)
    William V. Cruess. 1966 (University of California)
    Jack and Jamie Davies. 1990 (Schramsberg)
    Alfred Fromm. 1984 (Christian Brothers)
    Joseph E. Heitz. 1986
    Legh F. Knowles. 1990 (Beaulieu Vineyards)
    Louis M. Martini. 1967 and 1973
    Louis P. Martini. 1983
    Eleanor McCrea. 1990 (Stony Hill)
    Otto E. Meyer. 1971 (Christian Brothers)
    Peter E. Mondavi. 1990 (Charles Krug)
    Robert Mondavi. 1984
    E. Michael Moon. 1990 (Beringer)
    Myron S. Nightingale. 1988 (Beringer)
    André Tchelistcheff. 1979 and 1983
    Brother Timothy. 1971 and 1973 (Christian Brothers)
    Albert J. Winkler. 1970 and 1972 (University of California)

Camp, Charles L., ed. "Chronicles of George C. Yount." *CHSQ* (April 1923) 3-67.

Camp, Charles L. *George C. Yount and His Chronicles of the West.* Denver, 1966.

Carosso, Vincent. *The California Wine Industry, 1830-1895.* Berkeley, 1951.

Conaway, James. *Napa.* Boston, 1990. A controversial, close-up view of Napa wine celebrities and issues since World War II. Very useful for environmental issues.

Crane, George Belden. *A Life History.* San Jose, 1886. (NVWL)

Cruess, William V. "What Shall We Do With Our Wine Grapes?" *Pacific Rural Press* (March 13, 1920) 419. (UCB)

Dana, Richard Henry, Jr. *Two Years Before the Mast.* Los Angeles, 1964. This Ward Ritchie edition includes material from Dana's 1859-1860 notes with specific references to the Napa Valley and George Yount.

Darlington, David. *Angels' Visits: an Inquiry into the Mystery of Zinfandel.* New York, 1991. A light-hearted analysis with some good history.

Davidson, W. M. and R. L. Nougaret. "The Grape Phylloxera in California." USDA Bulletin No. 903. April 22, 1921.

de la Peña, Donald Joseph. "Preservation of Vineyards and Wineries in the San Francisco Bay Area." Unpublished master's thesis in city planning. U.C. Berkeley, 1962.

Department of Treasury (BATF). *U.S. Viticultural Areas.* October, 1983. Updated June 1, 1986.

Directory of Wineries, in *Wines & Vines,* Buyers Guide, 1952-1991. Various titles. Essential statistical and personnel data for all U.S. wineries.

Engelhardt, Zephyrin. *Missions and Missionaries of California*. 4 vols. San Francisco,1908-1915.

Faust, Albert B. *The German Element in the United States*. Boston, 1909.

Ford, Gene. *The Benefits of Moderate Drinking*. San Francisco, 1988. Contains an awesome bibliography on neo-temperance issues.

Gabler, James M. *Wine into Words*. Baltimore, 1985. An invaluable bibliography of works on and grapes. Particularly good for California materials.

Galet, Pierre. *A Practical Ampelography*. Ithaca, 1978. A good translation by Lucie Morton with excellent reference to California varieties, based on Galet's personal experience there.

Gates, Paul W. *California Ranchos and Farms, 1846-1862*. Madison, 1967.

Gould, Francis L. *My Life with Wine*. St. Helena, 1972.

Gregory, Thomas Jefferson. *History of Solano and Napa Counties*. Los Angeles, 1911. A very useful chapter on "Viticulture of Napa County."

Haraszthy, Arpad. "Wine-Making in California." *Overland Monthly*. 7:489-497; 8:34-41, 105-109, 393-398 (1871-1872). Published together in 1978 by the Book Club of California. The introduction by Ruth Teiser and Catherine Harroun provides important biographical information on this controversial industry leader.

Hardy, Thomas. *Notes on the Vineyards in America and Europe*. Adelaide (Australia) 1885. Portions on California winegrowing were reprinted in Wines & Vines, September, 1966 to September 1968.

Haynes, Irene. *Ghost Wineries of Napa Valley*. San Francisco, 1980. A tantalizing photo study.

Heintz, William F. *Wine Country; A History of Napa Valley, 1838-1920*. Santa Barbara, 1990.

Hilgard, Eugene. *Report of Experiments of Fermenting Red Wines. . .1886-7*. Sacramento,1888.

Hoch, Irving and Nicholas Tryphonopoulas. *A Study of the Economy of Napa County, California*. Giannini Foundation Research Report No. 303, August, 1969.(NVWL)

Howie, Mildred, ed. *The Long Memory*. Geyserville (CA) 1983. Recollections of California wine men, ca. 1920-1950.

Husmann, George. *American Grape Growing and Wine Making*. New York, numerous editions, 1880-1919.

Husmann, George. *Grape Culture and Wine Making in California. . . .* San Francisco, 1888.

Husmann, George C. "The Present Condition of Grape Culture in California," in *Yearbook of the USDA, 1898*. (Washington DC, 1899) 551-562.

Husmann, George. "Viticulture in California." *Sunset* (February 1910) 132-137.

Hutchinson, Ralph Burton. "The California Wine Industry." Unpublished doctoral dissertation economics. UCLA, 1969. (NVWL)

Hutchinson, Ralph Burton and Sydney Blummer. *The Williamson Act and Winegrowing in the Napa Valley*. Pomona (California Polytechnic College) 1970. (NVWL)

Hyatt, Thomas Hart. *Hyatt's Hand-Book of Grape Culture*. San Francisco, 1867. California's first book on viticulture.

Jacobs, Julius. "California's Pioneer Wine Families." CHSQ (Summer 1975) 139-174.

Jones, Idwal. *Vines in the Sun*. New York, 1949. Some good history mixed with fanciful fiction.Often difficult to separate the two.

Jordan, Rudolf, Jr. *Quality in Dry Wines. . . .* San Francisco, 1911. Based on the author's own work at Mt. Veeder's Castle Rock Vineyard and on that of Professor F. T. Bioletti. (UCD)

Kassimatis, A. N., et al. *Wine Grape Varieties in the North Coast Counties of California*. University of California, Division of Agricultural Sciences (January 1977).

Laube, James. *California's Great Cabernets*. San Francisco, 1989.

Laube, James. *California's Great Chardonnays*. San Francisco, 1990.

Laughridge, Jamie. *Rising Star: Domaine Chandon. . . .* New York, 1983.

Leggett, Herbert B. "Early History of Wine Production in California." Unpublished master's thesis, U.C. Berkeley, 1939. Wine Institute mimeo, 1941.

The Louis M. Martini Winery, 1982. A beautiful in-house history, lavishly illustrated.

Lyon, Richards. *Vine to Wine*. Napa, 1985. A beautiful photo analysis of contemporary Napa Valley viticulture and winemaking.

Mabon, Mary Frost. *ABC of American Wines*. New York, 1942.

McKee, Irving. "Historic Napa County Winegrowers." *California - Magazine of the Pacific* (September 1951) 14-15, 22-24. (NVWL)

McLachlan, Anne. "The Wine Grape Industry of Napa, California, 1964-1979."
Unpublished master's thesis in geography, University of London, 1980. (NVWL)

McNeil-Draper, Mary-Ellen, ed. *Vintners Club.* San Francisco, 1988. An interesting compendium of the results of hundreds of blind tastings conducted between1973 and 1987. There are also numerous articles on California wine by such as André Tchelistcheff, Warren Winiarski, Ann Noble, Gerald Asher and Paul Draper.

Meers, John R. "The California Wine and Grape Industry and Prohibition." *CHSQ* (March 1967) 19-32.

Melville, John Robert. *Guide to California Wines.* Garden City, 1955. Many subsequent editions.

Menefee, Campbell A. *Historical and Descriptive Sketch Book of Napa, Sonoma, Lake and Mendocino Counties.* Napa City, 1873.

Munson, Thomas Volney. *Foundations of American Grape Culture.* Denison (TX) 1909.

Muscatine, Doris, et al (eds.). *The California Wine Book.* Berkeley, 1984.

Napa County. *Agricultural Crop Report.* Napa, 1922-1991. Various titles.

Napa Valley Wine Library Association. "History of Napa Valley." 4vols. 1974-1985. Transcripts of the Association's oral history interviews. (NVWL)

Oldham, Charles F. "California Wines." *Journal of the Society of the Arts.* (February 2,1894) 195-201.

Ordish, George. The Great Wine Blight. New York, 1972 and 1987. A history of the phylloxera problem in Europe and North America.

Ostrander, Gilman M. *The Prohibition Movement in California, 1848-1933.* Berkeley, 1957.

Parker, Tom and Charles L. Sullivan. *Inglenook Vineyards; 100 years of Fine Winemaking. Rutherford, 1979.* A well illustrated in-house history.

Peninou, Ernest P. and Sydney S. Greenleaf. *A Directory of California Wine Growers and Wine Makers in 1860.* Berkeley, 1967.

Peters, Gary L. *Wines and Vines of California.* Belmont (CA) 1989. A geographer's approach.

Pinney, Thomas. *A History of Wine in America.* Berkeley, 1989.

Pouget, Roger. *Histoire de la lutte contre le Phylloxera de la Vigne en France.* Versailles, 1990.

Ray, Cyril. *Robert Mondavi of the Napa Valley.* London, 1984.

Robinson, Jancis. *Vines, Grapes and Wines.* New York, 1986. Perhaps even more useful than Galet's scholarly work.

Rossati, Guido. *Relazione di un viaggio d'instruzione negli Stati Uniti d'America.* Rome, 1900. (UCD)

Schoonmaker, Frank and Tom Marvel. *American Wines.* New York, 1941.

Slocum, Bowen & Co. *History of Napa and Lake Counties, California.* San Francisco, 1881. A treasure trove of local winegrowing data.

Smilie, Robert S. *The Sonoma Mission.* Fresno, 1975.

Smith, Clarence L. and Wallace W. Elliott. *Illustrations of Napa County with Historical Sketch.* Oakland, 1878. Reproduced by Valley Publishers, Fresno, in 1974.

Sorensen, Loren. *Beringer.* St. Helena, 1989. A beautiful photo-history.

Starr, Kevin. *Inventing the Dream; California through the Progressive Era.* Chapter 5 has an excellent discussion of the place of winegrowing in California history.

Stellman, Louis J. *Sam Brannan, Builder of San Francisco.* New York, 1953.

Stevenson, Robert Louis. *The Silverado Squatters.* London, 1883. The section titled "Napa Wine" (pp. 34-47) has been printed separately by several California publishers.

Stoll, Horatio. "Napa Valley Pioneer Winemakers." *Wines & Vines* (April 1937) 6-7,10.

Stuller, Jay and Glen Martin. *Through the Grapevine.* New York, 1989. An analysis of the modern California wine industry.

Sullivan, Charles L. "A Man Named Agoston Haraszthy." *Vintage.* A three part series, February-April, 1980.

Sullivan, Charles L. "A Viticultural Mystery Solved." *California History (CHSQ),* (Summer 1978) 114-129. Traces the Zinfandel from the East Coast of the United States to California.

Sullivan, Charles L. *Like Modern Edens.* Cupertino (CA) 1982.

Teiser, Ruth and Catherine Harroun. *Winemaking in California.* New York, 1983. Much of this solid history derives from the authors' work on the Bancroft oral history project.

Thompson, Virgil L. "Wine Industry in Napa County, Past Present and Future." Unpublished monograph, Pacific Coast Banking School, University of Washington, 1971 (NVWL)

Topolos, Michael and Betty Dopson. *Napa Valley* . St. Helena, 1975. Contains the best collection of graphics related to Napa wine history.

Truman, Benjamin C. *See How It Sparkles*. Los Angeles, 1896. A California bon vivant 's view of several Napa wines.

Unwin, P. T. H. (Tim). *Wine and the Vine*. London, 1991. A historical geography of wine.

Verardo, Denzil. *Napa Valley, from golden fields to purple harvest*. Northridge (CA) 1986. Very useful local history.

Viala, Pierre. *Une Mission viticole en Amerique*. Montpellier, 1889. (UCB)

"La Viticulture en Californie." *La Nature: Revue des Sciences*. (Paris 1886) 215-218. Several fine lithographs. (UCD)

Wait, Frona Eunice (Colburn). *In Old Vintage Days*. San Francisco, 1937. (UCD)

Wait, Frona Eunice (Colburn). "Vintage Day." *Sunset* (February 1910) 2, 206-210.

Wait, Frona Eunice (Colburn). *Wines and Vines of California*. San Francisco, 1889. Reprinted in 1973 by the NVWLA.

Wallace, W. F. *History of Napa County*. Oakland, 1901.

Waugh, Harry. *Diary of a Winetaster*. New York, 1972. French wine is Mr. Waugh's chief interest as a writer, but his visits to the California wine country, particularly Napa Valley, in the sixties and seventies, give the reader a very personal picture of the wine scene there during the "great revolution."

Waugh, Harry. *Harry Waugh's Wine Diary, 1982-1986*. San Francisco, 1987.

Waugh, Harry. *Pick of the Bunch*. London, 1970.

Waugh, Harry. *Winetaster's Choice*. New York, 1974.

Webb, Edith Buckland. *Indian Life at the Old Missions*. Los Angeles, 1952.

Wickels, John. "A Brief Biography of Charles Hopper. . . ." *Napa County Historical Society, 1979*. (NPL)

Wickels, John. "Footsteps in the sands of 'Vintage 1870'." *Napa County Historical Society, 1979*. (NPL)

Winkler, Albert J. *General Viticulture*. Berkeley, 1962.

Wood, Ellen. *George Yount*. San Francisco, 1941. (BnL)

INDEX

AxR-1 rootstock, 371
  hybrid, 117, 123 n. 17
  susceptibility of, 123 n. 17,
    369

B

Baade, Herman, 215, 220
Bale, Carolina (Mrs. Charles
    Krug), 22, 34, 42, 96
Bale clay loam, 359
Bale, Edward Turner, 22–23, 29 n.
    9
Bale Rancho, 26
Ballentine, John, 212
Balzer, Robert, 255
Bancroft Vineyard, 340
bankruptcies and closures,
    winery, 39, 89, 93, 155, 225,
    250, 292–294, 370
Barbera, 226
barrels. *See* cooperage
Barrett, James L., 287
Barrett, James P. (Bo), 288
Barth, George, 27, 76
Bartholomew, Frank, 241
Bartolucci Brothers Winery, 294,
    387
Bartolucci family, 211
BATF (Bureau of Alcohol, Tobacco
    and Firearms):
    appellation approvals,
      327–329, 358–362
    hearings, 334 n. 23, 361–362,
      377 n. 30
    label regulations, 368
Battista, John, 158
Bauer, J. A., 76
Bay Area:
    settlement of the, 3–8, 11–13,
      22–27
    winegrowing districts, 329,
      386
Beard, James, iii, 242, 253, 269–270
bearing acreage. *See* acreage,
    planted
Beaulieu Vineyard (BV), 89, 97–98
    n. 36, 146, 156, 162–164, 170,
    211, 221–224, 245, 258–259,
    273–275, 285, 364
    great wines, 216, 390

Heublein purchase of,
    290–291
  and Prohibition, 196–198
Becker, Peter, 294
Beckstoffer, Andrew, 291,
    322–323, 351, 356, 364, 378
    n. 35
Bell, Theodore, 114, 158, 183–185,
    190, 191, 195
bench land, 361–362
benchgrafts, 118, 124 n. 21, 143,
    161
Benson, John, 50, 59, 67 n. 4, 94
Berg, Harold, 284, 286
Bergfeld Winery, 165, 173, 215, 353
Beringer Brothers Winery, 73,
    102–103, 118, 168, 198, 212,
    230, 239, 272
    State Fair awards, 390
Beringer, Frederick (Fritz), 35,
    59–60, 89, 96, 157, 188
    funeral, 157
Beringer, Jacob, 55, 59–60, 89, 188,
    317
Beringer-Nestlé, 291–292, 293, 363
    purchases by, 60, 293, 348
Berkeley. *See* University of
    California
Bernstein, Michael, 296
Berrouet, Jean-Claude, 331
Bianchi, Adam, 199
"Big Co-op." *See* Napa
    Cooperative Winery
"Big Five" wineries, 237, 240, 251,
    255, 366, 390–391
    takeovers of, 277, 291,
      363–364
    in the 1960s, 270–277
    See also Napa Valley wineries
"Big Four" wineries, 220, 237
Bioletti, Frederic T., 77
Bisceglia family, 203, 212, 225
Bissonette, Greg, 311
Black community, 44
Black, J. F., 81
Black Malvoisie, 32
Blanc de Noir, 281, 297
blends, wine, 58, 87, 102, 134–142,
    229, 271
Blue, Anthony Dias, 292
Board of State Viticultural

Commissioners. *See*
    California State Viticultural
    Commission
Bodega Bay, 4
Boeger, Greg, 364
Bohler, Montana, 174
bonded winery, numbers, 387,
    392–397
Bonetti, William, 252
Bonnet, Leon, 218, 222
books on wine, 255, 269–270
boom times, 64–65, 200, 238, 245,
    302–303, 338, 370, 373
    of 1880s, 71–96, 374, 399
Bordeaux (France), 44, 136, 150 n.
    35, 309, 321, 337
Bordeaux varieties, 86, 136, 278,
    282, 405–406
Borel, Antone, 53, 155
Bornhorst & Eberling Winery, 157,
    199
Bosché, John, 285
botrytis cinerea, 141, 150 n. 35,
    279, 292
Bottles and Bins, 253
bottling:
    by wine merchants, 107
    estate, 79, 236, 238, 256, 257,
      277
Bouchaine Vineyards, 324, 327
boundaries, appellation. *See*
    appellations of origin
Bourn, Mrs. Sarah, 59
Bourn, William B., 90, 91, 93
Bowen, Charles, 42, 159
Brakeman, Robert and Susan,
    339–340
brand names, 79, 88, 109–110, 177
    recognition of, 246, 271
Brandlin, Henry, 244
brandy, 26, 58, 73, 89, 212, 364
    alambic, 330, 341
    attitudes toward wine and,
      57, 82
    blackberry, 50
    mission wine and, 10, 128–129
    prorate program, 224–225,
      229, 231 n. 34
    taxes, 36, 39, 45, 93–94, 96, 164
    warehouses, 43, 63
Brannan, Sam, 36, 38–39

San Francisco cellar, 63, 107, 114, 169
Carpy, Charles (grandson), 57, 285, 293
case goods, 221–222, 236
Cask wines, Inglenook, 257, 408
Castle Rock Winery, 77
Catawba, 24
Catholic Church, 219–220
Caymus Rancho, 12
Caymus Vineyards, 312–313, 361, 374
cellars, wine, 51, 55, 73, 95
    practices, 132–133, 145–149, 281
    tunnel caves for, 41, 59–60, 249, 279–280
    See also fermentation
Central California wineries, 229
Central Coast, wine evaluations & prices, 407, 408
Central Coast wineries, 363
Central Valley grapes, 200, 217, 319, 349, 350, 386
CGPA, 183–188
"Chablis," 140, 222, 274, 279, 384
Chaix, Jean, 156, 157
Chalone Vineyards, 314, 315, 324
Champagne, 249–250, 271, 280–281, 281, 295–297, 348, 389
    A. Finke's Widow "Champagne," 52
    méthode champenoise, 249, 330
    Millerway process, 279
Chandon Brut, 297
Chappellet winery, 259, 286, 326
chaptalization. *See* fermentation, sugar addition controversy
Charbono, 78, 226, 383
Chardonnay, 242, 244, 246, 287, 310, 321, 323, 342, 384
    award-winners (lists), 382, 388
    nomenclature, 140, 261
    quality and reputation of, 261, 288, 315, 407–409
Charles Krug Winery, 34, 117, 157, 210, 220, 239–240, 250–254, 389

the Mondavi family and, 275–276, 283–284, 342
    retrospective tasting, 342–343
    State Fair awards, 391
Chase, Horace, 155, 315, 358–359
Chasselas, 14 n. 7, 32, 86, 383
Chateau Bouchaine Winery, 324
Chateau Chevalier Winery, 95, 311, 341
Château d'Yquem, 150 n. 35
Chateau La Salle, 271
Chateau Montelena, 90, 159, 199, 214, 259, 287–288, 314, 315
Château Petrus, 331
Chateau Souverain, 348
Chateau Winegrowers Association, 249
Chateau Woltner, 339
Chauché noir, 137
Chavoor, Walt, 371–372
Chenin blanc, 253–254, 261, 271, 286, 381
Chevalier, Fortune, 91, 95
Chevalier Winery, 158, 170
Chicago Exposition of 1893, 110–112, 177
Chiles, Joseph B., 23, 76
Chiles Valley, 76, 84, 174–175, 212, 328, 361, 378 n. 31
    area owners, 66, 105, 395
Chiles Valley appellation, 361
Chimney Rock Winery, 345
Chinese community, 44, 59–60
    contract labor, 112, 145, 159, 161
Chotteau Treaty, 63–64
Christian Brothers, 93, 166, 203, 212, 219–220, 237, 248–249, 260, 341, 389
    brandy, 225
    profile of, 270–272
    sale to Heublein, 220, 363–364
    State Fair awards, 390
Christie's Auction House, 342
Churchill, E. S., 155, 211
Churchill, E. W., 88
Cinsaut, 32, 128
CK label, 251
claret, 63, 72, 128, 135–136, 137, 165, 170, 408–409
    varieties included in, 382

Clark, David and Kinta, 339
Clark, Mrs. Stephen, 269
classes, wine history, 269–270
cleanliness in processing, 88, 148–149
climate, Napa Valley, 21–22, 137, 144–146, 223
    microclimates, 308–309
Clos du Val, 309–310, 315
Clos Pegase Winery, 343–344
Coca-Cola Co., 289, 317–318, 333
Cognac, 39, 330
Coit, Lillie Hitchcock, 92, 98 n. 47
collectors and investors, wine, 248
Columbian Exposition, Chicago of 1893, 110, 111–112, 177
commercial wine shipment, first Napa Valley, 25
Commonsense Book of Wine, 255
community distillery, 93
competition:
    with European wines, 236, 326
    industrial, 375
    See also imports, wine; tastings
Concepción, Jorgé, 12
conglomerates. *See* corporations
Conn Creek Winery, 310, 347
Conn, Donald, 201
Conn Valley, 59, 76
    area owners, 66, 105, 395
connoisseur investors, 248
Connoisseur's Guide to California Wine, 406–407, 408
Connor, C. W., 212
Connors, S. P., 86
Connors/Furniss Winery, 92
Conradi family, 212
Conradi, Peter, 158
Conradi Winery, 318
conservation. *See* environment
conservationist issues, 298–299
consolidation, industrial, 113–114, 201, 225, 229
    of 1900-1915, 160, 363–364, 375
Consumer Reports evaluations, 254
consumption of alcohol, 182–183, 347, 367–368
consumption of wine, 367–368

Draper, Virginia, 242, 243
Dresel, Emil, 28, 61, 139
Dresel, Julius, 83, 139
drinking. *See* alcohol abuse
droughts, 37, 121, 313, 337, 367
Drummond, J. H., 136, 142
dry farming, 145
Duckhorn, Daniel, 318, 355
Duckhorn Winery, 318, 320
Duncan, Raymond, 311
Dunn, Randall, 312–313, 339, 340
Dunn Winery, 313, 332
Durán, Fr. Narciso, 10
Duriff. *See* Petite Sirah
Dwyer, Robert, 322

E

earthquakes, 44, 167, 167–170, 367
East Coast sales. *See* market, wine
East Coast viticulture, 24
Eckes Corporation, 311
Economic slump of 1890s, 101–123
Edelwein, 285
Edge Hill Winery, 43, 50, 58, 96, 137, 165
Eighteenth Amendment. *See* Prohibition
Eisele, Milton, 309, 354
Eisele, Völker, 348, 355
El Dorado County, 27
El Molino Winery, 23, 50
Elliot-Fisk, D. L., 29 n. 7
enologists, 222, 240, 247, 258, 259, 272, 279, 281, 287, 309, 331
entrepreneurs, wine, 208–209, 230, 364–366, 375
    1940-1975 Brand Name/Premium Wineries, 392–393
    1960s, 258–259, 266
    enologist, 259, 309
    failures, 292–294
    new breed of, 322–323, 330–331, 375
    post-war, 241–245
    second wave of, 277–290
    See also ownership of wineries
environment, Napa's natural, 20–22
    concerns for, 164, 266–267,

298–299, 338, 353–358, 376
Ephraim Light Winery, 199, 215
"equivalency" campaign, 347
"Ernie's" label, 330
Eshcol Winery, 24, 119, 146, 155, 197, 211, 239, 296
Esmeralda Winery, 117, 346
estate bottling, 79, 236, 238, 256, 257, 277
Estee, Morris M., 82, 85, 102, 363
ethnicity:
    changes in Valley population, 160–161, 208
    of Northern vs. Southern California, 182
    of winery owners c. 1880, 65–67
    See also specific group or country names
European vines. *See* vine cuttings
evaluation panels, wine. *See* tastings, wine
Evansen Winery, 322
Ewer, Frederick, 156, 168, 197
Ewer, Seneca, 57, 89, 114, 197
experiment stations, agricultural, 318, 324
    Krug estate, 121
    To Kalon Winery, 91, 167
    USDA, 167
exploration, Napa Valley, 6
exports, 53, 106–110
    See also market, wine
expositions and fairs, 24, 58, 110, 111–112, 216, 223–228
    Golden Gate Exposition (1939), 223, 225, 228
    Panama Pacific (1915), 175–177, 227
    Paris, 64, 94, 98 n. 53, 158
    See also California State Fair

F

failures, winery, 39, 89, 93, 155, 225, 250, 292–294, 370
fairs. *See* California State Fair; expositions and fairs
Falcon Crest label, 287
Falcon Crest (television series), 60, 134, 287

Far Niente Winery, 59, 94, 119, 146
    founding of, 50, 322
    restoration of, 322, 331
Fauré, Victor, 28
Fawver, James C., 155, 211, 239
Fay, Nathan, 358–359
Federal Alcohol Administration, 225
fermentation, 147–148
    cool, 77, 89, 211, 223, 251–252
    experiments in, 77, 251
    stainless steel tanks, 275
    stuck, 21, 45, 51, 89, 147–148, 319
    sugar addition controversy, 73, 81, 87, 148, 162, 169–170
    sulfur dioxide use in, 77, 173, 221
    techniques in, 89, 130–132, 136, 147–148, 221
    whole berry, 58–59
    in wood barrels, 33, 36, 90, 111, 148, 257, 278, 287, 289, 316
    yeast use in, 77, 147, 148, 173, 221
    See also cellars, wine
Ferriole, Vincent, 356
Fershko, Victor, 355
festivals, vintage or harvest, 96, 120, 174, 176, 187, 195, 217, 236
FI (Fruit Industries), 201–202
finances, low working capital and, 272, 273–275
fining practices, 148
Finke, Alois, 52
fires, forest, 174–175
fires, winery, 211, 326
    Charles Krug, 55
    Groezinger, 58
    La Loma Winery, 154
    To Kalon, 156
"First Growth" wines, 292
Fischer, J. H., 77
Fischer Winery, 155, 244
Fisher, M.F.K., 269
Flamant, Adolph, 84
Flame Tokay, 24
flavor factors, 145–149
    home winemaking, 193–194
    See also soils, Napa Valley

Hummel, Herman, 242
Huneeus, Augustin, 311
Huntsinger, Al, 252
Husmann, George, 27, 61, 76, 81, 85, 116–118, 132, 136, 157
Husmann, George C., 167, 179 n. 27
    influence of, 83–84

I

igneous alluvium. *See* soils, Napa Valley
image of Napa Valley. *See* marketing; public image
immigration. *See* population levels
imports, wine, 149 n. 24, 227
    French, 27–28, 53–54, 61, 135
    phylloxera-resistant, 117–118
    tariffs, 57, 63–64
    World War II absence of, 236
    See also vine cuttings
Indians, Northern California, 5, 6, 8, 10, 11, 12, 23, 29 n. 3
industry associations. *See* cooperative organizations; *specific group names*
industry, wine. *See* wine industry
information, viticultural:
    availability of, 79, 97 n. 36, 146, 247, 303 n. 4, 364–365
    on premium varieties, 260
    See also research, viticultural
Inglenook Winery, 50, 97 n. 9, 146, 173–174, 197, 212, 294
    founding, 50
    leadership by the, 77–80, 177, 216, 226–227, 237, 256–258
    modern, 225–227, 232 n. 38
    sale to volume producers, 276–277, 291
    State Fair awards, 390–391
Internal Revenue Service (IRS), 191, 194
International Wine & Food Society, 285
investors. *See* corporations; ownership of wineries
Italian community members, 65–67, 92, 160
Italian Swiss Colony, 110, 114, 165, 168, 214, 249, 277

J

Jacobi. *See* Lachman & Jacobi
Jacobs, Julius, 284
Japan, owners from, 352
Japanese community, 161, 377
Jeanmonod, August, 59
Jefferson, Thomas, 345
Johannisberg Riesling. *See* White Riesling
John, Brother, 214–215, 219, 237, 271
John Daniel Society, 331
Johnson, Hiram, 222
Jordan, David Starr, 188
Jordan, Robert, 77
Joslyn, M. A., 217
"Judgment of Paris," 313–314, 315
jug wines, 277, 292, 363
juice, grape, 191, 195, 386
juries. *See* tastings, wine

K

Kaltenbach, M., 76
Keenan, Robert, 158, 318
Keenan Winery, 318
Kellogg, Florentine (Frank), 23
Kelly, Harold, 355
Keseberg, Lewis, 39
Keyes, Erasmus Delano, 43, 50
Keyes, W. S., 75, 158, 169, 172, 340
Khoury, Tawfiq, 342
King, Charles. *See* Krug, Charles
Kingsburg Winery/distillery, 229
Kirin Brewery, 352
Knight's Valley, 42
Knowles, Legh (Lee), 248, 291
Kohler, Charles, 27
Kolm, Claude, 406, 408
Komes, Jerome, 316
Kornell, Hanns, 159, 249, 259, 269, 330, 370, 389
Kortum, Louis, 159, 191
Krug, Carolina Bale (Mrs. Charles), 22, 34, 42, 96
Krug, Charles, 37, 46, 73, 74, 75, 107, 140, 143, 174
    Agoston Haraszthy and, 34, 46 n. 4
    bankruptcy, 89

cellars, 51, 55, 59–60
first vintages for others, 25–26
grapes-buying by, 58, 59, 90
on phylloxera, 85, 86
sixtieth birthday, 89
in Sonoma, 28
winery fire, 55
Krug estate, 196, 198, 213, 228, 284
    experiment station, 121
    See also Charles Krug Winery

L

L. M. Renault Company, 239
La Jota Rancho, 158
La Jota Vineyard Company, 158
La Jota Winery, 320, 338, 339, 340
La Loma, 56–57
La Loma Vineyard, 64
La Loma Winery, 97 n. 25, 154
La Perla Winery, 158, 198, 242, 317
La Salle Institute, 219, 225, 271
labels:
    19th century nomenclature and, 134–142
    art, 344, 345
    "bottled at the winery," 236
    fake foreign, 107, 130
    health warnings on, 367–368, 374
    Mondavi "mission" statement on, 368
    Napa Valley appellations and, 177, 218, 228, 229, 359, 361, 362
    private reserve, 228
    varietal designation on, 218, 227, 237, 251, 256, 260, 274, 381–384
    vineyard designation, 278
    vintage dating and, 256, 271, 286
    wine characterization on, 368
labor, vineyard, 112, 145, 170, 237
Lachman & Jacobi, 92, 119
Lail, Robin Daniel, 325, 331
Lake County, 37, 329, 334 n. 23
Lamborn, Robert, 340
land ownership:
    determining, 364–366
    distribution by Vallejo, 11–12

York Creek Vineyard, 158
Yount, George Calvert, 12–13,
    17–20, 26, 29 n. 3, 75
Yountville, 18, 26, 65–66, 104, 123,
    360, 395

Z

ZD Winery, 318, 320, 329
Zellerbach, J. D., 278
Zierngibl, Louis, 93, 96, 111
Zinfandel, 32, 40, 76, 78, 81, 141,
    218, 310
        acreage changes, 261, 385
        award-winners (lists), 382,
        388
        comparing Napa and
        Sonoma, 398, 408–409
        grapes, 193–194, 382
        introduction of, 24, 135–136,
        150 n. 26
        reputation of, 63, 72, 128, 132,
        243, 319–320, 326, 408–408
        saving the red, 319–320
        spring frost and, 51
        white, 319, 342
"Zinfandel" (steamboat), 28
zoning, Napa Valley, 298–299
        See also appellations of origin